From the reviews of the First Edition:

'J.P. Sommerville's *Politics and Ideology in* Commendably short, it is both a monogra~~p.. ... ... p........ ... .~~ which preceded the Civil War and a judicious reconsideration of their role in causing it. . . . No one after reading him should be able to deny that the Civil War had long-term ideological antecedents (though no doubt many will go on doing so).'
Christopher Hill, English Historical Review

'All those interested in the field must become well acquainted with Sommerville's book, which represents the single most significant challenge to the revisionist thesis . . . It will as well likely have an extraordinary shelf life; long after the current furor over Parliament dies down, undergraduates and their teachers will still read it as the most convenient point of departure into the neglected ideological dimension of early seventeenth-century England.' *Thomas Cogswell, Journal of Modern History*

'In a stimulating, subtly argued and well written book, Johann Sommerville sets out to restore the role of ideology in the origins of the English Civil War . . . This is an important book, which revitalizes the debate on the origins of the Civil War. The interpretation is challenging, the detail largely accurate (this reader spotted very few factual errors). The author and publisher are to be congratulated on producing a cheaply priced, attractive and scholarly book. It deserves to be widely read.'
Kenneth Fincham, Parliamentary History

'Dr Sommerville is delivering a challenge to most of the English work published in this field in the past ten years. Such a challenge is a newsworthy event, and the beginning of a major new round of debate. The gauntlet has been thrown down with distinction: the scholarship is careful, the quotation accurate, the argument taut, the style courteous and succinct, and the whole bears the unmistakable stamp of quality. There are almost no passages in this work which will not survive a scrutiny of their source.' *Conrad Russell, London Review of Books*

'But those who disagree with Dr Sommerville will have to address themselves to the detailed substance of his case, and they will not find rebuttal an easy task. This is a powerful and persuasive work of considerable originality and importance.'
G.E. Aylmer, Times Higher Educational Supplement

'a thoughtful and well-organized set of essays' *James McSwain, History [US]*

'well researched, clearly thought through, and admirably written . . . Giving a fresh view of political ideas of seventeenth-century England, Sommerville shows their relationship to practical politics and emphasizes the fundamental disagreements on basic tenets. Students will find the book at once provocative and reliable – so too will their professors.' *Elizabeth Read Foster, American Historical Review*

'[fills] a yawning void, thereby forcing a revision in our thinking.'
Lamar M. Hill, Albion

'The 17th century remains one of the most contested periods of English history. This book, concerned with the relationship between political principles and political practice, aims to provide more light on the subject rather than fuel the heat of debate. It provides an incisive re-examination of the theories of divine right, government by consent and the ancient constitution, and relates them both to the crises and routine affairs of political and religious life under the first two Stuarts.'
R.C. Richardson, Times Educational Supplement

ROYALISTS AND PATRIOTS

Politics and Ideology in England 1603–1640

Second Edition

J.P. Sommerville

LONGMAN
London and New York

Pearson Education Limited
Edinburgh Gate,
Harlow, Essex CM20 2JE, United Kingdom
and Associated Companies throughout the world.

Published in the United States of America by Addison Wesley Longman, New York.

First published 1986
Second edition 1999

ISBN 0–582–32006–2 PPR

Visit Addison Wesley Longman on the world wide web at http://www.awl-he.com

British Library Cataloguing in Publication Data

A catalogue entry for this title is available from the British Library

Library of Congress Cataloging-in-Publication Data

Sommerville, J.P., 1953–
   Royalists and patriots : politics and ideology in England,
1603–1640 / J.P. Sommerville. — 2nd ed.
     p. cm.
   Rev. ed. of: Politics and ideology in England, 1603–1640. 1986.
   Includes bibliographical references and index.
   ISBN 0–582–32006–2 (pbk.)
   1. Political science—England—History—17th century. 2. Great
Britain—Politics and government—1603–1649. I. Sommerville, J.
P., 1953–   Politics and ideology in England, 1603–1640. II. Title.
JA84.G7S67   1999
320.5′0942—dc21   98–46176
                                             CIP

Set by 35 in 10/12pt Bembo
Transferred to digital print on demand, 2003
Printed and bound by Antony Rowe Ltd, Eastbourne

Contents

PART ONE   Principles

Handwritten annotations:
Hobbes → Locke → American founders.
government by consent
popular sovereignty
Absolutism
gov't by contract
law - common law → ANCIENT Parliament + King
England has no Constitution

Preface to the Second Edition

This second edition has been revised throughout to take account of research done since 1986, when the book was first published. Errors have been corrected in this edition and it contains much new material, dealing especially with current scholarship. There is a lengthy new chapter, discussing recent writings on early-seventeenth-century English politics and ideas, and especially the views of so-called 'revisionist' historians, some of whom have taken issue with this book's main arguments. The 'Suggestions for Further Reading' have been completely re-done to reflect the wealth of fine work that has appeared since the mid-1980s. There is a new 'Chronology' listing the main events mentioned in the text. The first edition sometimes used 'he' to mean 'he or she', but this one avoids such locutions except where they would be seriously misleading.

For funding which made possible this revision, I am most grateful to the Graduate School of the University of Wisconsin at Madison, and to the National Endowment for the Humanities. I am also much indebted to the staffs of the Folger Shakespeare Library and of Memorial Library here in Madison for their courteous and expert assistance. A particular word of gratitude is due to the ever-efficient Ed Duesterhoeft, the maestro of the microfilm at Memorial Library.

Johann P. Sommerville
Madison
June 1998

A final warm word of thanks is due to the Huntington Library for awarding me a fellowship. The proofs of the book and the index were completed in the congenial surroundings of the Huntington.

San Marino, California
December 1998

Acknowledgements

This book is about political ideas in England before the Civil War. Few of the men who feature in these pages were original thinkers. They borrowed their ideas from others. The same goes for the present writer. I owe a great deal of gratitude to many historians for whatever good ideas there are in this book. The bad ideas are, of course, my own. Debts for particular points are recorded in the notes and references but certain more general influences merit recognition here.

First and foremost, I would like to thank those who read and commented on drafts of the book. Professor G.R. Elton deserves additional thanks for the unflagging energy with which he faced the uphill struggle of instilling in me the elements of historical scholarship and a sense of the importance of English political history. Professor Quentin Skinner has been a kind and constant reader of my writings. He and Dr Richard Tuck guided my first faltering steps in political philosophy and the history of political thought. Their own works are a model of what can be achieved by a combination of historical sensitivity and precision in conceptual analysis. Dr John Morrill has freely shared his encyclopaedic knowledge of Stuart history and his boundless enthusiasm for the subject. Drs Mark Goldie and Glyn Parry and Mr Howard Moss have also made many telling criticisms of the book and saved me from blunders too horrendous to mention. I owe much to all of them.

Over the years, I have benefited from conversations with many friends and scholars, including Mr John Adamson, Drs Martin Dzelzainis and Jamie Hart, Professor Derek Hirst, Dr Peter Lake and Professor Linda Levy Peck. A special word of thanks is due to Dr Richard Cust for permission to draw on his important doctoral dissertation on the Forced Loan. More generally, I would like to thank the members of those seminaries of historical learning, the graduate seminars held at Cambridge and at the Institute of Historical Research. They have taught me a great deal, and so too have my undergraduate students.

Last, but not least, I would like to thank the staff of the Cambridge University Library for their unfailing courtesy and efficiency, and the Council of St

John's College Cambridge for electing me into a Research Fellowship and later extending that Fellowship. They have made possible the writing of this book, as have the long-suffering and rarely thanked British taxpayers. It is to them that scholarship in this country owes most. This book is an inadequate recompense for their generosity.

In the text of the book dates are old style but the year is taken to begin on 1 January. Quotations from original sources have been modernised where this aids comprehension. The term 'Prince' means 'supreme civil magistrate' and is usually but not always identical with 'king'.

Abbreviations and Bibliographical Note

APC	*Acts of the Privy Council.*
BL	British Library.
CD 21	W. Notestein, F.H. Relf and H. Simpson, eds, *Commons Debates in 1621*, 7 vols (New Haven 1935).
CD 29	W. Notestein and F.H. Relf, eds, *Commons Debates 1629* (Minneapolis 1921).
CJ	*Commons Journals* (references are to vol. 1).
CSPD	*Calendar of State Papers Domestic.*
CSPV	*Calendar of State Papers Venetian.*
CUL	Cambridge University Library.
DHC 25	S.R. Gardiner, ed., *Debates in the House of Commons in 1625* (1873).
EHR	*English Historical Review.*
HJ	*Historical Journal.*
HMC	Historical Manuscripts Commission reports.
JEH	*Journal of Ecclesiastical History.*
LJ	*Lords Journals* (references are to vol. 2).
PD 10	S.R. Gardiner, ed., *Parliamentary Debates in 1610* (1862).
PP 10	E.R. Foster, ed., *Proceedings in Parliament 1610*, 2 vols (1966).
PP 14	Maija Jansson, ed., *Proceedings in Parliament 1614 (House of Commons)* (Philadelphia 1988).
PP 25	Maija Jansson and William B. Bidwell, eds, *Proceedings in Parliament 1625* (New Haven 1987).
PP 26	William B. Bidwell and Maija Jansson, eds, *Proceedings in Parliament 1626*, 4 vols (New Haven) 1991–96.
PP 28	R.C. Johnson, M.F. Keeler *et al.*, eds, *Proceedings in Parliament 1628*, 6 vols (1977–83). The first four volumes are entitled *Commons Debates 1628*.
PSP 40	E.S. Cope and W.H. Coates, eds, *Proceedings of the Short Parliament of 1640* (1977).
SP	State Papers.

SRP	J.F. Larkin, and P.L. Hughes, *Stuart Royal Proclamations*, 2 vols (Oxford 1973).
ST	W. Cobbett and T.B. Howell, eds, *State Trials*, 33 vols (1809–26). References are to column numbers.
TRHS	*Transactions of the Royal Historical Society.*

In the notes, dates and places of publication are generally those (if any) given on the title page, but no place is given in the case of London. Fuller bibliographical details of books published before 1641 may be found in *A Short-title Catalogue of Books printed in England, Scotland, and Ireland and of English Books printed abroad 1475–1640*, ed. A.W. Pollard and G.R. Redgrave, second edn revised by W.A. Jackson, F.S. Ferguson and Katharine F. Pantzer, 3 vols, 1976–91.

many an ignorant subject hath been fooled into this faith, that a man may become a martyr for his country by being a traitor to his prince; whereas the new coined distinction of subjects into royalists and patriots is most unnatural, since the relation between king and people is so great that their well-being is reciprocal

Sir Robert Filmer, Patriarcha, c.1630

the Romanists labore to make a division of the land into regians & Republicans, under collour of standing for the Kings prerogative: the first of these are such as they cause to stand obstinately upon it, that to please the king is the chiefe thing to be regarded in state; and his absolute will the principall rule of all proceedings & obedience in the Commonwealth: intending thereby to cast the aspersion of blame & tyranny of all that by their meanes is done amisse, upon, *so the King will have it.* the latter they move pertenaciously to hold, that the peoples good is the chiefe end of all civill proceedings, and the rule of all such proceedings to be only the lawe of the land

Anonymous treatise of c.1624, Folger MS. V. a. 24, pp. 27–8

Introduction

What were the origins of the English Civil War? A century ago the answer seemed clear. In his monumental *History of England 1603–42*, S.R. Gardiner put forward an interpretation which was grounded in a mass of detail and built to last. He saw the war as the culmination of a long period of conflict between king and Parliament. The conflict began almost as soon as James I came to the throne in 1603, and had roots which stretched far further back. Indeed, he portrayed the quarrel between the first two Stuarts and their Parliaments as just one episode – though an extremely significant episode – in the long story of the English nation's progress towards Parliamentary democracy – the most civilised form of government. The historian's task was to chart this progress and to point out the signposts along the highway which led towards the present. There were plenty of such signposts to be found in the first half of the seventeenth century. As early as 1604 members of the House of Commons asserted English liberties and the rights of Parliament in their *Apology*. They returned to the same themes with increasing clarity in 1610, in the Addled Parliament of 1614, in the Protestation of 1621, in the Petition of Right of 1628, in the Grand Remonstrance of 1641, and finally, when words had failed too often, in the Civil War.

Gardiner was a political historian, and his account of English politics survived. But later writers added new dimensions. In particular, social and economic history – often with a Marxist tinge – came into fashion. Meanwhile, the idea that history is, or should be seen as, progress fell out of favour. Scholars continued to accept Gardiner's claim that increasing conflict was the keynote of politics throughout the first four decades of the seventeenth century. But they tried to locate the roots of conflict in the changing structure of English society, and in the shifting distribution of wealth, rather than in the notion of inevitable progress. An economic explanation of the origins of the Civil War had been advanced by James Harrington in the middle of the seventeenth century, and by Karl Marx in the middle of the nineteenth. By the mid-twentieth century it had won wide acceptance, though the details remained contested.

During the past four decades historical research has progressed, and old orthodoxies have come under heavy attack. No simple economic explanation of the war has survived the test of the evidence. It has proved impossible to find neat correlations between people's economic positions and the side they took when fighting started. Many, indeed, were reluctant to take either side and concentrated their efforts on keeping the war out of their locality. Moreover, it has turned out that Gardiner's account of English politics was far too crude. Close investigation has suggested that the signposts often pointed the wrong way. Many apparent examples of conflict between crown and Parliament, or between the Court and the Country, were in reality no such thing. At Court, people vied for power and they sometimes mobilised their allies in the House of Commons to help them attain their goal. The activities of the Commons, then, should be seen at least in part as functions of disputes within the Court rather than as expressions of opposition to it. The Commons' attack on the Duke of Buckingham in 1626, for example, was no mere spontaneous outburst of opposition to the king and his Court, but part of a carefully orchestrated campaign masterminded by Buckingham's great rival the Earl of Pembroke – himself a leading courtier.

Gardiner was eager to see conflict between crown and Parliament as the central feature of early Stuart politics. By contrast, a number of recent scholars lay stress on rivalries between factions, and on the clash of personality. They argue that there were few if any deep-rooted divisions of political principle in early-seventeenth-century England. The English, in short, were broadly united in their political attitudes. Given this, and given the inadequacy of social and economic explanations, they conclude that the Civil War had no long-term origins. A sudden and unexpected breakdown occurred in 1640–42. Before 1640 there had, indeed, been a few disagreements about particular policies, but for the most part England had been a harmonious, unified society.

Were the years between 1603 and the summoning of the Long Parliament in 1640 a period of political conflict or of consensus? Currently, this question is hotly disputed. The purpose of this book is to shed light rather than heat upon it. In particular, I want to investigate the ways in which early-seventeenth-century English people perceived their own political world, and how these perceptions affected their actions. In other words, this is a book about political ideas, or ideologies, and their relationship to practical politics.

In much recent work on early Stuart politics, the role of ideology has been largely neglected. There are several reasons why this is so. Firstly, historians of political thought have often concentrated on just a few major authors such as Hobbes and Locke. It is not surprising if students of politics conclude that they have little to learn from commentaries on the writings of these philosophers. Famous philosophers are rarely typical of the more humble mortals who shape political events. In this book, I have tried to avoid giving undue weight to the work of great political thinkers, and have instead taken most of my material from the pamphlets, treatises, sermons and speeches of lesser writers. They may not have possessed much philosophical acumen. But their

[handwritten: gives importance to smaller writers, not just great thinkers.]

pedestrian opinions mattered in politics. It is arguable that a knowledge of the works of such authors contributes to an understanding of what are commonly regarded as the classic tests of political theory. Locke's *Two Treatises of Government*, for example, owes a heavy debt to ideas which were current in the early seventeenth century. But the focus of the present book is on those ideas and on their relationship to politics, not on the great texts which they influenced.

A second factor in the recent neglect of ideology is the (rarely articulated) belief that ideologies do not matter in politics, since the essence of political life is naked self-interest: after the event people do indeed appeal to high-sounding ideas to justify their conduct, but what really motivates them are greed and ambition, not devotion to any ideology. This attitude is refreshingly cynical, *[handwritten: ha ha]* but does not stand up to criticism. Everyday experience shows that people are capable of acting selflessly. Moreover, they sometimes have ideas – or prejudices, if you like – which lead them to act in ways which are not in their own best interests. Again, ideas shape people's conceptions of what things are in their interests. Down the ages many Christians have been guided by a self-interested motive – the desire to be saved. Yet their ideas on how to get saved have differed, and so too have their actions. Some have fought crusades while others have condemned all wars. Some have persecuted heretics while others have preached toleration. Self-interest turns into action only after it passes through the filter of ideology. So even if it is true that early Stuart English people were self-interested, this provides no grounds for supposing that ideology had little role to play in their politics.

Thirdly, ideas have been neglected because it is commonly assumed that the English in fact shared a single political outlook. The purpose of the first section of this book is to question that assumption. I argue that there were several radically different outlooks. Of course, it is true that we can find a number of principles which almost everyone was willing to endorse. For instance, it was widely held that Roman Catholicism – or 'popery' – should be discouraged, and that innovation is evil. In almost every society, however politically divided, it is possible to find some (often very vague) principles of this sort which most people are willing to support. The existence of these principles is no evidence of political unity, since it is obviously possible for people to share some ideas and yet to differ on and even fight about a great many others. In the early seventeenth century people agreed that it would be wrong to change existing political and constitutional arrangements, but disagreed on what these arrangements in fact were. In particular, there was no unity on the questions of the nature and limitations of royal authority, the relationship between the law and the king, and the role of Parliament in church affairs.

In the first chapter I discuss one common approach to these questions. I *[handwritten:)λ]* have named this approach the theory of royal absolutism. This is a convenient label, since the theory gave supreme political power to the king alone. However, it is only a label. In using it I do not want to imply that the theory was

3

necessarily the same as absolutist doctrines which have existed in other times and places – though early Stuart absolutism was very like that which existed in contemporary France. Nor do I intend to imply that people in the seventeenth century used the term 'absolutism' in the same sense I do. In fact, they rarely talked about any '-isms', and never used the word 'absolutism'. But they knew what the thing was, and they did discuss 'absolute power' and 'absolute monarchy'.

I next outline two theories which imposed stringent limitations upon the king. One of these made him accountable to the people, while the other subjected him to ancient custom. These two theories were distinct from each other and the divergences between them became apparent in the 1640s. But before 1640 their similarities were more important than their differences. What mattered then was the stark disjunction between these ideas and the principles of royal absolutism.

It is unsurprising that rival ideologies existed in a society as sophisticated as early-seventeenth-century England. Indeed, differences of political principle exist in most societies. They may be a pre-condition of conflict, for it is difficult to see how dissension can occur if everyone agrees. But they do not invariably result in conflict. People of differing views can compromise with each other. In the second half of this book I discuss what happened when principles were brought to bear upon practicalities. I argue that formulae of compromise were developed, but did not succeed in overcoming the fundamental disagreements. Occasionally, the mere expression of political ideas was enough to cause trouble, but far more serious problems arose when people translated their opinions into practice. The actions which were most important were royal infringements of what many believed to be the liberties of the subject, and royal policies towards the church and religious affairs. Taxation without the subject's consent was particularly significant. In 1608 James I vastly extended extra-Parliamentary impositions on merchandise, and both he and his son drew more revenue from this source than they ever gained from Parliament. We might expect that some people, and especially merchants, would have found impositions objectionable. To understand the full depth of hostility towards them, however, and to understand why the king regarded such hostility as wholly unjustifiable, it is essential to grasp the ideological context of contemporary debates. In the last two chapters I examine the ways in which political principles were used to legitimate or attack particular royal policies – taxation without consent, imprisonment without cause shown, and the government of the church without Parliamentary advice.

There were, of course, developments in attitudes towards these questions. It is clear that Charles I was a far less able politician than his father, and that his policies resulted in a hardening of opinion on many issues. But early-seventeenth-century political debate did also possess a thematic unity. Ideologies which played a vital role on the eve of the Civil War had roots that went back at least to 1603. To this extent the war did have long-term origins.

4

Discussions in Parliament are not always the best place to look for these origins or for evidence about contemporary ideas. Speeches often survive in fragmentary form and are difficult to interpret. Pamphlets and treatises, on the other hand, give us a much clearer picture of contemporary opinion. They were written to be read and their authors used arguments which they believed that readers would find convincing. Pamphleteering and sermonising, just as much as participation in debate on the floor of the House of Commons, were political acts. Indeed, Parliamentary debates take on new meaning when seen in the light of wider English intellectual life.

In a relatively short book there are bound to be many omissions. Far more could be said about the transmission of ideas, and about the penetration down the social scale of ideologies which were voiced by the wealthy and literate. I have not been able to address these questions. I cannot claim to have given definitive answers even to those questions which I do address. Historical scholarship, unlike history itself, may progress inexorably towards perfection. But the goal is still a long way off, at least in the case of the present writer. If this book stimulates greater interest in the ideological dimension of English politics, in the principles for which the English argued and ultimately fought, then it will have achieved its objective.

PART ONE

Principles

CHAPTER 1

The Divine Right of Kings

In 1603 England was a monarchy in fact as well as name. This basic reality underlay the theory of royal absolutism, or, to give it its traditional title, the Divine Right of Kings. The king appointed Privy Councillors. With them he acted as the state's executive. He also appointed judges, bishops, Lord-Lieutenants, and local commissioners including Justices of the Peace. Under royal supervision these men controlled the administration of the realm. Government was the king's. Parliament met only occasionally and at the royal discretion. So it was natural that those who favoured firm and effective rule should look to a strong monarchy to provide it.

In 1603 there were many reasons why firm government seemed a necessity. Every Tudor monarch had faced at least one major rebellion. Poverty, faction and religious division were the causes. In the later 1590s bad harvests led to the gravest economic crisis of the century. Rioting was commonplace. The dangers of faction were illustrated when the Earl of Essex lost his head in an abortive bid for power in 1601. The dangers of religious division scarcely needed illustration. In France three decades of warfare resulted from friction between Protestant Huguenots and zealous Catholics. Religious disunity attracted foreign intervention. This was duly supplied by Spain. Philip II provided the Catholic League in France with troops and money. England escaped the French fate – but it was by no means obvious that she would do so. Philip sent fleets to conquer England and to assist the Irish in rebellion against Elizabeth. He also aided English Catholic exiles. These men set up seminaries on the Continent to train priests for service in England. The priests were suspected of inciting men to rebellion. Moreover, the mere fact that their activities fostered religious division was sufficient to make them politically dangerous.

The established church was criticised not only by Catholics but also by radical Protestants. After 1570 a number of such people argued for the introduction of a system of church government modelled on Presbyterian Geneva. If their ideas had been implemented, the Queen would have been deprived of effective control over the church. No doubt many Presbyterians, and many

Catholics, were loyal and law-abiding people. Yet from the 1570s foreign Presbyterians had produced a series of highly influential books which claimed that violent resistance was justified against kings who ruled tyrannically, especially by hindering the progress of the true religion. These books included the notorious *Vindiciae contra tyrannos*, published under the name of Stephanus Junius Brutus, and the Scotsman George Buchanan's *De jure regni apud Scotos*. The *Vindiciae* was written to justify Protestant revolt against the crown in France, while Buchanan's book defended the use of force against Mary Queen of Scots, who had been compelled to abdicate from the throne. Both works first appeared in 1579 and rapidly became best-sellers. Over the next three decades Catholics likewise printed many works permitting resistance to heretical or tyrannical rulers. The fact that such radical ideas circulated on the Continent underlined the question of the loyalty of English Catholics and Presbyterians. Did these people share the views of their foreign co-religionists? Even if they did not, it was imperative that the ideas be combated before they could lead to rebellion in England. English security required an antidote to theories of legitimate resistance.

To challenge resistance theory, and to strengthen royal power as a bastion against anarchy, some English writers claimed that the monarch was an absolute ruler. They held that he was accountable to God alone, and that he was above all human laws. In the early Stuart period absolutist doctrines became common, especially amongst the higher clergy. The church acted not only as a spiritual institution, but also as the king's ministry of propaganda. Leading churchmen had the intellectual skills needed to refute ideas of legitimate resistance. They also had a vested interest in controverting the views of their religious opponents. Moreover, they looked to the king to protect their own wealth and power. The king, as Supreme Governor of the church, defended the rights of the clergy. In return, clerics wrote in favour of absolute royal power. Most crudely, the king controlled ecclesiastical patronage and could promote men whose opinions he found congenial. In 1613 John Prideaux, Rector of Exeter College Oxford, was at work on a reply to a book by the Cretan Jesuit Eudaemon-Joannes. The Jesuit had said some harsh things about the authority of kings. James I let Prideaux know that he should take especial care to defend the rights of monarchs. Prideaux took the hint and shortly before the book was published he was promoted to the Regius Professorship of Divinity at Oxford. When Roger Maynwaring used absolutist ideas to defend the Forced Loan of 1627 he was impeached by Parliament, but rewarded by the king.[1]

1 Isaac Casaubon to John Prideaux, 23 March 1613, in Casaubon, *Epistolae* (Rotterdam 1709) 525; cf. Mark Pattison, *Isaac Casaubon, 1559–1614*, 2nd edn (Oxford 1892) 291. On Maynwaring cf. below, Ch. 4, pp. 119–24.

In this chapter, the theory of the Divine Right of Kings is equated with absolutism. But Conrad Russell has argued that many people who were *not* absolutists subscribed to the theory. He claims that it was 'held all the way across the political spectrum', and vigorously denies that it was 'a party creed': 'Divine rights in the early seventeenth century', in John Morrill, Paul Slack and Daniel Woolf, eds, *Public duty and private conscience in seventeenth-century England: essays presented*

The earliest defenders of the church of England against the attacks of papists
and Presbyterians did not always support royal absolutism. In 1559 John
Aylmer, later Bishop of London, published his *Harborowe for faithful and true
subjects*. He criticised ideas of legitimate resistance, but insisted that the government of England was not a 'mere monarchy'. It was, he claimed, a mixture
of monarchy, aristocracy and democracy. The monarch was bound by the
laws of the land. So the Queen was not an absolute sovereign – a 'mere ruler'
– for 'it is not she that ruleth but the laws'.[2] In 1585 Thomas Bilson, later
Bishop of Winchester, published a book entitled *The true difference between
Christian subiection and unchristian rebellion*. His general message was that resistance to Princes is evil. But he admitted that there are certain exceptions to this
rule. For kings, Bilson argued, are bound by the fundamental laws of the
states over which they rule. He took up this position not because he wanted to
show that Elizabeth's powers were limited, but because he wished to justify
the activities of England's allies, the French Protestants and the Dutch, both
of whom had resisted their sovereigns. In the hands of Charles I's opponents
Bilson's work was later used to prove that eminent Elizabethan churchmen
had admitted that royal power is subject to at least some limitations.[3]

The views that the monarch's authority is derived from the people, and that
it is limited by the law of the land, were still expressed by clergymen in the
early 1590s. In his *De presbyterio* of 1591 Matthew Sutcliffe, Dean of Exeter,
derived the Prince's power from an act of transference by the people. At about
the same time Richard Hooker was writing his great *Laws of ecclesiastical*

---

to G.E. *Aylmer* (Oxford 1993) 101–20, at 104–5. However, the ideas which Russell discusses are
not the same as the theory analysed in this chapter. Russell quite correctly notes that people of all
political views derived power from God, in accordance with St Paul's statement that 'the powers
that be are ordained of God' (Romans 13:1); he concludes that everyone endorsed the theory of
divine right and that they were in agreement on fundamentals. On Russell's definition, then, you
support the theory of divine right if you say that the king exercises power which is divine in
origin. According to this definition, people who maintain either of the following two views are
proponents of the doctrine of divine right, and are in fundamental agreement with each another:
(1) God initially granted power to a sovereign people, and they then transferred this divine power
to a king on conditions defined by contract, reserving to themselves the right to resist, depose
and execute him if he broke the contract; the king's power is divine in origin, but limited by
contract; (2) God granted power *directly* and *immediately* to the king and not to the people, so he
is accountable only to God, must always be obeyed except when his commands are contrary to
God's, and may not be actively resisted; his power is *not* limited by contract. In this chapter, the
'Divine Right of Kings' is used to refer to the second of these two views, while the very different
first view is discussed in Chapter 2. A third view was that even if kings originally got power from
God alone, they came in time to be limited by the customary law of the land: this theory is the
subject of Chapter 3. Fuller discussions of Russell's ideas are in Johann P.Sommerville, 'English
and European political ideas in the early seventeenth century: revisionism and the case of absolutism', *Journal of British Studies* 35 (1996) 168–94; and John Sanderson, 'Conrad Russell's ideas',
History of Political Thought 14 (1993) 85–102. See also 'Revisionism revisited: a retrospect', below.
2 Aylmer quoted in G.R. Elton, *The Tudor constitution*, 2nd edn (Cambridge 1982) 16.
3 Thomas Bilson, *The true difference between Christian subiection and unchristian rebellion* (Oxford
1585) 420, 520–1; Robert Baillie, *Ladensium ΑΥΤΟΚΑΤΑΚΡΙΣΙΣ, The Canterburians self-conviction*,
3rd edn (1641) 121; cf. John Locke, *Two treatises of government*, II, 239, and for a pre-Civil War
example of the use of Bilson to confirm resistance theory cf. John Floyd, *God and the king*
(St Omer 1620) 32.

polity, in which he maintained that the Queen's authority was derived from the consent of the commonwealth, that its extent was defined by the 'articles of compact' between the original commonwealth of England and its first king, and that it was limited by the laws of the land.[4]

The eighth book of Hooker's *Laws* is often treated as typical of contemporary thinking on the English constitution. In fact, by 1593, when Hooker published the first four books of his work, such ideas were going out of vogue among the higher clergy. Hooker's *Laws* had little to say about the resistance theories of the French Huguenots. Indeed, its basic premises were not far removed from those of such writings as the *Vindiciae contra tyrannos*. A work published in 1593, and written by Richard Bancroft – later Bishop of London and Archbishop of Canterbury – took a far more vigorous line against Calvinist resistance theories. Bancroft accused the Presbyterians of maintaining ungodly and seditious political opinions, and of plotting to put them into practice in England. Although he left his readers in no doubt that resistance theories were false, he devoted little space to spelling out his own ideas on the origins and extent of the Queen's authority.[5]

Bancroft's book was a work of polemic rather than political theory. The same was not true of another treatise published in 1593 – Hadrian Saravia's *De imperandi authoritate*. Saravia was born at Hesdin in Artois, but he was naturalised as an Englishman in 1568, and later held various livings in the English church. He was a translator of the Authorised Version of the Bible. In 1590 he published a book asserting that bishops derive their spiritual powers from God alone. This work had a great impact upon the development of English ecclesiastical thought. The *De imperandi authoritate* was perhaps equally significant. It was published by the Queen's Printer, an indication of official approval. In the *De imperandi* Saravia put forward a systematic set of alternatives to the resistance theories of Catholics and Calvinists. He argued that the Queen derived her power not from the people but from God alone, and claimed that she was bound by no purely human laws. These views contrast strongly with those expressed by Hooker at about the same time. It is worth noting that whereas Saravia's work was reprinted in 1611 by the Company of Stationers of London, Hooker's eighth book, in which he voiced his political opinions most clearly, remained in manuscript until after the Parliamentarians had triumphed over Charles I in the Civil War.

The doctrine that kings derive their powers from God alone was the orthodox teaching of the early Stuart clergy. It was officially endorsed by their representative organs, the Convocations of York and Canterbury, in 1606.[6] It

4 Matthew Sutcliffe, *De presbyterio, eiusque nova in ecclesia Christiana politeia* (1591) 155: 'At primis temporibus populus cum nullo certo teneretur imperio, ad unum aliquem summam detulit potestatem, eumque regem constituit.' Richard Hooker, *The laws of ecclesiastical polity*, VIII, ii, 5, 11.
5 Richard Bancroft, *Daungerous positions and proceedings* (1593) especially 14–18.
6 *The convocation book of MDCVI. Commonly called Bishop Overall's convocation book* (Oxford 1844) *passim*. Hooker and Saravia are compared and contrasted in J.P. Sommerville, 'Richard Hooker, Hadrian Saravia, and the advent of the Divine Right of Kings', *History of Political Thought* 4 (1983) 229–45.

was voiced in countless treatises and sermons.[7] It was the key proposition in a little dialogue entitled *God and the king* which was published in 1615 and compiled at James I's command as a textbook for the instruction of the young in their political duties.[8] The contention that the king drew his authority from God alone was the central plank on which absolutist theory rested. For this reason the theory is often referred to as the 'Divine Right of Kings'. This term is a misnomer, for absolutists asserted the natural right of all governments. They held that whatever the form of government – monarchy, aristocracy or democracy – the powers of the governor were derived from God alone. Secondly, they believed that these powers arose not in some mysterious supernatural way, but as a consequence of human nature. Reason showed that human nature was constructed in such a way that men needed government. Since God was the creator of nature, it could be said that He was the author of government. Nevertheless, it was not upon the revealed will of God, expressed in the Bible, but upon the law of nature, inscribed in the heart of everyone and discoverable by reason, that government was based. The concept of the law of nature was crucial in the thought of the absolutists. Any serious investigation of early Stuart political ideas must begin with an account of it.

THE LAW OF NATURE

English political thinkers did not work in a historical vacuum. Their conceptual apparatus was the product of tradition. Specifically, they were educated as Christians and Aristotelians. Theology took pride of place in the curriculum of the universities they attended. The division of subjects and the logic applied to their study was Aristotelian. To understand their substantive political doctrines it is vital to grasp at least the outlines of late-medieval Christian and Aristotelian teaching on the law of nature. It is difficult to understand modern communism unless we possess some acquaintance with the work of Karl Marx. It is equally difficult to understand early Stuart absolutism without some knowledge of the natural law tradition.

In the early Middle Ages many thinkers held that human nature was too corrupt for people unaidedly to construct a just political society. The only such society which existed, they believed, was the church, which had been set up by Christ. The views of these thinkers have become known as political Augustinianism. In the thirteenth century the rediscovery of the political writings of the ancient Greek philosopher Aristotle led to an intellectual revolution

---

7 For example, Lancelot Andrewes, *Tortura Torti*, ed. J. Bliss (Oxford 1851) 472–3; *Responsio ad apologiam Cardinalis Bellarmini*, ed. J. Bliss (Oxford 1851) 97; Richard Sheldon, *Certain general reasons, proving the lawfulness of the oath of allegiance* (1611) 11–12; John Buckeridge, 'The Lord Bishop of Rochester his defence of the power of kings', St John's College Cambridge Mss James 305(3), 1; Theophilus Field, 'Duae quaestiones', BL Royal Mss 18.A.XXXIX, f. 21a; Anon, 'Quaestio: rex in regno suo est minor solo Deo', CUL Addit. Mss 3320, f. 40a; Lord Chancellor Ellesmere, *The speech of the Lord Chancellor of England, in the eschequer chamber, touching the post-nati* (1609) 98–9.

8 *SRP*, I, 355–6. The book is sometimes ascribed to Richard Mocket.

in Europe. Aristotle had claimed that we are by nature political animals and
his ideas were used to launch a vigorous attack on the doctrines of the political
Augustinians. The Augustinians argued that the pope, as Christ's vicar on earth,
was the sole possessor of just and valid political power. Using Aristotle's
idea that political society is natural, their opponents argued that the states of
Europe were autonomous and independent of papal control. Since political
society was natural to all people, both pagans and Christians, the fact that the
pope was Christ's vicar on earth gave him no claim to a monopoly of political
power. The general tendency of the thought of the Aristotelians was to reduce
the authority of the pope and the clergy. In the hands of such an extreme
Aristotelian as Marsiglio of Padua, who completed his *Defensor Pacis* in 1324,
the clergy were shorn of almost all their powers.

By far the most influential figure to devote his attention to the dispute
between the Augustinians and the Aristotelians was the thirteenth-century
theologian and philosopher St Thomas Aquinas. Aquinas translated Aristotle's
ideas into Christian terms and effected a compromise between them and the
theories of the Augustinians. He claimed that God had given humans certain
goals and had implanted in their nature the means by which they could perceive and achieve these objectives. One such objective was well-being and
happiness in this life. By following reason, with which God had endowed
everyone, it was possible to attain temporal felicity. The precepts of reason
could be called the law of nature, since it was our natural objectives which the
precepts were designed to promote. The law of nature was God's law since it
consisted of a set of instructions which God had imprinted in human nature at
the creation.

One of these instructions was that people should join together in political
societies, for these were essential to securing the material welfare of humans.
Government was, therefore, natural to everyone. So the pope was not the
temporal lord of the world, and kings did not derive their authority from
him. However, the law of nature, upon which civil government was based,
was a part of God's law and as such was compatible with the teachings of
Christianity and with the authority of the church. The function of the church
was to fulfil people's spiritual purposes. The means by which we might attain
salvation could not be discovered through reason alone, but had been revealed
by Christ. Revelation – the law of grace – was inscribed in the Bible, not in
human nature. Its precepts concerned spiritual welfare and applied only to
Christians, not to all people. It was from the law of grace that the church
derived its powers, for these had been granted to it by Christ himself. Since
spiritual goals were of greater importance than temporal aims, the spiritual
powers of the church were superior to the temporal powers of civil commonwealths. Aquinas' theory vindicated both the autonomy of political societies
in the temporal sphere – which had been asserted by the Aristotelians – and
the supremacy of the pope – for which the Augustinians had argued.

In the later Middle Ages the theory of Aquinas, taken broadly, became the
orthodox teaching of universities throughout Europe. It was upon the law of

nature that civil society was grounded. Moreover, the law of nature was held to supply a set of moral imperatives which could not justly be infringed by any human authority. A human law which was incompatible with the superior law of God was simply void and not really a law at all. People were obliged to obey God rather than man. Of God's laws some were regarded as natural to humans, and hence as applying at all times and in all places. These natural laws included certain elementary religious principles which even pagans could recognise, but they did not include any essentially Christian duties. Christianity did indeed confirm people's political obligations. But it was from the law of nature that these obligations were derived, for humans were by nature political animals.

It might be thought that in post-Reformation England humanism combined with Protestantism to destroy the dependence of political thinking upon theories of natural law. Certainly, humanists such as Erasmus hoped to revive the true Christian message by returning to the original texts of the Scriptures and other ancient writings. They believed that over the centuries this message had been obscured by the endless pedantic quibblings of monks, and they attacked many aspects of the learning purveyed in medieval universities. Protestants likewise assaulted this learning, at least inasmuch as it supported Catholic conclusions. So it is true that the advent of humanism, and later of Protestantism, represented a break with the traditions of scholasticism – the academic system which prevailed in the Middle Ages. Many old dogmas were abandoned. It does not follow that the specific doctrine of the natural law was rejected. In fact, as we shall see, belief in natural law remained strong in early-seventeenth-century England, and was central to much of the political thinking of the period. Nature, people said, instilled a basic knowledge of moral absolutes in everyone. Political truths could be deduced from this knowledge.[9]

9 For different interpretations see J.N. Figgis, *The divine right of kings*, 2nd edn (Cambridge 1914) 152; Richard Tuck, *Natural rights theories: their origin and development* (Cambridge 1979) 144; James Daly, *Sir Robert Filmer and English political thought* (Toronto 1979) 139; J.D. Eusden, *Puritans, lawyers, and politics in early seventeenth-century England* (New Haven 1958) 131.
  A recent account which de-emphasises traditional scholastic natural law thinking and instead stresses the importance of scepticism and the so-called 'new humanism' is Richard Tuck, *Philosophy and government 1572–1651* (Cambridge 1993). According to Tuck, many major seventeenth-century writers on natural law – such as Grotius and Hobbes – were not really working in the old scholastic tradition of natural law at all. Rather, their background was in the Renaissance scepticism of Montaigne and Charron, and in theories of reason of state connected with Machiavelli and Tacitus. Tuck claims that Montaigne was sceptical about most things, but that he did acknowledge the central importance of self-preservation to human conduct (51); Grotius, whose main intention was to refute the scepticism of Montaigne and Charron, was 'fully conscious of the salience of the principle of self-preservation in the sceptics' account of how man should actually live' and placed it at the centre of his own work, showing how a whole 'theory of ethical conduct (including a theory of justice)' could be generated from this one principle (173).
  This interpretation is open to the objection that self-preservation did not in fact play much of a role in the thinking of Montaigne and Charron. Montaigne praised people who preferred death to loss of freedom or to dishonour (*The essays of Michel de Montaigne*, translated by M.A. Screech (1991) 236–7, 1030), and Charron stated that only the 'vulgar unlearned sot' accounts life 'a sovereign good, and preferreth it above all things', affirming that 'wisdom itself teacheth us' that death 'is a freedom from all evils' (Pierre Charron, *Of wisdome, three bookes* (no date, *c.*1612) 330,

There was very wide agreement on the existence of a natural law inscribed by God in our hearts and discoverable by reason. Indeed, the notions that the law of nature is reason, implanted in humans by God at the creation, that it is the rule of right and wrong, and that it is superior to any human law, were commonplaces. William Pemberton, a Jacobean cleric, asserted that God had 'instamped in mans nature' a rule by which he might 'live well' and added that this 'law of workes, called the morall law, is grounded on nature'. John Donne, the poet and theologian, referred to 'rectified reason, which is the law of nature'. According to the common lawyer Sir Henry Finch, 'the law of nature is that soveraigne reason fixed in mans nature, which ministreth common principles of good and evill'. Finch believed that human laws 'which are contrarie to the Law of nature' were void, citing as examples a law of the ancient Egyptians which kept men at home and sent women out to work, and any law which permitted adultery.[10]

The law of nature was frequently equated with God's moral law, set out in the Ten Commandments. The cleric Francis Mason spoke of 'the law of human nature', asserting that it was 'the same in substance with the Law Morall', and claiming that those things which it commanded 'are in their own nature good and everlastingly to bee imbraced'. According to the layman Edward Forsett 'whatsoever nature by her uncorrupted rules doth induce or perswade us unto, touching our duties in Morall actions, the same, as it was written by the finger of God, in the heart of man at the Creation, so was it also reduced and comprised by the Wisedome of God, into the Tables of the Moral Law'. In a sermon of 1606 John Buckeridge, later Bishop of Rochester and Ely, adopted the same position. The churchman Foulke Robarts referred to 'things Morall, and founded on the law of nature'. This equation of the law of nature with the moral law was not intended to show that natural law was equivalent to any narrow construction of the Ten Commandments, for the Commandments were held to have implications far beyond their literal sense. All forms of civil obligation, and not merely the duty to honour parents, were commonly held to be deducible from the Fifth Commandment. Again, the theologian George Carleton maintained that tithes were due to the clergy by the law of nature although there is no specific mention of them in the Ten Commandments. In the Parliament of 1621, Sir Edwin Sandys asserted that 'the Lawe of nature teacheth to repell force with force, and no civill Lawe can dissolve the Lawe of nature'. The principle that self-defence is permissible or

114). Moreover, it is unclear that Grotius' principal concern was to refute scepticism, or that he gave particular weight to self-preservation. Accounts which stress the affinities between Grotius' thinking and traditional Aristotelianism/scholasticism include Charles S. Edwards, *Hugo Grotius: the miracle of Holland* (Chicago 1981) 148–55; M.M. Goldsmith, 'Hobbes: ancient and modern', in Tom Sorell, ed., *The rise of modern philosophy* (Oxford 1993) 317–36, at 326–30; and John A. Trentman, 'Scholasticism in the seventeenth century', in Norman Kretzmann *et al.*, eds, *The Cambridge history of later medieval philosophy* (Cambridge 1982) 818–37, at 828, 833.
10 William Pemberton, *The charge of God and the king* (1619) 2–4; John Donne, *Pseudo-Martyr* (1610) 171; Sir Henry Finch, *Law, or, a discourse thereof* (1627) 3–4, 75.

even obligatory was one of the major tenets of natural law thinking, though it was only with considerable ingenuity that it could be deduced from the Decalogue.[11]

Did the idea of natural law appeal to all Protestant groups or only to some? It has been suggested that in the early seventeenth century it was 'Anglicans' who adopted natural law theories, while 'puritans', taking a much gloomier view of human nature, relied on Scripture alone as a guide to moral truths.[12] In fact, this is difficult to support. The puritan Robert Bolton accepted the distinction of the 'Schoole Divines' – medieval scholastics – between the law of nature, the law of nations, and human laws. William Prynne held that the wickedness of stage plays was one of the 'divine truths founded in the law of nature, of which heathen men by the light of nature are competent judges'. William Ames, a very influential puritan writer and Professor of Theology at the Dutch university of Franeker, held wholly conventional views about the law of nature. 'Divine Right', he wrote, is divided into Right Naturall, and Right positive. Right Naturall is that which is apprehended to be fit to be done or avoided, out of the naturall instinct of Naturall Light; or that which is at least deduced from that Naturall Light by evident Consequence.' Ames affirmed that 'that in morality is called Right, which accords with right practicall reason, and Right practicall is the Law of Nature'. He held that the Ten Commandments were a summary of natural law.[13]

It might be supposed that the Protestant emphasis on the corruption of human nature would have led to a rejection of natural law. In fact, Protestants believed that corruption had not entirely obliterated people's ability to distinguish between good and evil. The doctrine of natural law was held to be compatible with a Calvinist theology of grace. The Fall had indeed corrupted people's nature to such an extent that it was now impossible for them to merit salvation by their own efforts. Salvation, the Calvinists argued, could be obtained only through God's grace which was given freely and not as a consequence of our works. Human nature was totally corrupted in the sense that on their own people could do nothing to achieve salvation. Yet nature was not so corrupt that pagans, lacking grace, were wholly blind to God's laws. The light of nature was sufficiently strong to give pagans some knowledge of God's will, and to condemn them for not doing all they could to obey it. Of course, Protestants insisted that God's revealed will was more excellent than

11 Francis Mason, *The authority of the church in making canons*, 2nd edn (Oxford 1634) 5; Edward Forsett, *A defence of the right of kings* (1624) 25; John Buckeridge, *A sermon preached at Hampton Court* (1606) sig. C3a; Foulke Robarts, *Gods holy house and service* (1639) 15; George Carleton, *Tithes examined and proved to bee due to the clergie by a divine right* (1606) ff. 9a, 35a–37a; *CD 21*, v, 159–60. The political uses of the Fifth Commandment are discussed in G.J. Schochet, 'Patriarchalism, politics and mass attitudes in Stuart England', *HJ* 12 (1969) 413–41.
12 J.F.H. New, *Anglican and puritan* (1964) *passim*, especially 13, 47, 78–91.
13 Robert Bolton, *Two sermons preached at Northampton* (1635) 8; William Prynne to William Laud, 11 June 1634, in S.R. Gardiner, ed., *Documents relating to the proceedings against William Prynne, in 1634 and 1637* (1877) 39; William Ames, *Conscience with the power and cases thereof* (1639) 100, 105, 107; cf. John Davenport, *An apologeticall reply* (1636) 66.

the dictates of mere reason. According to Ames, there is nowhere to be found 'any true right practicall reason, pure and complete in all parts, but in the written Law of God'. This was not, however, a particularly Protestant doctrine. The Jesuit Thomas Fitzherbert admitted that 'the light of nature is almost extinct in man' and held that the precepts of God's written law – the Ten Commandments – had been 'given to recall men to the law of nature, by terrour of penaltie'. He believed that even pagans were able to detect the corruption of human nature, but that unlike Christians they could not perceive 'the only true remedy thereof'. This remedy, which could be 'learned by the veritie of holy scripture', was 'our conversion and returne to God, by the helpe of his grace'.[14]

The existence of the law of nature was not at issue in the controversies between predestinarian Calvinists and their opponents, whether Catholic or Protestant. Nor was the fact that since the Fall human nature was corrupt, so that the law of nature could not now be fully obeyed or perceived. The real issue was whether fallen humans could ever do anything to merit God's grace. This question was of great theological interest, but had few implications for political theory. It was precisely because of this that the resistance theories of Catholics and Calvinists were so similar. The political thinkers of the early seventeenth century needed no Intellectual Revolution to free them from the trammels of authority and usher in a new Age of Reason. Reason – the law of nature – was already their guide. Both absolutists and resistance theorists shared many fundamental assumptions about the contents of the law of nature. The most basic was the doctrine of the necessity of government.

THE NECESSITY OF GOVERNMENT

Natural law was held to comprise principles which were evident to reason. There was wide agreement on what these principles were. A case in point is the notion that government is necessary. To people in early-seventeenth-century England this was an obvious fact. There was no police force or standing army. Gentlemen wore swords and used them on little provocation. Poverty led to vagrancy and crime. 'Everyone', says Peter Laslett, 'was quite well aware . . . that the poorer peasantry might at any time break out into violence'. The number of serious crimes probably rose under Elizabeth to reach 'a peak between 1590 and 1620'.[15] In these circumstances, the necessity of government seemed manifest. The notion that too little government is better than too much is modern.

According to Robert Bolton, 'Government is the prop and pillar of all States and Kingdoms, the cement and soule of humane affaires, the life of society and order, the very vitall spirit whereby so many millions of men doe

14 Ames, *Conscience*, 108; Thomas Fitzherbert, *The second part of a treatise concerning policy and religion* (Douai 1615), 209, 411.
15 Peter Laslett, *The world we have lost* (1971) 53; Keith Wrightson, *English society 1580–1680* (1982) 149.

18

breathe the life of comfort and peace; and the whole nature of things subsist.' The ideas that human nature requires society and that society requires government were wholly conventional. As the churchman Nicholas Byfield put it, 'man by the instinct of God, and by the nature given him, tends to society'. John Selden, the eminent scholar and common lawyer, traced the origins of the English commonwealth to 'the first peopling of the land, when men by nature being civil creatures grew to plant a common societie'. Even if society consisted of only two men, argued Hadrian Saravia, it would not long survive unless one commanded and the other obeyed. If everyone is allowed 'the freedome of his own sword', claimed the cleric William Dickinson, 'there will soone be an end of all civill society, and good order amongst the affaires of man'. James I held that without government there would be anarchy, and that this was worse than the worst form of government, which was tyranny. He believed that there was order even in Hell and that the devils had their chieftains.[16]

Like the Calvinist Bolton, the Arminian theologian Thomas Jackson held that society and government were natural to humans. He claimed that 'the imperfection of man's corrupted nature makes the society and help of others more necessary to him than it is to any other creatures by nature sociable'. People require the help of their fellows to achieve even simple objectives. 'If we consider but the preparation of that food which is necessary to every one that will live as a man, this alone is a greater task than any one man can perform.' But 'every man's affections being principally set upon himself and his' human society would collapse through 'strife and debate unquenchable' if a ruler were not set up to govern men. 'So then the imperfection of human nature, the necessity of society which this imperfection requires, and the occasions of discord which this necessity breeds, do all by God's providence and ordinance impel men to seek after and admit some power of jurisdiction which may compel all and every one to observe the rules of society in peace.'[17]

Of course, Calvinists took a gloomy view of human nature. Yet they held that government served not only to curb people's sinfulness, but also, and much more positively, to enable them to fulfil the potentialities of their nature. Robert Bolton did indeed claim that if 'Soveraignty' were taken from the face of the earth 'men would become cut-throats and Canibals one unto another' and 'all kinds of villanies, outrages, and savage cruelty, would overflow all Countries'. Nevertheless, strict Calvinist though he was, Bolton believed that government not only has the negative purpose of repressing sin, but also that 'it giveth opportunity by Gods blessing, for the free exercise, and full improvement of all humane abilities, to their utmost worth and excellency'.

16 Bolton, *Two sermons*, 10; Nicholas Byfield, *A commentary upon the first three chapters of the first epistle generall of St Peter* (1637) 441; John Selden, 'Notes upon Fortescue', 19, in Sir John Fortescue, *De laudibus legum Angliae* (1616); Hadrian Saravia, *De imperandi authoritate* in *Diversi tractatus theologici* (1611) 122, 159; William Dickinson, *The kings right; an assize sermon* (1619) sig. D3a; James I, *The true lawe of free monarchies* (Edinburgh 1598) sig. D6a–7a; in *Political writings*, ed. Johann P. Sommerville (Cambridge 1994) 79 (anarchy); *A premonition* (1609), 44 (devils).
17 Thomas Jackson, *A treatise of Christian obedience*, in *Works*, 12 vols (Oxford 1844) XII, 311.

Protestants normally dated *coercive* government to the period after the Fall, but held that government itself had existed even in Eden. As Buckeridge put it, 'order of superioritie and subjection is the instinct of purest nature: For in heaven there is order among blessed Angels. . . . And in the state of innocencie there was superioritie and subjection not only betweene man and all other creatures, but betweene man and woman.' The Civil lawyer Calybute Downing said much the same thing in virtually the same words. According to John Donne 'if the world had continued in the first Innocency, yet there should have been Magistracie'.[18]

Even before the Fall, the pursuit of co-operative enterprises necessitated government. If human nature had not been corrupted, however, there would have been no need for the enforcement of the magistrate's commands by temporal penalties, since everyone would willingly have obeyed them. 'Even in innocencie', wrote the clergyman William Sclater, 'there was a subordination of one to another, though without paine as now it is.' Edward Boughen, another churchman, insisted that if people had continued in the state of innocence 'there should have beene a power directive, though not coercive, to have prescribed order'. In support of this point Boughen cited 'a great learned man', the sixteenth-century Catholic theorist Vitoria. There was, indeed, little difference between Protestant and Catholic views on the necessity of government. It is true that Protestants deduced the need for coercion from the sinfulness of man's fallen nature. 'So servile and vicious is the nature of man', wrote Pemberton, 'that it hath neede to be curbed and restrained from evill, by threat and execution of correction and punishment.' Catholics, however, likewise dated coercive authority from the Fall.[19]

So society and government were natural. Little was heard in early-seventeenth-century England of the doctrine that government is an artificial and not a natural creation. Sclater noted that according to Cicero it was oratory, and not natural sociability, which 'first drew into civill communion the dispersed and brutish companies of men'. But he argued that people would not have responded to the orator's appeals that they gather together in society unless nature had predisposed them to a social life: 'some principle there must be acknowledged in man's nature fit to acknowledge the equitie of such constitutions'. John Selden attacked the Ciceronian picture in a different way. He pointed out that people who lived before the first societies had been set up could not have been subject to human laws. It could not, therefore, have been from human law that they acquired the obligation to abide by the norms of society, when once they entered it. A ground of obligation separate from human laws must exist to explain the obligation to obey human laws themselves.

18 Bolton, *Two sermons*, 10–11; Buckeridge, *Sermon*, sig. C3a; Calybute Downing, *A discourse of the state ecclesiasticall*, 2nd edn (Oxford 1634) 68; Donne, *Pseudo-Martyr*, 83.
19 William Sclater, *A sermon preached at the last generall assize holden for the county of Sommerset* (1616) 6; Edward Boughen, *A sermon concerning decencie and order* (1638) 15; Pemberton, *The charge of God and the king*, 83; cf. St Thomas Aquinas, *Summa Theologiae*, Ia.q.96, art. 3–4, in *Selected political writings*, ed. A.P. D'Entrèves (Oxford 1959) 102–5.

According to Selden, this ground was the law of nature, enacted by God and inscribed in the heart of everyone.[20]

To explain the historical origins of civil society many writers thought it sufficient to observe that people are by nature sociable. This was the position of Marc'Antonio De Dominis, the former Catholic Archbishop of Spalato who served James I as Dean of Windsor and Master of the Savoy. De Dominis, like many other authors, followed Aristotle closely on the question of natural sociability. Government, considered abstractly, was commonly regarded as a prescription of God, the author of nature. As the clergyman John White put it, 'Government and eminency is of God, by his own ordinance, for the benefite of mankind, and the maintenance of civill societie.'[21]

Since government was the ordinance of God, consent was unimportant in explaining its origins. The consent of individuals might indeed explain how they at first came to be members of the society. 'A Common-wealth', said the Civil lawyer William Vaughan, 'is a society of free men, united together by a generall consent.' But consent did not explain how the power of governing arose. For the power of governing included the right to execute criminals, and by nature no individual possessed this right. So the power was derived from God's law of nature and not from any act of transference on the part of individuals.[22]

In his *De jure praedae* of around 1606 the great Dutch theorist Hugo Grotius put forward the view that individuals had originally possessed the power to punish criminals, and that the state had been set up when they first transferred this power to the whole community. Writing in the 1680s, John Locke likewise embraced what he called the 'strange doctrine' that each individual originally possessed the 'executive power of the law of nature'. Thomas Hobbes adopted a similar stance in the middle of the seventeenth century, though his argument was slightly different from that of Grotius and Locke. For Hobbes claimed that the state began when individuals authorised not the community but the sovereign (who could be one or a few people) to act in their name. Grotius and Locke, on the other hand, claimed that individuals transferred their rights to the society as a whole.[23]

20 Sclater, *Sermon*, 4; Selden, *De jure naturali et gentium* (1640) 92–4; cf. William Barret, *Ius regis* (1612) 10. There are contrasting interpretations of Selden's ideas on the law of nature in Tuck, *Natural rights theories*, 82–100, and Johann P. Sommerville, 'John Selden, the law of nature, and the origins of government', *HJ* 27 (1984) 437–47. Recently, Tuck has claimed that Selden grounded human knowledge of natural law upon 'an *external* force, a god or angel, capable of giving illumination to the human mind' and especially prone (apparently) to reveal things to 'the posterity of Noah through Shem': Tuck, *Philosophy and government*, 216. It is true that Selden – writing about Hebrew ideas on natural law – reported a number of Jewish traditions, but there seems little reason to suppose that he endorsed this rather exotic one.
21 Marc'Antonio De Dominis, *De republica ecclesiastica pars secunda* (1620) 519; John White, *Two sermons* (1615) 18.
22 William Vaughan, *The golden-grove, moralized in three bookes*, 2nd edn (1608) sig. R5a–b.
23 Hugo Grotius, *De jure praedae*, tr. G.L. Williams (Oxford 1950) 91–2; Locke, *Two treatises*, II, 13; Thomas Hobbes, *Leviathan*, ed. C.B. Macpherson (Harmondsworth 1968) 227. Contrasting views on whether Grotius later repudiated the doctrine are in Tuck, *Philosophy and government*, 177, and James Tully, *An approach to political philosophy: Locke in contexts* (Cambridge 1993) 20.

Early Stuart English writers, by contrast, did not derive political power from any transference of rights by individuals. A partial exception to this rule is William Barret. As chaplain of Gonville and Caius College Cambridge, Barret caused a sensation in 1595 by preaching a sermon against the orthodox Calvinist theology of grace. Soon afterwards he became a Catholic, but he later supported James I in his controversies with Jesuits on political theory. Barret claimed that by nature individuals had originally possessed some transferable rights over themselves (though not over others) and that in order to set up a king it was necessary that these rights be transferred to him. Yet Barret held that the king's powers were greater than the sum total of the powers he had received from individuals, for the king could execute his subjects, while they had not had the right to execute themselves or each other. So Barret derived the king's authority to inflict the death penalty from God alone. The same argument recurs in the writings of royalist thinkers of the 1640s.[24]

According to early Stuart theory, people did not have the power to coerce each other into joining society. So societies arose by consent – or by birth. Once they had arisen, however, political power came into existence within them without any further human act. 'If a companie of Savages should consent and concurre to a civill manner of living', wrote John Donne, 'Magistracie, and Superioritie, would necessarily, and naturally, and Divinely grow out of this consent.' Society and government were not just institutions which people happened to have set up for their own comfort, but prescriptions of God's law of nature. The 'Lawes of soveraigntie and subjection', wrote the common lawyer Thomas Nash, 'had their originall from the beginning of times, long before the Lawes of Moses were written, even from the Law of nature.'[25]

Though the law of nature enjoined that humans live in society and under government it did not follow that they had always done so. People could break laws, including the law of nature. The clergyman Robert Pricke did, indeed, adopt the extreme thesis that 'there was never people or Nation so barbarous and savage: never assembly of men so void of the light and knowledge of God' that it did not admit 'some Prince or Superior', and declared that this was 'a matter cleare by the experience of all times'. The Civil lawyer and historian Sir John Hayward, on the other hand, took the opposite point of view, rejecting the claim that 'there was never people found, either in ancient time, or of late discoverie, which had not some magistrate to governe them'. But he hastened to observe that 'it is not necessarie to have so large a consent of nations', maintaining that the law of nature could be deduced from 'the received custome, successively of all, and alwaies of most nations in the world'. The example of recently discovered tribes of American Indians was, as Saravia noted, sufficient to indicate that not all people lived in political societies, but it

24 Barret, *Ius regis*, 127; Tuck, *Natural rights theories*, 108–9.
25 Donne, *Pseudo-Martyr*, 83; Thomas Nash, *Quaternio or a foure-fold way to a happy life* (1636) 138.

did not serve to undermine the thesis that government was natural, for the law of nature could be broken.[26]

The belief that government was natural was widely accepted in early-seventeenth-century England. The fact that God had ordained through the law of nature that there be government did not, however, serve to prove anything in particular about the nature and limitations of contemporary governments. If government had at first arisen as a consequence of God's natural law, and not as a result of any transference of individual rights, it might be necessary to conclude that the powers of the first governors had been derived from God alone, and that it was only to God that these governors were accountable for their exercise. It was by no means obvious, however, that such conclusions would apply to contemporary governments.

Most Catholic and Calvinist resistance theorists accepted that government was natural. But they claimed that in every particular society the power of governing had at first resided in the community as a whole. The authority of kings, they argued, was derived from the consent of the community. Each community, they believed, had at first possessed sovereign power over its members. In setting up a king, the community had transferred this power to a single man. This act of transference took place upon whatever conditions the community chose to stipulate. If the king's actions infringed these conditions, power would revert to the community. The practical implications of this view were that the king's authority was limited by the original conditions – or fundamental laws – set down by the people, and that in certain circumstances the king could be resisted and even deposed by the community.

In order to rebut these conclusions, the advocates of absolutism denied that political power had originally resided in the community as a whole. They claimed that whoever now possessed authority, derived it from God alone, and not from the people. Drawing a strong distinction between a ruler's power and his title, they claimed that his authority itself was derived immediately from God, though his title might be derived from the people. Some authors also attacked the notion that political power had originally resided in the community by suggesting that the first political societies had been families. It was widely accepted that power over a family was in the hands of the father. But the father's power was often regarded as non-political, since it did not include the power to execute his wife or children. By claiming that fathers had at first possessed the right to inflict the death penalty upon members of their families, a number of authors tried to show that the earliest political societies were not self-governing democracies, but monarchies ruled over by a father and king.

In the early seventeenth century the majority of Catholic political theorists, including such major figures as Francisco Suarez, a Jesuit who has been

---

26 Robert Pricke, *The doctrine of superioritie, and of subiection* (1609) sig. C1b–C2a; Sir John Hayward, *An answer to the first part of a certaine conference* (1603) sig. B2a; Saravia, *De imperandi authoritate*, 166.

described as the teacher of early modern Europe,[27] and Robert Bellarmine, a Saint and Doctor of the Catholic church, maintained that the powers of kings were derived from an act of transference – or 'translation' – to them by the people. In modern Catholic writings on political theory this view has become known as 'translation theory'. After the French Revolution of 1789, a number of Catholic theorists abandoned the translation theory because of its implication that the people might in certain circumstances depose their kings. These writers claimed that the people had not at first *transferred* power to the king, but had merely *designated* the person of the ruler. It was God alone, they held, who granted the ruler his power. Modern Catholics refer to this approach as 'designation theory'. In the early seventeenth century Protestant absolutists such as James I and his supporters adopted strikingly similar views. Indeed, 'designation theory' was the orthodoxy of early Stuart absolutists.

DESIGNATION THEORY

Writing in 1649, the puritan theologian John Goodwin recalled that

> between thirty and forty years since, when I was a young student in Cambridge . . . such doctrines and devises as these: . . . that the interest of the people extends only to the nomination or presentation of such a person unto God, who they desire might be their king, but that the regal power, by which he is properly and formally constituted a king, is, immediately and independently in respect of any act of the people derived unto him by God – these, I say, or such like positions as these were the known preferment-divinity of the doctorate there, and as the common air, taken in and breathed out by those who lived the life of hope in the king and sought the truth in matters of religion by the light of his countenance.[28]

Goodwin was right to think that these views were standard in academic circles before the Civil War. Moreover, designation theory remained a staple doctrine of royalism in the 1640s.

'In the first original of kings', James I admitted in 1610, 'some had their beginning by conquest and some by election of the people.' Though election might account for how a man had become king, however, it did not account for how he acquired his power. James believed that popular consent might originally have made a particular man a king, but he held that the king's power came directly from God. Thomas Morton, who lectured in logic at Cambridge in the 1590s and served the first two Stuarts as Bishop successively of Chester, Lichfield and Durham, admitted 'election of people to have been upon necessitie usuall', but thought that 'wheresoever a king is established

---

27 Leroy Loemker, *Struggle for synthesis: the seventeenth-century background of Leibniz's synthesis of order and freedom* (Cambridge, Mass. 1972) 119.
28 John Goodwin, *The obstructours of justice* (1649) 28–9.

by consent of the Kingdom, this ordinance is of God, and the people must obey'. Consent might give the king his title, but it did not confer authority upon him. Morton stated that the Catholic theologian Bellarmine 'erreth . . . by not distinguishing betweene the Title of authority, and the authority it selfe. . . . For the title unto an authority is not without the meanes of man, but the authority it selfe is immediately from God.' The same position was publicly maintained by another churchman at Cambridge in 1614: 'To have this or that king is by human law. Election makes the king capable of dominion', but 'to obey a king once constituted is by divine law. God himself gives the right of dominion to the man who has been elected.'[29]

This distinction between a king's title and his authority was commonly made throughout the first half of the seventeenth century. Speaking of kings, William Sclater affirmed that 'the persons are sometimes intruders, as in case of usurpation; sometimes abusers of their authoritie, as when they tyrannize: but the powers themselves have God for their author'. Similarly, Robert Bolton informed his audience that 'the question is not, by what meanes, whether by hereditary succession, or election, or any other humane forme, a Prince comes into his Kingdome, but whether by the ordinance of God we ought to obey him, when he is established'. Bolton resoundingly answered this question in the affirmative. He drew an analogy between the origins of royal power and the Catholic theory of papal power. Catholics claimed that a man became pope when he was elected by the cardinals, but that he derived his papal powers from God alone: 'I hope the Pope is hoisted into his chaire of pestilence by the election of the Cardinals or worse meanes, and yet that hinders not our adversaries from holding it a divine ordinance.' Precisely the same analogy was drawn by John Buckeridge and William Barret.[30]

The same distinction between the king's authority and his title was reiterated in the 1640s. The continuity between royalist theories before and after the outbreak of the Civil War is striking. On the question of the origins of royal authority few royalist writers of the Civil War period had much to add to the arguments of their predecessors. Writing in 1642 Sir John Spelman endorsed designation theory by claiming that it was lawful for an ungoverned multitude 'to designe the particular person or persons' who were to rule over them, but that 'the power so determined by their vote . . . is from God still'. Henry Hammond, one of Charles I's chaplains, similarly maintained that the power of the people extended no further than the designation of the person(s) of their ruler(s): 'And in case it were the act of the People, and not of God

29 James I, *The kings maiesties speach to the Lords and Commons the xxj. of March 1609* (1610) sig. B3a, in *Political writings*, ed. Sommerville, 183; Thomas Morton, *A full satisfaction concerning a double Romish iniquitie* (1606) I, 29; *The encounter against M. Parsons* (1610) II, 49, I, 246. CUL Mss Addit. 3320, f. 12b: 'Habere regem hunc vel illum est de jure humano. Electio facit regem capacem dominii. Parere regi jam constituto est de jure divino. Deus ipse dat electo jus dominii.'
30 Sclater, *Sermon*, 2; Bolton, *Two sermons*, 16; Buckeridge, *De potestate papae in rebus temporalibus* (1614) 291; Barret, *Ius regis*, 28; cf. Sheldon, *Certain general reasons*, 11–12.

immediately, that designs or nominates the Person to that Office, yet doth not this nomination bestow this power, but God who alone hath that power, bestows it on him who is thus nominated.' Again, Henry Ferne, another chaplain to Charles I – and previously chaplain to Thomas Morton – wrote of kings in the following terms: 'though hee [sc. God] doth not now immediately designe those his Vicegerents, but by other meanes, bee it by the choice of the People; yet have they their power not from the People . . . but from God'.[31]

The most proficient defender of designation theory in the early Stuart period was Marc'Antonio De Dominis. Most of his arguments can be paralleled in other writings, but the sustained treatment which he gave to the question of the origins of government was unequalled in contemporary English political literature. At several crucial points De Dominis anticipated the arguments of Sir Robert Filmer, one of the most famous of all Stuart absolutists. De Dominis saw that the key doctrine of those who favoured original popular sovereignty was this: because natural law prescribes that government should exist in every society and because no individual by nature possesses a better claim than anyone else to rule, political power originally resided in the community as a whole. De Dominis argued that this theory was blasphemous in that it implied that God was responsible for giving human societies the worst form of government, namely democracy. Filmer later repeated this allegation against Bellarmine, arguing that 'he makes God the author of a democratical estate'. Again, De Dominis contended that if the theory were correct, communities could not lawfully alter their form of government, but would be obliged to suffer democratic rule for ever. Once more, Filmer repeated the argument, deducing from the premise that every society was originally a democracy the conclusion that 'not only aristocracies but all monarchies are altogether unlawful, as being ordained . . . by men, when as God himself hath chosen a democracy.'[32]

The crucial argument in favour of the original sovereignty of the people was that natural law required that there be government in every society, but gave no one a greater right to govern than anyone else. Since everyone had an equal right to govern, political power was at first possessed by the society as a whole. According to De Dominis, this argument involved a *non sequitur*. Natural law, he claimed, gave everyone an equal right to govern only in the sense that it gave no one any right to govern. The law of nature did, indeed, require that there be government, but was perfectly silent on who should govern. Nothing could be deduced from this silence. Natural law showed that the community should be governed, but *not* that it had the power to govern. 'On this matter', he stated,

---

31 Sir John Spelman, *A view of a printed book intituled Observations* (Oxford 1642) sig. B3a; Henry Hammond, *To the right honourable the Lord Fairfax* (1649) 11; Henry Ferne, *A reply unto severall treatises* (Oxford 1643) 13.
32 De Dominis, *De republica ecclesiastica pars secunda*, 919–20; Sir Robert Filmer, *Patriarcha and other political writings*, ed. Johann P. Sommerville (Cambridge 1991) 5–6.

some theologians and jurists have spoken a great deal of nonsense, not perceiving the distinction between passive and active government, and not seeing that by natural law only passive and not active government is set up in the people; and that by natural consequence it does not follow that anyone in particular should rule, but only that the multitude should be ruled.[33]

In other words, God had constructed human nature in such a way that communities needed to be governed (passive government), not that they had the power to govern (active government). Of course, some mechanism was needed by which a governor could actually be appointed. De Dominis thought that original election by the people was one possible mechanism. But his point was that such election did not involve any transference of power from the people to the king, since the people did not have power in the first place. The king drew his authority from God alone, and so it was to God alone that he was accountable for its exercise. De Dominis confirmed his theory by drawing an analogy between government and marriage. In matrimony the power of the husband sprang not from any transference of power by the wife, but from God. The wife's consent made the man her husband, but did not give him power – for husbandly power was natural, and had been imprinted by God in man's nature at the creation. Similarly, the powers of the civil ruler were derived immediately from God as the author of nature, though his person might be chosen by the multitude. Thomas Morton employed the same analogy in precisely the same way.[34]

The proponents of designation theory aimed to show that kings did not derive their authority from the people. Their rebuttal of the doctrine of *original* popular sovereignty was not sufficient by itself to establish this conclusion. For early Stuart writers admitted that aristocracy and democracy were valid forms of government, though less excellent than monarchy. This left their theory open to the following objection. Even if the people had not at first been sovereign, was it not possible that they had *designated* themselves as rulers? God would then have given them political power. If, at some later date, they had chosen to set up a king, they could have done so by transferring their power to a single man upon whatever conditions they cared to impose. De Dominis evaded this objection to his theory by construing cases in which sovereignty had changed hands as involving not a transference of

33 De Dominis, *De republica ecclesiastica pars secunda*, 919: 'Et in hac re nonnulli tam Theologi, quam Jurisconsulti plurimum hallucinati sunt, non advertentes discrimen inter regimen passivum et activum, et in populo jure naturae solum constitui regimen passivum, non activum; et ex naturali consequutione non sequi ut quis regat, sed tantummodo ut multitudo regatur.'
34 Ibid., 527–8; Morton, *Full satisfaction*, I, 31; Dudley Digges was still using the same analogy in 1644: Richard Tuck, '"The ancient law of freedom": John Selden and the Civil War', in J.S. Morrill, ed., *Reactions to the English Civil War 1642–1649* (1982) 137–61, at 159. See also Mary Lyndon Shanley, 'Marriage contract and social contract in seventeenth century English political thought', *Western Political Quarterly* 32 (1979) 79–91, and Constance Jordan, 'The household and the state: transformations in the representation of an analogy from Aristotle to James I', *Modern Language Quarterly* 54 (1993) 307–26. An excellent discussion of the role of women in early-modern political thought is Margaret R. Sommerville, *Sex and subjection: attitudes towards women in early-modern society* (1995).

power but merely the designation of a new ruler or rulers, upon whom God immediately conferred authority. If the form of government changed from democracy to monarchy, for example, the people would have abdicated and then elected a king – whose authority would stem from God alone. By arguing in this way, De Dominis was able to avoid the possibility that a ruler was accountable to the people for the exercise of his power. Underlying his theory at this point was the crucial doctrine that mixed government is impossible. A constitutional arrangement by which the king *was* accountable to the people would not be an example of monarchy, but of a democracy in which kingship was purely titular. Many other authors – including Sir John Hayward, Hadrian Saravia and David Owen – also specifically stated that a king who is accountable to his people is not really a king at all, but an inferior magistrate in a democracy.[35]

The designation theorists were far more concerned with the powers of established kings than with the means by which a man could become king. This is not to say that they failed to distinguish between legitimate rule and usurpation. The mere fact that a man was administering the kingdom did not make him a king, for, as the clergyman Burhill noted, 'it is not administration but authority which makes a king, and authority can be retained though the power of administration is lost'.[36] A number of claims to authority were commonly recognised as legitimate. These included original election by the people, victory in a just war, and gift from a sovereign ruler. It was widely agreed that the best form of government was a monarchy in which succession proceeded by primogeniture in the male line, but no one argued that this was the only valid type of government. God could punish an evil king or a wicked people by altering the form of government or the person of the ruler. Providence sometimes employed such unlawful means as rebellion or usurpation in accomplishing this end. Saravia believed that almost all the states of contemporary Europe had at first arisen either by conquest or by usurpation. Legitimate rule was distinguished from usurpation, but it was sometimes acknowledged that if a usurper and his descendants succeeded in establishing their rule for a sufficient length of time, it would become legitimate. Barret held that the usurper's line became legitimate in the third generation. Others claimed that a full century was required.[37] The canons passed by the clergy in 1606 were rather more radical on this point, asserting that 'new forms of government' which arose after a rebellion became valid as soon as they were 'thoroughly settled'. James I was unimpressed by this doctrine, which implied that mere success legitimated rebellion, and this was one reason why he withheld his consent to the canons.[38]

35 De Dominis, *De republica ecclesiastica pars secunda*, 527, 920; Hayward, *Answer*, 36; Saravia, *De imperandi authoritate*, 163–4; David Owen, *Anti-Paraeus* (Cambridge 1622) 45.
36 Robert Burhill, *Contra Martini Becani controversiam* (1613) 79: 'Regem enim facit, non administratio, sed auctoritas, quae vel in desperata administrandi facultate constare potest.'
37 Saravia, *De imperandi authoritate*, 178; Barret, *Ius regis*, 417–18; Sir John Eliot, *De jure majestatis*, ed. A.B. Grosart (1882) 104; Thomas Preston, *Last reioynder to Mr. Thomas Fitz-herberts reply* (1619) 134.
38 *The convocation book of MDCVI*, 51, preface 6–9.

The central contention of designation theory was that by whatever means a ruler acquired his title, his authority came from God alone. To substantiate this claim, some authors argued that originally fathers had been kings, and that political and kingly power were essentially the same thing. This approach, known as patriarchalism, is familiar to modern scholars primarily through Sir Robert Filmer's *Patriarcha*, written about 1630 but first published in 1680, and through John Locke's *Two treatises of government* – a blistering attack on Filmer's ideas, published in 1689.[39] Filmer did not, however, introduce patriarchalism into English political thought. In fact, patriarchalist ideas were common in early Stuart England and, along with designation theory, formed the basis of absolutist thinking.

PATRIARCHALISM

The strength of patriarchalist political theory lay in its appeal to the common social assumptions of contemporaries. Early modern English society was patriarchal. The basic social unit was the family, and the head of that unit was the father. In the words of Keith Wrightson, 'the family was fundamental'. Peter Laslett describes pre-industrial England as an association between the heads of families, and argues that 'the village community was a patriarchal matter, even if it cannot itself have been a family'.[40] Only the heads of families – fathers – were admitted to any share of political power. Servants, women and children were 'subsumed' into the personalities of their fathers and masters. Obedience was seen as the principal duty of children and it was instilled in them by all the religious, emotional and social pressures available.

Conventional morality contemplated filial disobedience with horror – a point nowhere better illustrated than in Shakespeare's *King Lear*. Its theme is all the more relevant to patriarchal notions of royal authority since in it disobedience to a father is also disobedience to a king. In *Lear* Regan's and Goneril's disobedience to their father leads to a breakdown of all moral norms, plunging the state into civil war. Throughout the play, Lear's disobedient daughters are portrayed as 'unnatural', while only Cordelia's loyalty 'redeems nature from the general curse'. Through the words of the Duke of Albany, Shakespeare made explicit the assumption that human society cannot prosper if family ties are dishonoured. Albany complains that if God does not punish Lear's ungrateful daughters ('Tigers, not daughters'), then 'Humanity must perforce prey on itself, Like monsters of the deep'. *King Lear* dramatically

39 Filmer's *Patriarcha* used to be dated to 1635–42 – Peter Laslett, ed., *Patriarcha and other political works of Sir Robert Filmer* (Oxford 1949) 3 – or later – John M. Wallace, 'The date of Sir Robert Filmer's *Patriarcha*', *HJ* 23 (1980) 155–65, argued for a date of 1648 at the earliest. There are two distinct versions of the work. The consensus of recent scholarly opinion favours a date of around 1630 for one of them and between 1635 and 1642 for the other: Richard Tuck, 'A new date for Filmer's *Patriarcha*', *HJ* 29 (1986) 183–6; Filmer, *Patriarcha and other political writings*, ed. Johann P. Sommerville, pp. viii, xxxii–xxxiv.
40 Wrightson, *English society*, 66; Laslett, *The world we have lost*, 82. The fullest discussion of patriarchalism is G.J. Schochet, *Patriarchalism in political thought* (Oxford 1975).

embodied the contemporary belief that the father's authority is natural, and that any attack upon it would inevitably lead to the disruption of society.[41]

Shakespeare was not the only writer to express such notions. In his *First anniversary* John Donne argued that chaos was upon the world, by pointing to the breach of the strongest bonds he recognised:

'Tis all in pieces, all cohaerence gone;
All just supply, and all Relation:
Prince, Subject, Father, Sonne, are things forgot.

In a play of the 1590s, *Edward III*, King John of France attempts to persuade his son to break an oath, by arguing that

Thou and thy word lie both in my command;
What canst thou promise, that I cannot break?
Which of these twain is greater infamy,
To disobey thy father or thyself?

His son prefers to obey God rather than man, and honours his oath. But the fact that such arguments could plausibly be mounted testifies to the strength of patriarchalist sentiment – sentiment on which the theorists built.[42]

A father's power was held to extend over the whole of his 'family' – servants and wife as well as children. The individual who lived outside the family – the 'masterless man' – was treated as a dangerous social anomaly. Moralists were tireless in reminding wives of their duties of subjection and obedience to their husbands. In *King Lear* the only permissible limitation on Cordelia's duty to her father is her duty to her husband:

Haply, when I shall wed
That lord whose hand must take my plight shall carry
Half my love with him, half my care and duty.

The degenerate Regan and Goneril are unfaithful to, and disrespectful of, their husbands as well as their father.[43]

It was not only absolutists who accepted the importance of paternal power. Even those who rejected absolutist ideas were imbued with the assumption that only fathers should have full political power and rights. Puritans who asserted that the 'people' should choose their own ministers of religion almost invariably meant heads of households by 'people'. The leading Elizabethan Presbyterian Thomas Cartwright rebutted the charge that he wanted women or children to have any say in the election of ministers, for 'all men understand that where the election is most freest and most general, yet only they have to doe, which are heads of families'. Another puritan, William Stoughton, qualified his argument for popular election in the same way: 'For when we

41 Shakespeare, *King Lear*, iv. vi. 206, ii. 40, ii. 48–9.
42 Donne, *Complete poetry and selected prose*, ed. John Hayward (1929) 202; *The reign of King Edward III*, iv. v. 80–4.
43 Shakespeare, *King Lear*, i. i. 100–2.

saye, that the people of every Parish ought to choose and elect their Pastour, wee meane not that the election should solely be committed to the multitude, but we intend onely that the chiefe Fathers, Ancients and Governours of the Parish in the name of the whole should approve the choyse made.'[44]

Even when Charles I had been defeated in the Civil War and when the demands for a broader Parliamentary franchise reached their height in the Putney Debates of 1647, the Leveller Maximilian Petty was willing to admit that 'servants and apprentices . . . are included in their masters'. Patriarchal attitudes were deeply embedded in social beliefs. It was on this unquestioned basis that patriarchal theories of royal authority were founded.[45]

Comparisons between the king and the father of a family were common-place in early Stuart literature. William Tooker – a royal chaplain – and David Owen – chaplain to one of James I's favourites – said that the king was the father of his country, and the political writer Edward Forsett made the same hackneyed claim, referring to it as a 'similitude in Nature'.[46] The Fifth Commandment – 'Honour thy father and thy mother' – was interpreted as enjoining obedience to the king as well as to natural fathers. But the belief that royal and fatherly power were in some respects similar did not imply any particular view of the origins and nature of political society. In ancient Rome the emperors adopted the title of 'pater patriae' – 'father of the fatherland' – though their powers were held to stem from an act of transference by the people. A father's power, by contrast, was not derived from the consent of his children. It is difficult to deduce much of consequence from vague analogies between kings and fathers. Of far more significance were a second group of statements, *equating* royal with paternal authority. The authors who made these statements had two objectives. Firstly, they wanted to show that the king's power was derived from God alone. Secondly, they intended to demonstrate that the earliest political societies had not been self-governing democracies, but absolute monarchies ruled over by a king and father.

Sixteenth-century Catholics admitted that fathers derive their power from God, and not from their families. But they distinguished between the *domestic* power of a father and the *political* power of a king, arguing that the king's power *was* derived from his subjects. The same position was adopted by Richard Hooker, who used it to support his claim that the authority of kings was limited by the conditions upon which the people had granted it to them. The Elizabethan political writer Thomas Floyd also distinguished between royal and paternal power: the first king was not Adam – the first father – but Nimrod, who acquired dominion by conquest long after the Flood. Others who drew the same distinction include the absolutists Sir John Hayward and Marc'Antonio De Dominis. So not all absolutists were patriarchalists.

44 Thomas Cartwright, *A replye to an answer made by M. Doctor Whitgifte* (1574) 42; William Stoughton, *An assertion for true and Christian church-policie* (1604) 246–7.
45 A.S.P. Woodhouse, *Puritanism and liberty* (1938) 83.
46 William Tooker, *Duellum sive singulare certamen cum Martino Becano Iesuita* (1611) 87; Owen, *Anti-Paraeus*, 25; Forsett, *A defence of the right of kings*, 23.

Nevertheless, patriarchalism in the strict sense – the equation of royal and fatherly power – had its advocates throughout the period.[47]

If kingly and paternal power are identical, it follows that fathers must have the authority to punish their children with death. 'As for the father of a family', James I told Parliament in 1610, 'they had of old under the Law of Nature *patriam potestatem* [fatherly power], which was *potestatem vitae et necis* [the power of life and death], over their children or family, (I mean such fathers of families whereof kings did originally come).' John Ap-Robert argued that 'a family is a civill society, yea the only commonweale which God and Nature first ordayned', and supported his thesis by claiming that God had given fathers the power to punish their offspring 'by death it selfe'.[48] The assertion that fathers had originally possessed the right to inflict the death penalty made it possible for the patriarchalists to conflate domestic and civil power and hence to argue that the civil authority of kings was granted to them directly by God, and not by the people. Patriarchalism was at once an account of the origins of government and a description of the nature of political power. It served to show that humans had not originally been free, but were born into civil subjection. It also showed that if at some later period people had set up kings by consent, the power of these kings, as distinct from their titles, was from God alone – for it was fatherly.

Many writers equated royal with patriarchal power and claimed that the first fathers were kings. '*Jus Regium*', said Andrewes, 'cometh out of *jus Patrium*, the Kings right from the Fathers, and both hold by one Commandement.' Even more explicit were the ecclesiastical canons passed by both Convocations – the representative bodies of the northern and southern clergy – in 1606. They asserted that God

> did give to Adam for his time, and to the rest of the patriarchs and chief fathers successively before the flood, authority, power, and dominion over their children and offspring, to rule and govern them; ordaining by the law of nature, that their said children and offspring (begotten and brought up by them) should fear, reverence, honour and obey them. Which power and authority . . . although we only term it fatherly power (*potestas patria*); yet, being well considered how far it did reach, we may truly say that it was in a sort royal power (*potestas regia*); as now, in a right and true construction, royal power (*potestas regia*) may be called fatherly power (*potestas patria*).

Many writers – including Donne, Maynwaring, Willan, Rawlinson and Field – endorsed the view that Adam's power had been kingly. Field also claimed that the law of nature prescribed primogeniture, and others agreed though some held that the succession could be altered at the king's discretion. Among

47 Hooker, *Laws of ecclesiastical polity*, ɪ, x, 4; Thomas Floyd, *The picture of a perfit common wealth* (1600) 21; Hayward, *Answer*, 29, 46; De Dominis, *De republica ecclesiastica pars secunda*, 580, 938–9.
48 James I, *The kings maiesties speach to the Lords and Commons*, sig. B2a, in *Political writings*, ed. Sommerville, 182; J. Ap-Robert, *The younger brother his apology by it selfe* (St Omer 1618) 44.

the latter was Ap-Robert who launched a vigorous attack on primogeniture in *The younger brother his apology*. He was himself a younger brother.[49]

If the power of the first fathers had been kingly, it followed that the doctrines of original democracy and of the contractual origins of regal authority were false. Since 'the first government that was in the world among men, was the government of a family', argued George Carleton, 'it is absurd to thinke, and impossible to proove, that the power of government was in the multitude'. The canons of 1606 rejected the ideas that the people had once been sovereign and that political authority was in any sense derived from or dependent on their consent. These canons represented the official teaching of the clergy, and their conclusions were frequently repeated by churchmen. One example is a sermon of 1610 by Thomas Ireland. Peter Laslett has also detected their influence in the writings of Sir Robert Filmer.[50]

The Arminian Thomas Jackson held that man's sinful nature made coercive government necessary. The right to punish, he argued, was at first in the hands of fathers:

> The regal power, which in process of time did spread itself over whole nations and countries, had its first root from that power which the fathers of families had over their children, their grandchildren, and their posterity; which power did extend itself much further in ancient times than now it can, because the age of man was much longer, and mankind did multiply much faster than now it doth.

The Calvinist Robert Bolton gave a very similar account of the origins of government. He claimed that 'before Nimrod, fathers and heads of families were Kings', and argued that in those early times 'men lived five or six hundred yeares' so that it was 'an easie matter for a man to see fifty, yea a hundred thousand persons of his posterity, over whom he exercised paternall power, and by consequence, soveraigne power'.[51]

Since fatherly power extended over all the father's descendants, it followed that not every natural father held full paternal (and therefore royal) power. What, then, was the nature of the powers of natural fathers who were subjects? According to Ap-Robert, the king was 'the Father of all Fathers', and could use his paternal authority to 'abate' the powers of those of his subjects who were fathers. The patriarchalists regarded every kingdom as a family,

49 Andrewes, *A sermon preached before his maiestie, on Sunday the fifth of August last* (1610) 13; *The convocation book of MDCVI*, 2–3; Donne, *Pseudo-Martyr*, 83; Roger Maynwaring, *Religion and alegiance: in two sermons* (1627) I, 13; Robert Willan, *Conspiracie against kings, heavens scorne* (1622) 30; John Rawlinson, *Vivat rex* (Oxford 1619) 1; Richard Field, *Of the church, five books*, 4 vols (Cambridge 1847–52) II, 3. Arguments in favour of primogeniture are in Vaughan, *Golden-grove*, sig. S1b–S2a, and in Hayward, *Answer*, sig. A1b–3a, C2b–D1a, but at sig. P2b Hayward gives the king the right to alter the succession, as does Saravia, *De imperandi authoritate*, 167.

50 Carleton, *Iurisdiction regall, episcopall, papall* (1610) 12; Thomas Ireland, *The oath of allegiance, defended by a sermon* (1610) sig. B2b–3b; Filmer, *Patriarcha*, ed. Laslett, 58n.

51 Jackson, *Treatise of Christian obedience*, 311–12; Bolton, *Two sermons*, 15. Another patriarchalist account, stressing Adam's princely power, is in Robert Gomersall, *Sermons on St Peter* (1634) 55–63.

ruled over by a king whose power was fatherly. The only difference between a kingdom and a family was one of size. According to Jackson, 'how great soever a kingdom may be for circuit of lands, or multitude of persons, yet kingly authority and fatherly authority, as they are both the ordinance of God, differ not in nature or quality, but only in quantity or extent'. John Buckeridge similarly claimed that 'paternal and regal power are the same in substance and essence, even if they differ in size and extent'. No one specified how large a family had to be if it were to count as a kingdom. This scarcely mattered, since an autonomous family was *essentially* the same thing as a kingdom.[52]

Like other absolutists, the patriarchalists were relatively indifferent to the question of titles. The important point, they believed, was that however a man became king, his power was fatherly. 'Fatherly power', said Buckeridge, 'is the origin of all power, and all power is founded upon it; and likewise, all true, just, and lawful power is fatherly.' According to Filmer, 'it skills not which way Kings come by their power'. The first kings had, indeed, been Adam and his heirs, but it was not necessary for modern kings to prove succession by primogeniture from Adam, for Providence could alter the royal line and even the form of government. One slightly odd implication of this view was that even in a democracy the rulers would hold fatherly power. Whether it is a king who rules, wrote Filmer, 'or whether some few or a multitude govern the commonwealth, yet still the authority that is in any one, or in all of these, is the only right and natural authority of a supreme Father'. Filmer was not the first theorist to equate royal with patriarchal power. The theory was common in Jacobean England. Moreover, most of the character- istic patriarchalist doctrines had already been lucidly expressed by Saravia in 1593. Like Filmer, he claimed that the book of Genesis showed that 'supreme power began at the same time as men themselves', for 'whoever examines the course of sacred history attentively will easily perceive that the first progen- itors of mankind were also the first kings'. Since fatherhood and kingship had originally been identical, it followed that 'men did not elect but received Princes'. When the original king (and father) died, the right of appointing a successor did not devolve upon his subjects (and children), for 'the prerog- ative of primogeniture' gave the kingship 'to the first-born, unless his father, who had possessed supreme power, disposed of it otherwise'. A king could alter the succession, but if he did not do so the crown would descend to his eldest son.

Saravia traced the history of kingship from the earliest times, concluding that 'fatherly power was kingly, that is to say supreme, amongst the first authors of the human race'. Paternal power, he claimed, extended not only over a man's children, but over all his descendants. Since the powers of the original father were passed on to his successors by right of primogeniture,

---

52 Ap-Robert, *The younger brother his apology*, 47; Jackson, *Treatise of Christian obedience*, 312; Buckeridge, *De potestate papae*, 282: 'Potestas enim patria et regia, quoad essentiam et rem eadem sunt, etsi ambitu et extensione differant.'

supreme power over the whole kinship group remained in the hands of one person. Saravia's book was still read in the 1640s, for Bishop Williams of Ossory, one of Charles I's chaplains, cited it to prove the patriarchal nature of early kingship in 1644. That Filmer was directly indebted to Saravia is, however, impossible to demonstrate.[53]

The main conclusion of both designation theory and patriarchalism was that the powers of every supreme magistrate were derived *directly* from God and not from the people. In the early seventeenth century it was widely agreed that government was prescribed by God's natural law. Political authority, considered abstractly, was the creation of God, not man. What caused disagreement was the question of whether the power of every *particular* Prince was derived immediately from God, or immediately from the people and only indirectly, or intermediately, from God. The standard absolutist view was that the king drew his authority from God alone. The Prince was the vicegerent, or deputy, of God – not of the people. James I thought that kings were God's lieutenants, accountable to him alone, and a host of clergymen endorsed this opinion. 'Kings have their Authority from God', wrote David Owen, 'and are his Vicegerents on earth, to execute justice and judgement for him amongst the sonnes of Men.' 'The King', Thomas Ireland assured his readers, 'is Gods Vicegerent to judge and execute his judgements upon earth.' Sebastian Benefield, a strict Calvinist, and Lady Margaret Professor of Divinity at Oxford, affirmed that 'kings hold their kingdomes immediately from God'. Peter Heylin, an Arminian and one of Charles I's chaplains, similarly stated 'that Kings do hold their Crownes by no other Tenure, then *Dei gratia*: and that what ever power they have, they have from God'. According to the Civil lawyer Thomas Ridley, every king was 'Gods immediate Vicar upon earth' in his own kingdom. The anonymous *God and the king* of 1615 claimed that the king 'receiving his Authority only from God . . . hath no Superior to punish or chastise him but God alone'.[54]

Scriptural texts were, of course, pressed into service to confirm the thesis that kings derive their authority from God alone. Examples are Proverbs 8:15 – 'By me kings reign, and princes decree justice' – and Psalms 82:6 – 'I have said, Ye are gods.' The assertion that kings were gods was not intended

---

53 Buckeridge, *De potestate papae*, 531: 'Potestas enim patria, origo est omnis potestatis, in qua potestas omnis fundatur: et omnis potestas vera, justa et legitima, patria itidem est.' Filmer, *Patriarcha*, ed. Sommerville, 11, 44; Saravia, *De imperandi authoritate*, 167: 'summam potestatem cum ipsis simul hominibus incepisse'. 'Seriam sacrae historiae qui considerabit attentius, priores hominum progenitores primos quoque fuisse Reges facile inveniet.' 'accepisse Principes non elegisse'. 'Primogeniturae praerogativa principatum . . . dabat maximo natu, nisi parens, penes quem summa erat potestas, aliud statuisset'; 168: 'patriam potestatem regiam, hoc est, summam fuisse apud primos humani generis authores'; Gryffith Williams, *Jura majestatis, the rights of kings* (Oxford 1644) 143.
54 James I, *The kings maiesties speach to the Lords and Commons*, sig. A4b, Bla, in *Political writings*, ed. Sommerville, 181–2; Owen, *The power of princes and the dutie of subiects*, BL Royal Mss 18.B.V., f. 4a; Ireland, *Oath of allegiance*, sig. E4a; Sebastian Benefield, *A sermon preached in St Maries church in Oxford* (1613) 4; Peter Heylin, *A briefe and moderate answer, to the seditious and scandalous challenges of Henry Burton* (1637) 33; Thomas Ridley, *A view of the civile and ecclesiasticall law*, 2nd edn (Oxford 1634) 103; *God and the king* (1615) 31.

literally. It was not the king himself, but his authority which was divine. 'Kings and Princes therefore are termed Gods . . . in regard of honour, authority and power conferred upon them from God', argued the clergyman Thomas Gataker, and Charles I's chaplain Isaac Bargrave warned his royal master that 'though kings be Gods before men, yet, they are but men before God'.[55] Perhaps the most frequently cited of all biblical texts was Romans 13:1 – 'Let every soul be subject unto the higher powers. For there is no power but of God: the powers that be are ordained of God.'

All these passages were regarded as *confirming*, and not *creating* the Prince's authority and the subject's duty of obedience. The obligations of subjects towards their kings arose from the law of nature, which applied to everyone, and not from the law of grace, which applied only to Christians. Samuel Collins, Provost of King's College and Regius Professor of Divinity at Cambridge, pointed out that Romans 13 merely confirmed an already existent duty of obedience, for 'meere Naturalists' – that is to say, people guided only by natural law – were able to perceive the same obligation. Civil authority, argued Francis Mason, was 'given immediately from God, both unto Christian Princes, and also unto Ethnickes which are guided only by the light and law of nature'. Matthew Wren, Master of Peterhouse and later Bishop successively of Hereford, Norwich and Ely, claimed that political obligations were 'charged upon us, not so much by any written Law, as by a Law within us also, by the Rule of Reason, and the Divine Law of Conscience'. According to Heylin, 'the law of Monarchie is founded on the law of nature'. The *Constitutions and canons ecclesiasticall* of 1640 summed up the official teaching of the church, claiming that royal power was 'the ordinance of God himself, founded in the prime Laws of nature, and clearly established by expresse texts both of the old and new Testaments'.[56]

By arguing that the king derived his power from God alone, early Stuart thinkers were able to lay the foundations for a fully fledged theory of royal absolutism. Since God had granted coercive authority to the king alone, his subjects possessed no power to coerce him. Moreover, the king was accountable to God alone for the use which he made of royal authority. From their theory of the origins of government, the early Stuart absolutists deduced a general account of the nature and limitations of political power, applicable to all governments. They also, though more rarely, spelled out the implications of their views for the English constitution. It was their particular conclusions, especially on the private property of the subject, which brought the wrath of the House of Commons to bear upon the clergy. In 1628 Roger Maynwaring was impeached for defending Charles I's Forced Loan. Maynwaring was

55 Thomas Gataker, *Certaine sermons* (1637) II, 74; Isaac Bargrave, *A sermon preached before King Charles, March 27. 1627* (1627) 16.
56 Samuel Collins, *Epphata to F.T.* (Cambridge 1617) 60; Francis Mason, *Of the consecration of bishops in the church of England* (1613) 118; Matthew Wren, *A sermon preached before the kings maiestie* (Cambridge 1627) 34; Heylin, *Briefe and moderate answer*, 32; *Constitutions and canons ecclesiasticall* (1640) sig. B4b.

unusually explicit in driving home the consequences of absolutist theory, but the principles on which he based his argument were widely accepted, especially among the clergy.

Since God alone was the king's superior, the king could not be coerced or judged by his subjects, and was under no obligation to account to them for his actions. Charles I did publish an account of the reasons which led him to dissolve the Parliaments of 1625 and 1626. But he was careful to explain that he was not *bound* to give an account of his 'Regall Actions' to anyone except God 'whose immediate Lieutenant and Vicegerent Hee is'. He reiterated this point after the dissolution of each of his next two Parliaments, asserting in 1629 that 'Princes are not bound to give accompt of their actions but to God alone', and saying the same thing in much the same words in 1640.[57]

The notion that the king was accountable only to God did not, however, imply that his powers were wholly unlimited, for like everyone else he was subject to divine law. If a royal command conflicted with God's law, it would be necessary to obey the superior authority of God, and, in so doing, to disobey his deputy the king. As Thomas Morton put it, 'whensoever the immortal God shall Command any thing, and any Power on earth shall give it a Countermand, then must the Law of the earthen and mortall God be rejected, justly'. So if the king told you to lie, or blaspheme, you would have a duty to disobey him. David Owen summed up the conventional view when he stated that 'subjects ought not to obey in those cases where the Prince commands against God' and added that 'there is no controversy about this in the Church of God'. It is worth noting three important points in connection with this doctrine. Firstly, it was the *only* exception to the rule that subjects are bound to obey their Prince. As Robert Sanderson put it in 1634, 'Gods Vice-gerents must bee heard and obeyed in all things that are not manifestly contrary to the revealed will of God'.[58]

Secondly, the doctrine that subjects could disobey the king if his commands conflicted with divine law was interpreted strictly. In order to have adequate grounds for disobedience, a subject had to *know*, and not merely to believe, that his Prince's commands were ungodly. 'It is cleare', wrote Nicholas Byfield, 'that if I know the Magistrate commands a thing unlawfull, I must not doe it, because in that case I am bound to obey God, and not men: but suspition or doubting of the lawfulnesse of things, is no discharge for obedience.'

57 Charles I, *A declaration of the true causes which moved his maiestie to assemble, and after inforced him to dissolve the two last meetings in Parliament* (1626) 2; *His maiesties declaration to all his loving subiects, of the causes which moved him to dissolve the last Parliament* (1628) 9; *His maiesties declaration to all his loving subiects, of the causes which moved him to dissolve the last Parliament* (1640) 1–2.
58 Morton, *A sermon preached before the kings most excellent maiestie* (Newcastle upon Tyne 1639) 13–14; Owen, *Anti-Paraeus*, 63–4: 'non debere subditos in iis parere, quae princeps imperaverit contra Deum . . . de quo in ecclesia Dei nulla controversia est'; Robert Sanderson, *Two sermons* (1636) 91.

'Infinite confusion', he remarked, 'would follow if the conjectures and suspitions of the Inferiors might warrant their refusall of subjection.' Clearly, if the king were obliged to provide each of his subjects with a justification of his commands, good government would become impossible. Indeed, in some circumstances the public interest required that the king keep secret the reasons for his decrees. Since 'reasons of state and policie' sometimes necessitated secrecy, argued John Everard, 'it doth not belong . . . to every private man, to make too curious a disquisition into the causes and occasions of his Soveraignes command'.[59]

Thirdly, subjects could never actively resist their kings. If the king's command was incompatible with the law of God, subjects were bound to obey God and not the king. But they were also obliged meekly to accept whatever penalties the king might choose to impose upon them for their disobedience. 'It becomes not good Subjectes', wrote William Barlow, 'to bee their owne Revengers. Christianity teacheth Patience, not Rebellion.' In 1610 James I warned Parliament that prayers and tears were the only arms which subjects could employ against their king.[60] The doctrine that subjects could never justifiably use force against the king was the most commonly expressed political principle in early Stuart England. Officially sanctioned in the church's

---

59 Byfield, *Commentary upon . . . St Peter*, 437–8; cf. Jackson, *Treatise of Christian obedience*, 291; John Everard, *The Arrierban* (1618) 31–2. See also Johann P. Sommerville, *Thomas Hobbes: political ideas in historical context* (1992) 88. Everard was one of many who suggested that for 'reasons of state', or in a case of necessity, or for the public good (*salus populi*), rulers could do things which would otherwise be unjustified. In his *Philosophy and government* (*passim*, esp. 118) Richard Tuck argues that such claims are straightforward expressions of Tacitist humanism, which he contrasts with both Aristotelian scholasticism and Ciceronian humanism, and which (he says) rose to great prominence in late-sixteenth- and early-seventeenth-century Europe. But these contentions are difficult to sustain. The idea that necessity and the public good justified the king in taking measures which infringed individual rights was central to medieval arguments in favour of extraordinary royal taxation, and was widely expressed by canon and Civil lawyers, and by scholastics including St Thomas Aquinas. G.L. Harriss, *King, Parliament, and public finance in medieval England to 1369* (Oxford 1975) speaks of 'an incipient notion of *raison d'état*' in the 1100s and argues that it was defined more explicitly by Aquinas in the following century (21); from the early twelfth century, he claims, canonists regularly argued that 'necessity overrode the law'; the idea that royal authority 'might transcend private rights in defence of the common good found expression first as a doctrine of emergency', and Aquinas argued that rulers are justified in imposing taxes on their subjects when this was '"necessary to promote the common interest"', and especially in wartime (22); all of these notions about necessity and royal power were commonplace from the 1200s at the latest (24, 33–5 and *passim*).

Seventeenth-century English debates on royal rights in cases of necessity arguably owed more to medieval arguments, and to the thinking of canonists and scholastics, than to any new Tacitist insights of the late sixteenth century. The medieval position was that in emergencies governments are justified in taking extraordinary action, but that there are limits to what they can do, for God and nature have instituted some unchangeable laws, which all must obey: there are moral rules which no one should flout, even in a good cause (for instance, the king can tax in emergencies, but cannot lie or murder). The Tacitist and Machiavellian view was that in the state's interest kings may break virtually any law (and may lie and murder). There is little reason to think that this view was adopted by most of the people who used arguments from necessity or the public good in early Stuart England: see references in the index of this book under 'necessity', 'public good', and 'reason(s) of state'. A good discussion of early modern Machiavellian thinking is Peter S. Donaldson, *Machiavelli and mystery of state* (Cambridge 1988).

60 William Barlow, *A brand, Titio Erepta* (1607) sig. F1a; *PP 10*, ii, 103.

Book of homilies, the duty of non-resistance was enjoined upon numberless hearers in countless sermons throughout the early seventeenth century. The Vicar of Bray was merely aping the practice of his ancestors when, in the reign of Charles II, he taught his flock that

Kings are by God appointed,
And damn'd are those who dare resist,
Or touch the Lord's anointed.[61]

Absolutists magnified royal power. They did this to protect the state against anarchy and to refute the ideas of resistance theorists. They did not want the king to rule in a lawless, arbitrary manner. In absolutist theory the king had a duty to abide by the laws of God and nature. He also had a duty to rule in the public interest. Natural law – reason – demonstrated that the purpose of government was the maintenance of the common welfare. People joined together in society in order to procure temporal welfare. Natural law prescribed that the king should govern in the interests of his subjects. This meant governing in an orderly, law-abiding fashion. It was obviously in the public interest that we should be governed by settled, known rules. So the king had a moral obligation to abide by established law. But if special circumstances arose in which the public interest required that the king flout established law, he had a duty to do so.

Since the king alone possessed political power, he alone was the lawmaker in England. This general principle was frequently stated. 'The law is the worke of the King, to whose regall dignitie it appertaines to make Lawes', said James's chaplain William Wilkes, and he claimed that established laws had been 'enacted by his Majesties most noble Progenitors, the Kings of these most famous Islands'. Clerics, said Nicholas Byfield, should 'often teach their hearers their duty to Magistrates, and . . . show the power that Princes have to make Lawes'.[62] 'Kings make lawes', declared another churchman in 1638. The ecclesiastical canons of 1604 were endorsed by the king but not by Parliament, yet Francis Mason argued that they 'may be justly called the Kings Ecclesiasticall lawes'.[63] The king's power to make laws was a straightforward consequence of absolutist theory. Subjects had a duty to obey royal commands provided that they were not contrary to the unalterable principles of justice. As William Barlow told James I, they were bound to obey his majesty not only in matters 'absolutely necessarie as enjoyned by God', but also in matters 'in themselves indifferent, but authoritatively necessarie, as commanded by your selfe'. When God was silent, the king had to be obeyed. The Prince, said Thomas Ridley, 'is supreme soveraigne above the rest, and whom they ought in all things to obey, so it be not against the Law of God, and common Justice'. He concluded that the king 'is the Law it selfe, and the only interpreter

---

61 Quoted in W.H. Auden, ed., *The Oxford book of light verse* (Oxford 1938) 260.
62 William Wilkes, *A second memento for magistrates* (1608) 56, 50; Byfield, *Commentary upon . . . St Peter*, 423. On Wilkes see also 'Revisionism revisited: a retrospect', p. 240 below.
63 Boughen, *A sermon concerning decencie and order*, 18; Mason, *The authority of the church*, 16.

thereof'. Legislative power was vesed in the king and not Parliament, said Saravia and James I himself. When Cowell and Maynwaring argued that the king could make law outside Parliament they were only spelling out an implication of this general principle. It was an implication which many in Parliament found unacceptable.[64]

In practice kings usually abided by the law. They often allowed the courts to control the exercise of royal power – or, as lawyers put it, the royal prerogative. They did not accept that the prerogative was wholly subject to the law. Absolutists, including the first two Stuarts themselves, admitted that kings should ordinarily rule according to law. So in normal circumstances they should permit the courts to decide on the legality of royal acts – say, of proclamations. It is one thing for a king generously to permit his subjects to discuss and define his powers in some specific matter. It is quite another for all royal power to be defined by law. Absolutists held that the king possessed powers outside the law. He could justly use these powers to flout human law if the public interest demanded such action.

As we shall see in Chapters 2 and 3, many people believed that royal power was limited by law. The prerogative, they said, was subject to legal definition and subordinate to the subject's legal liberties. Absolutists denied this. It would be 'high presumption' said Godfrey Goodman – chaplain to James I's wife and later Bishop of Gloucester – to attempt to set bounds to the royal prerogative: 'to prescribe a limitation of power would argue a kind of subjection in a free Monarch.' The essence of *free* monarchy was that royal power was limited by no human law. Just as God ordinarily governed the universe according to the rules of nature – which could be defined – so the king usually ruled by known laws. But God had miraculous supernatural powers which broke the rules, and the king had the prerogative: 'Nature is the Common law by which God governs us', said John Donne, 'and Miracle is his Prerogative. . . . And Miracle is not like prerogative in any thing more than in this, that no body can tell what it is.'[65] According to the Civil lawyer Calybute Downing, the king had 'an unwritten, unrestrained right of Dominion', by which he could 'make legall propositions of validitie, or void in their first institution', and by which he could later interpret or dispense with them. In 1637 Peter Heylin inveighed against the puritan Henry Burton, whose views on the constitution he regarded as false and seditious. 'For the obedience of the Subject', he wrote, 'you limit it to positive laws; the King to be no more obeyed than there is

---

64 Barlow, *The first of the foure sermons preached before the kings maiestie, at Hampton Court* (1607) sig. A2a; Ridley, *A view of the civile and ecclesiasticall law*, 104. Saravia, *De imperandi authoritate*, 276. James I, *Political writings*, ed. Sommerville, 73–4, 183; *CD 21*, I, 4.
65 Godfrey Goodman, *The fall of man, or the corruption of nature, proved by the light of our naturall reason* (1616) 180; Donne, *Essays in divinity*, ed. E.M. Simpson (Oxford 1952) 81; cf. Sir Benjamin Rudyerd in *PP 28*, III, 128, and Francis Oakley, 'Jacobean political theology: the absolute and ordinary powers of the king', *Journal of the History of Ideas* 29 (1968) 323–46; Oakley, *Omnipotence, covenant, and order: an excursion in the history of ideas from Abelard to Leibniz* (Ithaca, NY 1984). An interesting discussion of Donne's politics is Annabel Patterson, 'John Donne, Kingsman?', in Linda Levy Peck, ed., *The mental world of the Jacobean Court* (Cambridge 1991) 251–72.

speciall Law or Statute for it: the Kings Prerogative Royall being of so small a value with you, that no man is to prize it, or take notice of it, further than warranted by Law.' Heylin did not believe that the prerogative was defined or limited by law. The subject, he said, owed the king 'absolute obedience', and the king possessed 'unlimited power'.[66] Chief Baron Fleming expressed very similar ideas in giving judgment on Bate's Case in 1606. He held that over and above his ordinary power, guaranteed to him by the law of the land, the king also possessed absolute power which he could use at his discretion for the common good. Nor was Fleming the only common lawyer to argue in this way. Less well known, but equally forthright, were the claims of Sir John Davies, James I's Attorney-General for Ireland. Davies maintained that at first kings had held 'an absolute and unlimited power in all matters whatsoever'. Later, they had agreed to abide by established laws in ordinary cases, but had reserved an absolute power to act as they saw fit in extraordinary circumstances – and they defined what counted as an extraordinary circumstance. The king, he said, had reserved

> in many points that absolute and unlimited power which was given unto him by the Law of Nations, and in these cases or points, the Kings Prerogatives do consist; so as the Kings Prerogatives were . . . reserved by himself to himself, when the positive Law was first established; and the King doth exercise a double power, viz. an absolute power, or *Merum Imperium*, when he doth use Prerogatives only, which is not bound by the positive Law; and an ordinary power of Jurisdiction, which doth co-operate with the Law.

Prerogative, then, was not limited by law.[67]

The effect of absolutist theory was to make the king sovereign in England. The concept of sovereignty was perfectly familiar to English thinkers. It is sometimes supposed that the concept was first formulated by the Frenchman Jean Bodin in his *Six livres de la république* of 1576, and that the question of its reception in England is synonymous with the question of Bodin's influence. Bodin did not invent the concept, though he did express its implications – that sovereignty must be unlimited and indivisible – with particular clarity. So English writers had no need to turn to Bodin's work for the idea. Some nevertheless did so, an example being the Civil lawyer William Vaughan. Others used the concept quite happily without mentioning Bodin. Saravia thought it obvious that in every state there must be an indivisible, unlimited sovereign. Christopher Lever maintained that 'the Prince is the Soveraign or principall of every State: by whom the lawes have authority, and the life of execution'. Apparently without Bodin's aid he had reached the conclusion that lawmaking is the characteristic feature of sovereignty. David Owen declared that 'royal power is free and absolute', and glossed this as meaning that

---

66 Downing, *Discourse of the state ecclesiasticall*, 104; Heylin, *Briefe and moderate answer*, 179, 156.
67 *ST*, ɪɪ, col. 389; Sir John Davies, *The question concerning impositions* (1656) 30–1.

it was supreme under God and subject to no human authority.[68] Nor did he subject it to the laws. The English had no difficulty whatever in understanding the idea of sovereignty. Problems arose because some of them believed that it was a bad idea – for they held that the king's power was limited by an original contract or by ancient custom – while others thought that it was a very good idea.

Those who argued that the king possessed sovereignty were aware that he might use his powers against the public interest. Yet they held that if there were no sovereign, anarchy would inevitably result – and tyranny was better than anarchy. Any government, however bad, was preferable to no government at all. 'Any King is better than no King, Tyranny is better than Anarchie.'[69] Of course, tyranny was not very palatable. But absolutist theory provided no safeguard against it. At this point in their argument absolutists turned to the idea of Providence. God, they claimed, would punish a ruler who flouted divine law or acted against the interests of his subjects. Such punishment was certain to be meted out in the after-life, but God might also choose to inflict it here on earth. Rebellion, assassination and invasion awaited the evil ruler. The *Mirror for magistrates*, an Elizabethan best-seller, recorded the awful fates of wicked rulers. The same theme was frequently explored by playwrights. In Massinger's *Roman actor* the immortal powers look down on a tyrant's evil actions, and

> in their secret judgements, do determine
> To leave him to his wickedness, which sinks him
> When he is most secure.

In Thomas Preston's *Cambises, King of Persia*, a tyrannical ruler meets a bloody end, and while undergoing it, speaks in verse:

> Thus, gasping, here on ground I lie; for nothing I do care.
> A just reward for my misdeeds my death doth plain declare.[70]

In plays, as in absolutist theory, tyrants have sovereign power and are punished by God for misusing it. They are not limited monarchs, whose unlawful edicts are ruled out of court by lawyers. The absolutist notion of Providence was identical with that of the dramatists – who were usually laymen writing for a lay audience. Absolutist ideas on the necessity of government

68 Vaughan, *Golden-grove*, sig. R6b; Saravia, *De imperandi authoritate*, 159, 163–4; Christopher Lever, *Heaven and earth, religion and policy* (1608) 56; Owen, *Anti-Paraeus*, 99: 'Regiam vero potestatem solutam esse et absolutam.' The reception of Bodin in England is discussed in U. Krautheim, *Die souveränitätskonzeption in den englischen verfassungskonflikten des 17. jahrhunderts; eine studie zur rezeption der lehre Bodins in England* (Frankfurt am Main 1977).
69 Thomas Adams, *A commentary or, exposition upon the divine second epistle generall, written by the blessed apostle St Peter* (1633) 240 (quotation). James I, *True lawe*, sig. D6a–7a, in *Political Writings*, ed. Sommerville, 79; Henry Valentine, *God save the king* (1639) 14; Hayward, *Answer*, sig. L3a–b; Owen, *Anti-Paraeus*, 18; William Goodwin, *A sermon preached before the kings most excellent maiestie at Woodstocke* (Oxford 1614) 25.
70 Philip Massinger, *The Roman actor*, III. i. 64–6; Thomas Preston, *A lamentable Tragedie, mixed full of plesant mirth, containing the life of Cambises King of Persia* (no date, *c.*1584), sig. F4a.

and on patriarchalism were also rooted in attitudes common among England's laity. We have seen that absolutism was most volubly asserted by clerics. But not all clerics were absolutists and not all absolutists were clerics. To understand the historical significance of absolutism we must look a little more closely at the influence and development of the theory.

THE INFLUENCE AND DEVELOPMENT OF THE THEORY
OF ROYAL ABSOLUTISM

In the early days of English printing few books were published on subjects other than religion. By the later sixteenth century theological works were still the most common, with the exception of such ephemeral items as almanacs and prognostications, but large numbers of books had begun to appear on topics of purely secular interest. They ranged from chess to fishing and from navigation to accountancy. This literature catered for laypeople eager to polish whatever skills they needed in their occupations or hobbies. Its concern was to teach readers the expertise they desired, and not to prove the ethical merits of that expertise – though few authors resisted the temptation to claim that the reader would receive not only instruction but also spiritual comfort from mastering the book's contents.

Among writings of this kind perhaps the most popular were those dealing with the means by which the state could be made wealthy and secured from its enemies at home and abroad – a subject known to contemporaries as politics or political science. In 1579 the poet Gabriel Harvey claimed that at Cambridge 'You can not stepp into a schollers study but (ten to one) you shall lightly finde open either Bodin de Republica or Le Royes Exposition uppon Aristotles Politics or sum other like French or Italian Politic Discourses.' Ben Jonson satirised the lay devotee of political learning in the person of Sir Politic Would-be, who derived his opinions from the works of 'Nic. Machiavel, and monsieur Bodin'.[71] Machiavelli's political works were published at London in 1584. In 1606 Bodin's *Six livres* appeared in an English translation. Lay interest in the practicalities of political life was also reflected in books by English writers. The works of Sir Francis Bacon and Sir Walter Raleigh are examples, and an excellent though neglected instance is the anonymous *State of Christendom*, attributed on no very good grounds to Sir Henry Wotton.

It is reasonable to draw a broad distinction between a clerical and a lay approach to politics. The cleric was concerned with rights and duties, in a word with morals, while the layman was interested in means. Of course, there are many exceptions to this rule, and lawyers were interested both in matters of expediency and in questions of right. But the important point is that even lay political writers, who devoted their attention to practicalities, accepted much of the moral framework which informed the works of their

---

71 E.J.L. Scott, ed., *Letter-booke of Gabriel Harvey* (1884) 79; Ben Jonson, *Volpone*, IV. i. 28.

clerical brethren. Expediency was subordinated to morality. Machiavelli was Christianised – or rejected.

Contemporary plays reveal much about the opinions of the lay audiences for whom they were produced. Of course, playwrights were primarily concerned to entertain rather than instruct, but certain moral principles are writ large in the political drama of the period. Thomas Nash defended the theatre against puritan attack by pointing out that plays 'shew the ill-success of treason', and that 'no play . . . encourageth any man to tumults or rebellion, but lays before such the halter and the gallows'. 'Plays', said Thomas Heywood, 'are writ with this aim . . . to teach their subjects obedience to their king, to shew the people the untimely ends of such as have moved tumults . . . to present them with the flourishing estate of such as live in obedience.'[72] Dramatists insisted that the king's misconduct could not justify his subjects in rebellion. 'No ill', wrote Ben Jonson,

> should force the subject undertake
> Against the sovereign more than hell should make
> The gods do wrong,

while in *The Roman actor* Massinger condemned the assassination of the tyrant Domitian, for

> he was our prince,
> However wicked.

John Ford's *Perkin Warbeck* conveyed the same message:

> But Kings are earthly gods, there is no meddling
> With their anointed bodies, for their actions
> They only are accountable to heaven.

In *King John* Shakespeare associated the doctrine that kings could be deposed with popery, but his most extensive analysis of resistance and its consequences occurs in the plays dealing with Richard II and his successors. Richard violated established laws and ignored the public good of the realm, yet he was a king,

> the figure of Gods majesty,
> His captain, steward, deputy, elect

and as such could never 'be judg'd by subject and inferior breath'. The rebellion against Richard brought God's wrath to bear upon England, and more particularly upon Richard's successor Henry IV and his line. The Bishop of Carlisle's prophecy that Henry's usurpation will lead to dire consequences, and that 'The blood of English shall manure the ground', is brought to pass in

---

72 Thomas Nash, *Complete works*, ed. A.B. Grosart, 6 vols (1883–85) II, 90–1; Thomas Heywood, *An apology for actors* (1612) sig. F3b.

the Wars of the Roses when 'tumultuous wars' did 'kin with kin and kind with kind confound'.[73]

The twin themes of the evil of rebellion and the intervention of Providence in human affairs were also explored in Samuel Daniel's verse chronicle, the *History of the civill warres* – which dealt with the same period as Shakespeare's plays – and in Sir Francis Hubert's *Deplorable life and death of Edward II*. Hubert's poem, published in 1628 when the questions of royal tyranny and favouritism were highly topical, was pedestrian in both style and content – and all the more historically significant for that. He claimed that it was Edward's errors which led to his downfall, for Edward overlooked the fact that

> Kings must observe a just and rightfull course:
> God is their king, by whom they stand or fall.

Inevitably, a king who flouted the divine law would be punished by

> God, who ruines and erects,
> Sets up a David, and pulls downe a Saul.

Nevertheless, however tyrannical the actions of the king, he could not be actively resisted. Despite the incompetence and injustice of the king's rule the deposition of Edward II was a 'hatefull crime'.

Hubert informed his readers that there was no

> better way
> Whereby a Prince may with assurance reign
> Than to be truly just

and recommended that kings rule in the public interest and according to law.[74] He had nothing to say about the possibility of a conflict between the common good and the law. Would it be truly just for a king to disregard the laws of the land if, in his opinion, the security and welfare of the realm depended on such action? The poets and dramatists said little of direct relevance to this crucial question. Shakespeare gave a high priority both to the common good – for which Brutus killed and died – and to established laws – which Henry VIII refused to violate. But he did not tell his audience which principle should ultimately take precedence. *poets tend to be conservative*

According to absolutist theory the king was a sovereign ruler with a moral obligation to abide by established laws. The works of the poets and play-wrights were less explicit on the king's relation to the laws. Nevertheless, their views correspond more closely to those of the absolutists than to the opinions of such common lawyers as Sir Edward Coke. The kings of early Stuart drama were true rulers, not legal cyphers. It is interesting to compare Shakespeare's treatment of the Amicable Grant of 1525 with some of the views expressed by lawyers on a very similar measure of 1627 – Charles I's

hers slightly dismissive about the play. Wright's engagement with their political theory

73 Jonson, *Sejanus*, IV. iii. 71–3; Massinger, *Roman Actor*, v. ii; John Ford, *Perkin Warbeck*, III. ii. 57–9; Shakespeare, *Richard II*, IV. i. 125–6, 128, 141.
74 Bernard Mellor, ed., *The poems of Sir Francis Hubert* (Hong Kong 1961) 10, 90, 77.

Forced Loan. The lawyers held that the Loan was illegal and that the refusers were guilty of no offence. Since illegal royal actions were automatically invalid there was no need for the king to annul the Loan or to pardon the refusers. In Shakespeare's play, on the other hand, Henry VIII discovers that there are no legal precedents for the Amicable Grant, and decides to cancel it and to pardon those who refused to pay. The implication is that the king is the judge and interpreter of the laws, not the laws of the king. The same implication is evident in Heywood's *Edward IV*, where Matthew Shore accepts the king's seduction of his wife:

> Oh, what have subjects that is not their Kings?
> I'll not examine his prerogative.

In *The tragedy of Chabot*, George Chapman portrayed the king as acting wrongly in enforcing an unlawful order, and Chabot as acting rightly in refusing to acquiesce. Yet Chabot accepts that the king and his officers can never be resisted actively. People were bound meekly to accept the penalties which the king inflicted upon them for disobedience to his unlawful commands.

> Subjects are bound to suffer, not contest
> With princes, since their will and acts must be
> Accounted one day to a Judge supreme.[75]

Princes should obey the laws and rule well, but if they did not do so only God could call them to account.

Poems and plays may give a reasonable indication of popular opinion, but to gauge the mentality of more educated people we must turn to their books and speeches. Writing in 1640, Henry Parker drew attention to the insidious effects of absolutist ideas which ascribed 'all to Soveraignty, nothing at all to popular libertie'. He claimed that such views were held not only by papists and bishops but also by 'court parasites', and argued that 'the common Court doctrine is that Kings are boundlesse in authority'. In Parker's opinion, this doctrine was responsible for the ills which beset the commonwealth in 1640. It was 'that venemous matter which hath lain burning and ulcerating inwardly in the bowels of the common-welth so long'. Lay courtiers did indeed voice absolutist ideas throughout the period. In James's reign the Earl of Northampton parroted the ideas of his royal master, and as we shall see in the second section of this book royal servants frequently expressed absolutist ideas in Parliamentary debates and in the courts of law.[76]

75 Shakespeare, *Henry VIII*, I. ii. 88–102; Heywood, *The first part of King Edward IV*, v. iv; George Chapman, *The tragedie of Chabot admirall of France*, III. 164–6.
76 Henry Parker, *The case of shipmony briefly discoursed* (1640) 8, 33–4; Linda Levy Peck, *Northampton: patronage and politics at the court of James I* (1982) 181–4; Peck, 'The mentality of a Jacobean grandee', in Peck, ed., *The mental world of the Jacobean court*, 148–68. Other essays in Peck's collection are also highly informative on the cultural and intellectual life of the early Stuart Court, as are Peck, *Court patronage and corruption in early Stuart England* (Boston 1990); R. Malcolm Smuts, ed., *The Stuart Court and Europe: essays in politics and political culture* (Cambridge 1996); and Smuts, *Court culture and the origins of a royalist tradition in early Stuart England* (Philadelphia 1987).

Of course, it is not surprising that courtiers magnified the authority of the king. Few monarchs are immune to judicious flattery, and the more powerful a king is, the better can he reward his loyal servants. Yet it would be a mistake to suppose with Parker that courtiers were the only laymen to be infected with absolutist ideas. Henry Peacham, author of the best-selling *Compleat gentleman*, was no courtier, yet his attitude to royal authority, expressed in *The duty of all subjects to their king* of 1639, was uncompromisingly absolutist. Writing in opposition to the Scottish Covenanters, who had taken up arms against Charles I, Peacham repeated the conventional sentiments on rebellion, warning the reader that 'many times the disloyalty and unfaithfulnesse of subjects toward God and their lawfull Princes, draweth downe the vengeance of God upon the land'. Of course, the Scots denied that their actions had been unlawful or rebellious. They claimed that they were fighting in defence of the established laws, and denied that this could be construed as rebellion. Peacham would have no truck with this argument. If laws conflicted with the royal will, he asserted, we should obey the king and not the law: 'if therefore wee must live under and obey the law, how much more the Prince, that made and establisht it, yea who gives vigor and life unto the Law?' The king was above the law, for kings made the law, while God and not the law made the king: 'the Law is the Act or Ordinance of the Prince, and the Prince is the Vice-gerent of God, having sovereign power over those whom hee hath given in charge'.

Peacham wrote in support of Charles I's Scottish policy, but the theory of the Divine Right of Kings did not appeal only to those who happened to endorse royal policies. Sir Walter Raleigh was a critic of many of James I's actions. He believed that as a matter of expediency the king should ensure that his policies commanded the people's support, and abandon such unpopular measures as impositions – new duties on imports and exports, which James had levied without Parliamentary consent. The Commons of England were too powerful to be ignored with impunity, and a king who failed to please them ran the risk of rebellion. Raleigh's main interest lay in the area of practical politics, but his work also had a philosophical dimension – and the philosophy was absolutist. The king ought indeed to consult the wishes of his subjects, he argued, but any attempt to force him to do so would be morally ineffective: 'All binding of a King by Law upon the advantage of his necessitie, makes the breach it selfe lawfull in a King.' Laws were made by the king's 'unconstrained will'. They were not imposed upon him. In England kings had agreed to legislate in Parliament, but it was 'the Kings absolute power', not the consent of Lords and Commons, which made law. The state's welfare required the existence of a sovereign above the law, for emergencies would make it necessary that laws be broken: 'the immortal policie of a state cannot admit any law or privilege whatsoever, but in some particular or other, the same is necessarily broken'. The king's power to rule the country effectively could not be limited or taken away by law: '"Saving the right of our crown"

(*Jure salvo Coronae nostrae*) is intended inclusively in all oathes and promises exacted from a Soveraigne.'[77]

Raleigh provides a persuasive instance of someone who subscribed to absolutist notions while opposing royal policies. Clearly, the theory of the Divine Right of Kings exercised an appeal which transcended crude material interests and intentions. No doubt the logical force of absolutist arguments was one reason for their popularity. Another, and very important, reason lay in English people's detestation for all things popish. From the earliest days of the English Reformation anti-papal propaganda had stressed not only the irreligious nature of Roman Catholic theology, but also the seditious and anti-monarchical character of its political doctrines. In his *Acts and monuments* – the most influential Tudor indictment of popery – John Foxe was at pains to show that Roman Catholicism diminished royal power. From the 1590s onwards the equation of popery with anti-absolutist theories became one of the commonest themes in English political writing. Such works as Buchanan's *De jure regni apud Scotos* and the *Vindiciae contra tyrannos* were condemned for putting forward views which were essentially popish, though their authors were Protestant.

The roots of modern democracy are sometimes traced back to early modern Calvinism. It is true that some Calvinists permitted active resistance to tyrants. But many did not. Under James I the doctrines of royal accountability to the people and of legitimate resistance were commonly equated with Catholicism rather than Calvinism. An event of especial importance in this context was the Gunpowder Plot of 1605, which threw into high relief the practical implications of Catholic theory. The king himself took up the pen against papists, and a host of clergymen followed suit, including such orthodox Calvinists as Bolton, Morton, Prideaux and Robert Abbot, whose brother George became Archbishop of Canterbury in 1611. While Abbot ruled the church, such men were zealous defenders of the royal prerogative, but in the 1620s Abbot's authority declined as that of William Laud increased. In 1627 Abbot was deprived of the right to exercise his powers as archbishop.

Royal policies in the 1620s were ill-calculated to please doctrinal Calvinists. In the early years of the decade James I attempted to negotiate a Spanish marriage for his son, Prince Charles. To many zealous Protestants this policy appeared misguided, for Spain was the most powerful Catholic state in Europe, and Spanish troops seemed set to destroy Protestantism on the Continent. Moreover, the king's policy had unpalatable domestic consequences, for, in response to Spanish demands, he extended a far greater degree of toleration to his Catholic subjects than had been customary. In fact, the project for a Spanish marriage collapsed, and Charles I began his reign by going to war

---

77 Henry Peacham, *The duty of all true subiects to their king: as also to their native countrey* (1639) 12, 4, 3; Sir Walter Raleigh, *The prerogative of parliaments in England* (1628), sig. A3a, 57, 42, 15. A different approach to Raleigh's political thought is taken in Christopher Hill, *Intellectual origins of the puritan revolution*, paperback edn (1972) 131–224.

with Spain. But the new king's religious policies were even less acceptable to orthodox Calvinists than those of his father, since Charles gave effective control over the church to men who were hostile to the Calvinist theology of grace, and whose attitude towards ceremonies seemed to many to smack of popery. Led by William Laud and Richard Neile, these men used their newly acquired power to conduct a vigorous campaign against rigid Calvinism, preventing the publication of Calvinist books and redefining the pejorative term puritans to mean not nonconformists or Presbyterians but doctrinal Calvinists. In these circumstances it is hardly surprising that many Calvinists began to revise their views on royal power. They countered Laud's efforts to brand them as puritans by claiming that Laud and his followers were papists. Though popery had often been associated with opposition to royal authority, it had also traditionally been associated with tyranny – particularly with the spiritual tyranny of the pope. In the hands of Laud's opponents, theories of royal absolutism were identified with popery. Thus began the equation of popery with arbitrary government which was to be of the utmost importance in seventeenth-century politics. The twin themes of anti-popery and limited monarchy informed the writings of Thomas Scott, a best-selling puritan pamphleteer, in the early 1620s.[78] After 1625 the same ideology acquired still greater significance, binding together people who opposed Charles's secular policies and Laud's religious innovations.

Laud's ecclesiastical measures had the full support of the king, and Laudian tracts naturally defended royal absolutism. The bishop's opponents portrayed absolutist theory as itself a Laudian innovation, but with little justification. In fact, as we have seen, absolutist doctrines flourished long before Laud rose to power. Moreover, a number of Calvinists continued to take a high view of royal authority after 1625, though they disapproved of the king's ecclesiastical policies. A striking instance is Thomas Morton. As a bishop, he was notoriously lax in suppressing nonconformity. As a theologian, he was a rigid Calvinist. In 1626 Morton was a leading proponent of doctrinal Calvinism at the York House conference which discussed the outspokenly anti-Calvinist views of Laud's protégé Richard Montagu. Yet Morton did not allow his distaste for royal policies to affect his attitude to the king's authority. In the first two decades of the century he had been a zealous defender of royal sovereignty against the Catholics. In 1639 he repeated his arguments in a sermon preached against the Scots Calvinists, condemning their political opinions as popish, and their actions as seditious. Delivered before the king, the sermon was published at Newcastle as anti-Scots propaganda, and was all the more telling in view of its author's known Calvinism.[79]

78 Scott's ideas are discussed in P.G. Lake, 'Constitutional consensus and puritan opposition in the 1620s: Thomas Scott and the Spanish match', *HJ* 25 (1982) 805–25, and, from a different perspective, in Markku Peltonen, *Classical humanism and republicanism in English political thought, 1570–1640* (Cambridge 1995) 229–70.
79 Morton, *A sermon preached before the kings most excellent maiestie.* Morton equates ideas of active resistance with popery on, for example, pp. 3–4, 9, and quotes Calvin against resistance at 38–9.

Another Calvinist who opposed Laud's ecclesiastical policies, but adopted high views on the king's powers, was Edward Bagshaw. Lecturing at the Middle Temple in 1639, Bagshaw had some harsh things to say about the conduct of the Laudian bishops. He was silenced by Laud, but his lectures had already won him the affections of the London populace, and in 1640 he was elected to the Long Parliament as burgess for Southwark. In the Civil War he went over to the king's side, and while taking a stance close to Coke's on the royal prerogative, rejected ideas of contractual monarchy and legitimate resistance as popish. Filmer's influence has been detected in his work, but Bagshaw's ideas bear a still closer resemblance to those of his 'deare friend' Robert Bolton who had been his tutor at Oxford. Bagshaw wrote a life of Bolton and edited a number of his works for publication in the 1630s. Both men combined a conventionally Calvinist approach to questions of theology with a sturdy rejection of theories of contractual monarchy. Jailed by the Parliamentarians, Bagshaw wrote a book denouncing their political ideas in the later 1640s.[80]

In the first two decades of Stuart rule, absolutist ideas were enunciated primarily against Catholics and only secondarily in the context of domestic political disputes. After 1625 the anti-Catholic element remained strong in the writings of such Calvinists as Morton. But the sermons and treatises of Laud and his protégés increasingly identified anti-absolutist doctrines not with popery but with puritanism and with opposition by the king's subjects to his ecclesiastical policies. As a propagandist, Laud displayed an almost complete lack of awareness of the cohesive force of anti-popery. He was quick to detect ideas of limited and contractual monarchy in the writings of his opponents, but slow to identify these with Roman Catholicism though such an identification was entirely plausible, since in the early seventeenth century Catholic polemicists were among the most vigorous assertors of the notion that kings are accountable to their people. In Stuart England there was much political capital to be made from convicting one's opponents of popery. Laud's enemies were aware of this, but Laud was not, and he sold the pass needlessly.

CONCLUSIONS

The first, most obvious and most important conclusion about absolutist theory is that it existed – and existed in the minds of many English people, not just in the ravings of a few eccentric clerics. The notion that absolutism was a typically Continental doctrine, which had little or no influence in England, is groundless. The writings of foreign absolutists – Bodin, Barclay, Bédé – found English publishers. The works of James I and other English authors sold well abroad. There is little to distinguish the ideas of Buckeridge, Bolton

---

80 Daly, *Filmer*, 178–9; Bagshaw's 'To the reader' in Bolton's *Two sermons*, sig. A2a. Bagshaw, *The rights of the crown of England* (1660) sig. A3a–5a, 12. Although the book was written against Parliamentarian theories, Conrad Russell tells us that the purpose of Bagshaw's ideas was 'to exclude the Pope': Russell, *The causes of the English Civil War* (Oxford 1990) 150.

or Morton from those of Continental – say, French – absolutists. French kings succeeded in imposing absolute rule during the seventeenth century. The Stuarts failed. This was not because of any differences between absolutist theories in the two countries. Nor was it a foregone conclusion.

Secondly, it is apparent that absolutist ideas were expressed far more frequently in early Stuart than in Tudor England. Of course, there were Tudor advocates of strong monarchical authority. Examples from the first half of the sixteenth century are the Protestant William Tyndale and the Catholic Stephen Gardiner. Elizabethan instances are furnished by Charles Merbury and Hadrian Saravia. It has been suggested that constitutionalist thinking was already under pressure from absolutism by the time that Hooker set pen to paper in the early 1590s.[81] This may well be true. Certainly, Hooker's markedly constitutionalist attitudes were fast becoming unfashionable among leading clergymen in the final decade of Elizabeth's reign. But the succession of James I – himself an outspoken absolutist – accelerated the shift towards absolutism. This shift can be detected in the writings of Lancelot Andrewes, who at one time held that kings derive their power from the community. Under James he unswervingly maintained that monarchs draw their authority from God alone. Similar developments occurred in the writings of Alberico Gentili, Regius Professor of Civil Law at Oxford, and in those of Sir John Hayward, the historian and Civil lawyer. In the opening years of James's reign ideas of mixed and limited monarchy, and of the legitimacy of resistance in extreme circumstances, were still just occasionally expressed by highly placed clergymen – such as William Tooker in 1604 and, rather more equivocally, Robert Abbot in the previous year. These ideas were the exception not the rule, and were rapidly disappearing from the armoury of apologists for the established church.[82]

Fears that the Stuarts intended to rule England as absolute monarchs – subordinating the law of the land to their own wishes – were closely associated with the fact that absolutist theories were voiced with increasing frequency in the early seventeenth century, particularly by clergymen. What made this especially alarming was that James and Charles themselves subscribed to absolutist notions. Absolutism was defended on the grounds that God had prescribed it by the law of nature, and confirmed it in Scripture. To put this another way, absolutists believed that their theory could be expressed in – and proved by – purely rational arguments. They used the Bible only to support these arguments. Obviously, pagans who had never come into contact with Scripture or with Christian teachings were ignorant of the biblical message. Yet these pagans were none the less obliged to obey their governors. So the

81 Brendan Bradshaw, 'Richard Hooker's ecclesiastical polity', *JEH* 34 (1983) 438–44.
82 Douglas Macleane, *Lancelot Andrewes and the reaction* (1910) 37–9; M.F. Reidy, *Bishop Lancelot Andrewes: Jacobean court preacher* (Chicago 1955) 188; B.P. Levack, *The civil lawyers in England 1603–1641* (Oxford 1973) 112–13 and, more generally, Levack, 'Law and ideology: the Civil law and theories of absolutism in Elizabethan and Jacobean England', in Heather Dubrow and Richard Strier, eds, *The historical Renaissance: new essays on Tudor and Stuart literature and culture* (Chicago 1988) 220–41; William Tooker, *Of the fabrique of the church* (1604) 99–100; Robert Abbot, *Antichristi demonstratio* (1603) 92–3.

obligation to obey kings – and other superiors such as fathers – could not have arisen through Scripture alone. The Bible confirmed but did not create such duties. Pagans did possess *reason*, and it was reason which informed them of their political obligations. The key piece of reasoning for absolutism ran like this. By nature people need to live in society. But society cannot survive unless it is directed by a sovereign governor. So nature requires sovereignty. It was the law of nature, then, which made governors absolute sovereigns. Since God was the author of nature, and since natural law was a subdivision of God's law, it followed that rulers derive their sovereign power from God alone.

Of course, English Protestants were fond of corroborating their political views by quoting Scripture. They were also fond of using analogies to illustrate their ideas. It is sometimes suggested that the key to early Stuart political thought lies in the habit of thinking *analogically*. Another notion is that the English were obsessed with history, and that their political thought was essentially historical thought. Certainly, early Stuart writers filled up much space with historical examples. Absolutists liked to cite historical precedents to confirm the claim that royal power was limited by God alone. They frequently employed analogies to illustrate the same conclusion. But the crucial point is that the analogies, and the historical examples, were regarded as *illustrations*, not as proofs. They reinforced conclusions which had been reached by other means. They did not themselves generate conclusions.

Perhaps the commonest analogies were those drawn between the king and the head of a body, or between human and animal societies. The state was often compared with a hive of bees, ruled, so it was supposed, by an absolute king. From the point of view of traditional patriarchal values this analogy turned out to be rather unfortunate, for in 1609 Charles Butler published a work showing that the hive was a *feminine* monarchy.[83] Analogies of this sort meant far more to people in the early seventeenth century than they would today. The universe was often viewed as an orderly hierarchical structure, or Great Chain of Being, in which each part was related by correspondence or analogy to all other parts. However, the importance of analogical thinking should not be overrated.[84] Early Stuart writers were well aware of the obvious point that analogies hold water only if the things compared are relevantly similar. 'An argument by analogy (*a similibus*)', said Hayward, 'is not good, if any difference can be assigned.'[85] The use of analogy presupposed relevant

83 Charles Butler, *The feminine monarchie: or the historie of bees*, revised edition (1623) nevertheless continued to draw political analogies from the case of bees, arguing that the hive was 'an expresse patterne of a perfect monarchie' (sig. B2b), and warning the reader against 'nimble tongued Sophisters' who tried to draw any general conclusions from the gender of the queen (sig. I1b). The queen was commonly treated as male until much later. In the early eighteenth century Bernard Mandeville's famous *Fable of the bees* still called their ruler a king: *The fable of the bees*, ed. F.B. Kaye, 2 vols (Oxford 1924) I, 17 and elsewhere.
84 Emphasis is placed on the importance of analogical thinking in W.H. Greenleaf, *Order, empiricism and politics* (Oxford 1964) 1–94.
85 Hayward, *Answer*, sig. O2a.

similarity. The analogy between God and the king, for example, *presupposed* that both held sovereignty over their subjects. It was all very well to argue that creation was a Great Chain of Being. But the fact that the universe was a hierarchy did not prove anything at all about political society. Was the pope, or were the people superior to the king in the Great Chain? The mere existence of the Chain was of little use in answering this question.

It is difficult to find any early Stuart writer who believed that analogies did more than illustrate points which had been independently established. In 1610 James I used analogies when lecturing Parliament on the rights of kings. But he pointed out that the analogies were 'similitudes that *illustrate* the state of Monarchy'. One writer who was particularly addicted to fanciful analogies was Edward Forsett, author of *A comparative discourse of the bodies natural and politique*. Forsett's book was an idiosyncratic and rather foolish work which had no discernible influence, but it did emphatically and repetitively employ arguments by analogy. Yet even Forsett stated that it was 'for the better apprehension and illustration' that the commonwealth was 'set forth by sundry fit resemblances' and described such similitudes as 'familiar and well pleasing illustrations'.[86] Analogies were held to be illustrations, not proofs. The patriarchalist ideas of Filmer and others were not based on analogy: royal and fatherly power, these thinkers held, were identical, not merely similar. Again, there was nothing analogical about the reasoning which underlay designation theory or the doctrine of the necessity of government.

While there is little evidence that early Stuart writers placed any particular weight on arguments by analogy, there is evidence that some of them rejected such arguments as worthless. Richard Field, Dean of Gloucester under James I, accused Catholic publicists of folly for arguing from 'similitudes, which serve only for illustration'. Thomas Bilson pointed out that 'similitudes be no syllogisms'. Isaac Casaubon, the great classical scholar who spent the last few years of his life in England advising James I on matters relating to the king's controversies with the papists, took issue with Catholic arguments from analogies made by the Fathers of the Church: 'the allegories of the fathers teach but do not prove'. Again, Thomas Morton devoted a chapter in one of his anti-papist works to demonstrating that 'an argument drawn from a similitude illustrates rather than proves'. 'A reason drawn from a similitude', he said, 'is the weakest of all kinds of argument.' Analogies, he held, might be useful in 'vulgar everyday teaching', but they were 'rarely if ever of any use in convincing and accurate argument.'[87]

86 James I, *The kings maiesties speach to the Lords and Commons*, sig. A4b in *Political writings*, ed. Sommerville, 181; Forsett, *A comparative discourse of the bodies natural and politique* (1606) sig. π 3a, 4b.

87 Field, *Of the church*, iii, 507; Bilson, *True difference*, 525; Casaubon, *De rebus sacris et ecclesiasticis exercitationes* (1614) 292: 'allegoriae patrum docent non probant'; Morton, *Causa regia, sive de authoritate et dignitate principum Christianorum, dissertatio* (1620) 236–7: 'Argumentum, a similitudine ductum, illustrare magis quam probare.' 'ratio a Similitudine ducta, sit omnium maxime imbellis'. 'Rectius Dialectici, qui Similitudinem ad genus docendi exotericum et populare accommodant, cuius in acroamatico et accurato genere rarus ac fere nullus est usus.'

Absolutists used history to confirm their theories. For example, they claimed that the history of relations between the pope and monarchs supported the view that kings were independent of the church in temporal matters. Again, some of them argued that William of Normandy had ruled England as an absolute conqueror. But such contentions had little special significance in their thinking. History might show that the truth about royal power had been recognised in the past. It did not establish the truth. By divine law all sovereigns derived their power from God alone, and were accountable only to Him. For this reason, history was largely irrelevant to politics. The manner by which the king's ancestors had at first come to power was of minor interest. James I did indeed believe that William had won the crown 'by force, and with a mighty army'. Yet he placed little emphasis on this point. For in James's opinion 'the same ground of the king's right over all the land, and subjects thereof remaineth alike in all . . . free Monarchies'. Divine right rendered history immaterial.[88]

What lay at the heart of absolutist thinking was not an odd devotion to analogies or historical precedent, but a set of simple rational arguments. These arguments purported to show that kings were subject to God alone and that they could never actively be resisted. Though kings had a moral obligation to abide by settled laws, they could justly rule outside the law if the public good demanded such action. There was a strong communitarian and anti-individualist bias in natural law thought. In the public interest, it was held, the sovereign could infringe any of the legal rights of his subjects.

Absolutism was not the only form of natural law thinking current in the early seventeenth century. There were many reasons why subjects – both on the Continent and in England – resented the grandiose claims of their rulers, and why they expressed constitutionalist views. In England some based their ideas of limited monarchy upon notions typical of the thought of common lawyers. Others drew on natural law theory. In their hands, the theory retained its communitarian and ahistorical character, but was given a radically anti-absolutist twist.

---

88 James I, *Workes* (1616) 202, in *Political writings*, ed. Sommerville, 74; cf. Saravia, *De imperandi authoritate*, 288. That historical examples are insufficient to establish moral or political truths is stated or implied in Hayward, *Answer*, sig. P1b; De Dominis, *De republica ecclesiastica pars secunda*, 818; Burhill, *Contra Martini Becani controversiam*, 72; Owen, *Anti-Paraeus*, 52. Two modern interpretations which stress the importance of historical thinking are J.G.A. Pocock, *The ancient constitution and the feudal law* (Cambridge 1957; revised edn 1987) and Martin Dzelzainis, 'The ideological context of John Milton's *History of Britain*', unpublished Cambridge University Ph.D. dissertation, 1983.

CHAPTER 2

Government by Consent

Early Stuart England was a monarchy. But the king could govern effectively only with the assistance of the nobility and landed gentry. Modern states possess large paid bureaucracies, standing armies and police forces, swift communications, and all the resources for efficient government – or tyranny – which technology has placed at their disposal. The early Stuart state possessed none of these things. The enforcement of royal policy required the active co-operation of local élites. No king could afford to ignore the wishes of country gentlemen, whose wealth and social standing commanded the deference – and obedience – of the king's own subjects. Conversely, local gentlemen and communities were well advised to keep on good terms with the Court and the Privy Council, which could promote or undermine the interests of individuals or localities by patronage or executive action. The Court and the country were not mutually exclusive and opposed entities, but two aspects of a single whole, linked by a myriad of subtle connections. Whatever the theoretical merits of absolutist doctrine, it misdescribed English political practice, for the king and his subjects were in fact bound together by mutual dependencies. It was to this idea of mutual dependency that the doctrines of mixed and limited government gave formal expression.

There were several separate strands of anti-absolutist thinking current in early modern Europe. One was the set of ideas associated with ancient and immemorial custom, and voiced in England by common lawyers. A second was the movement known as civic humanism. Deriving inspiration from ancient Roman writings, a number of late-medieval Italian authors espoused the ideals of republican government, and of the active participation of citizens in political life.[1] Prominent among these humanists was Leonardo Bruni – and

1 The classic modern study of civic humanism is J.G.A. Pocock, *The Machiavellian moment* (Princeton 1975). Only a relatively brief section – 333–60 – is devoted to early-seventeenth-century England, an indication that civic humanism was buried if not dead in England before the Civil War. Pocock's interpretation has recently been questioned in Markku Peltonen's excellent *Classical humanism and republicanism in English political thought 1570–1640* (Cambridge 1995). Peltonen admits that there was no 'coherent republican tradition' in England before the 1640s (12) but argues that some key civic humanist ideas were quite commonly expressed in the Elizabethan and

Bruni was one of the very few writers cited by the fifteenth-century English anti-absolutist Sir John Fortescue in his highly influential *De Laudibus Legum Angliae* (In praise of the laws of England).[2] But republicanism acquired little hold in England. The idea of active involvement in political affairs did survive, but came to mean service to the king, not direct participation in political decision-making. Nakedly republican sentiments were rarely expressed before the Civil War. Until the 1640s monarchy of some sort seemed inevitable. Moreover, given royal control of the press, it was difficult and dangerous to voice republican ideas. Significantly, one of the very few books to suggest – albeit tentatively – that republics were superior to monarchies was published from the safety of St Omer. Its author approvingly noted that Aristotle, the 'great Philosopher', discussed 'whether a Monarchy or Commonweale is the better forme of Policy' and came down on the side of 'a Commonweale' (or republic), 'because the wisest and best men are admitted to sway therein'. When the book was reprinted at Oxford this passage underwent an important change. Aristotle was now said to favour not a republic, but 'that Forme of Politie, where the Wisest and Best are admitted to the Manage of State-Affaires: (as at this day is most conspicuous, in the Blessed Raigne and Regiment of our Most Gracious and Glorious Soveraigne, whom God preserve)'.[3] Fledgling republicanism turned into sycophancy towards the king as soon as it crossed the Channel.

Though there is little sign that classical learning was exploited to republican ends in the years before 1640, the writings of the ancient Greeks and Romans *were* used to mount arguments against absolutism. The works of Cicero, Tacitus and Plutarch were staple items in the English gentleman's education. Tacitus' damning analysis of absolute rule appeared in English in the 1590s and was reprinted four times between the accession of James I and the outbreak of the Civil War. In 1628 two separate translations of the Frenchman Pierre Matthieu's *The powerfull favorite, or, the life of Aelius Sejanus* – largely derived from Tacitus – were illicitly published. The translators' aim was to attack Charles I's unpopular favourite the Duke of Buckingham. Of course, if Buckingham were Sejanus, Charles must be the tyrant Tiberius. In 1642 an English translation of the Italian Malvezzi's commentaries on Tacitus was dedicated to Viscount Saye and Sele – one of the most outspoken critics of royal policy.[4]

Jacobean periods. Amongst the most important of these ideas were the notions that true nobility consists in virtue, and that virtue is a matter of action rather than contemplation. Peltonen demonstrates that these claims were frequently voiced. However, there was nothing particularly republican about such ideas, and absolutists could happily accept them. James I held that virtue lies in action not contemplation (*Political writings*, ed. Sommerville, 34, 222), and the most famous of French absolutists, Jean Bodin, believed that we should 'measure true nobility by virtue' – a point which he thought uncontroversial: *The six bookes of a commonweale*, translated by Richard Knolles (1606) 394.

2 Sir John Fortescue, *De laudibus legum Angliae*, ed. S.B. Chrimes (Cambridge 1942) pp. xc, xcii n., 11, 148.

3 Ap-Robert, *The younger brother his apology* (St Omer 1618) 59; (Oxford 1635) 52.

4 Virgilio Malvezzi, *Discourses upon Cornelius Tacitus* (1642) is dedicated by the publisher to Saye and Sele at sig. A2a–b.

Like Tacitus' writings, the *Lives* of Plutarch contained much that could be used to attack absolute rule. Plutarch's work first appeared in English in 1579 and was printed four more times before 1640. It was Shakespeare's main source on the classical world. We all know that early Stuart gentlemen were fond of quoting from the classics. They did not always do so merely to parade their learning. For instance, Sir John Eliot told the House of Commons in 1629 that

> I find by Plutarch of the great Antiochus of Asia, who . . . sent messengers and letters to all his Provinces, that if there were any letters or dispatches sent under his name that came to them, that were not warrantable by law and agreeable to justice, it should not be conceived to be done by him, and therefore they should not give way to it.[5]

Eliot was using Plutarch's story to support a radically anti-absolutist contention: royal officers who acted against law and justice could always be resisted by the king's subjects.

A love of the classics is sometimes associated with the movement known as humanism, and contrasted with scholasticism. This way of looking at things may be useful when dealing with the fifteenth and early sixteenth centuries. Its validity is limited once we reach the later sixteenth century. The Jesuits combined classical learning with adherence to medieval scholastic ideas. Similarly, Calvinist resistance theorists were as much at home in the world of ancient Rome as in that of the medieval universities. The *Vindiciae contra tyrannos*, for instance, is full of classical references. The pseudonymous name chosen by the author itself alludes to Roman times, and in particular to the assassination of Caesar by Brutus and his confederates. Yet the *Vindiciae* also derived its claims from the natural law tradition of medieval scholasticism. Indeed, it was to this tradition that the book made its major appeal. By the later sixteenth century the leading mode of anti-absolutist argument current in Europe was no longer civic humanist, or overtly republican, but was based upon a particular reading of the law of nature.

St Thomas Aquinas anchored his account of political society upon the law of nature, ordained by God, and eternally binding on humans. His theory was vastly influential, not only in its general structure, but also in a myriad of details. As late as the early seventeenth century he was still one of the authors most frequently quoted in English literature. But his writings were of little use in solving the most pressing problem of early modern political thought: did kings derive their power from God alone or from the people? Aquinas gave scant attention to this question. 'The later ideals of the Sovereign People expressing itself through universal suffrage', it has rightly been said, 'can be forced out of him only less easily than the doctrine of the Divine Right of Kings.'[6]

---

5 *CD 29*, 25–6.
6 St Thomas Aquinas, *Summa Theologiae*, ed. Thomas Gilby *et al.*, 60 vols (1964–) xxviii, 176.

In the later Middle Ages and early modern period, however, the most famous intellectual heirs of Aquinas – including Gerson, Almain, Suarez, Grotius and Locke – claimed that royal power was derived from the community, not from God alone. This was the commonest theory among Catholics at the beginning of the seventeenth century. At first sight it seems a little odd that Catholics defended such ideas, for popes claimed to be absolute rulers over the church, accountable to God alone. Two points are important here. Firstly, not all Catholics were advocates of the pope's ecclesiastical monarchy. The conciliarists of the fifteenth and early sixteenth centuries – such men as Gerson and Almain – rejected papal claims to sovereignty, arguing that the whole church, represented in a General Council, was superior to any of its members, including the pope.[7]

Secondly, natural law theorists distinguished sharply between God's eternal law of nature and his positive laws, holding that ecclesiastical authority was derived from revelation while civil society was a purely natural institution. Since the two forms of power – civil and ecclesiastical – were grounded upon different laws, it was plausible to argue that their general characteristics were also different. Thus anti-absolutist writers often claimed that Christ had set up absolute papal monarchy in the church, while God's natural law had granted original sovereignty in every society to the people. This was the attitude of many Counter-Reformation Catholics, in Spain and elsewhere. We often think of early modern Spain as an absolute monarchy. But in theory the powers of the king were strictly limited, even in Castile. The diplomat Dudley Carleton contrasted England, where the king possessed wide powers, with 'Spaine, where all the actions of the prince, great and small, are bounded and limited by express statutes to tie prerogative, and to set the subject at liberty'.[8]

In the later sixteenth century, notions of limited kingship and of the legitimacy of resisting a ruler who exceeded his powers were frequently adopted by Protestants whose Catholic kings refused to grant them toleration. Cases in point are the French Huguenots in the years after the massacre of St Bartholomew's day 1572, and the Dutch Calvinists in revolt against the king of Spain. During the late sixteenth and early seventeenth centuries some Continental Protestants continued to maintain similar positions. Of these, the most notorious was David Paraeus, while the best-known is Johannes Althusius.[9]

7 A good introduction to constitutionalist natural law theories is Quentin Skinner, *The foundations of modern political thought*, 2 vols (Cambridge 1978) II, 113–84; cf. J.H. Burns, '*Jus gladii* and *jurisdictio*: Jacques Almain and John Locke', *HJ* 26 (1983) 369–74 for an important correction.
8 *PD 10*, 111. In 1614, Sir Roger Owen argued that 'The parliament in Spain has more liberty than here': *PP 14*, 344. Cf. L. Pereña et al., *Francisco Suarez de iuramento fidelitatis: estudio preliminar, conciencia y politica* (Madrid 1979) 174–91.
9 On Paraeus, see also pp. 76, 79, 122, 251–4 below. Althusius is the subject of Otto von Gierke's highly important *The development of political theory* translated by Bernard Freyd (New York 1939). References to Althusius in early Stuart writings include Thomas Owen, *The copie of a Letter sent from Paris to the Reverend Fathers of the Society of Iesus, who live in England* (1611) 65; James Pateson, *The image of bothe churches, Hierusalem and Babel, unitie and confusion* (Tournai 1623) 351–2; David Owen, *Anti-Paraeus sive determinatio de iure regio* (Cambridge 1622) 72–3; John Buckeridge, Bishop of Rochester, 'The Lord Bp. of Rochester his defence of the power of kings against papa-puritanicall expositions of texts of Scriptures', St John's College, Cambridge, James Ms 305(3), 22. Buckeridge's treatise has an imprimatur dated 1623.

In England such ideas ran counter to the prevailing orthodoxy of the universities and the clergy. The bishops controlled – or rather attempted to control – the press, and on occasion suppressed books which contained politically objectionable passages. In particular, efforts were made to confiscate English Catholic literature, though with only partial success. Books written in Latin were allowed to circulate unless they contained material encouraging rebellion.[10] The majority of Continental works of political theory, both Catholic and Protestant, were thus available to English readers. Anti-absolutist natural law ideas were not confined to Catholics – a relatively small proportion of the population, whose legal disabilities reduced their political importance still further – but circulated widely among the educated. Such politically significant laymen as Selden, Sandys, Phelips and Pym all gave expression to ideas of this sort.

The natural law theory of original popular sovereignty was often employed to show that the powers of monarchs were limited. The people had set up monarchy by transferring their power to a single individual upon whatever conditions they chose. If the king failed to abide by these conditions his actions would automatically be invalid and might even lay him open to resistance and deposition. However, it was possible that the community had failed to impose any conditions on its ruler and arguably this was always the case if the king had gained power by conquest. In England the claim that the monarch ruled by conquest was often expressed by Civil lawyers. Justinian's *Digest* and *Institutes* – major texts of the Civil law – endorsed the view that the Roman emperors had derived their power from a grant made by the people.[11] A number of Civil lawyers denied that the same analysis applied to English kings. A king who ruled by conquest, they held, manifestly did not derive his powers from the consent of his subjects. So his power was absolute. The main function of the Civil lawyers was to staff the ecclesiastical courts. Consequently, they found themselves in close alliance with the clergy and the crown. Their intellectual heritage, combined with their actual political position and interests, led them to adopt a theory which married the notions of original popular sovereignty and current royal absolutism.

In the hands of the Civil lawyers the notion of original popular sovereignty was given an absolutist twist, but in general the idea was exploited to diminish royal power. Its proponents distinguished between royal and paternal authority, rejecting the patriarchalist claim that kingly power was essentially the same thing as fatherly power. They denied that God and nature had originally granted power over the commonwealth to a specific person or persons (for example, the eldest father), and concluded that political authority had at first resided in the community as a whole. Since the community had originally

10 In 1609 Wotton told the Venetian Cabinet that 'provided books do not endeavour to destroy loyalty they are not prohibited' in England: *CSPV 1607–10*, 322. This is confirmed by the list published in C.R. Gillett, *Burned books: neglected chapters in British history and literature*, I (New York 1932).
11 *The Institutes of Justinian*, translated by J.B. Moyle, 5th edn (Oxford 1913) 5. *Digest* I, iv, 1.

possessed power, it followed that kings had at first received authority from the hands of the community, and that the extent of royal authority was defined by the terms on which the grant took place. Of course, it was possible that the community had transferred power without imposing any conditions at all upon the king. Some writers argued that even in this case the king's powers were limited, for the natural law gave him a duty to rule in the public interest, since the very purpose of political society was the promotion of the public good. Even if the community had imposed no express limitations on royal authority, then, the king was still bound to act in the interests of his subjects. If need arose, the community could enforce this condition. These were the main elements in the theory of government by consent. Each deserves further discussion.

THE ORIGINS OF GOVERNMENT

Thinkers who advocated the theory of government by consent adopted the same broad account of natural law as their absolutist adversaries. They held that human nature rendered society and government necessary. They admitted that by nature fathers hold power over their families. But they denied that fatherly power is kingly. This view was commonly expressed by Counter-Reformation Catholics. Matthew Kellison, President of the English College at Douai, was typical in asserting that Adam 'had the power called Oeconomica, yet had he no power of governing a Citie or Common wealth'. Among non-Catholics who adopted the same position was John Selden. He distinguished between 'Oeconomique rule' over a particular family, and political government over 'the common state' – that is to say, a community consisting of many families. The same distinction occurs in the writings of Richard Hooker.[12]

This distinction between domestic and political power served to rebut the patriarchalist version of absolutist theory, but it left intact the alternative – designation theory. To refute this it was necessary to show that the community had at first possessed civil authority itself, and not just the right to nominate the person or persons to whom God would then grant authority. The main argument employed at this stage ran as follows. Since natural law did not mark out any particular person or persons to rule the commonwealth, and since it was necessary that the commonwealth be ruled, it followed that political power had at first resided in the community as a whole. Matthew Kellison expressed this attitude concisely: 'seeing that Nature made all equall, and that there is no more reason why this power should be in one rather than another, it followeth that it is first in the communitie.'[13]

12 Matthew Kellison, *The right and iurisdiction of the prelate and the prince*, 2nd edn (Douai 1621) 44; John Selden, *Titles of honor* (1614) 2; Richard Hooker, *The laws of ecclesiastical polity*, I, X, 4. Sixteenth- and early-seventeenth-century Catholic examples of the distinction between royal and paternal power are discussed in Quentin Skinner, *The foundations of modern political thought*, II, 156, and in J.N. Figgis, 'On some political theories of the early Jesuits', *TRHS* new series 11 (1897) 89–112, at 104.
13 Kellison, *Right and iurisdiction*, 43.

When families congregated together to form a political society, Kellison held, 'power was resident in the communitie'. The Catholic Robert Parsons likewise claimed that 'temporall power is given first of all by God, in the law of Nature, unto the people or multitude'. Monarchy, in Parsons's view, arose only when the sovereign people decided to transfer political power (upon conditions of its own choosing) to a particular person. The monarch's powers were, in consequence, derived from the people, and not from God alone. Once again, John Selden took a similar line, arguing that when 'inbred sociablenesse' drove people to congregate together in some society larger than the family, 'a Popular state first rais'd it selfe'. Selden rejected the absolutist contention that monarchy was the original form of government, claiming, in his rather cumbrous way, that this could not 'be conceived as truth, otherwise than with a presupposition of a Democracie, out of which . . . a Monarchie might have originall'.[14]

Selden believed that democracy was the first form of government, but it would be a mistake to suppose that he, or others who adopted such ideas, were democrats in the modern sense. Their point in arguing that power had originally resided in the people was to show that the authority of kings was limited, not that the people should govern. Political thinkers of all persuasions were agreed that the mass of the people was fit only to be ruled. The giddy or many-headed multitude was incompetent to make political decisions. Democracy, it was held, was the worst form of government, monarchy the best. Yet, if democracy was so much inferior to all other forms, how was it that God (whose insight into political matters was profound) at first set up democratic government? As we have seen, Filmer and De Dominis made precisely this objection to the notion of original democracy. Yet the objection is not as strong as it seems. The Spanish Jesuit Francisco Suarez anticipated and countered it in a work written against the political ideas of James I and publicly burned at London in 1613. Suarez argued that natural law permitted all three of the possible forms of government, but did not prescribe any of them. Since God had ordained that society be governed but had not insisted on any particular form of government, it followed that societies were at first self-governing democracies. This did not at all imply that God preferred or prescribed democracy. Original democracy was simply a consequence of the failure of God – and natural law – to prescribe any particular form of government. Suarez distinguished between the permissive and the obligatory decrees of the law of nature – that is to say, between what natural law permitted and what it forbade or commanded – arguing that original democracy was according to the permissive law. Selden later made much of this

14 Ibid., 44; Robert Parsons, *An answere to the fifth part of reportes lately set forth by Syr Edward Coke* (St Omer 1606) 358; Selden, *Titles of honor*, 3; in the second edition of this book Selden changed his mind: *Titles of honor* (1631) 4–5, 11; cf. J.P. Sommerville, 'John Selden, the law of nature, and the origins of government', *HJ* 27 (1984) 437–47, at 445. A recent discussion of Selden's views on English constitutional history is Paul Christianson, *Discourse on history, law, and governance in the public career of John Selden, 1610–1635* (Toronto 1996).

same distinction between the two kinds of natural law in his *Mare Clausum* of 1635.[15]

Sovereignty over any political society had originally resided in the society as a whole. But there was no reason why it should continue to do so. Indeed, since democracy was an inferior form of government, the wisest course for the people was to set up aristocracy or monarchy by transferring power to one or a few men. If they chose, the people could impose conditions upon their ruler's exercise of power. Historical evidence in favour of this account of the origins of government was provided by the fact that the powers of European kings varied. According to Kellison, 'the Kinges power in divers countries is diversely limited'. Another Catholic, Edward Weston, pointed out that some rulers could make laws and levy taxes without the consent of their subjects, while others – such as the kings of England – did not have these powers. It was possible, of course, that such kings had voluntarily accepted limitations on their authority, but Kellison thought this implausible, for 'who seeth not how unlikely it is that Kinges should thus restraine their owne power, and tie their owne hands?' He concluded that limitations had been imposed by the people upon their king: 'as the people gave the king his authoritie; so it was the people that thus limited and restrained him for their owne preservation: for to the same Authoritie that giveth power, it pertaineth to restraine it'. The extent of the king's authority, and of the subject's duty of obedience, could be deduced from the conditions upon which power had been transferred to him. 'The power of the king', wrote Suarez, 'is greater or less, according to the pact or agreement between him and his subjects.'[16] The law of nature proved that the king's power was derived from the people, but the specific limitations to which he was subject had to be deduced from the text of the original contract, or from equally compelling evidence.

THE ORIGINAL CONTRACT

The main problem with the original contract, from the practical point of view, was that it did not exist. Theory might insist that the king's powers were derived from the people's grant and that conditions imposed by the commonwealth defined their limits. Yet there was no reason why the people should have written down these conditions, still less why such a document should have survived the ravages of time. Richard Hooker admitted that the original 'articles of compact' between the king and his subjects were often 'clean worn out of knowledge'. How, then, could subjects gain information

15 Francisco Suarez, *Defensio fidei Catholicae*, II, ii, 8, in *Opera*, 28 vols (Paris 1856–78) XXIV, 208–9; Selden, *Mare clausum*, translated by Marchamont Nedham as *Of the dominion, or ownership of the sea* (1652) 12–13; cf. Tuck, *Natural rights theories*, 87.
16 Kellison, *Right and iurisdiction*, 54; Edward Weston, *Iuris pontificii sanctuarium* (1613) 199; Suarez, *De legibus*, III, iv, 5, translated in G.L. Williams *et al.*, eds, *Selections from three works of F. Suarez*, 2 vols (Oxford 1944) II, 386.

on their ruler's powers and their own liberties? The answer was twofold. Firstly, though the original contract might not survive, evidence did exist of later and equally binding agreements between the two contracting parties – king and people – in the form of statutes and the coronation oath. Secondly, the nature of the original constitution could be deduced from 'custom reaching beyond the memory of man' – the assumption being that if no one knew when an institutional arrangement had been introduced it was original.[17]

John Selden believed that laws were contracts between the king and his subjects, and claimed that 'to know what obedience is due to the prince you must looke into the contract betwixt him and his people'. In England, he held, laws were either Acts of Parliament or customs. Another author asserted that the king's power was 'gotten by grant of the commonwealth', and claimed that 'the common received customs must be our guide' in gauging its extent. Sir Robert Phelips expressed similar ideas in a striking speech delivered in the Parliament of 1628. 'It is well known', he told his audience, 'the people of this state are under no other subjection than what they did voluntarily assent unto by the original contract between King and people.' This contract, he believed, guaranteed the subject 'many necessary privileges and liberties, as it appears by the common laws and acts of parliament'. For Phelips, legal precedents were interesting less because of their antiquity than because they furnished evidence of the original contract.[18]

The notion that the laws of the land imposed contractual obligations upon the king was frequently expressed by educated people under the early Stuarts – and a number of them were vocal opponents of royal policies. Selden and Phelips are examples. In 1640 an anonymous puritan critic of the king's religious measures (probably the cleric Henry Burton) argued that 'both Prince and People are bound by mutuall Covenant and Sacred Oath' to maintain the subject's 'ancient Rights and liberties and those good laws of the land, which as the ligatures doe bind, unite, and fasten the Head and Body, the King and his Subjects together'. This author believed that in taking the coronation oath the king accepted contractual obligations which had been imposed upon his ancestors. In this he was not alone. The Catholic Robert Parsons viewed the coronation oath as a repetition of the original contract. Another Catholic work, published in 1616, claimed that kings were 'bound to their subjects' 'by a mutuall and reciprocall oath'. On the eve of the Civil War, the Scotsman

---

17 Hooker, *Laws of ecclesiastical polity*, VIII, ii, 5, 11, 13.

18 Selden, *Table talk of John Selden*, ed. Sir Frederick Pollock (1927) 137; F.S. Fussner, ed., 'William Camden's "Discourse concerning the prerogative of the crown"', *Proceedings of the American Philosophical Society* 101 (1957) 204–15, on p. 210. The attribution to Camden is doubtful. It is notable that the author relies heavily on the Catholic theorists Alphonsus a Castro and Molina. *PP 28*, III, 33, II, 61 (Phelips). That kings are elected for the good of the electors, and that they are bound not only by natural law but also by fundamental laws which provide for '*salus populi*' is stated in Phelips's notes 'De regimine politico', Somerset Record Office, Phelips Mss 221/38, f. 63a. These notes are Latin extracts from a variety of classical and Continental authors, including Bodin and Lipsius.

Robert Baillie asserted that the oath was a 'true convenant or paction . . . betwixt the King and his subjects'. In the Parliament of 1628 John Pym took a similar line.[19]

This approach to the coronation oath differed strikingly from that of the absolutists. In absolutist theory, the king's powers were limited only by the laws of God – his one superior. The coronation oath was a promise to the people to rule well. If the king broke this promise he sinned, and God might punish him. But the oath did not limit the king's powers or the subject's duty of obedience. According to the theory of government by consent, on the other hand, the king and his subjects were bound by *reciprocal* conditions. Obedience was due to the king only in so far as he kept his part of the bargain. Preaching in favour of the Forced Loan of 1627, the absolutist clergyman Roger Maynwaring insisted that the subject's duty of obedience was unconditional. John Pym attacked this point of view, claiming that Maynwaring 'hath acted the part of the Romish Jesuits'. His reasoning was amusing. Just as the Jesuits 'labour our destruction by dissolving the Oath of Allegiance taken by the people', he argued, so Maynwaring 'doth the same work by dissolving the oath of protection, and justice, taken by the King'. The logic of Pym's case was weak – for his own ideas on royal authority were far closer than those of Maynwaring to the teaching of the Jesuits – but his rhetoric was persuasive and his campaign to brand absolutism as popish was ultimately successful.[20]

The text of the early Stuart coronation oath supported the absolutist rather than the contractual interpretation – largely because it incorporated two important revisions of medieval precedent. The first was an addition. Instead of simply undertaking to observe the old law, the king now consented to do so only if the law was compatible with 'the prerogative of the Kinge'. The second was an alteration. The king agreed to maintain the 'laws and customs which the communalty . . . have', and not 'which the communalty have . . . chosen'. The implication of the latter version was that the laws had been imposed upon the king by an originally sovereign people – an implication which absolutists were keen to avoid, but which others willingly accepted. The lawyer Oliver St John, for example, claimed that the 'Lawes of the Realme' bound the king precisely because they had been 'instituted at first, and freely assented unto' by the commons. When the Civil War began, Parliamentarians were quick to note the ideological dimension of Charles I's coronation oath, and

---

19 Henry Burton, *Lord bishops, none of the Lords bishops* (1640), sig. K4a; the book is attributed to Burton by W.M. Lamont, 'Prynne, Burton, and the puritan triumph', *Huntington Library Quarterly* 27 (1964) 103–13; Peter Holmes, *Resistance and compromise: the political thought of the Elizabethan Catholics* (Cambridge 1982) 149–50; Jacques Davy, Cardinal Du Perron, *An oration made on the part of the lordes spirituall* (St Omer 1616) 82; Robert Baillie, *Ladensium ΑΥΤΟΚΑΤΑΚΡΙΣΙΣ, The Canterburians self-conviction*, 3rd edn (1641) 123; *PP 28*, III, 271; for evidence that Pym thought in terms of *enforceable* limitations, cf. ibid., IV, 107. See also p. 126 below.
20 Pym quoted by Conrad Russell, 'The parliamentary career of John Pym, 1621–9', in Peter Clark, Alan G.R. Smith and Nicholas Tyacke, eds, *The English commonwealth 1547–1640* (Leicester 1979) 163.

accused Laud of responsibility for the revisions – though these in fact pre-dated Charles's reign.[21]

The theory of government by consent struck at the central doctrine of absolutism – the contention that kings derive their power from God alone. Pym took Maynwaring to task for preaching that 'kings are ordained of God without the people', and in the Parliament of 1610 the lawyer John Hoskins declared that while regal power itself was from God, the 'actuating thereof is from the people'. In other words, God first gave regal power to the people, who then decided on the form in which it should be exercised. John Floyd expressed the same idea in 1620, arguing that 'regall authority was created immediately of God together with mans nature, and is formally in every absolute and free state'. The people created a king by transferring to a single man 'the royall Sovereignty which God created and bestowed upon them'.[22] As we have seen, the theory construed the laws of the land as limitations placed upon the king's power by the people, either at the time of the original transference or later. But what if it could be shown that the king had not acquired power by a grant from the people, or that the grant had been unconditional? Most theorists in the early seventeenth century admitted that there was one means by which a king could gain power without the consent of his subjects – namely conquest. Unfortunately, there was rather strong historical evidence that England had been conquered, by Charles's ancestor William of Normandy.

CONQUEST THEORY

If a state were conquered in a just war, it forfeited its autonomy and became subject to the conqueror. This principle was accepted by virtually everyone as a decree of the law of nations, which took precedence over the laws of particular states. Sir Edwin Sandys and John Floyd did indeed claim that even in a case of conquest, the victor gained no power over the defeated population until they consented to his rule.[23] But this attitude was exceptional. On the question of conquest, Coke, Davies and the Civil lawyers were in agreement. A conqueror acquired power over his vanquished subjects not from their consent but from God alone. He was, in consequence, bound only by the laws of God and nature and not by any merely human laws. As Richard Hooker put it, 'Kings by conquest make their own charter: so that how large their power . . . is, we cannot with any certainty define, further than only to set them in general the law of God and nature for bounds.' The lawyer Robert Mason, who acted as Sir John Eliot's defence counsel in 1629, contrasted the 'absolute power of a conqueror', who 'was bound by no laws but has power

21 Christopher Wordsworth, ed., *The manner of the coronation of King Charles the First of England at Westminster, 2 Feb., 1626* (1892) pp. lvii–lxv; Oliver St John, *Mr S.-John's speech to the lords in the upper house of parliament January 7. 1640* (1640) sig. A2b.
22 *PP 28*, IV, 37; *PD 10*, 76; Floyd, *God and the king*, 36–7.
23 Floyd, *God and the king*, 29; *CJ* 186, 493; *PP 14* 312, 316.

to make laws' (*dare leges*), with the limited power of a king who derived his authority from the people, and ruled 'by contract' (*ex pacto*). If the king of England conquered another state he could rule it as he pleased. Ireland, argued Sir Francis Bacon, was subject to the laws of England only because King John had chosen to introduce them. In the Parliament of 1621 the same argument was used to show that James I could govern Virginia as he chose, since he ruled it by right of conquest.[24]

Thinkers who claimed that the king of England was bound by contract to rule within the law were obliged to deny that he ruled by right of conquest. So they had to adopt one of two positions. Either they could argue that there had been no conquest, or they could admit that there had been a conquest but deny that it had conferred power upon William. Thus, Richard Hooker affirmed that the Conqueror had come to the crown by lawful succession, and was consequently bound to abide by the laws of the realm. William tried, indeed, to exempt himself from the laws by claiming to rule as a conqueror, but Hooker left the reader in little doubt that this claim was unwarranted. Similarly, Robert Mason argued that William had at first asserted a legitimate title to the throne. It was only later 'that the title of conquest – to introduce that absolute power of a conqueror – was claimed'. In England, Mason believed, 'the extent and limits of the king's power . . . depend on human will and on the ancient agreement or contract between the kings and the kingdom'. These words were a direct quotation from the Jesuit Suarez.[25]

John Pym took the second line – admitting that there had been a conquest, but denying that it had given the Conqueror his authority. Though William 'conquered the kingdom', said Pym, 'he conquered not the law'. The clergyman Maynwaring had used the biblical text 'Render to Caesar the things that are Caesar's' to show that subjects have an obligation to pay taxes. Pym disagreed with this interpretation of Christ's words, arguing that He was dealing only with the case of the ancient Jews, who had been conquered by the Romans. Since the English were not a conquered nation, Christ's command did not apply to them: the Jews 'were at that time a conquered province, governed by such laws as the conqueror put upon them; wherein their case is different from us'. In Pym's opinion, William obtained the crown by consent, not conquest. His victory 'gave him first hope, but the assurance and possession of the crown he obtained by composition, in which he bound himself to observe . . . the . . . ancient laws and liberties of the kingdom, which afterwards he likewise confirmed by oath at his coronation'.[26]

24 That conquest gives absolute power is stated in Sir Edward Coke, *The reports*, ed. G. Wilson (1776) 7, f. 17b; Sir John Davies, *Le primer report des cases & matters en ley* (Dublin 1615) f. 30b; Hooker, *Laws of ecclesiastical polity*, VIII, ii, 11; *PP 28*, III, 528–9 (Mason); *ST*, II, 592 (Bacon); *CD 21*, III, 82, IV, 256. On Davies, see Hans S. Pawlisch, *Sir John Davies and the conquest of Ireland: a study in legal imperialism* (Cambridge 1985).
25 Hooker, *Laws of ecclesiastical polity*, VIII, vi, 1; *PP 28*, III, 528–9: 'Amplitudo et restrictio potestatis regum . . . pendet ex arbitrio hominis et ex antiqua conventione vel pacto inter reges et regnum': Suarez, *De legibus ac Deo legislatore*, v, xvii, 3 (with minor variations).
26 *PP 28*, II, 106; John Rushworth, *Historical collections*, 7 vols (1659–1701) I, 596.

As we have seen, most absolutists placed little weight upon the Norman Conquest.[27] The same goes for many common lawyers. Sir Edward Coke, for example, claimed that England had been conquered by the Normans (and others), but drew few political conclusions from this fact. Coke did indeed believe that the conquerors had at first been absolute sovereigns, empowered to alter the English law, though they chose not to do so.[28] But he held that in the course of time absolute rule became subject to *customary* limitations. So it simply did not matter that there was once a conquest. Conquest, however, *did* matter to anyone who believed that limitations on royal authority arose when a sovereign people transferred its powers to a single man. If there was a conquest, then there was no transference of power and, in consequence, no limitations. So Hooker and Pym denied that William ruled by right of conquest, and concluded that the power of his descendants was limited by the law of the land. Working within the same framework of ideas a number of Civil lawyers reached the opposite conclusion by turning the argument on its head. William, they said, had ruled as an absolute conqueror. So the Stuarts were likewise absolute monarchs. They also claimed that the Conqueror had made radical changes in the English laws – cocking a snook at Coke and his cronies.

The Civil lawyer Calybute Downing argued that there were three ways by which kings came to power – succession, election and conquest. Kings by succession, he stated, 'have as much power as their ancestors'. To assess the extent of a king's powers, then, it was necessary to trace back his ancestry until we came to a ruler who reached the throne either by election or by conquest. Downing took a contractual view of election. The power of kings who ruled 'onely by election', he asserted, 'is restrained and curbed with cautionary conditions, and stands limited by them'. The king of England, however, ruled by conquest, not mere election. Charles I, asserted Downing, possessed power 'by lineall succession from an absolute Conqueror'. In words that echoed Hooker, he affirmed that kings who rule 'by the right of conquest, may have as much power as they will take; they make their owne Charters'.[29]

27 Cf. above, Chapter 1, p. 54.
28 Coke, *Reports*, 2, preface, p. x; 8, preface, p. iv. A different interpretation is put forward in Pocock, *The ancient constitution and the feudal law* (Cambridge 1957; reissued, with retrospect, 1987), especially 31, 36, 52, 53. At p. 53, Pocock argues that people were 'tirelessly and monotonously insistent that the establishment of the Normans in England did not constitute a conquest' since to 'admit a conquest was to admit an indelible stain of sovereignty upon the English constitution'. These claims are open to the objections that many people – including Coke – thought that the Normans had conquered England, but did not draw the conclusion that the constitution was indelibly stained with sovereignty. Relevant discussions include Johann P. Sommerville, 'History and theory: the Norman Conquest in early Stuart political thought', *Political Studies* 34 (1986) 249–61; Glenn Burgess, *The politics of the ancient constitution: an introduction to English political thought, 1603–1642* (1992) esp. 82–6; and Johann P. Sommerville, 'The ancient constitution reassessed: the common law, the court and the languages of politics in early modern England', in R. Malcolm Smuts, ed., *The Stuart Court and Europe: essays in politics and political culture* (Cambridge 1996) 39–64, esp. 52–3.
29 Calybute Downing, *A discourse of the state ecclesiasticall*, 2nd edn (Oxford 1634) 50–1. A different interpretation of Downing is in Glenn Burgess, *Absolute monarchy and the Stuart constitution* (New Haven 1996) 112–13. A response to Burgess is in Johann P. Sommerville, 'English and European political ideas in the early seventeenth century: revisionism and the case of absolutism', *Journal of British Studies* 35 (1996) 168–94, at 183–4 n. 49.

Another Civil lawyer, Sir John Hayward, stated that after the Norman Conquest 'Saint Edwards lawes were abrogated, and not onlie new lawes, but newe language brought into use'. Hayward regarded William's claim that he had acted on a grant from Edward the Confessor as a mere pretence 'which had neither probabilitie nor force', and asserted that he had obtained the crown 'by dinte of sworde'. It was from the Conquest that Hayward derived the powers of the current king, James I.[30]

John Cowell – again, a Civil lawyer – believed that William had altered the English laws as he pleased, retaining some but adding to them 'of the Norman laws, such as he thought good'. The resulting amalgam, he maintained, had survived largely unchanged into the seventeenth century. Cowell thought it plausible that subsidies – taxes voted to the king by Parliament – were not free gifts but grants owed to the king 'in recompence or consideration, that whereas the Prince of his absolute power, might make lawes of himself, he doth of favour admit the consent of his subjects therein'. William Fulbecke – yet another Civil lawyer (and also a common lawyer) – took a similar line on taxation, claiming that since 'the universal conquest of William, who first commanded and imposed tribute upon this land (for conquerors may command)', subsidies had been paid 'as a remembrance of a conquest'.[31]

Conquest, these Civil lawyers said, had made William absolute. Others denied the Conquest and subjected the crown to contractual limitations. The nature of the constitution in England and other unconquered countries depended upon the original and later agreements between the king and the people. Any such agreement was possible and binding, provided that it did not infringe God's natural or positive laws. An agreement to commit adultery, for example, would bind no one, since adultery was against the law of God. An agreement imposing drastic restrictions upon the power of the ruler, however, would be perfectly valid, since God's law was silent on the form that government should take. But what about a contract which imposed no limitations whatever upon the king? At first glance, it would seem that such a contract too would have been viewed as binding – though regrettable from the people's point of view. But a good many thinkers argued that an agreement giving the king absolute power would be invalid. Their basic claim was that the law of nature itself gave certain duties to rulers and certain rights to subjects. No contract could erase these rights and duties. All those who argued in this way appealed to one central concept: the public good, or *salus populi*.

THE PUBLIC GOOD AND RESISTANCE

Natural law theorists were agreed that the purpose of the commonwealth was to promote the public welfare and not the interests of private groups or

---

30 Sir John Hayward, *An answer to the first part of a certaine conference* (1603), sig. R2a–b, pp. 33–4; cf. Hayward, *The lives of the III. Normans kings of England* (1613) esp. 44, 90–1. Hayward is discussed in D.R. Woolf, *The idea of history in early Stuart England* (Toronto 1990) 106–15.
31 John Cowell, *The interpreter: or book containing the signification of words* (Cambridge 1607) sig. 2R2b, 3R1a; William Fulbecke, *The pandectes of the law of nations* (1602) f. 69b.

individuals. Proponents of Divine Right kingship, and advocates of original popular sovereignty both believed that the object of government was the common weal. According to absolutists, the king had a duty to rule in the common interest, but no one could compel him to do so. The reason for this was simple. The common interest itself required that the king possess absolute power, for if he possessed anything less the state would collapse in anarchy – and anarchy was clearly not in the public interest. By contrast, those who founded royal authority upon a grant from the people rejected the absolutist argument, and drew on the concept of the public good to show that the power of all kings was limited, and that they could in certain circumstances be resisted.

The author of an anonymous *Discourse concerning the prerogative of the crown* admitted that it was logically possible for a commonwealth to transfer all its power to a king unconditionally. 'But that the grant of a commonwealth should be so general', he wrote, 'I think it was never seen.' Moreover, he added, even kings who possess absolute power 'cannot force their subjects by unjust laws, nay not by burdensome laws'. In his view, not only unjust laws – that is to say, those which contravened God's will – but also laws which the people found 'grievous' were *ipso facto* invalid. As John Hoskins put it in the Parliament of 1610, 'the king cannot doe any thinge against the common peace or common proffit'.[32]

No contract could diminish the king's duty to rule in the public interest or the people's right to be ruled in this way. For this reason, some authors held that the original agreement between king and people necessarily included the provision that royal power be exercised for the common good. A Catholic work of 1616, for example, argued that this provision was 'necessarily, I say, implied', since 'it were a Barbarous conceipt to thinke that it were in' the Prince's 'lawful power, to Tyrannize over' his subjects 'at his pleasure, without respect either to their defence in time of warre, or to the administration of Justice in time of peace'. Similarly, the puritan William Ames thought that it was 'against all naturall inclination' for a people to enslave itself to a king. Such a society would not 'constitute a City or Body Politick, but rather a Lordly Domineering, and a monstrous slavery'. Moreover, the Prince would still retain the 'duty chiefely to have an eye upon the common advantage of his subjects'.[33] According to this line of approach, the commonwealth possessed an inalienable right to be ruled in its own interest. This did *not* mean that individuals possessed an analogous right, and most natural law theorists were perfectly willing to allow that private persons could sell or give themselves into slavery. Natural law permitted the enslavement of an individual, but not of a whole commonwealth.

Two alternative views on this question were expressed in the early seventeenth century – one radical, the other conservative. The radical view, voiced

32 Fussner, 'William Camden's "Discourse concerning the prerogative of the crown"', 210; *PD* 10, 77.
33 Du Perron, *An oration made on the part of the lordes spirituall*, anonymous English preface, sig. 3*2a–b; William Ames, *Conscience with the power and cases thereof* (1639) 164.

by John Floyd in 1620, was that even individuals, and not just communities, had certain inalienable rights. 'Slaves', he wrote, 'have some rightes and liberties by the law of nature inviolable, which (if they be able) they may defend by force against even their owne Maisters.' The second and conservative view was put forward by Sir John Hayward, who argued that not only individuals but also whole commonwealths could enslave themselves: 'as a private man may altogether abandon his free estate, and subject himselfe to servile condition, so may a multitude passe awaye both their authoritie and their libertie by publicke consent'.[34]

Hayward's argument – which fitted in very well with his general absolutist position – was intended to rebut the suggestion that all kings were subject to at least some limitations, and that all peoples had some rights against their king. Most of the theorists who grounded royal power in a grant from the people were willing to accept both of these suggestions. The notion that the king had a contractual obligation to rule in the public interest was used to show that every commonwealth had the right to resist its king in certain circumstances. The Jesuit Thomas Stephenson spelled out this conclusion in a manuscript book written for the Gunpowder Plotter Robert Catesby. A Prince who governed badly, he argued, could be 'deprived of his kingdom by the authority of the assembly of the people', for 'reason ordains that he who has been chosen to maintain the honour and safety of the commonwealth should not have charge over it to its destruction'. It was in accordance with this principle, Stephenson believed, that Richard II had been deposed by Parliament.[35]

The original contract and later agreements between the king and his subjects might guarantee the people rights of resistance to their ruler, but even if they did not, natural law empowered the people to resist in certain circumstances. The people had an inalienable right to be ruled in the public interest. They also had an inalienable right of self-defence. The precept that unjust force could justly be met by force – *vim vi repellere licet* – was accepted by all as a prime law of nature. Absolutists, however, held that this principle did not apply against the king. In other words, a private individual could use force against the onslaught of another private individual, but could never use force against the king. For if individuals could resist the king whenever they believed that he was unjustly attacking them, anarchy would result. In fact, the notion that force could never be employed against the *person* of the king circulated widely in England, even among those who wished to limit his power most stringently. The English way was to neuter the king's authority while leaving his person inviolate. Yet even English writers occasionally expressed the view that kings themselves might be resisted in defence of the realm.

---

34 John Floyd, *God and the king* (St Omer 1620), 19; Hayward, *Answer*, 22.
35 Thomas Stephenson, *Cyclopaedia aut compendium omnium scientiarum*, BL Mss Royal 12.E.X., f. 170a: 'Si male gubernat . . . privari a regno est authoritate comitatis, a qua delectus est. nam ratio iubet ut is, qui delectus est ad reipublicae procurandam dignitatem et salutem, non praesit ad reipublicae perniciem. Quo more Richardus 2dus privatus factus est, et Henricus 4us rex appellatus in regni Comitiis parliamentaribus, anno 1400.'

Kellison, for example, argued that God and nature gave societies 'power to rule, conserve, and defend themselves'. He cited the maxim *vim vi repellere licet* to confirm his thesis that all peoples possessed the power to resist their rulers in certain circumstances.[36] Of course, Kellison was a Catholic. In the writings of non-Catholics ideas of legitimate resistance were rarer until the outbreak of the Civil War. But they did circulate. This point deserves emphasis, since resistance theories are often regarded as a relatively late development in English political thinking. When circumstances forced civil war upon a reluctant English people in 1642, so the common argument runs, the Parliamentarians were ill-equipped to justify their actions. They resisted first, but only later proclaimed that what they had done was resistance, and that resistance could be legitimate. Though widely accepted, this argument deserves to be examined afresh.

In 1610, when the opinions of the absolutist Civil lawyer John Cowell were under attack in the House of Commons, Cowell's patron Richard Bancroft, Archbishop of Canterbury, counter-attacked by pointing to the greater dangers portended by the circulation of works by such authors as the Scottish resistance theorist George Buchanan. Bancroft, like many absolutist clerics, was quick to detect ideas of resistance in any writing which limited the king's prerogative, especially in ecclesiastical matters. Doubtless he exaggerated the influence of Buchanan and like-minded authors. Yet they plainly exercised some influence. Buchanan's *Rerum Scoticarum Historia*, together with his *De jure regni apud Scotos*, was frequently reprinted on the Continent, and imported into England. In 1622, for example, Thomas Wentworth sent a copy of the book to Lord Clifford, hoping that his lordship would find it 'a meanes to passe over some sad hours with contentment'.[37]

Of course, the mere fact that a book circulated does not show that anyone took notice of the ideas which it contained. The English knew about resistance theories, but did they express such ideas in the years before 1640? The answer is that they did, though infrequently. Dudley Fenner, the Elizabethan puritan, had no hesitation in allowing the deposition of tyrannical rulers, either by inferior magistrates or by a representative assembly. He approvingly cited the biblical example of Athaliah, a queen ousted for tyranny. The case of Athaliah was a great favourite with Continental resistance theorists. In 1594 another Englishman declared that erring Princes could be punished by Parliament. 'There is a High Court of Parliament', he said, 'unto which Princes either can be contented, or be constrained to submit themselves.' Not the Prince, but Parliament – or rather the two Houses of Parliament – was supreme in England. 'If Princes offend', he added, 'they may be chastened according to the nature and quality of their offences; and it cannot justly or

36 Kellison, *Right and iurisdiction*, 43.
37 *PP 10*, ɪ, 29; Bancroft associated Calvinist resistance theories with the seditious practice of English puritans in *Daungerous positions and proceedings* (1593), especially 14–17, 34–41; J.P. Cooper, ed., *Wentworth papers 1597–1628* (1973) 176.

truly be said, that that is against a Law or without Law which is done by an high Court of Parliament.'[38]

In 1622 a young cleric named John Knight delivered a sermon in Oxford, maintaining that tyrannical rulers could be resisted. Shortly afterwards the king commanded Archbishop Abbot to issue a set of directions to preachers, forbidding them 'to declare, limit, or bound out, by way of positive doctrine, in any lecture or sermon the power, prerogative, and jurisdiction, authority, or duty of sovereign princes'. In 1618 Ralph Brownrig, a Fellow of Pembroke College Cambridge, discussed the question of whether kings who broke the fundamental laws might be deposed. Though he debated this delicate subject in the privacy of a college room, he only narrowly escaped punishment for his audacity. Brownrig later mended his ways, was appointed Bishop of Exeter, and in the Civil War became a royalist.[39]

A more consistent advocate of resistance theory was the Civil lawyer Isaac Dorislaus, who lectured on history at Cambridge University in 1627. Commenting – significantly – on Tacitus, Dorislaus used contractual ideas to show that subjects could sometimes resist their sovereigns. Though his arguments were avowedly intended to justify the Dutch revolt against Spain, he gave no reasons for supposing that they would not apply equally to England. In 1627 – the year of the Forced Loan – such views had very crude practical implications, and Dorislaus was promptly silenced by the Vice-Chancellor Matthew Wren. When civil war came, Dorislaus joined the Parliamentarian side. It was he who prepared the charge of treason upon which Charles was tried and executed. Shortly afterwards, Dorislaus was assassinated by royalists at The Hague.[40]

Justifications of resistance became commoner in the years immediately preceding the Civil War, particularly though not exclusively in connection with the activities of the Scottish Covenanters. In 1638 some Scots ministers asserted that 'subjects may defend their Ancient and Christian liberties, covenanted and agreed upon by those Princes to whom they first submitted themselves'. Defence of the laws, they argued, could not be rebellion against the king. The same attitude informed the work of the Englishman – probably Henry Burton – who published a book entitled *Lord bishops, none of the Lords bishops* in November 1640. Subjects, the author argued, were bound to obey their rulers only 'according to Gods law, and the laws of the land'. Obedience

---

38 Dudley Fenner, *Sacra theologia* (1585) 186. Absolutists claimed that Athaliah was not a legitimate queen but a usurper who was removed on the authority of the true ruler: John Buckeridge, *De potestate papae in rebus temporalibus* (1614), 233, 918–23; Thomas Hobbes, *Leviathan*, ed. C.B. Macpherson (Harmondsworth 1968) 639. Sir Henry Wotton, *The state of Christendom* (1657) 205, 207; the attribution to Wotton is doubtful.

39 J.B. Mullinger, *The university of Cambridge from the royal injunctions of 1535 to the accession of Charles the First* (Cambridge 1884) 564–6; J.P. Kenyon, *The Stuart constitution* (Cambridge 1966) 146. It was David Owen who informed on Brownrig.

40 B.P. Levack, *The civil lawyers in England 1603–1641* (Oxford 1973) 91–5, 224; cf. Kevin Sharpe, 'The foundation of the Chairs of History at Oxford and Cambridge: an episode in Jacobean politics', *History of Universities* 2 (1982) 127–52, especially 139–40; Woolf, *The idea of history* 174, 198.

to the laws could not be rebellion against the king, so the English should think twice before condemning the actions of the Scots as treasonable. He appealed to Parliament to decide whether the Scots had rebelled or had merely stood 'to defend their ancient Rights and liberties'.[41]

In fact, a number of Charles's more vocal opponents in England had established political contacts with the Scots well before the summoning of the Long Parliament. How large a number remains unclear, but it almost certainly included Lord Saye and Sele and Lord Brooke. When, in the spring of 1639, Charles required his nobles to take an oath promising that they would have no dealings with the Scots, Saye and Brooke refused.[42] In the Short Parliament of 1640, the House of Commons displayed few signs of haste either to condemn the Scots as rebels – which is how Charles regarded them – or to supply the king with money to fight them. The arguments which had been used to legitimate Scottish resistance to the king were soon employed to show that the English, too, could forcibly defend their liberties against royal aggression.

A Scottish work, written for English consumption in 1640, and entitled *The intentions of the army of the kingdome of Scotland, declared to their brethren of England*, made no bones about the justifiability of resistance in extreme circumstances. The Scots, it argued, had been pushed to the limits of human endurance by the recent oppressions. In such a case it would be quite wrong to 'sit still in senselessnesse and stupiditie', for nature itself commanded 'us to study our own preservation'. Necessity, which 'is said to have no Law', permitted resistance, for 'where Necessity commandeth, the Lawes of Nature and Nations give their consent, and all positive Lawes are silent and give place'.[43]

The same argument was applied to English affairs by Calybute Downing, who by 1640 had abandoned his earlier absolutism – though his ideas remained within the contractualist tradition. Preaching on 1 September 1640, Downing affirmed that all peoples possessed a right to resist their rulers in extreme circumstances, arguing that '*salus populi* should be *sola, & suprema lex*', and citing 'Rationall Grotius' to confirm his views. Henry Parker maintained the same position at about the same time, proclaiming that 'rather than a Nation shall perish, any thing shall be held necessary, and legal by necessity'. He too declared that 'the supreme of all humane lawes is *salus populi*'. In 1641 Pym similarly spoke of 'that universall, that supreme law, *Salus Populi*'. This idea was not new. As early as 1621 Sir Robert Phelips affirmed that 'an act of Parliament or a Charter no longer bindes a state than the reason of State that grounded it'. Reason of state could be employed against as well as for the

---

41 'The answers of some brethren of the ministrie', sig. C4a, in *Generall demands concerning the late covenant* (Edinburgh 1638); Burton, *Lord bishops*, sig. B4b, K4a.
42 Edward Hyde, Earl of Clarendon, *The history of the rebellion and Civil Wars in England*, ed. W.D. Macray, 6 vols (Oxford 1888) I, 99, 154–5. Later contacts are discussed in David Stevenson, *The Scottish revolution 1637–1644: the triumph of the Covenanters* (Newton Abbot 1973) 205.
43 *The intentions of the army of the kingdome of Scotland, declared to their brethren of England* (Edinburgh 1640) 11, 14–15.

king. The claim that necessity or the public weal might justify the breach of literally any human laws obviously had very radical implications, though few of these were explored in detail before the outbreak of the Civil War. At the beginning of 1641 Oliver St John did indeed claim that 'for the common good' Parliament might enact laws which were 'derogatory to the Crowne' and which contradicted the common laws.[44] Many country gentlemen were soon to find, to their cost, that Parliament was quite as capable as the king of contravening traditional liberties in the name of necessity.

The principle of the supremacy of the public good could be used to justify not only resistance but also the deposition and even execution of the king. In a work published in 1621, and written before 1617, the Cambridge clergyman Paul Baynes remarked that in the case of kings who were 'not absolute Monarchs, it was never esteemed as absurd, to say that their people had power in some cases to depose them'. In 1642 the lawyer Peter Bland posed a rhetorical question: 'hath no man heard of a king deposed by a Parliament?' 'Surely yes', was his answer, and he declared that 'convenience and the common good' legitimated deposition. Bland staunchly denied that he wanted Charles to be deposed, and it is plain that in 1642 few believed that such a drastic step was either necessary or politic. But it would be naïve to suppose that people who justified resistance in the early days of the Civil War were ignorant of the fact that their arguments could be employed to advance far more radical remedies: deposition and regicide.[45]

A glance at the political literature of the early seventeenth century reveals a wealth of arguments in favour of limited monarchy on the one hand, and, on the other, in favour of the thesis that in the final analysis the king's powers were not limited by any human law. Yet apologies for active resistance were rare, at least until 1640. The logic of anti-absolutist natural law ideas did, indeed, point in the direction of resistance theories. Why, then, were detailed expositions of such theories so uncommon? There are three simple answers to this question. Firstly, freedom of expression – especially on sensitive political issues – was discouraged. Anyone who wrote or spoke in favour of active resistance to kings ran the risk of condign punishment for sedition or treason. When John Knight preached in justification of resistance, he studiously refrained from applying his ideas to contemporary England. Yet he was imprisoned for two years in the Gatehouse, and died within months of his release. In 1615 the Catholic John Owen was convicted of treason for affirming that excommunicated Princes could be killed by their subjects, though he denied

---

44 Downing, *A sermon preached to the renowned company of the artillery, 1 September 1640* (1641) 37; Henry Parker, *The case of shipmony briefly discoursed* (1640) 7; John Pym, *The speech or declaration of John Pym esquire: after the recapitulation or summing up of the charge of high-treason, against Thomas, Earle of Strafford* (1641) 3; *CD 21*, III, 106, cf. V, 110; St John, *Mr S.-Johns speech to the lords in the upper house of parliament Ianuary 7. 1640*, sig. F2b.
45 Paul Baynes, *The diocesans tryall* (Amsterdam 1621) 88; Peter Bland, *Resolved upon the question* (1642) 16. In another work of 1642 Bland argued that deposition was against the common law, but that Parliament might temporarily abrogate any royal right in a case of necessity: *A royall position* (1642) 8–9.

that his words had referred to the king of England.[46] In an age when men lost their ears for less, it took uncommon bravery – or idiocy – to assert that subjects could lay violent hands upon the Lord's anointed.

Secondly, there was little point in advocating resistance to the king unless it had some chance of success. Those who did admit the legitimacy of resistance were unanimous in declaring that it had to take place on *public*, not private authority. That is to say, the king had to be resisted by the whole common-wealth or its representative institutions, or, according to the Catholic point of view, by the church acting through the pope. No private individual, it was agreed by all, could actively resist his ruler. Applied to English circumstances, this meant that only Parliament could possibly have the authority to resist the first two Stuarts. As long as the king retained the power to dissolve Parlia-ment whenever he pleased, resistance was obviously impossible. Yet until 1640 – when the presence of a victorious Scottish army in the field decisively broke the mould of English politics – Parliament lacked the means effectively to challenge the dissolving power. Talk of resistance became more common after 1640 not because of the sudden discovery of resistance theory, but be-cause resistance had become a practical possibility.

Thirdly, there was little to be gained by advocating ideas of resistance – which Protestant propaganda had long condemned as popish – when the same effects could be obtained by other and apparently milder means. The king's power could be limited while his person was left untouched. The essence of this approach was to declare that illegal royal commands were invalid and that those who obeyed them would be punishable. The king himself was absolved of responsibility for such commands, but his counsellors or anyone else who enforced his will would suffer for breaking the law. As Speaker Glanville put it in the Short Parliament, a royal command

> contrary to Lawe . . . will bee void and the king innocent even in his very person defended by his prerogative. Nevertheless the . . . actors in these abuses will stand liable and exposed to strict examination and just censures as having nothing to defend themselves but the colour of a void command made void by just prerogative according to fundamentall and true reason of State and Monarchy.[47]

In other words, the law and not the king ruled in England. 'I was only obey-ing orders' was no defence if the orders were illegal. Since the king himself was immune from punishment, the buck stopped with his servants.

There was nothing new about this idea in 1640. Glanville himself had said much the same thing in 1628: 'Our law says that the King's command con-trary to law is void, and the actor stands single.' Others agreed with him.

46 Mullinger, *The university of Cambridge*, 566; A.J. Loomie, ed., *Spain and the Jacobean Catholics*, 2 vols (1973–78) ii, 47–8; John Godbolt, *Reports of certain cases, arising in the severall courts of record at Westminster* (1652) 263–4.
47 *PSP 40*, 127.

Fuller, speaking in the Parliament of 1610, went still further, claiming not only that people who obeyed illegal royal commands were punishable but also that in at least some cases the king could not pardon them. For example, someone who killed on the king's orders could be executed despite a royal pardon: 'The King commandeth I.S. to kill A.B. being not condemned, which I.S. performeth according to the King's commandment. This is felony in I.S. for which by the laws of England I.S. shall be hanged notwithstanding the King's pardon if an appeal be sued upon the death of A.B.'[48]

Richard Hooker claimed that 'though no manner person or cause be unsubject to the king's power, yet so is the power of the king over all and in all limited, that unto all his proceedings the law itself is a rule'. An illegal royal grant, he held, was void. The king could not validly do anything contrary to the law: '*Rex nihil potest nisi quod jure potest.*' Hooker may have thought that kings could be resisted by their subjects. He said that the commonwealth was superior to its ruler. He spoke of 'the king's dependency in power upon the body' of the commonwealth. These passages are difficult to explain if he believed in strict non-resistance. But the important point is that in Hooker's theory resistance was unimportant. As long as the king's commands were obeyed only inasmuch as they accorded with law, he could not act as a tyrant. Hooker's message was that the English constitution – 'the foundations of this commonwealth' – prevented tyranny by setting the laws above the king. Unfortunately, to make this workable it was necessary that the judges act independently of royal control, and that in making their decisions they eschew the doctrine of royal absolutism. Under Charles I, the judges failed conspicuously on both counts. This was another reason for the shift towards resistance theory in 1640. Yet the concept of a limited but irresistible monarch remained strong, particularly in the thought of common lawyers.[49]

Natural law ideas of the public good could easily be exploited to justify resistance to kings. They could also be used to eradicate individual liberties. Since the public good was the supreme law, individual rights gave way before it. Ordinarily, indeed, no individuals could be deprived of their property without their consent, but this rule did not hold in a case of public necessity. In England, the king justified his unorthodox levies – for example the Forced Loan of 1627 – precisely on the grounds that they were for the public good. Defending the Loan, Roger Maynwaring was able to show that such anti-absolutists as David Paraeus and Francisco Suarez had admitted that taxation did not always require the consent of the taxed. When Robert Mason and John Pym attacked Maynwaring's ideas in the Parliament of 1628, they did not challenge this contention. Instead, they denied that his reasoning applied to England. They placed particular emphasis upon the contractual ideas of Suarez, claiming that Maynwaring had distorted the Spaniard's theory. In

---

48 *PP 28*, IV, 393; *PP 10*, II, 154.
49 Hooker, *Laws of ecclesiastical polity*, VIII, ii, 13. The role of the judges is discussed in W.J. Jones, *Politics and the bench: the judges and the origins of the English Civil War* (1971).

their view, Suarez did indeed allow that taxes could sometimes be levied without the people's consent. But he believed that in Spain popular consent was essential, for, said Pym, he 'declares that, about 200 years past, Alfonso, by special pact, brought in the consent of the people there, before which time it was not requisite by the law there'. 'Suarez's opinion', asserted Mason, 'is that by that agreement the kings of Spain are bound and can impose no tribute without such consent.' 'If the law so brought into Spain by special pact of Alfonso ought to bind', remarked Pym, '*a fortiori*, the law of England, which is original and fundamental, ought to be observed.'[50]

Both Mason and Pym quoted Suarez's work at length and in Latin. Both approved of his ideas, despite the fact that he was a Spaniard and a Jesuit. In the Parliament of 1628 even the Duke of Buckingham found it convenient to pay lip-service to the authority of Suarez.[51] This may come as something of a surprise to those who believe that the keynote of English political thinking in the early modern era was insularity. In fact, with the partial – and only partial – exception of common law thought, there was nothing in the least insular about English political ideas.

THE INFLUENCE AND SIGNIFICANCE OF THE THEORY

English thought, it is often said, was parochial. In religious matters, the English were narrow-mindedly Scripturalist; on secular questions they were equally hidebound, but looked for guidance to the common law rather than the Bible. This view has little to recommend it. Perhaps the most frequently cited sources in the whole of early-seventeenth-century English literature were Calvin, Beza, Aquinas and Bellarmine – none of whom was English. Books written in Latin, the international language of learning, circulated widely. Gentlemen visited the Continent in increasing numbers. The poet John Donne not only travelled abroad, but in his prose works displayed a vast knowledge of Continental literature – as did Robert Burton, Sir Thomas Browne, Milton, and a great many others. J.H.M. Salmon has drawn attention to the large number of French political works which were translated into English during the later sixteenth century. The same trend continued throughout the early seventeenth century – and France was not the only area of Europe to attract interest. Political tracts relating to such events as the papal Interdict of Venice in 1606 and the Thirty Years War found a ready market in England. A high proportion of books printed in English were translations either from Latin or from Continental vernaculars.

Internationalism, not nationalism, was the keynote of Protestant ecclesiastical thought. John Foxe saw history as a struggle of the elect everywhere – and not just in England – against the popish Antichrist. James I's ambitions to

---

50 *PP 28*, IV, 108, III, 528.
51 *PP 28*, V, 649. It is possible that this part of the speech is not by Buckingham: ibid., 648, n. 13.

restore the unity of Protestantism, indeed of Christendom, are well known. The correspondents of George Abbot, Archbishop of Canterbury, included Cyril, Patriarch of Alexandria.[52] The learning purveyed by the universities – the seminaries of the English clergy – was cosmopolitan. Topics such as English history, literature and law were conspicuous by their absence. A number of foreigners found a welcome in the English church – the most famous being Isaac Casaubon and Marc'Antonio De Dominis. Casaubon, perhaps the greatest contemporary classical scholar, left a correspondence which provides first-rate evidence on the world of learning in England and Europe. The main lesson which it teaches is that these two worlds were one. William Laud and Richard Montagu, it is true, did place the parochial interests of their national church before those of international Protestantism. But their learning was not insular, though it served insular ends. Moreover, their lack of fervour for the cause of Continental Protestantism was a major cause of their unpopularity.

The classic example of an insular Englishman is Sir Edward Coke – as Professor Pocock argued over forty years ago. Yet Coke was not representative even of common lawyers, far less of all English people. A glance at the works of John Selden underlines the extent to which cosmopolitan learning was attainable even by a common lawyer, and the extent to which such learning could transcend confessional barriers. Selden drew on a staggering range of Continental authors, and expressed his views on these sources in conversation: 'The Jesuits and the lawyers of France and the Low Country men have engrossed all learning', he said, while 'the rest of the world make nothing but homilies'. Far from being a narrow-minded Protestant, Selden affirmed that 'Popish books teach and inform what we know', and asked rhetorically 'if you take away them, what learning will you leave?' These views do little to confirm the conventional opinion that English attitudes were insular.[53]

Contractual ideas are commonly associated with the works of Continental or Scottish, but not English theorists. It has been suggested – on the basis of the abortive canons drawn up by Archbishop Bancroft and accepted by Convocation in 1606 – that contractualist ideas were 'sturdily rejected' in England. Certainly, Bancroft and like-minded clerics did reject such theories. But the canons were not representative of English thinking as a whole. James I suppressed them for reasons which are obscure, though he was doubtless aware that the clergy's absolutist ideas would meet with hostility in the House of Commons. Speaking in the Commons a few days after Bancroft's death, Richard Martin referred to 'a book lately offered to the convocation House'. This book, which would have confirmed absolutism, was probably

---

52 J.H.M. Salmon, *The French religious wars in English political thought* (Oxford 1959) *passim*. Ephraim Pagitt, *Christianographie, or the description of the multitude and sundry sorts of Christians in the world*, 2nd edn (1636) 74–80, prints a letter from Cyril to Abbot.
53 Selden, *Table talk*, 71, 23. The thesis that English (legal) scholarship was insular is well stated in Pocock, *The ancient constitution and the feudal law*, especially 30–69, and in D.R. Kelley, 'History, English law and the Renaissance', *Past and Present* 65 (1974) 24–51.

the abortive canons. 'Let that book die', he said, 'with all ill memory of the book and of him that was the author of it.'[54]

Martin did not spell out his own political theory, though he certainly believed that the king's powers were limited by the law of the land. Anti-absolutists grounded their views either on a contractual theory – the notions that the king derived his power from the commonwealth, not immediately from God, and that the king and people were bound by reciprocal conditions – or on Coke's theory of an immemorial common law which had been created by neither king nor people and stood above both. The third, and most frequently exercised, option was simply to state that royal power was limited without bothering to defend the proposition. It is sometimes supposed that anyone who regarded the king's power as limited subscribed to Coke's theory of the ancient constitution. This is mistaken. The vocabulary of contract was almost as common as that of immemorial law.

In the Parliament of 1614 Sir Edwin Sandys declared that there were 'reciprocal conditions between King and People'. These conditions, he held, prohibited the king from taking the property of his subjects without their consent. Sandys claimed that not only the person, but also the power of the king had at first been introduced by popular consent. The authority of the current king was therefore subject to the limitations which had been imposed upon his ancestors. The influential puritan William Ames similarly derived royal power from a grant by the commonwealth, and not from God alone, while his friend Paul Baynes maintained much the same thing: 'True it is', he wrote, 'all civil power is in the body politicke', and only derivatively in the king. Puritans in New England voiced similar ideas. According to John Cotton, the magistrate's authority was derived from 'the People, in whom fundamentally all power lyes'. In a sermon of 1638 Thomas Hooker likewise claimed that 'the foundation of authority is laid firstly in the free consent of the people'.[55]

William Ames was a professor at the Dutch university of Franeker, and his writings – most of which were in Latin – drew on Continental as much as English sources and ideas. John Knight was quite candid in admitting a foreign source for his views on legitimate resistance – the German theologian David Paraeus. His admission so impressed the ecclesiastical authorities that they ordered Paraeus' book to be burned in Oxford, Cambridge and London.[56] Ideas of contractual monarchy and legitimate resistance circulated in England

---

54 Kenyon, *The Stuart constitution*, 7; *PP 10*, ΙΙ, 328. It is sometimes assumed that James withheld his assent to the canons because they included a clause prescribing obedience to usurping governments which were 'thoroughly settled': cf. the King's letter to Abbot printed in *The convocation book of MDCVI*, preface, 7–8. But James could have excised the clause. So it is doubtful that its inclusion was the only reason for his decision to suppress the canons.

55 *CJ* 493; cf. ibid., 186 and *PP 14* 312, 316; Ames, *Conscience*, 164; Baynes, *Diocesans Tryall*, 83; John Cotton quoted in P.G.E. Miller and T.H. Johnson, eds, *The puritans* (New York 1938) 213; Thomas Hooker, 'Letters and abstracts', *Collections of the Connecticut Historical Society* 1 (1860) 1–21, at 20.

56 *Decretum universitatis Oxoniensis damnans propositiones neotericorum infrascriptas* (Oxford 1622) sig. B2a; Mullinger, *The university of Cambridge*, 567; *CSPD, 1619–23*, 400.

because Continental books circulated. There were, indeed, English writings of the sixteenth century in the same tradition, but they exercised relatively little influence. The final three books of Richard Hooker's *Laws* remained in manuscript until after the Civil War. The first book did indeed contain some passages which were incompatible with the Divine Right of Kings. In James I's reign the Jesuit John Floyd made use of this in his attack on English absolutism, and in 1640 Calybute Downing drew on the book to support his arguments in favour of resistance. The ideas of two Marian exiles and resistance theorists, Christopher Goodman and John Ponet, were frequently criticised by absolutists, but attracted few supporters – though Ponet's treatise was secretly republished at the time of the Scottish troubles in 1639.[57]

The general structure of contractual theory was the same in England as on the Continent, but the liberties which the English defended were peculiarly their own. In the years before 1640, the main goal of anti-absolutists was to secure these liberties against royal aggression. The differences between those who used arguments derived from natural law to this end and those who, like Coke, appealed to an immemorial constitution were of minor practical signi-ficance until the outbreak of the Civil War. They soon acquired importance thereafter. Coke's ideas were essentially static, dealing with how the constitu-tion should function, but saying little about what could be done if it failed to do so. Constitutional innovation, popular resistance and the deposition of the king were all quite alien to Coke's way of thinking, but fully compatible with contractual ideas of government and with the natural law theory of the public good. In 1628 John Selden told the House of Commons that 'an act of Parlia-ment may alter any part of Magna Carta'. Many learned by bitter experience in the 1640s that Parliament, claiming to represent the people and to act in the public interest, could be as dangerous an enemy to the subject's liberty as ever the king had been. *Salus populi* was invoked against Parliament itself – a development which to some seemed anarchic, but came as no great surprise to absolutists, who had long insisted that the only alternative to royal sover-eignty was anarchy.[58]

---

57 Floyd, *God and the king*, 32; Downing, *A sermon preached to the renowned company of the artillery*, '28' = 34. References to the unpublished eighth book of Hooker's *Laws* occur in Sir Robert Filmer, *Patriarcha and other writings*, ed. Johann P. Sommerville (Cambridge 1991) 22, and in Parker, *The true grounds of ecclesiasticall regiment* (1641) 42. Ponet and/or Goodman are attacked by e.g. Bancroft, *Daungerous positions*, 34–41; David Owen, *Herod and Pilate reconciled* (Cambridge 1610) epistle dedicatory; Henry Howard, Earl of Northampton in *A true and perfect relation of the whole proceedings against the late most barbarous traitors, Garnet a Iesuite, and his confederats* (1606) sig. 2E4b; Donne, *Ignatius his conclave*, ed. T.S. Healy (Oxford 1969) 77.
58 *PP 28*, III, 439 (Selden). An excellent discussion of Magna Carta and *salus populi* in the 1640s is Robert Ashton, 'From cavalier to roundhead tyranny', in J.S. Morrill, ed., *Reactions to the English Civil War, 1642–1649* (1982) 185–207.

CHAPTER 3

The Ancient Constitution

Common lawyers exercised a far greater influence upon English political life than any other professional group of laymen. Their importance was threefold. Firstly, a legal career was one of the major routes to high office in the service of the king. In Parliament, too, lawyers were unusually well represented, and their influence was out of all proportion to their numbers. Parliament was still widely regarded as a High Court. Moreover, statutes needed to be properly drafted if they were to hold water in lower courts, and this was a job for lawyers. Secondly, the law provided the sole effective barrier against absolutism available within the established constitution. No one could prevent the king from spouting absolutist rhetoric, but this did not matter greatly as long as the subject retained legal remedies against the practice of absolutism. The eventual failure of the law to uphold the subject's liberties was a major reason for the dissolution of the old constitution.

Thirdly, the common law had an immense cultural and intellectual influence. In an age when almost every gentleman could expect to be involved in one or more often protracted legal cases, familiarity with the fundamentals of the law was inevitable among England's ruling classes. Of course, familiarity could breed contempt, and satire on the pedantry and greed of lawyers was a stock literary theme, well exemplified in Ruggle's play *Ignoramus* – a great favourite with James I. Yet it was from the lower ranks of society that lawyers received the harshest criticism: 'The first thing we do, let's kill all the lawyers', says Dick the butcher in Shakespeare's *Henry VI*. Among the gentry at least, resentment of high legal fees often gave way to admiration for the laws. Law-books, though lagging behind religious works in popularity, sold well to the reading public. Many of the sons of the gentry attended the Inns of Court – England's third university, and socially more prestigious than either Oxford or Cambridge. There they acquired at least a smattering of legal learning, though they often expended more of their energies on dancing and fencing. Again, gentlemen who served as Justices of the Peace needed to acquaint themselves with the rudiments of the law that they enforced.[1]

1 Shakespeare, *The Second Part of Henry the Sixth*, IV. ii. 73; Wilfrid R. Prest, *The Inns of Court under Elizabeth I and the early Stuarts* (1972) *passim*, especially 31, 153.

Lawyers often made high claims for the English common law. It was, they said, the best of all human legal systems, and approached God's own law in excellence. They believed that no amount of abstract reasoning could rival the wisdom of the law. So questions about the subject's rights and the Prince's powers were to be answered by reference to the common law, not by airy theorising. Formally, lawyers recognised the existence of laws superior to their own – in particular the law of nature. Substantively, they were sceptical. The lawyers' tendency was to reduce these higher laws to terms of such wide generality that they became vacuous. Such attitudes did not imply any particular doctrine on what the king's powers were. It was perfectly possible to argue that the common law itself gave nigh-unlimited discretionary powers to the monarch, and some lawyers did just this. But others, including Sir Edward Coke, held that the law imposed rigid restrictions upon his majesty's authority. It is with the ideas of Coke and like-minded thinkers that we shall be primarily concerned in this chapter.

Coke gained high legal office under Elizabeth. He became Solicitor-General in 1592 and Attorney-General a year later. Under James he was promoted to the position of Chief Justice of the Common Pleas, and later transferred to the King's Bench. He was also a Privy Councillor. In 1616, however, he was sacked from the Bench and the Council. In the following year he was restored to the Council, but his failure to support royal policies in the 1621 Parliament earned him a second dismissal and a spell of imprisonment in the Tower. It is true that Coke's fortunes were closely linked to the machinations of Court factions. His dismissal in 1616 was engineered by his old enemy Sir Francis Bacon and by George Abbot. His partial restoration to favour in 1617 was the work of his new friend George Villiers, later Duke of Buckingham. Stephen White has shown that it was not until the reign of Charles I that Coke became 'a consistent, dogmatic opponent of court policies'.[2] But the judge's dismissal, and his disagreements with James I cannot be wholly explained in terms of factional manoeuvrings. There was an ideological dimension.

As early as 1608 Coke offended the king in the Privy Council by denying that the ultimate right of interpreting laws lay with his majesty. James lost his temper at these words and claimed they were treasonable. The judge fell to his knees, but the king was placated only when his kinsman Cecil also knelt to intercede for him. Later, Coke refused to purge his printed *Reports* of passages which James considered ideologically unsound. He also denied that the king could stop common law proceedings by a writ *de non procedendo rege inconsulto*.[3] These actions, which certainly contributed to Coke's dismissal in 1616, were symptomatic of deep-rooted differences of opinion between the judge and James. The whole tenor of Coke's thinking was radically anti-absolutist.

2 Louis A. Knafla, *Law and politics in Jacobean England: the tracts of Lord Chancellor Ellesmere* (Cambridge 1977) 176; Stephen D. White, *Sir Edward Coke and 'the grievances of the commonwealth', 1621–1628* (Chapel Hill 1979) 45.
3 R.G. Usher, 'James I and Sir Edward Coke', *EHR* 18 (1903) 664–75, at 669–73; White, *Sir Edward Coke*, 7–10.

Coke's greatest intellectual debt was to Sir John Fortescue, a fifteenth-century judge whose *De laudibus legum Angliae* (In praise of the laws of England) was first printed around 1545. Translated into English twenty-two years later, it rapidly established itself as an Elizabethan best-seller. In many respects Fortescue's views were close to those of St Thomas Aquinas, an author whom he frequently quoted, and whose ideas on the law of nature he accepted wholesale. As a political theorist in the broad sense, Fortescue was unoriginal. But his ideas on the law and institutions of England proved highly influential.[4] He claimed that the customary laws of the land had survived unchanged since the days of the ancient Britons. In his opinion the fact that none of the nations which conquered England had altered these laws testified to their excellence. Fortescue believed that the purpose of government was the protection of the persons and property of the governed. This purpose was best served by the laws of England, which prohibited the king from legislating or levying taxes without the consent of his subjects. In England, he held, the king ruled as a constitutional monarch. The English system of government was an amalgam of monarchical and populist elements – a *regimen politicum et regale*. This implied no slur upon the king, for a monarch who ruled over free and prosperous subjects was likely to be both wealthier and more powerful than such a ruler as the king of France, who governed downtrodden, impoverished slaves.[5]

The outlines of Fortescue's ideology survived largely unchanged into the seventeenth century, but its details underwent a number of important, and sometimes contradictory modifications. Although Fortescue had regarded Parliament as the institution in which subjects expressed their agreement to royal legislation or taxation, he gave little emphasis to its powers. By contrast, Sir Thomas Smith was able to write in 1565 that 'the most high and absolute power of the realm of England consisteth in the Parliament',[6] and the lawyers of early Stuart England frequently repeated his sentiments. Yet the aggrandisement of Parliament and statute law was accompanied by a contrary but equally important development – the elevation of custom to the status of the supreme form of law.

In natural law thinking, custom could abrogate existing laws, and itself acquire the force of law, only if it was admitted by some sovereign authority, whether prince or people. The lawyers' notion of custom was quite different, for it elevated the common law, which was customary, above both prince and people. If a practice had existed for long enough it could be assumed that it was ideally suited to the needs of the commonwealth. To abrogate a custom which had proved its merits over the ages would be dangerous and presumptuous, for the distilled wisdom of past ages was far greater than that which

4 E.F. Jacob, 'Sir John Fortescue and the law of nature', *Bulletin of the John Rylands Library* 18 (1934) 359–76, at 376; Max Adams Shepard, 'The political and constitutional theory of Sir John Fortescue', in *Essays in history and political theory in honor of Charles Howard McIlwain* (Cambridge, Mass. 1936) 289–319, at 304, 308.
5 Sir John Fortescue, *De laudibus legum Angliae* (1616) ff. 38b–39a, 78a–86b; in Sir John Fortescue, *On the laws and governance of England*, ed. Shelley Lockwood (Cambridge 1997) 26–7, 49–54.
6 Sir Thomas Smith, *The common-wealth of England* (1635) 72.

moderns could unaidedly attain. The common law, it was argued, was the best of all possible laws precisely because it was ancient custom. But this was only part of the story. A second and rather different claim made for the common law was that it excelled all other human laws in rationality, corresponding most closely to the supremely rational laws of God.

Lawyers liked to think of the common law as the quintessence of reason. Since English law was so rational it was obviously superior to foreign laws, including Roman (or Civil) law. However, the equation of the common law with reason was a double-edged weapon. Everyone possessed reason. So it could be argued that all people were equally capable of understanding and interpreting the common law – a conclusion which Coke and others were anxious to avoid, partly to protect the privileged status of lawyers as the custodians of the law, and partly because they were well aware that their own ideas of what was rational did not tally with those of such men as the king and bishops. So the lawyers resorted to the notion that what was required to understand the law was not plain, ordinary reason, but 'artificial' reason, which, they claimed, could be acquired only by those who had spent long years studying the law, or, in other words, by lawyers.

Formally, common lawyers regarded their law as rational custom or 'tried reason'. Substantively, they held that its purpose was the maintenance of individual rights, particularly to property: 'the declaring of *meum* and *tuum* . . . is the very object of the laws of England'.[7] While natural law theorists believed that the purpose of government was the welfare and survival of the community as a whole, many common lawyers held that the aim of the state was the protection of the individual's property. They did, indeed, appeal to the rhetoric of the common good, but, like Fortescue, they argued that the public good could be maintained only if the rights of individuals were safeguarded. Free and prosperous subjects, the claim ran, would lead to a wealthy and powerful state. The main elements of common law political thinking, then, were the ideas of custom, of the rationality of English laws, and of the sacrosanctity of private property. Underpinning, or perhaps contradicting, all these ideas was the notion that Parliament was the supreme legislative institution in the land. Each of these concepts is worth considering in more detail.

THE COMMON LAW AS ANCIENT CUSTOM

'The Common Law of England', wrote Sir John Davies, Attorney-General for Ireland, 'is nothing else but the Common Custome of the Realm.' When the people found a practice 'good and beneficiall', he argued, they decided to retain it. In due course the practice became a custom, 'and being continued time out of mind, it obtaineth the force of a law'. In Davies's view, custom was the best form of law precisely because it was not instituted by a sovereign. To gain the status of law, custom had to win the acceptance of the people, and

7 F.S. Fussner, ed., 'William Camden's "Discourse concerning the prerogative of the crown"', *Proceedings of the American Philosophical Society* 101 (1957) 206.

there could be no stronger proof that it was in fact suited to their needs. 'A custome doth never become a Law to bind the people, untill it hath been tried and approved time out of mind, during all which time there did thereby arise no inconvenience.' By contrast, the edicts of a sovereign were imposed 'upon the Subject before any Triall or Probation made, whether the same be fit and agreeable to the nature and disposition of the people'. The enactments of a sovereign might or might not turn out to benefit the commonwealth – only time would tell. But the common law, being ancient custom, had by definition passed the test of time.[8]

'Time', said the lawyer Thomas Hedley, 'is the trier of truth, author of all human wisdom, learning and knowledge.' It was from time, he argued, that 'all human laws receive their chiefest strength, honor, and estimation'.[9] What was meant by the claim that the common law was the product of time? There are two plausible answers to this question. Firstly, the common law could be regarded as a set of customs which had existed from the earliest times and which still flourished, while other usages had fallen by the wayside. The common law, in short, could be viewed as unchanged since the remotest antiquity. Secondly, and very differently, the law could be seen as in a state of constant development, forever adjusting itself to the needs of the people, and ever sensitive to changes in those needs. On this view, it was quite possible that the laws existing in the seventeenth century were wholly different from those of earlier periods.

Lawyers found it tempting to portray their law as exceedingly old, and none succumbed to the temptation more wholeheartedly than Sir Edward Coke. He argued on the flimsiest evidence that the common laws, including their most detailed procedural provisions, dated from the earliest times. Even Coke, however, admitted that certain legal institutions had relatively modern origins. He confessed, for example, that Justices of the Peace dated only from 1337 – disagreeing on this point with John Selden who was in general far more sceptical about the antiquity of the law than Coke, but who traced the origin of Justices to the time of William the Conqueror.[10] The important point is that Coke's talk of the law's prehistoric antiquity was really just so much window-dressing. The essential doctrine of the lawyers, including Coke, was that because the common law was customary, and not enacted by a sovereign, it was better suited to the English people than any other law. So it was the supreme law in England and the fact that it did not proceed from the arbitrary decree of a sovereign meant that it could not be abrogated by any claimant to sovereignty, whether king or Parliament. To count as customary, a usage had to date from 'time immemorial' or from 'time out of mind'. But this did *not* mean that the origins of the usage were necessarily shrouded in the mists of

8 Sir John Davies, *Le primer report des cases & matters en ley* (Dublin 1615) preface, sig.* 2a; in David Wootton, ed., *Divine Right and democracy: an anthology of political writing in Stuart England* (Harmondsworth 1986) 131–43, at 131.

9 *PP 10*, ii, 175.

10 Sir Edward Coke, *The reports*, ed. G. Wilson (1776) 3, preface, f. va; John Selden, *Jani Anglorum facies altera* (1610) 73.

most distant antiquity. Strictly, 'time immemorial' perhaps meant (as, to law-yers, it still means) before 1189.[11] But, of course, a strong *prima facie* case could be constructed to show that even later practices possessed the force of custom – in the sense that their survival demonstrated their excellence.

Coke's opinion that most of the common law could be traced to the time of the ancient Britons was widely rejected. William Lambarde, Sir Dudley Digges and Sir Roger Owen looked to the Saxons rather than the Britons as the founders of the common law. Others argued that the historical origins of the law were many and various, and that some of its major elements might even date from after the Norman Conquest. Sir Francis Bacon, for example, be-lieved that the common law was an amalgam of the customs of Romans, Saxons, Danes and Normans. William Hakewill asserted that 'the laws of the Britaines were utterly extinct by the Romans; their laws again by the Saxons; and lastly, theirs by the Danes and Normans much altered'. John Selden, perhaps the greatest legal historian in early Stuart England, gave his authorit-ative vote to Coke's opponents, claiming that many new and lasting laws had been introduced by and after the Conqueror. Coke did find supporters for his notion that English customs had survived largely unchanged since the days of the Britons, and these included such eminent lawyers as Sir John Dodderidge and Sir John Popham as well as the ignorant populariser George Saltern. But the idea that the common law had not been altered since prehistoric times was neither dominant nor, indeed, very important. The law's binding force was derived from its customary nature, not from its prehistoricity.

Indeed, the fact that the common law was unwritten, and thus subject to change, was held to be a main reason for its superiority to other laws. Unlike, say, the Civil Law of the Roman emperors, the common law was not a rigid set of rules inherited from the distant past, but a flexible system which had developed along with the English people itself. 'It is the work of time', said Thomas Hedley, 'which hath so adapted and accommodated this law to this kingdom as a garment fitted to the body or a glove to the hand or rather as the skin to the hand, which groweth with it.' Judges were not rigidly bound by a written code, nor even by the decisions of their predecessors. For this reason, the law was in a state of constant development and refinement. In Hedley's view, the pronouncements of contemporary judges were not the mere expres-sions of personal opinion, but the culmination of a long historical process. The judges spoke not for themselves alone, but for their predecessors, and their decisions encapsulated the distilled wisdom of bygone generations. No modern assembly – not even Parliament – could match the wisdom of the dead. To claim to be wiser than the laws was boastful folly. 'Our rule is in

11 J.H. Baker, *An introduction to English legal history*, 2nd edn (1979) 125 states that the statute of Quo Warranto of 1290 fixed 1189 as the date from which prescriptive claims could be made; G. Padfield and F.E. Smith, *Law made simple*, 6th edn (1981) 285 asserts that in modern legal usage '"time immemorial"' means 'since 1189'. Different views on when it came to mean this are expressed in Glenn Burgess, *The politics of the ancient constitution* (1992) 256 n. 60, and Corinne C. Weston, 'England: ancient constitution and common law', in J.H. Burns and Mark Goldie, eds, *The Cambridge history of political thought, 1450–1700* (Cambridge 1991) 374–411, at 387.

this plain commonwealth of ours', said James Whitelocke, '*oportet neminem esse sapientiorem legibus*' (let no one presume to be wiser than the laws).[12]

Despite his views on the history of English law, Coke adopted the same line, arguing that the common law had been 'fined and refined' 'by the wisdom of the most excellent men, in many successions of ages'. The evident implication of this – and one spelled out by Selden – was that the law might be very different now from what it had been in previous centuries, and yet still, in some sense, be the same law. The common laws of England, wrote Selden, 'are not otherwise than the ship, that by often mending had no piece of the first materialls, or as the house that's so often repaired, *ut nihil ex pristina materia supersit* [that none of the original material survives], which yet . . . is to be accounted the same still'.[13]

Yet even Selden admitted that the common laws possessed an immutable rational core. All human laws had, by definition, to conform to the higher laws of God and nature. So, strictly speaking, the common law was not mere custom, but godly and rational custom. As Lord Chancellor Ellesmere put it, 'custome cannot allow that which is unreasonable in it selfe'. Not every ancient practice had the force of law, for evil actions remained evil however often they were repeated. A custom became law only if it was sanctioned by reason: 'how long soever it hath continued', wrote Coke, 'if it is against reason it hath no force in law'.[14]

12 William Lambarde, *Archeion or, a discourse upon the high courts of justice*, eds C.H. McIlwain and P.L. Ward (Cambridge, Mass. 1957) 11–12; *PP 28*, ii, 33 (Digges); *PD 10*, 115 (Owen); Sir Francis Bacon, 'A proposition to his majesty . . . touching the compiling and amendment of the laws of England', in *Resuscitatio*, 3rd edn (1671) i, 203–11, at 204; Thomas Hearne, ed., *A collection of curious discourses*, 2 vols (1771) i, 8, 283 (Hakewill, Doddridge); Selden, *Jani Anglorum facies altera*, 63–73; *ST*, ii, 569 (Popham); George Saltern, *Of the antient lawes of Great Britain* (1605) sig. B3a, I3a, L3b; *PP 10*, ii, 180 (Hedley); *ST*, ii, 518 (Whitelocke). In his *Historie of tithes* (1618) Selden was careful to avoid the implication that English kings ruled as absolute conquerors: the Norman invasion had not been a conquest but 'a violent recovering of the Kingdome out of the hands of Rebels' (482), and the laws which were changed 'were not at all abrogated by his Conquest but either by the Parliaments or Ordinances of his time and of his successors, or else by non-usage or contrarie custom' (484).
Selden's views on English legal history and the Norman Conquest are discussed in Paul Christianson, 'Young John Selden and the ancient constitution, ca. 1610–1618', *Proceedings of the American Philosophical Society* 128 (1984) 271–315, and Christianson, *Discourse on history, law, and governance in the public career of John Selden, 1610–1635* (Toronto 1996). Another lawyer who dissented from Coke's theory that English law had remained largely unchanged since the earliest times was Robert Hills, who wrote a manuscript treatise 'Of tenures in knights service' for the Earl of Salisbury about 1610 (Folger Library Mss G.b.16); Hills argued that many laws had been changed after the Conquest, and that as a conqueror William of Normandy had been fully authorised to introduce new laws, since that was a privilege of conquerors: ff. 12b–13a. He held that English *tenures* pre-dated the Conquest, however: ibid., and see also William Klein, 'The ancient constitution revisited', in Nicholas Phillipson and Quentin Skinner, eds, *Political discourse in early modern Britain* (Cambridge 1993) 23–44, at 38–9.
13 Coke, *Reports*, 7, f. 3b; Selden, 'Notes upon Fortescue', 19, in Sir John Fortescue, *De laudibus legum Angliae* (1616).
14 Selden, 'Notes upon Fortescue', 17–18, in Fortescue, *De laudibus legum Angliae*; Sir Thomas Egerton, Lord Ellesmere, 'A coppie of a wrytten discourse by the Lord Chancellor Elsmere concerning the royall prerogative', in Knafla, *Law and politics in Jacobean England*, 197–201, at 200; Coke, *The first part of the institutes* (1628) f. 62a.

THE COMMON LAW AS REASON

In the opinion of the lawyers, the common law derived its excellence not only from its customary nature, but also from its supreme rationality. It was based, said Coke, 'upon a rock of reason'. William Noy believed that it was 'grounded on the Rules of reason', while for Sir Henry Finch it was 'nothing els but common reason'. Equally frequent were claims that the common law corresponded more closely than other human systems to the law of God set out in Scripture. Coke reported that 'the common law was grounded on the law of God', and George Saltern argued that twelve-man juries were modelled upon Scripture – presumably because there were twelve Apostles. Nicholas Fuller dated the common laws to 'the first preaching of the Gospel in this island', and declared that 'they have their foundation as well from the laws of God as from approved reason'. Similarly, Lord Chancellor Ellesmere proclaimed that 'the common law of England is grounded upon the law of God, and extends it selfe to the originall Law of Nature, and the universal Law of Nations'.[15]

The common law was held to be rational not only in the negative sense that its provisions were compatible with natural law, but also in a much more positive sense. All human laws had to conform to the law of nature. What was special about the common law was that it not only conformed to, but actually *was*, or at least came close to being natural law. 'Coming nearest to the law of nature, which is the root and touchstone of all good laws',[16] the common law of England was manifestly superior to its rivals. The common law was regarded as a product of reason and custom, and each of these two elements strengthened and contributed to the other. Customs had to square with reason if they were to become laws. But equally, reason had to pass the test of time. So the common law was 'tried reason' – a set of norms which not only were rational but also had proved to be so over the centuries.

Common law was case-law, built on precedents. It was also much more than this. Precedents had little meaning on their own. They had to be interpreted, and to do this lawyers resorted to a set of general principles which they called maxims or reasons of the common law. Maxims had a dual quality. They were precepts of reason, 'drawne out of the Law of Nature', and they were also general rules derived from and applicable to a vast mass of particular cases, 'containing in a short summe the reason and direction of many particular and speciall occurrences'. Maxims were taken from a wide variety of sources, including the Civil Law: 'out of the Civill Lawes there are also very many Axiomes and Rules, which are likewise borrowed and usually

15 *CD 21*, III, 319 (Coke); William Noy, *A treatise of the principall grounds and maximes of the lawes of this kingdom* (1641), 1; Sir Henry Finch, *Law, or, a discourse thereof* (1627) 75; Coke, *Reports*, 3, f. 40a; Saltern, *Of the antient lawes of Great Britaine*, sig. I2a; *PP 10*, II, 152 (Fuller); Lord Chancellor Ellesmere, *The speech of the Lord Chancellor of England, in the eschequer chamber, touching the post-nati* (1609) 31–2. The same thesis was well stated by Christopher St German in the 1520s: *A dyalogue in Englysshe betwyxt a Doctoure of Dyvynyte and a student in the lawes of Englande*, f. ixb: 'the lawe of Englande is grounded . . . on the lawe of reason'.
16 Davies, *Le primer report*, preface, sig.* 2a.

frequented in our Law'. Indeed, one reason why the law was held to be superior to other branches of human learning was that it was parasitic upon them, adopting their conclusions as its own maxims. English law was 'the Science of Sciences', said Dodderidge, because it was 'holpen and assisted almost of all other Sciences'.[17]

In the opinion of lawyers, years of study were required to achieve an understanding of the laws. To comprehend and interpret case-law, a lawyer needed not mere reason but 'artificial reason'. In his posthumous twelfth report Coke related how he had bearded James I on this point. The king had argued that he could act as a judge, since 'he thought the law was founded upon reason, and that he and others had reason as well as the Judges'. Coke replied by praising the king's natural gifts, but pointing out that legal cases 'which concern the life or inheritance or goods or fortunes of his subjects are not to be decided by natural reason but by the artificial reason and judgment of law, which law is an act which requires long study and experience before that a man can attain to the cognizance of it'. The accuracy of Coke's account is questionable, but it is clear that he and other lawyers drew a sharp distinction between the uneducated reason of ordinary mortals and the 'artificial reason' of a lawyer.[18]

Finch said that the law was 'common reason' but glossed this as meaning 'refined reason', not the reason 'which everie one doth frame unto himself'. Dodderidge declared that the common law 'is called reason, not for that every man can comprehend the same; but it is artificiall reason'. Artificial reason was, in essence, natural reason informed by a knowledge of English customs and by the arts and sciences which supplied legal maxims. It was not merely a knowledge of precedents, for the common law was not mere custom. Custom and common law, said Hedley, 'differ as much as artificial reason and bare precedents'. In the view of the lawyers, then, the common law developed along two distinct but intimately connected lines. Firstly, the general customs of the land were recorded in precedents. Secondly, these precedents were interpreted according to the light of reason. The dictates of reason were generalisations drawn from particular legal decisions, but also imported from other disciplines including logic, theology and even the Civil Law. English legal attitudes were insular inasmuch as the substance of the common law was English custom. But custom was only one aspect of the law, and there was nothing particularly insular about the lawyers' use of reason.[19]

Case-law combined with reason to produce high-level general principles or fundamental points of the law. These principles were treated with far greater

17 Sir John Dodderidge, *The English lawyer* (1631) 124–5, 153, 158, 35. An important discussion of the use of Civil Law principles particularly by Sir John Davies is H. Pawlisch, 'Sir John Davies, the ancient constitution, and the Civil law', *HJ* 23 (1980) 689–702.

18 Coke, twelfth report, quoted in J.R. Tanner, ed., *Constitutional documents of the reign of James I* (Cambridge 1930) 187; Usher, 'James I and Sir Edward Coke', 664–75, casts doubt on this account. James commented at length on Coke's ideas in his speech to Star Chamber of 1616: *Political writings* ed. Johann P. Sommerville (Cambridge 1994) 204–28.

19 Finch, *Law, or, a discourse thereof*, 75; Dodderidge, *The English lawyer*, 242; *PP 10*, II, 175.

reverence than mere precedents. While precedents had to be interpreted in terms of maxims, maxims were self-sufficient: 'Every Maxime is a sufficient authoritie to himself.' Maxims were the essential core of the common law, woven so closely into the fabric of English life that they could never be ignored with impunity: 'I never sawe a maxim of the Common lawe altered but much losse and harme did ensew', Coke told the House of Commons in 1621, and in 1628 John Bankes reminded the same body that it was 'dangerous to shake any maxim at the common law'. What were the maxims or funda-mental principles of the law? Hedley insisted that they could all be found written in law-books: 'there is no principle or maxim of law which is not found in some of our books'. In fact, the situation was rather more fluid than Hedley allowed, and the early seventeenth century witnessed the elevation of several new principles to the status of maxims. Free trade was declared a maxim of the law by Coke in 1621, and by 1628 the doctrine that no subject could ever be imprisoned without cause shown was widely recognised as fundamental, though in 1621 it had been equally widely rejected.[20] But some principles received consistent support from a high proportion of lawyers throughout the early Stuart period. The maxim that you could not be a judge in your own case is one example, but of far greater political interest were the two allied contentions that subjects could not be deprived of their property nor bound by a new law without their consent.

These two principles, purportedly derived from a combination of reason and custom, constituted the core of what lawyers took to be the fundamental liberties of the subject, which, they held, were enshrined in Magna Carta. Both principles implied the existence of Parliament, for it was to Parliament that lawyers looked as the institution in which subjects expressed their con-sent to legislation or taxation. Parliament consisted of the king, the House of Lords and the House of Commons, but it was the House of Commons alone which was held to represent the broad mass of the English people. The notion that the Commons represented the people was a Tudor commonplace, un-questioned until the later 1640s when the Levellers began to demand what was by contemporary standards a very radical reform of the franchise. Moreover, it was a relatively realistic notion if we take the people to mean the politically significant portion of the population. In the early Stuart period it was the gentry who enforced law in the counties and who paid taxes. The House of Commons successfully represented the interests of the gentry.

Legislation, the lawyers believed, could not take place without the consent of the subject in Parliament. Furthermore, Magna Carta – the quintessential repository of the liberties of the subject – was itself regarded as an Act of Parliament. In the words of Finch, Parliament possessed 'an absolute power in all causes'.[21] Common lawyers elevated Parliament to a position of

---

20 Noy, *Treatise of the principall grounds and maximes of the lawes*, 21; CD 21, III, 304; PP 28, IV, 227; PP 10, II, 186; White, *Sir Edward Coke*, 113. On imprisonment cf. below, Chapter 5, pp. 153–63.
21 Finch, *Law, or, a discourse thereof*, 233.

near-sovereignty, while at the same time insisting that unwritten custom was superior to statute law. This looks very much like a contradiction. What, then, did the lawyers mean?

THE COMMON LAW AND STATUTE

'The Parliament', said Thomas Hedley in 1610, 'hath his power and authority from the common law, and not the common law from the Parliament. And therefore the common law is of more force and strength than the Parliament.' The power of Parliament to make statutes could not itself be derived from statute. So there had to be some law higher than statute upon which Parliament's authority ultimately rested – and this, according to the lawyers, was the common law. Since Parliament's authority was derived from the common law, it was plain that Parliament could not abolish the whole of the common law without abolishing itself. 'That the parliament may abrogate the whole law, I deny', said Hedley, 'for that were includedly to take away the power of the parliament itself, which power it hath by the common law.' However, Parliament could justly correct particular deficiencies in the common law: 'the parliament may find some defects in the common law and amend them (for what is perfect under the sun?)'. But Parliament's power to do this was itself derived from the common law, so the supremacy of the common law was safeguarded.[22]

The essence of English legal thinking was to elevate rational custom above all written, man-made laws, including Acts of Parliament. This was all very well in theory, but difficult to apply. Before common law could be enforced it was necessary to decide what it was. Disagreements about whether a certain precept was enjoined by the common law were clearly possible and threatened to create legal anarchy unless some means of resolving them was devised. The vital question, then, was not whether the common law was superior to statute but who should decide what the common law was. Lawyers countenanced two answers to this question – the judges and Parliament.

The judges, declared Nicholas Fuller, 'are and always have been thought the most carefull, judicious and jelous preservers of the lawes of England'. For this reason, he argued, 'the exposition of all statutes' was left to the judges, who could interpret them 'contrary to the common sense of the words of the statute, to uphold the meaning of the common lawes of the Realme'. A far more famous exposition of the same doctrine was that of Sir Edward Coke in Bonham's Case of 1609. Coke not only set aside a statute, but also enunciated the principle that 'in many cases the common law will control acts of Parliament'. The precise significance of Coke's assertions remains debatable, but if, as seems plausible, he intended to give judges the power to ignore any statute

22 *PP 10*, II, 174.

which they deemed contrary to the fundamentals of the common law, his project was short-lived, and that for two reasons.[23]

If the judges could definitively interpret statute they could in effect alter and add to the laws as they pleased. A judicial power to review the laws would, in the end, amount to legislative sovereignty. The notion that the judges should be sovereigns in England found few supporters. James I pointed out, in his homely way, that 'if the Judges interprete the lawes themselves and suffer none else to interprete, then they may easily make of the laws shipmens hose'. In James's view, Coke's argument undermined royal power. In the view of Lord Chancellor Ellesmere, it 'derogateth much from the wisdome and power of the parliament'. If judges could set aside a statute which 'agreeth not in their particular sense with Common right and reason', then the judgments of 'a particular Court' would be superior to those 'of all the Realme' assembled in Parliament.[24] It was one thing to say that the common law was superior to statute and quite another to say that the judges were superior to Parliament. The common law forbade legislation without the consent of the subject. If the judges were the supreme interpreters of the law, then by interpreting they might change it – and so legislate without the subject's consent.

The second reason for rejecting the notion that judges could set aside those statutes which they held to be against common law was purely political. The judges – royal appointees – were too easily subjected to political pressure from the king to be reliable defenders of the subject's liberties. As Edward Alford put it in the Parliament of 1621, 'it is dangerous that the judges, a fewe persons, dependant and timorous some of them, should judge betweene the king and the state of their liberties'. 'If this should be suffered', he asked, 'what will become of us?' In 1627 (in the Five Knights' Case), and again in the 1630s (over Ship Money), the judges failed to protect the subject's liberties against what many saw as royal encroachment. Well aware that he could more easily manipulate the judges than Parliament, Charles I told them in 1628 that 'to you only, under me, belongs the interpretation of laws'.[25] Judicial review of statutes was workable only if the judges were politically independent. Once the Bench fell under royal control, judicial review would become a tool of royal absolutism.

The dominant legal opinion, then, was that Parliament and not the judges had supreme power to interpret the laws. As one author put it, 'the most general use of interpreting doubtful laws and statutes hath been by Parliament, whereof yet if any man doubt let him see the statutes made in the time of King Henry the 8th. And let no king desire to be accounted worse than

23 Nicholas Fuller, *The argument of Master Nicholas Fuller, in the case of Thomas Lad, and Richard Maunsell* (1607) 28. A different interpretation of Bonham's Case is S.E. Thorne, 'Dr Bonham's Case', *Law Quarterly Review* 54 (1938) 543–52. See also Glenn Burgess, *Absolute monarchy and the Stuart constitution* (New Haven 1996) 181–93.
24 James I quoted in Usher, 'James I and Sir Edward Coke', 669; Ellesmere in Knafla, *Law and politics in Jacobean England*, 306–7.
25 *CD 21*, v, 195; *PP 28*, iv, 481. Alford is discussed in R. Zaller, 'Edward Alford and the making of country radicalism', *Journal of British Studies* 22 (1983) 59–79.

Henry 8.' This allusion to Henry VIII is significant, for it was, in fact, the events of the 1530s – masterminded by Thomas Cromwell – which 'gave to Parliament a permanent place of political importance and, so to speak, finally incorporated it in the English system of government.'[26]

Once Parliament had decided on a point of law, it was not open to the judges to reverse its decision. So the enactments of Parliament defined what was actually enforceable as law in the courts. Parliament was 'absolute' in the sense that there was no human authority – except a later Parliament – which could reverse its decrees. But this did *not* mean that there was no law above statute. Everyone agreed that the laws of God and nature were superior to Acts of Parliament. Many lawyers believed that at least the fundamental points of the common law were likewise above statute.

Speaking of the law of God and reason in 1621, Sir William Fleetwood declared that 'to make a law contrary to that is to make a void thing'. In the Parliament of 1610 Heneage Finch cited the judgment in Calvin's Case, asserting that kings had a natural duty to protect their subjects, and that 'an act of parliament cannot take away that protection which the law of nature giveth'. 'We that are now the household of God', said Nicholas Fuller in the same year, 'hold that every law of this realm against the laws of God (although it were by act of parliament) is a void law.'[27] A statute which failed to conform to the superior decrees of God and nature would impose no obligations upon the subject, and, in this sense, was void. People might, indeed, be punished for disobeying such a statute. Until the statute was repealed, disobedience would be legally (though not morally) punishable. Yet an ungodly statute *ought* to be disobeyed, for it was better to obey God than man.

Since people were fallible, it was possible for them to adopt and enforce laws which were contrary to God's. Such laws had no moral validity and their very existence threatened to bring God's displeasure to bear upon the land. The wisest course was for Parliament to abolish them as swiftly as it could. In the view of lawyers, equally calamitous results would follow if Parliament ignored any of the fundamental points of the common law. 'It is a maxim in policy, and a trial by experience', wrote Coke, 'that the alteration of any of them is most dangerous.' 'Shake Magna Carta', he told the House of Commons in 1628, 'and we know what will come of it.'[28]

Coke admitted that Parliament could *in fact* set aside at least some of the fundamental points of the common law. In other words, Parliament could enact that a maxim of the common law no longer applied in England, and was no longer enforceable in the courts. In the same way, Parliament could decide (quite wrongly) that some precept of the law of God was not in fact according to God's law. For instance, Parliament might decide that theft was condoned by God, and pass an act permitting the practice. If this occurred, no court

---

26 Fussner, ed., 'William Camden's "Discourse concerning the prerogative of the crown"', 215; G.R. Elton, *The Tudor constitution*, 2nd edn (Cambridge 1982) 234.

27 *CD 21*, III, 306; *PP 10*, II, 244, 152–3.

28 Coke, *Reports*, 4, preface, p. v; *PP 28*, III, 96.

would have the power to punish theft. But, of course, theft would still be wrong, for human laws could not abrogate the decrees of God. The effect of a statute allowing theft would be to set God's law on this matter in abeyance within the realm of England, but not to abolish it. Should a later Parliament decide that theft was not, after all, permissible, it could merely declare what God's law was upon this question. Declarative acts tacitly admitted the existence of law superior to statute.

People could decide not to enforce divine law, but they could never abolish it. Could they abolish the fundamental precepts of the common law? Parliament could set these precepts in abeyance. But the precepts themselves retained a moral superiority to any statutes which discontinued them. The subject's rights were based upon customary not statute law. Magna Carta was, indeed, a statute, but a statute declaring old, not enacting new, law. 'The ancient law of England', wrote Coke, was 'declared by the great charter.' 'I do not take Magna Charta to be a new grant or statute', said Hedley in 1610, 'but a restoring or confirming of the ancient laws and liberties of the kingdom.' 'The liberties of all', said Crew in 1621, were 'confirmed in Magna charta.'[29] So the rights of subjects existed independently of any statute. Magna Carta made these rights enforceable at law, but did not itself create them. Statute might prevent the enforcement of ancient liberties, but it could not abrogate them, for the liberties existed by virtue of a law higher than statute.

The same reasoning applied to those rights which the king possessed by ancient common law, for example Supremacy over the church. When Parliament made Elizabeth Supreme Governor of the church in 1559, it declared that it was merely 'restoring and uniting to the imperial crown of this realm the ancient jurisdictions, authorities, superiorities and preeminences to the same of right belonging and appertaining'. The Act of 1559 did not create a new law, but made an existing law enforceable; it was, said Coke, 'not a statute introductory of a new law, but declaratory of the old'.[30] Coke's conclusion was that throughout the ages of popish darkness and in the benighted days of Queen Mary the monarchs of England had by law been supreme over the church, though the law had not been enforced. Not even the statute of 1554, restoring papal supremacy, had been able to change the law. Statute, then, could not strictly speaking abrogate the fundamental precepts of the common law, any more than it could abolish the laws of God and nature, though it might foolishly and for a while set these laws in abeyance.

The fact that judges did not habitually overthrow statutes indicates that Parliament and not the Bench was regarded as the supreme interpreter of the law. It does not show that statute was regarded as the supreme form of law. Statute was inferior to the laws of God and nature, and (said the lawyers) to the fundamental tenets of the common law. Parliament could declare what these laws and tenets commanded, but could not change them. This does not

29 Coke, *Reports*, 2, preface, p. x; *PP 10*, ɪɪ, 190; *CD 21*, ᴠ, 239.
30 Act of Supremacy quoted in Elton, *Tudor constitution*, 372; Coke, *Reports*, 5, f. viiia.

mean that Parliament's *sole* function was to declare law. It used to be argued that in medieval England 'the law was declared rather than made', and that there was no conception of 'law-making' until the advent of 'the new idea of legislative sovereignty' in the Civil War.[31] Certainly, it is true that many statutes were merely declarative of old law. But the notion of lawmaking was entirely familiar to the English in the early seventeenth century. Where superior laws were silent, or permitted more than one application, people could make and unmake laws. Parliament, said Sir Henry Finch, had the power 'to make Lawes', and he spelled out the implications of this, pronouncing that 'one and the self same lawes may be altered and changed in themselves', provided of course that such changes were not 'against the two maine Lawes, of Nature, and Reason'.[32] In Finch's view, and that of many lawyers, the law of reason was broadly equivalent to the maxims of the common law. So one law might be unmade and another made unless the first was prescribed or the second prohibited by the superior laws of God and nature or by the fundamental principles of the common law. Concretely, Parliament could not make adultery permissible, or give the king a right to take his subjects' property without their consent, but it could, say, regulate the conduct of rogues and vagabonds, or even make it a punishable offence to get up before nine o'clock in the morning.

From the 1530s the Tudor Parliament was in many respects a sovereign legislature. Early Stuart lawyers believed that Parliament was the supreme judicial and legislative authority in the land. In this sense, it was sovereign. But it had an obligation to tailor its edicts to superior laws. In the theory of Bodin and the English absolutists the king was a sovereign, accountable to no human authority, but having a duty to abide by the laws of God and nature. In the theory of the lawyers, it was not the king alone but the king-in-Parliament who was sovereign, and Parliament's decrees were inferior not only to those of God and nature, but also to the fundamental precepts of the common law. Indeed, it was from the common law that Parliament derived its sovereignty. The English did not have to wait for the Civil War to become acquainted with the concept of a supreme human authority. On the other hand, the notion that there were laws superior to those enacted by the sovereign persisted long after the war. Even in the work of Hobbes, the most famous apologist for nigh-unlimited sovereignty, the will of the sovereign was not able to eradicate the subject's right or duty of self-defence which was grounded upon a higher authority than any human law, namely the law of nature. As the Parliamentarians were forced to ever more extreme expedients in the Civil War they came to abandon the claim that fundamental common laws were superior to statute. But they did not adopt any notion of strictly unlimited sovereignty, for they acknowledged that human sovereigns were bound by the laws of God and nature, and it was indeed upon these laws that

31 C.H. McIlwain, *The High Court of Parliament and its supremacy* (1910) p. vii, 94.
32 Finch, *Law, or, a discourse thereof*, 233, 76.

they based their claim that Parliament could abrogate the common law. Reason and nature, they held, permitted the commonwealth to change all purely human legal arrangements if such a course was in the public interest. Parliamentary thought in the Civil Wars witnessed the triumph of the law of nature over the common law, not the advent of any idea of unlimited sovereignty.

Just as the common law granted supreme legislative and judicial authority to Parliament, so, the lawyers held, it guaranteed certain powers to the king. These powers were known as royal prerogatives. As Coke put it, reporting a legal decision of 1610, 'the King hath no prerogative but that which the law of the land allows him'.[33] Essentially, the king possessed certain executive powers, but could not use these to undermine the liberty of the subject.

THE COMMON LAW AND THE ROYAL PREROGATIVE

Absolutists believed that the king's power was derived immediately from God as the author of nature. Natural law, they held, prescribed that there be a sovereign authority in every commonwealth. In England it was the king who held this authority. The law of nature gave the king a duty to do whatever he thought necessary to provide for the security and welfare of his subjects. In ordinary circumstances he might execute this duty by ruling within settled limits to which he had agreed. But where the law of the land did not spell out how he should act, the prior law of nature left him free to rule as he pleased – provided, of course, that his decrees conformed to those of God and nature. Moreover, the king might justly flout even the known law of the land if special circumstances arose in which it turned out that the security of the commonwealth necessitated such action. According to this view, the king always possessed absolute, extra-legal rights, though he could only justly exercise these if he believed that the common and statute laws of the land did not sufficiently provide for the public good. So it was not open to lawyers, or anyone else, to define or circumscribe royal power. Lawyers might point out what the law was, but if the king judged it appropriate he could rule outside or even against the known law. It was sedition, said James I, for 'subjects to dispute what a king may do in the height of his power'.[34]

Many lawyers, by contrast, believed that the king had no extra-legal powers whatever. In their opinion, the king's prerogative was nothing more than those rights which he possessed at law. 'I never knew the prerogative but as a part of the common law', said Christopher Sherland in 1628, while Sir Henry Finch affirmed that the king's prerogative 'groweth wholly from the reason of the Common law, and is as it were a finger of that hand'. Selden argued that the royal prerogative was simply that which the law allowed the king to do. 'The King's prerogative', he insisted, 'is not his will, or – what divines make it – a power to do what he lists.' If the king possessed any powers outside and

33 Coke, twelfth report, quoted in Tanner, *Constitutional documents*, 188.
34 James I's speech of 21 March 1610 in *Political writings*, 184.

above the law, argued the lawyers, he could use them to subvert and finally abrogate the whole of the common law. In 1610 James I warned his subjects not to dispute what a king could do. The lawyer Thomas Wentworth ignored the warning, observing that subjects would lose their liberty if royal actions could not be questioned: 'if we shall once say that we may not dispute the prerogative, let us be sold for slaves.'[35]

Lawyers agreed that the king himself could not be prosecuted for his illegal actions. But anyone who executed a royal command which was against the law was liable to prosecution. The basic principle according to which the king's prerogative powers were held to be limited was summed up in the dictum that the king could do no wrong. This did not mean that whatever the king did was right, but that if an action was wrong the king could not possibly have done it. In other words, lawyers held that the king could only command things that were lawful. 'The laws of England', said Sir Dudley Digges in 1626, 'teach us that Kings cannot command ill, or unlawful things. Whenever they speak, though by Letters Patent, if the thing be evil, those Letters Patent are void, and whatsoever ill event succeeds, the executioner of such commands must ever answer for them.' The royal prerogative was derived from and wholly circumscribed by the law. 'That which the King would doe', said Sir George Croke in 1638, 'if it be against the common lawe or stattuts, the lawe doth not judge to be a prerogative in the Kinge.' More particularly, the king could never infringe the personal or property rights of his subjects. 'If any graunt or Commission from the King doth tend to charge the body, landes, or goods of the subjects unlawfully', wrote Nicholas Fuller in 1607, 'the Judges will redresse the same.'[36] Events did not fulfil this pious expectation, for the judges were too easily persuaded to decide cases in favour of their royal master.

According to the lawyers, the king possessed a large number of prerogative powers, all of which facilitated good government, though otherwise they might have little in common. Of these powers, a good many were more or less irrelevant to the subject's liberties. For example, the king could choose the design of the coinage. In doing so he might offend his subjects' aesthetic sensibilities, but could hardly invade their rights. Other prerogatives affected the subject's welfare more closely, but indirectly. For instance, the king could specify the fineness of the coinage, and also set the ratio at which gold coins would be valued against silver. Using the first prerogative, Henry VIII had debased the coinage in the 1540s. Using the second, James I revalued gold in 1612. On both occasions the consequences were grave. Lacking economic sophistication, however, the English paid relatively little attention to James I's

---

35 *PP 28*, III, 99; Finch, *Law, or, a discourse thereof*, 85; Selden, *Table talk of John Selden*, ed. Sir Frederick Pollock (1927) 112; *PP 10*, II, 82–3.

36 *CD 21*, V, 59; Digges quoted in Clayton Roberts, *The growth of responsible government in Stuart England* (Cambridge 1966) 59; S.R. Gardiner, ed., *Notes of the judgment delivered by Sir George Croke in the case of ship-money*, 11, in *The Camden miscellany*, volume the seventh (1875); Fuller, *The argument of Master Nicholas Fuller*, 15.

monetary policy – even in the Parliament of 1621, which debated the country's economic problems at length – and concentrated instead upon the more direct ways in which the exercise of the royal prerogative might infringe the liberty of the subject.

From this point of view, the most dangerous prerogatives were those which permitted the king to flout known law in emergencies. A straightforward case was that of war. As Cicero put it – in a much-quoted adage – '*silent leges inter arma*': 'the laws are silent in war'. Sir Thomas Smith, the Elizabethan commentator on the English constitution, summed up the conventional wisdom, declaring that 'in war time and in the field the prince hath . . . absolute power, so that his word is law; he may put to death or to other bodily punishment whom he shall think so to deserve, without process of law or form of judgment'.[37] It would be inconvenient to maintain established legal procedures, with their accompanying delays, in wartime. But the king's right to rule as he pleased during a war could be abused. For example, if the king's word defined what was war, he could declare that a state of affairs which seemed perfectly peaceful to his subjects was in fact war, and could rule accordingly.

To circumvent this possibility, the lawyers insisted that it was not the king but the law that decided what was war. The law, said Heneage Finch in 1610, defined 'what shall be called war at home and abroad'. The same principle was endorsed by lawyers in the 1628 Parliament – at a time when the king's recent use of martial law made the question of intense practical interest to his subjects. When the Civil lawyer Sir Henry Marten claimed that 'execution of martial law is necessary where the sovereign and state think it necessary', Coke vigorously rejected his opinion, declaring that 'martial law must be bounded by the law of England' – that is to say, the common law. The lawyers argued that where the courts were open and the common law could in fact be executed, martial law could never apply. The king's emergency powers, then, could not be exercised at his discretion, but only when the law permitted.[38]

The function of the law, it was held, was to protect the life, liberty and especially property of the subject, not only against other subjects, but also against the king himself. As Richard Martin noted in 1610, if the king possessed powers to ignore the law in special circumstances, and to decide what these circumstances were, his authority would be absolute, and the law would have failed in its purpose. The law was valuable because it was certain, letting everyone know precisely what their rights were, and providing a remedy for every injury. To allow discretionary powers above the law was to undermine its certainty, and so, as Hakewill observed in 1610, 'to leave a way open to oppression and bondage'. The royal prerogative remained indisputable only as long as it did not affect the liberty of the subject.[39]

37 Smith, *The common-wealth of England*, 93.
38 *PP 10*, ɪɪ, 235; *PP 28*, ɪɪ, 548, 555, 363, 576, ɪɪɪ, 307.
39 *PD 10*, 89; William Hakewill, *The libertie of the subject: against the pretended power of impositions* (1641) 12, 22; *CD 21*, ɪɪ, 193, ɪᴠ, 79, ᴠ, 59.

The common law was (under God) the ultimate arbiter of justice in England, and the supreme guardian of the subject's liberties. It was, said Coke, 'the most ancient and best inheritance that the subjects of this realm have', while Fuller regarded it as 'the high inheritance of the Realme, by which both the King and the subjects are directed'.[40] Except in Parliament, the king could never abrogate the slightest provision of the common law. Nor could he dispense anyone from the obligation to obey it. He did indeed possess a prerogative to dispense from statute, but not from the common law, for what was forbidden by the common law was *malum in se* – evil in itself – and had to be avoided by everyone and always. The common law attitude to the prerogative was not the invention of Coke and like-minded lawyers, but had a venerable Tudor and medieval ancestry. Indeed, the idea that the royal prerogative was derived from and limited by law was orthodox among Tudor lawyers. Moreover, the Tudor monarchs themselves accepted legal limitations upon their powers in practice, whatever high views of their authority they may have held in theory. James and Charles, by contrast, proved far more willing to test their theoretical claims at law, with results that some found catastrophic. For, succumbing to royal pressure, the judges failed to uphold the liberties of the subject – especially in Bate's Case of 1606 and the Five Knights' Case of 1627. The result was that a gulf opened between legal theory and practice.

Parliament was the one institution which could bridge this gulf – by reversing the decisions of the judges. But traditionally Parliament met only at the king's pleasure. Moreover, an Act of Parliament required the king's assent. While these prerogatives remained intact, the king could block any attempt to overrule the judges. From an early date a number of lawyers did in fact argue that it was (or should be made) law that Parliament meet regularly and not at the king's pleasure. In 1610 the House of Commons discussed proposals that Parliament be held every four, five or seven years. In 1621 Coke told the House that according to statutes dating from the reign of Edward III, Parliaments should be held annually. He also claimed that by precedents from King Alfred's reign they 'ought to be twice a year or oftner', and brought in a manuscript to prove it, 'because he was suspected by some malevolent persons to have devised them of his own head'. Parliament, Alford roundly told the same House of Commons, 'by the lawes of the kingdome ought to be kept everye yeare'. In 1628 Coke yet again insisted that annual Parliaments were prescribed by statutes of Edward III. By 1640 this idea had become commonplace. County petitions to the House of Commons at the time of the Short Parliament requested that measures be taken to put in force the laws requiring annual Parliaments, and Pym told the Commons that the 'intermission of Parliaments' was not only the foundation of all the subject's grievances, but itself a grievance, for 'by two statuts not repealed nor expired, a

---

40 Coke, *Reports*, 5, preface, f. iiia; Fuller, *The argument of Master Nicholas Fuller*, 3; cf. *PP 10*, ɪɪ, 152.

Parliament ought to bee once a yeare'. The statutes in question were Coke's old favourites – 4 Ed. III, c. 14 and 36 Ed. III, c. 10. When Parliament passed the Triennial Act in February 1641 it was merely acting on ideas that had long been familiar.[41] What was new was that the Long Parliament possessed the coercive power to ensure that these ideas were put into practice.

The second prerogative, namely the king's power to veto legislation, was not attacked until the Civil War and it is difficult to see how it could have been as long as the English believed that their country was a monarchy in something more than name. Yet Charles detected tendencies in this direction in the Commons of 1629: 'some have not doubted to mainteine, that the resolutions of that House must binde the Judges; a thing never heard of in ages past'.[42] If the decisions of the Commons bound the judges, there would be no need for statute – or for the king. Clearly, such ideas were innovatory, and so too was Coke's notion of annual Parliaments, despite his attempts to provide them with a respectable heritage. Yet, in the eyes of the lawyers, it was Charles who had innovated by undermining the rule of law and invading the property rights of his subjects. In principle, the common law was held to guarantee rights not only to individual subjects but also to the king. But it was the rights of the individual which took priority. When the judges failed to enforce the legal rights of the subject, the fundamental principles of the common law could only be vindicated extra-legally. Politics, and ultimately war, continued the rule of law by other means.

THE COMMON LAW AND NATURAL LAW

From Aquinas to Locke philosophers turned to the idea of natural law in order to delineate the contours of political society. The rights and duties of princes and subjects, they held, were deducible from certain fundamental principles which God had made self-evident to human reason. Using reason, everyone could understand how and for what purpose society and government had come into being. Once a general account of the philosophical origins of all government had been established, it was possible to speak with confidence of the extent and limitations of the powers of particular governments. As we have seen, there was a sharp division among writers in the natural law tradition between those who located original political sovereignty in the whole community and those who did not. But all agreed in placing the utmost weight upon the abstract philosophical question of the origins of government.

Many common lawyers, by contrast, paid little attention to the problem of origins. In their view, it simply did not matter a great deal how kings had first

41 *PP 10*, i, 279, ii, 71, 382; *CD 21*, ii, 22, iii, 136, v, 36, 116; *PP 28*, ii, 64–5, iii, 283; *PSP 40*, 275–7, 258–9. The idea that the law required annual Parliaments was proclaimed in print by Finch in 1627 – *Law, or, a discourse thereof*, 233 – and in court by Sir George Croke in 1638 – Gardiner, ed., *Notes of the judgment delivered by Sir George Croke*, 10. See also Pauline Croft, 'Annual Parliaments and the Long Parliament', *Bulletin of the Institute of Historical Research* 59 (1986) 155–71.
42 Charles I, *His maiesties declaration to all his loving subiects, of the causes which moved him to dissolve the last Parliament* (1628) 30.

acquired their power, since even if they had at one time been absolute rulers their government would later have become subject to customary limitations. Writers in the natural law tradition admitted that custom could acquire the force of law, but held that this took place only with the consent (at least tacit) of the ruler. The will of the lawmaker, in other words, was required to transform custom into law. The common lawyers, by contrast, believed that customary law was not *made* by anyone, and that it was superior to all laws which *were* made. So they were able to concede that kings derived their power from God alone and that they pre-dated all human laws, and still argue that once laws came into being they limited royal power.

Reporting the judges' decision on Calvin's Case of 1608, Coke presented a very conventional natural law account of the origins of government. 'The law of nature', he wrote, 'is that which God at the time of creation of the nature of man infused into his heart, for his preservation and direction; and this is *lex aeterna*, the moral law, called also the law of nature.' This law, he asserted, was the foundation and root of government: 'Aristotle . . . proveth that magistracy is of nature: for whatsoever is necessary and profitable for the preservation of the society of man is due by the law of nature: but magistracy and government are necessary and profitable for the preservation of the society of man; therefore magistracy and government are of nature.'

In the beginning, he claimed, 'Kings did decide causes according to natural equity, and were not tied to any rule or formality of law, but did *dare jura*' (make laws).[43] At one time, then, not only conquerors but all kings had been absolute rulers, accountable to God alone and limited by no human laws. There is no trace in Coke's writings of the notions – espoused by Selden – that democracy was the original form of government and that kings owed their power to a grant from the people. Yet, like Selden, he insisted that in contemporary England the power of the king was limited. In Coke's opinion, rational custom imposed limitations upon rulers, whatever the means by which their ancestors had gained power. Since custom was supreme, talk of philosophical origins was irrelevant.

Most common lawyers accepted the standard natural law doctrine of the necessity of government, but some gave it a highly distinctive twist, arguing that government became essential only after the introduction of property. This was the position of Thomas Hedley, who traced the origins of government to all people's desire to conserve their own property, and not to any 'natural necessity of association'. Again, Sir John Davies declared that 'the first and principal cause of making Kings, was to maintain property and Contracts, and Traffique, and Commerce amongst men'.[44] This line of thinking could easily be developed to show that *by nature* people could not be deprived of their goods without their own consent. If God and nature had set up government in order to preserve each individual's property, it would be

43 Coke, *Reports*, 7, ff. 12b–13a.
44 *PP 10*, ɪɪ, 192; Davies, *The question concerning impositions* (1656) 29.

contrary to natural law for a governor to take away what was his subjects' without their consent.

Usually, common lawyers were concerned to defend the legal rights of the English, not the natural rights of people in general. Yet they viewed the common law as an amalgam of custom and reason, of past English practices and universal moral truths. In emphasising the rational nature of English liberties, the lawyers came close to asserting that these liberties did, in fact, belong to everyone by nature. On occasion, they put forward the purely insular claim that the common law was ideally suited to the people of England. But they also maintained that it was superior to all foreign competitors. Because the English were free while the French or the Turks were slaves, England was more prosperous, more stable and better able to defend itself than these peoples. The implication was that the English constitution was suited not only to England but to all countries. Only by safeguarding individual freedom – the liberty of the subject – could any country be prosperous. When John Locke claimed that absolutism had been responsible for the impoverishment of lands ruled over by the Turks he was merely rehearsing a theme that was familiar to the early Stuart lawyers and, indeed, to Fortescue. Locke, unlike many of the lawyers, argued for a contractual theory of the origins of government. His achievement was to combine such a theory with a philosophical justification of the liberties for which the lawyers had stood.

Though rejecting the idea that royal power arose by contract, Coke and his colleagues imposed stringent limitations upon the king's authority. Kings, in Coke's view, derived their power from natural law modified by custom. 'Faith, obedience, and ligeance', he declared, 'are due by the law of nature.' This law 'never was nor could be changed'. Allegiance was not only natural but also unconditional: 'in point of Allegiance none must serve the King with Ifs and Ands'. Yet – and this is the crucial point – allegiance bound the subject only to obey the law, not the king's extra-legal commands. Coke was prepared to admit that the king had no human superior. He declared 'that the kingdom of England is an absolute monarchy, and that the king is the only supreme governor'. The king, however, was under the law. As the medieval law-book attributed to Bracton put it in a much-quoted phrase, the king was not below any man, but below God and the law.[45] Coke's arguments imposed restrictions upon kings. So did the theory of government by consent. On other points, however, the two approaches differed. While legal thinking stressed the rights of individuals, the natural law theorists emphasised the public good and the authority of the community as a whole. Modern democratic ideas owe a great deal to notions of contract and popular sovereignty which were current in the natural law tradition. Modern liberalism owes as much to the English common law.

---

45 Coke, *Reports*, 7, f. 13b; John Godbolt, *Reports of certain cases, arising in the severall courts of record at Westminster* (1654) 264; Bracton quoted in e.g. Coke, *Reports*, 4, p. xix.

How widespread was the doctrine of the ancient constitution? It is sometimes supposed that the idea was universally accepted, for, it is said, people feared innovation and therefore looked to the past as the only reliable source of political truths. That the English expressed hostility to innovation is true but unimportant. Innovation was a pejorative term. It is no more surprising that early Stuart politicians failed to advocate innovation than that their modern counterparts so rarely profess their allegiance to totalitarian ideals, whatever they may do in practice. The crucial point is that the English were far from united on what constituted innovation, since they held radically divergent ideas on the past and present constitution of the realm. It is well known that early modern English people were fond of citing precedents. But it is insufficiently noted that no one – not even the common lawyers – relied on 'bare precedents'. Not everything that had happened in the past constituted binding precedent for the present, since not all that had been done had been rightly done. Precedent had to be interpreted. Coke believed that the 'artificial reason' of the lawyer was the only instrument capable of doing this. Clerics preferred to rely on Scripture and natural law. James I argued that precedents taken from the reigns of weak kings did not count, advising Coke in 1621 'to bring precedents of good Kings times', since a grossly misleading picture of the constitution would result from placing any great weight upon the troublesome reigns of such monarchs as Henry VI and Richard II, when 'the Crown tossed up and down like a tennis ball'.[46]

The ideas of Coke and Fortescue were incontestably influential in the House of Commons. Yet we should not overrate their importance. Conrad Russell has been unable to find more than a 'few vocal adherents of Coke's doctrine of the ancient constitution'[47] in the Parliament of 1628. Even among common lawyers themselves many dissented from Coke's views on the constitution. Chief Baron Fleming in Bate's Case and Judge Berkeley in the trial of Hampden displayed a clear bias towards absolutism. So too did Sir Francis Bacon – an intellectual as well as a personal enemy of Coke – and Sir John Davies was also willing to grant the king far greater powers than Coke thought acceptable.

There are more general reasons for doubting that the ideas of Fortescue and the common lawyers dominated the political attitudes of England's ruling classes. Only one of Fortescue's works was published before 1714, and its printing history suggests that Fortescue was declining in popularity by the early seventeenth century. Published three times between 1567 and 1599, it was reprinted only once more before 1660. Of course, many gentlemen were educated at the Inns of Court. Doubtless this did something to popularise

---

46 James I quoted in W.J. Jones, *Politics and the Bench: the judges and the origins of the Civil War* (1971) 155; cf. F.H. Relf, ed., *Notes of the debates in the House of Lords officially taken by Robert Bowyer and Henry Elsing* (1929) 14. According to the latter version James acknowledged that Parliaments were held continuously in King Alfred's time, but claimed that anyone who would now 'have all done by parliament is an enemy to monarchie and a traitor to the King of England'.
47 Conrad Russell, 'The parliamentary career of John Pym, 1621–9', in Peter Clark, Alan G.R. Smith and Nicholas Tyacke, eds, *The English commonwealth 1547–1640* (Leicester 1979) 161.

Coke's ideas. Yet, as Wilfrid Prest has shown, it would be a mistake to over-rate the legal learning which most gentlemen acquired at the Inns. Their function was not only to educate the gentry in the law, but also to provide a finishing-school in which they could polish their manners. 'The mere fact of an individual's admission to an inn', says Prest, 'certainly cannot be taken as evidence that he received there a legal education of any kind.'[48] Coke's ideas may have exerted more influence upon the gentry than upon other groups of Englishmen, but even among gentlemen they possessed no monopoly. Some members of every early Stuart House of Commons stiffly opposed Coke's beliefs.

In this and the previous two chapters we have discussed the abstract polit-ical ideas of the English in the early seventeenth century. As we have seen, there were at least three distinct theories current in England. Were these the-ories of any practical importance? Academics are forever debating abstruse theoretical points, but their opinions rarely have any effect in the domain of politics. Occasionally, however, what begins as a learned controversy ends as a political or even military conflict. The differences of opinion on the nature of God's grace between the Dutch theologians Arminius and Gomarus had the most profound political consequences, not only in Holland but also in England. In the next section of this book we shall see that the disagreements on matters of political and constitutional theory of, say, James I and Sir Edward Coke, had equally far-reaching effects.

48 Prest, *Inns of Court*, 153.

PART TWO

Applications

CHAPTER 4

Conflict and Compromise

Three major political theories divided the English in the early seventeenth century. The first – royal absolutism – received its most vociferous support from the clergy, while the third – Coke's doctrine of the ancient constitution – was usually expressed by common lawyers, particularly in the House of Commons. Of course, the mere existence of divergences of opinion on matters of political theory does not entail any sort of political conflict, far less civil war. It would be wrong to suppose that serried ranks of absolutists, armed to the teeth, stood ready to fight their ideological opponents in 1603, though it is clear enough that ideas which were familiar in 1603 had by 1642 acquired the greatest and most immediate political importance. Obviously, political co-operation is possible among people who hold divergent opinions. Old opponents enter into uneasy alliance in the face of common danger – say, from foreign fascists, or papists.

In the sixteenth century the Tudor monarchs generally ruled according to law, as Professor Elton demonstrated. This does not, of course, mean that the Tudors themselves believed that their powers were limited by the laws of the land. Since Henry VIII was usually able to effect his policies by legal means, he had no need to resort to extra-legal expedients. Moreover, under Henry and Elizabeth the crown had urgent and pressing concerns – the implementation of the Reformation, the Tudor revolution in government, and the defence of the realm against invasion. Success in these required the support of the political nation. So the Tudors steered clear of such sensitive questions as the ultimate origins of political authority and the relations between the crown and the law. By the 1590s, indeed, Elizabethan clerics were expressing nakedly absolutist ideas, but it was not until the accession of James I that an English sovereign gave unequivocal support to such views.

James was most unusual among English monarchs, for he was a scholar. In 1598 he published *The true law of free monarchies* in which he set forth a fully fledged theory of royal absolutism. When James came to England he republished this work, and throughout his reign he continued to maintain the same political ideas both in print and in a series of long, flowery, and exceedingly boastful speeches. Whatever his failings, undue modesty was not among them. Both James and Charles were convinced that God had entrusted them with sole and sovereign authority to govern their subjects. James lost few opportunities to preach this message, while Charles, though he made his opinions perfectly plain, took less delight in advertising them except when provoked. He stuttered, and had no love of speech-making. Of course, it is one thing to believe that you hold supreme power in England and quite another to govern in a lawless, arbitrary way. Both James and Charles were God-fearing men who thought that they had a duty to rule in an orderly, law-abiding manner. Moreover, without a paid bureaucracy or a standing army the crown was dependent upon the co-operation of the gentry for the enforcement of good government. In these circumstances it was often prudent to tone down the more controversial implications of absolutist theory and to adopt the rhetoric of compromise. The early Stuart kings believed that they possessed absolute power, but were quite willing to promise that they would rule in the public interest and with the consent of their subjects. 'The love of the people is the king's protection', declared some of Charles I's gold coins, while others insisted that 'kingdoms flourish through concord'.[1]

Unfortunately, the kings' promises to rule well did not always satisfy the more sceptical of their subjects. Firstly, the mere assertion of absolutist ideas by clergymen and by the kings themselves aroused suspicions. If the king thought that he could flout the law, what guarantee was there that he would not in fact do so? To anyone convinced that the subject's liberties were rights guaranteed by a law higher than the king's will, doctrines of royal absolutism seemed at best misguided and at worst pernicious errors which threatened the fundamental constitution of the realm. Few, except Catholics, had the temerity to attack the political writings of James I himself, but his ideas, as expressed by lesser men, came under heavy fire in the House of Commons. The attack on Cowell in 1610 and on Maynwaring in 1628 are examples of ideological conflict at its crudest. In this chapter we shall discuss such cases, in which the mere expression of political ideas served to arouse conflict. We shall also investigate the various ways in which attempts were made to reconcile the competing ideologies.

Secondly, it seemed to many that royal undertakings to safeguard the liberties of the subject were not borne out by the king's actions. The two liberties which attracted most attention were the subject's exemptions from taxation and legislation without consent. James I's impositions – new and extra-Parliamentary levies on exports and imports – were often construed as striking at both exemptions. Still more serious were the financial expedients of Charles I. The Forced Loan of 1627 was widely regarded as a violation of the most fundamental principles of the English constitution. The arrest (without cause shown) of refusers of the Loan dramatically raised the question of the king's power to

---

1 *Standard catalogue of British coins: vol. 1: coins of England and the United Kingdom*, 20th edn, ed. P. Frank Purvey (1984) 306–7.

imprison his subjects. Charles's obvious reluctance to allow the legality of the Loan to be tested in court suggested that he was prepared to subjugate the law to his own convenience. The billeting of troops, the enforcement of martial law, the purging of dissidents in the universities, and the introduction of religious policies which flouted the spirit if not the letter of statute law, confirmed the conclusion that Charles was, in fact, subverting the constitution and introducing absolute government. Under James, people had feared for the future. Under his son, it was the present which terrified them. Yet, by modern standards, Charles's rule does not look all that tyrannical. He was no Hitler. Why, then, did his policies arouse resentment? The answer is that within the framework of anti-absolutist theories Charles's rule was indeed tyrannical. In other words, it was because they held certain political views that people opposed the king's policies. Equally, it was Charles's own political outlook which led him to act as he did. This will be the theme of Chapter 5.

ABSOLUTISM: ATTACK AND COUNTER-ATTACK

Absolutist ideas were sometimes expressed in legal decisions and Parliamentary debates, but more often and more fully in sermons and treatises. The printed works of James I were perhaps the most famous expositions of the doctrine. In addition to the *True law*, the king also wrote three anti-Catholic works, namely *Triplici nodo triplex cuneus, or an apologie for the oath of allegiance* (1608), the *Premonition* (1609), and the *Remonstrance for the right of kings* (1616). These books were written in defence of the oath of allegiance which had been imposed upon Catholics in 1606, and which sparked off a prolonged war of words between papists and Protestants. James and his supporters in this controversy claimed that kings derived their powers from God alone and were therefore accountable to neither pope nor people. They portrayed kings as sovereign lawmakers, not as bound by the law of the land. When the exact meaning of some words in the oath was disputed, the king's supporters argued that James's interpretation had to be accepted as definitive, for he had made the law imposing the oath.[2]

As we have seen, Catholics denied the *jure divino* origins of royal authority, arguing that the king's power arose by an act of transference from the people. They claimed that the Divine Right theory of kingship was not only false but also innovative. John Floyd, replying to the absolutist dialogue entitled *God and the king*, took issue with its central thesis that 'Kings have power only from God', asserting that this was 'a paradox which scarce any Christian Divine holdes'. He contended that 'Catholicks, Puritans, forraine Protestants, even our English Conformitants, derive regall authority from the Commonwealth', and cited the Elizabethans Hooker and Bilson as English examples. Robert Parsons detected innovative errors in *Triplici nodo*, suggesting that the

2 Lancelot Andrewes, *Tortura Torti*, ed. J. Bliss (Oxford 1851) 11; Thomas Preston, *A new-yeares gift for English Catholikes* (1620) 89–90; William Warmington, *A moderate defence of the oath of allegiance* (1612) 67.

clergy must have seen it through the press without informing the king, since James was so learned that he could not have failed to correct its many mistakes. Since the book had been written by James, as Parsons was almost certainly aware, it is hardly surprising that the king was not amused by the Jesuit's comments, to which he thought that 'a rope is the fittest answere'.[3]

Catholic polemicists were able to avoid the rope by living and publishing abroad. Puritan authors in exile on the Continent occasionally made anti-absolutist statements, though they usually confined their remarks to the king's ecclesiastical policies. In the 1630s Prynne, Burton and Bastwick published secretly in England.[4] Their pamphlets attacked many aspects of government policy, and commented scathingly on the political ideas current among the higher clergy. They were severely punished for their efforts. As long as the bishops controlled the press, it was difficult and dangerous to publish anything outspokenly critical of absolutism. It could be perilous to possess even manuscripts hostile to the government, as the case of the Somerset clergyman Edmond Peacham demonstrated in 1615 (he was tortured and executed for writing an attack on James's regime, though he did not circulate it). So it was in the House of Commons – protected by its own privileges or rights of self-discipline – that the most vigorous indictments of absolutism were heard, though even in the Commons there were limits to what anyone could safely say.

'The differences between government and opposition', it has been argued, 'did not reflect radically different political philosophies', for the prevailing political theory was challenged only by 'the occasional wild clergyman – Cowell, Maynwaring or Montagu', and even in the case of these oddities their 'views, on close analysis, were rarely as revolutionary as their tone'.[5] A common modern attitude is that the ideas of Cowell and Maynwaring were highly unusual, and that their books were readily condemned by all. As we shall see, this latter contention is incorrect. Moreover, there was nothing exceptional about the absolutist ideas which they propounded, though both men were rather more explicit on the practical implications of these ideas than was usual. Absolutist ideas were common, particularly among the clergy, and this fact was frequently recognised – and bemoaned – in the House of Commons.

In 1610 Richard Martin warned the House that 'the Kings wants may drive him to extremities'. This was particularly likely, he argued, if the king listened to the advice of clerics. Absolutist ideas were rife among churchmen, he said, because 'the highway to get into a double benefice or to a higher dignity is to tread upon the neck of the common law'. There were 'sermons made

3 John Floyd, *God and the king* (St Omer 1620) 32; Robert Parsons, *The iudgment of a Catholicke English-man* (St Omer 1608) 2; James I, *Premonition*, in *An apologie for the oath of allegiance . . . Together with a premonition of his maiesties*, 2nd issue (1609) 13.
4 For obvious reasons the place of publication of these works is often difficult to establish. Stephen Foster, *Notes from the Caroline underground* (Hamden, Conn. 1978) especially 76, 78, argues that most of them were published in the Netherlands, but his evidence is not decisive.
5 Michael Hawkins, 'The government: its role and aims', in Conrad Russell, ed., *The origins of the English Civil War* (1973) 38, 42.

every day to rail upon the fundamental laws of the kingdom'. Martin drew up a bill to purge this evil. It proposed that clerics who preached against the subject's liberty should be hanged. Some of his friends suggested that this was rather harsh. Martin revised his bill. The second version replaced the death penalty with enslavement, so that the guilty ecclesiastics 'might feel that bondage which they would lay upon others'. But his friends once more dissuaded him. Finally, he proposed that the penalty for a first offence should be 'loss of all their dignities', while a second would result in a praemunire – loss of goods and imprisonment during the king's pleasure. 'If this may pass', he declared, 'it may, I hope, somewhat secure us; if it do not, yet we shall do well to leave a monument behind us that may shew to posterity we do unwillingly endure servitude.'[6]

There was no possibility that such a bill would be passed for law. The bishops were certain to vote against it in the Lords not only because they objected to its contents but also because they resented lay interference in the affairs of the clergy. The king was unlikely to give it his assent. So Martin's measure was quietly dropped. Yet his fears of clerical absolutism were shared by many. Cowell, and later Maynwaring, were attacked precisely because their views were known to be widespread. In 1610 Whitelocke warned the clergy not to attempt to 'overthrow the antient laws and liberties of the kingdom', citing the fate of the Amicable Grant and of its author, Wolsey. By 1628 it was clear that clerics had not heeded this advice, and the fact that promotion in the church was going to those ecclesiastics who 'preached (or rather prated) in our pulpits that all we have is the Kings' was noted with alarm. Sir Dudley Digges detected 'damnable danger' in Maynwaring's book because he thought that 'a great many churchmen are gone too far in this kind'. That the ecclesiastical authorities were bent upon a policy of subverting the laws was one of the most frequently voiced contentions in Commons' speeches of 1628–29. When Parliament was summoned again in 1640, members of the Lower House reverted to the same theme, attacking those who preached 'the Kings prerogative that the king hath an unlimmitted power and that the subjects have no property in their goods'. More specifically, Dr William Beale, Master of St John's College Cambridge and a royal chaplain, was summoned before the House to answer charges that in a sermon delivered five years earlier he had argued 'that all we had was ye Kings', and had inveighed against Parliament which, he said, 'seemed to give with one hand but did take away more with ye other, using the King as men did Apes, with a bit and a knock'.[7]

The bishops did not take kindly to attacks on the clergy or the royal prerogative. There were, of course, exceptions to this rule, especially in the years after 1625 when the rise of Arminianism created a major split among

6 *PP 10*, ii, 328–9; cf. *PD 10*, 131–2. The speaker is far more likely to have been the common lawyer Richard Martin than the careerist Civil lawyer Henry Marten.
7 *ST*, ii, 484–5; *PP 28*, ii, 56; iii, 405; cf. *CD 29*, 15–16, 52, 68–9; *PSP 40*, 142, 204. Digges made a similar point in 1614: *CJ* 496.

churchmen. George Abbot, for example, became a vigorous critic of royal policies, and, more mutedly, of absolutist ideas, in the later 1620s.[8] But on the whole the alliance between the king and the ecclesiastical authorities stood firm. This alliance was, indeed, a central feature of the political and intellectual history of the period. When the Commons questioned Cowell's ideas in 1610, Archbishop Bancroft returned their fire in the Lords. He knew, Bancroft said, that he was suspected of inclining too much towards the king's authority, but denied the charge. Nevertheless, he made his true feelings plain, at least on the question of taxation, by arguing that 'in speculative divinity' 'the King must be relieved in his necessity'. In other words, it was the duty and not the right of subjects to grant the king taxes when he needed them. He referred contemptuously to the common lawyers, who maintained the opposite point of view, and who arrogantly thought that their trivial learning was superior to theology: 'nowadays every man, though he have not read more than the first leaf of Littleton, is able to teach the best doctor of divinity'. As long as affairs remained in this state, he argued, the future looked bleak: 'what will come of it God knows, and wise men may foresee it'.[9]

This outburst may have allowed the aged prelate to unburden his soul, but, from the point of view of political expediency it was ill-advised. The king's interest in Parliament was to raise taxes, and speeches of the kind delivered by Bancroft were unlikely to put the Commons in a mood to vote them. This was amply illustrated by a speech delivered in the House of Lords in 1614 by Richard Neile, Bishop of Lincoln. Neile claimed that those who questioned the king's right to levy impositions – that is to say, the Commons – were guilty of breaking the oath of allegiance. The Commons angrily refused to continue business until the affair was settled.[10]

In print, clergymen concentrated their efforts upon refuting ideas of legitimate resistance and of the contractual origins of government. Outside the legal fraternity, few political writers paid much attention to Coke's theory of the ancient constitution. One reason for this was that from the perspective of natural law theory Coke's ideas did not make much sense. Lawyers' claims for the superiority and excellence of the common law seemed mere boastfulness. 'It were a foule disparagement', wrote Godfrey Goodman, 'to compare the learning of all ages, the learning of the whole world, the knowledge of God and nature, with any private or provinciall lawes.' The substance of human laws, he claimed, was taken from scholastic divinity, or, as he put it, 'school-learning': 'all their wisdom is onely borrowed from school-learning'. Human laws might vary on such ephemeral matters as 'the formes of their writs', or 'the manner of their proceedings', but 'the ground and reason of their law, is

---

8 Abbot's ideas are set out in his account of Sibthorp's book, *ST*, ɪɪ, 1453–80. He does not commit himself on the question of whether the laws of the land are superior to the king's will, but inclines to an affirmative answer on e.g. col. 1460.

9 *PP 10*, ɪɪ, 79; cf. ɪ, 81. Bancroft's repeated distinction between speculation and practice almost certainly alludes to the Commons' proceedings against Cowell: ibid., ɪ, 24–5.

10 *CJ* ɪ, 499; *PP 1614*, 361–4; cf. T.L. Moir, *The Addled Parliament of 1614* (Oxford 1958) 117ff.

onely taken from schoole-learning'. So, he concluded, 'our schoole-learning doth as farre exceed all the lawes in the world, in the excellencie of their wisedome and knowledge, as the lawes of God and nature, are much wiser then the lawes of men'.[11]

Since divinity was superior to law, the ideas of the lawyers were of no consequence in establishing the truth. The notion that custom was superior to man-made law was rejected by absolutists and contractualists alike. In their view, the concept of a law without a legislator was mere nonsense. Like many others, the Jesuit Robert Parsons dissented from Coke's opinion that the English common laws were literally immemorial: 'I, for my parte, finde noe memory of any of them extant, before the Conquest.' But his main grievance with Coke was theoretical. 'To avouch a Common-law', he wrote, 'without beginning, author, cause, occasion, or recorde of the introduction thereof, is a strange Metaphysicall contemplation; for that lawes doe not growe up without beginning, but must needs be made or admitted by some Prince or people.' The point could hardly have been put more clearly. Parsons was replying to a work in which Coke had claimed that by the ancient common laws of England the monarch was Supreme Governor of the church. In defence of the Supremacy, English churchmen often attacked Parsons on grounds drawn from God's natural and positive laws. But they rarely said anything in defence of Coke's ideas. Some, indeed, took secret delight in seeing the judge trounced by a Jesuit.[12]

Parsons, living in Rome, could mount a detailed attack on Coke's ideas with impunity. English clerics were in a less enviable position. Slighting comments on Parliament or the ancient liberties of the subject could result in trouble. In 1604 John Thornborough, Bishop of Bristol, was called in question by the House of Commons for belittling Parliament in a tract which advocated union between England and Scotland. But the most graphic illustrations of the difficulties which might be encountered by those who asserted absolutist ideas were the cases of Cowell and Maynwaring.

THE CASE OF JOHN COWELL

Few episodes in the ideological struggle between absolutists and their opponents have been so frequently misunderstood as the condemnation of John Cowell's *Interpreter* in 1610. The basic facts are these. John Cowell was an eminent Civil lawyer. In 1594 he became Regius Professor of Civil Law at Cambridge, and in 1598 he was appointed Master of Trinity Hall in the same university. He was a close friend of Richard Bancroft, who in 1604 became

11 Godfrey Goodman, *The fall of man, or the corruption of nature, proved by the light of our naturall reason* (1616) 136–7; cf. 171, and on Goodman's attitude towards lawyers cf. Sir Charles Ogilvie, *The king's government and the common law 1471–1641* (Oxford 1958) 86.
12 Parsons, *An answere to the fifth part of reportes lately set forth by Syr Edward Coke* (St Omer 1606) 12–13, 267; cf. Henry Parker, *The case of shipmony briefly discoursed* (1640) 15; Dennis Flynn, 'Irony in Donne's *Biathanatos* and *Pseudo-Martyr*', *Recusant History* 12 (1973) 59–60.

Archbishop of Canterbury, and who appointed Cowell vicar-general of Canterbury four years later.[13] Both men believed in strong royal power and a clergy independent of lay control. Cowell's absolutism was expressed as early as 1606 when at Bancroft's request he drew up arguments to show 'that the king hath power to hear and determine all kinds of causes when it shall so please his majesty'.[14] In 1607 Cowell published *The Interpreter: or booke containing the signification of words*, which was, for the most part, an innocuous academic work. Published at Cambridge, it was a law dictionary which set out in alphabetical order a number of common legal terms and provided definitions and brief commentaries. As a modern and straightforward introduction to the law, Cowell's book proved a best-seller in the seventeenth century. Its nearest present-day equivalents are perhaps such works as *Teach yourself law*, or *Law made simple*.

The reason why Cowell's book attracted attention in 1610 was threefold. Firstly, it poked fun at the medieval common lawyer Sir Thomas Littleton, whose *Tenures* Coke described as 'the most perfect and absolute work that ever was written in any human science'.[15] Secondly, it claimed that English legal practice did not adequately recognise the rights of the clergy. In particular, Cowell argued, the clergy had traditionally been represented in the House of Commons, and ever since this custom had been discontinued 'the Church hath daily grown weaker and weaker'. He added a prayer 'that her liberties be better maintained'. Cowell also disapproved of writs of prohibition by which cases could be withdrawn from ecclesiastical to common law courts. When papal jurisdiction had existed in England, he said, there had been some point in these writs, since they had allowed the king, acting through the temporal courts, to control the activities of the popish clergy. But since the Reformation, ecclesiastical jurisdiction had itself been brought under direct royal control, so that there was now no need for the king to govern the church indirectly through the secular courts. In these circumstances, prohibitions served little purpose other than 'to wearie the subject by many quircks and delayes, from obtaining his right'.[16]

Thirdly, and crucially, Cowell's *Interpreter* included a small number of passages in which he maintained that the king was an absolute monarch, whose powers were not limited by any human laws. The king, he remarked, 'is above the Law by his absolute power'. The liberties of the subject were not rights, but privileges held at the king's discretion. In practice, Cowell admitted, English kings usually made laws in Parliament and he regarded this custom as 'a mercifull policie, and also a politique mercie (not alterable without great perill)'. Yet he made it plain that the king could alter this arrangement if

13 B.P. Levack, *The Civil lawyers in England 1603–1641* (Oxford 1973) 221.
14 BL Lansdowne Mss 211, f. 141.
15 John Cowell, *The Interpreter: or book containing the signification of words* (Cambridge 1607) sig. 2S2b; Sir Edward Coke, *The first part of the institutes* (1628) preface, sig. 2 π 1b; cf. Coke, *The reports*, ed. G. Wilson (1776) 10, preface, f. xviib.
16 Cowell, *Interpreter*, sig. 3F3a–b.

he pleased: 'simply to binde the prince to or by these laws, were repugnant to the nature and constitution of an absolute monarchy'.[17]

Cowell's book was published after the end of the Parliamentary session of 1606–7. A new session did not begin until 9 February 1610. On the 15th Lord Treasurer Cecil delivered a long speech giving a detailed account of royal finances. His objective was to encourage the Commons to 'consider of some such supply as will make this state both safe and happy'.[18] In other words, he wanted them to vote the king a large amount of money. James's primary interest in the session was financial. He was reluctant to allow other issues to distract the Commons from voting taxes. It was in these circumstances that John Hoskins brought Cowell's book to the attention of the House on 23 February. It was possibly on the same day that he also 'produced several treatises containing as much as Dr Cowell's book'.[19] Hoskins was a common lawyer who had made his fortune by marrying a rich widow. In the Parliament of 1610 he proved himself a staunch defender of the subject's liberties, and a critic of various royal policies, notably the deprivation of ministers under the ecclesiastical canons of 1604 and the king's favouritism towards the Scots. He reverted to this latter theme in the Parliament of 1614, delivering a notoriously inflammatory speech for which he was imprisoned in the Tower.[20]

The House appointed a committee to investigate the *Interpreter* and decided to proceed against Cowell. With this in mind, the Commons sent a message to the Lords on 27 February. The *Interpreter*, they claimed, contained 'Matter of Scandal and offence towards the High Court of Parliament, and is otherways of dangerous Consequence and Example'.[21] The Commons asked for a conference between committees drawn from both Houses, and after some dispute the Lords agreed.[22] At the conference, on 2 March, Sir Henry Hobart, the Attorney-General, summed up the views of the Lower House on Cowell and his book. The argument that the king could legislate outside Parliament was, said Hobart, 'a presumptuous novelty' which struck at the *'lapis angularis'* – the cornerstone – of the English system of government. Richard Martin then read the passages to which the Commons objected. The proceedings of the conference were duly reported in the House of Lords on 3 March.[23]

One point that had emerged very clearly by this time was that a majority in the House of Commons was eager to see Cowell suffer. As early as 1 March

---

17 Ibid., sig. 2Q1a, 3A3b.
18 *PP 10*, ii, 9–27, on p. 24.
19 *CJ* 399; William Petyt, *Miscellanea Parliamentaria* (1680) 66. Petyt cites no evidence to confirm his claim that Hoskins produced treatises other than Cowell's.
20 *CJ* 399; *PP 14*, 422–3; *PP 10*, ii, 344; Moir, *Addled Parliament*, 138. An important reappraisal of the traditional but dubious thesis that Hoskins was an innocent tool of the Spanish faction is in Linda Levy Peck, 'The Earl of Northampton, merchant grievances and the Addled Parliament of 1614', *HJ* 24 (1981) 533–52, at 550.
21 *CJ* 399; *LJ* 557.
22 Robert Bowyer, 'The proceedings in Parliament anno 7° Jac: Imi against a booke writt by Dr Cowell', in Petyt Mss 538/2 ff. 158–65, f. 161b. Bancroft claimed that it was 'unfitt' for the Commons to 'fall upon a matter of this nature' when they should be discussing supply: ibid., f. 161a.
23 *PP 10*, i, 24–5; *LJ* 561.

a letter-writer noted that the Commons had petitioned the king, asking that they be allowed to 'proceed by their Authority against the said Cowell'. If the king permitted this, the writer added, 'it is thought they will go very near to hang him'. What is equally notable, however, is that the House of Lords was far less hungry for Cowell's blood. Indeed, it is doubtful that they ever intended to condemn the book. On 27 February, when the Commons first asked for a conference, Archbishop Bancroft told the Upper House that 'he knew Cowell to be a very honest man and sufficient scholar', and expressed the hope that the Lords 'would not deal sharply with him, seeing he assured himself he meant nothing in any evil manner'. Bancroft had a special interest in Cowell's case. The two men were close friends, and the *Interpreter* had been dedicated to the archbishop – though Bancroft cautiously denied any responsibility for the book's contents. Yet there is little evidence that the other Lords dissented from Bancroft's views.[24]

On 5 March the Upper House resumed its deliberations. Cecil spoke to particularly telling effect. On what grounds, he asked, could Cowell be punished? The only answer he could find was that the book might have breached Parliamentary privilege, though he was sceptical about this since it had been written when Parliament was not sitting: 'the book, being written out of parliament, and touching no particular member of the body, for to punish in this particular, not knowing whether there were any the like precedent or any near hereunto, he liked not'. If Cowell had not infringed privilege, Cecil continued, there was no reason to punish him: 'for else he could not for any reasons he saw yet give consent for his punishment'. Cecil suggested that precedents be consulted, and that in the meantime good relations be maintained with the House of Commons. The Lords liked this motion, asking their clerk Bowyer to 'search precedents in this nature', and inviting the Commons to a second conference to be held on 8 March.[25]

Before this conference took place the situation changed dramatically with the personal intervention of the king. On the morning of 8 March Cecil told the Lords that 'the King doth take exceptions at Cowell's book and is pleased to give me leave to deliver this that followeth'. He then summarised the king's criticisms of the *Interpreter*. Cowell, said James, was 'too bold with the common law, which being the law he enjoyeth, he and all others ought to reverence that law under which government he breatheth'. Moreover, 'he mistaketh the dignity of parliament and over-curiously writes in that subject, which is out of his proper element'. James asserted that 'by the law of Latin nations and the law of this realm he hath as absolute power as ever any monarch in this kingdom'. Yet he admitted that 'in a settled state and commonwealth' – such as contemporary England – it was dangerous to question accepted constitutional procedures, and he expressed his dislike of Cowell's doctrines that the king could legislate or levy taxes without the consent of

24 Beaulieu to Trumbull, 1 March 1610, in E. Sawyer, ed., *Memorials of affairs of state . . . collected chiefly from the original papers of Sir Ralph Winwood*, 3 vols (1725) III, 125; *PP 10*, I, 18, 29.
25 *PP 10*, I, 27.

Parliament. For his own part, said James, he never meant to rule arbitrarily, but would always 'prefer the public good to his own wishes' (*anteponere salutem populi ante voluntatem*). Most significantly, the king reprimanded Cowell for discussing the royal 'power and prerogative', declaring that these things should not be brought into question. He would be 'careful and anxious', he said, 'that the parliament shall not be troubled hereafter with such businesses'.[26]

Cecil expressed his own agreement with his royal master's views, observing that 'there are some things in the book very idle'. At the conference that afternoon Cecil told the Commons' committee of the king's decision to suppress the *Interpreter*. Henceforth the Lower House dropped its case against Cowell. James had already interviewed the professor, and on 17 March it was reported that he had seen him again, this time to question him on 'some other Passages of his Book, which do as well pinch upon the Authority of the King, as the other Points were derogatorie to the liberty of the Subject'. Finally, on 25 March, James issued a proclamation condemning the *Interpreter*. This proclamation bemoaned the idle curiosity of the times, which led people to 'go out of their element, and meddle with things above their capacity'. The book, it claimed, was a striking example of the errors to which this could lead. Cowell had said things which were 'derogatory to the supreme power of this crown'. He had also mistaken 'the true state of the Parliament of this kingdom', and had spoken 'unreverently of the common law of England'. In order to prevent 'the said errors and inconveniences' from being repeated in the future, the king prohibited the buying, selling or reading of the book and commanded all those who possessed copies to hand them in.[27]

It is commonly supposed that Cowell's ideas were highly unusual, that they were willingly denounced by all, and that they had little or no influence.[28] According to one recent account, for example, it is 'well known' that 'both Parliament and James I agreed readily in condemning the book just because of his statements on the prerogative, a plain acknowledgement of what the right doctrine was thought to be'. This 'right doctrine' was that the king's prerogative is 'governed by the law', indeed that it is 'a department of the law'. Deluded by 'non-English laws and precedents', and influenced by Bodin, Cowell went astray. So his ideas stand outside the orthodox tradition of English constitutional thought.[29]

There are several problems with this account. As we have seen, Parliament did not condemn the *Interpreter*, and it cannot be shown that the House of Lords ever intended to do so. Moreover, it is not clear that it was because of its arguments in favour of an unlimited prerogative that James I took exception to the book. The proclamation against Cowell did not even mention the

26 Ibid., 28–9.
27 Ibid., 30, 31; Sir Thomas Edmondes to Winwood, 17 March 1610, in Sawyer, ed., *Memorials of . . . Winwood*, iii, 137; *SRP*, i, 244.
28 The best account of Cowell's thought is S.B. Chrimes, 'The constitutional ideas of Dr John Cowell', *EHR* 64 (1949) 461–87. It stresses his originality.
29 G.R. Elton, 'The rule of law in sixteenth-century England', in *Studies in Tudor and Stuart politics and government: papers and reviews 1946–1972*, 2 vols (Cambridge 1974) i, 260–84, at 268.

prerogative, and was studiously vague on the reasons for which the *Interpreter* was suppressed. Of course, it is true that the king's message of 8 March criticised Cowell for discussing the prerogative. The point that James was trying to get across was that he did not want his subjects to debate his powers. As Cecil told the Commons' committee, the 'Prerogative of Princes is a thinge which will admitt no disputacion'. 'It was dangerous', said James, 'to submit the power of a kinge to definition.' In short, what the king objected to was the fact that Cowell had discussed the prerogative at all, not that he had adopted the 'wrong' view of the matter.[30]

When Hoskins introduced the subject of the *Interpreter* on 23 February, his intention was to bring into the open what he considered to be the subversive ideas of Cowell and like-minded writers. He was interested in Cowell precisely because he believed that such ideas were becoming widespread. He – and the majority of the Commons – hoped to condemn the ideas along with the book. This project did not succeed. The king intervened in order to prevent Parliament from wasting on Cowell's case precious time which could be better devoted to debating financial measures, and in particular the Great Contract whereby James proposed to forgo certain customary revenues in return for a regular income from Parliament. He was also eager to avoid public discussion of the prerogative. By promising to suppress the book James achieved both objectives. In fact, the proclamation against Cowell was so worded that it was far from clear for what his book was being condemned. It said that Cowell had misconstrued the true nature of Parliament, but gave no indication of how the professor had erred, or what Parliament's true nature was. In passing, it is worth noting that the proclamation probably had little effect, and James may well have been aware of this. On 1 April 1609 the king himself published a book against Catholic political ideas. A week later, having found that the volume contained many printing errors, he suppressed it by proclamation and demanded that copies which had already been bought be returned. Of the 800 copies sold, only 15 were handed back.[31]

Cowell's book was not published illicitly, but by the press of one of England's most influential institutions – Cambridge University. It escaped criticism for more than two years. Its arguments were unoriginal, though it explored the constitutional implications of absolutist theory in more detail than was customary. This was the reason why it proved such an inviting target for the House of Commons in 1610. Of course, the *Interpreter* was not primarily a work of political theory. It should not surprise us that later theorists rarely quoted it. If we ask whether Cowell's ideas were influential, the answer must be that absolutist ideas were well known while Cowell was not. Yet the *Interpreter* was sometimes quoted. Civil lawyers drew upon it occasionally, but more interesting is a passage from a work on Parliament by Ralph Starkey, first published in 1628 and reprinted in revised form in

30 *PD 10*, 23, 24.
31 *CSPV 1607–10*, 297.

1641.[32] In this book Starkey asserted that according to Civil lawyers 'of these two one must needs be true, that either the King is above the Parliament, that is the positive Law of the Kingdom; or else that he is not an absolute King'. The Civil lawyers, he continued, believed that it was 'a merciful policy, and also a politick mercy, not alterable without great peril' that kings legislate only in Parliament, 'yet simply to bind the King to or by those Laws, were repugnant to the nature and constitution of an absolute Monarchy'. With minor variations these were direct quotations from the *Interpreter*. Starkey was a singularly ignorant commentator on Parliamentary procedure, and, as such, perhaps more representative of lay opinion than many men of greater learning. The facts that he took Cowell's views to be typical of the ideas of Civil lawyers as a whole, and that he regarded these ideas as plausible – he said nothing to refute them – are sufficient to suggest that the *Interpreter*, despite its condemnation, left its mark upon the minds of later generations.[33]

As a footnote to the episode of John Cowell and his book, it is worth pointing out that the *Interpreter* was republished in 1637. Later, his enemies rather dubiously laid responsibility for this at the door of Archbishop Laud. Some writers have equally dubiously supposed that the edition of 1637 had been shorn of the politically sensitive passages. They have, presumably, relied upon the notion that Cowell's un-English absolutism was universally condemned in 1610 and could not, therefore, have been revived at a later date. The myth of the expurgation of the second edition of the *Interpreter* was first launched upon the world in 1701 and has often been repeated since. In fact, nothing was changed.[34]

Cowell took an absolutist line on the question of the king's power, but did not intend, in writing the *Interpreter*, to defend any particular royal policy. Roger Maynwaring and Robert Sibthorp, by contrast, composed their notorious sermons of 1627 to encourage payment of the Forced Loan. Yet the general theory underlying the sermons was much the same as that informing Cowell's work. Like the *Interpreter*, the sermons incurred the wrath of the House of Commons.

MAYNWARING AND SIBTHORP

Denouncing absolutist theory in the first of his *Two treatises*, John Locke looked back in anger on its origins in England. 'By whom this Doctrine came

32 Ralph Starkey, *The privileges and practice of Parliaments* (1628) was reprinted in *The manner of holding Parliaments in England* (1641) 42–95. These books are discussed in S. Lambert, 'Procedure in the House of Commons in the early Stuart period', *EHR* 95 (1980) 753–81, at 756–7 n. 3.
33 *The manner of holding Parliaments*, 91, reprinted from Starkey, *Priviledges*, 41. Like Cowell, the Civil lawyers Gentili and Zouch 'placed legislative sovereignty with the king alone': Levack, *Civil lawyers*, 103.
34 Chrimes, 'The constitutional ideas of Dr John Cowell', 474; Cowell, *Interpreter* (1701) preface, sig. b2b; W.S. Holdsworth, *A history of English law*, v (1924) 21 n. 2; Faith Thompson, *Magna Carta: its role in the making of the English constitution 1300–1629* (Minneapolis 1948) 236; Christopher Brooks and Kevin Sharpe, 'History, English law and the Renaissance', *Past and Present* 72 (1976) 133–42, at 138 and n.

at first to be broach'd', he wrote, 'and brought in fashion amongst us, and what sad Effects it gave rise to, I leave to Historians to relate, or to the Memory of those who were contemporaries with Sibthorp and Maynwaring to recollect.'[35] Recent scholars have likewise portrayed the ideas of the two clerics – and especially Maynwaring – as innovatory. Their high-flown notions, we are told, exerted little influence, even on Charles himself. The king may have 'listened complacently enough to Maynwaring's absolutist theories', but 'he did not necessarily agree with' such opinions, for his own political thought was 'entirely conventional, and essentially the same as that voiced by the opposition to his regime'.[36] In fact, Maynwaring and Sibthorp said little that had not frequently enough been asserted by their predecessors of the cloth, though – like Cowell – they did indeed make the practical implications of royal absolutism more plain than was usual. Moreover, the king fully endorsed their ideas.

In 1626, having failed to obtain money from Parliament, Charles decided to raise a Forced Loan – that is to say, to compel his subjects to lend him large sums with dubious prospects of repayment. Since England was at war, and the king's financial needs were desperate, this decision was understandable. Yet it was obvious that many subjects would not take kindly to such a policy. Those infected by anti-absolutist ideas would regard the king's action as invalid, believing that kings possessed no authority to take property without consent. Even among absolutists, a number would hold that a Forced Loan was imprudent and unjust, though valid. In absolutist theory a king could justly break the positive law of the land only if public necessity required such a course. In 1626 it was arguable that no necessity existed. Charles could have obtained money from Parliament, but dissolved it in order to protect his favourite, the Duke of Buckingham.[37] To anyone who believed that Buckingham should be removed, or that the welfare of a favourite was not a matter of public necessity, the Forced Loan must have seemed a highly questionable measure.

In order to justify the Loan, Charles commanded the bishops to see that the clergy preached in its favour.[38] A cleric named Titley did so, and a complaint was lodged against him in the House of Commons of 1629. Furthermore, printed sermons clearly though cautiously defending the Loan survive by Isaac Bargrave, a royal chaplain, and by Matthew Wren, Master of Peterhouse in Cambridge.[39] It is very likely that these examples represent a tiny minority of the sermons which were in fact delivered in defence of Charles's policy.

35 John Locke, *Two treatises of government*, I, 5.
36 J.P. Kenyon, *The Stuart constitution* (Cambridge 1966) 9.
37 The reasons for the dissolution are explored in J.S. Flemion, 'The dissolution of Parliament in 1626: a revaluation', *EHR* 87 (1972) 784–90.
38 S.R. Gardiner, *History of England from the accession of James I to the outbreak of the Civil War, 1603–42*, 10 vols (1883–84) VI, 143; *PP 28*, V, 635, n. 13.
39 *CD 29*, 52, 133; Isaac Bargrave, *A sermon preached before King Charles March 27 1627* (1627) 18–20; Matthew Wren, *A sermon preached before the kings maiestie* (Cambridge 1627) 37–8; Peter Titley is discussed in Clive Holmes, *Seventeenth-century Lincolnshire* (Lincoln 1980) 112–14; I owe this information to Dr Richard Cust.

The sermons of Maynwaring and Sibthorp were exceptional not because they defended the Loan, but because they were printed, and, more particularly, because of the circumstances surrounding their publication.

Robert Sibthorp, vicar of Brackley in Northamptonshire, responded to the king's instructions to the clergy by working out arguments showing that subjects had a duty to pay the Loan. On 12 January 1627, when the king's commissioners for the Loan were in Northampton, Sibthorp and other divines were commanded to deliver their opinions on the measure's lawfulness. He wrote up his views and preached the result as an assize sermon at Northampton on 22 February. So far there was nothing very remarkable in all this. A minor cleric had obeyed the orders of his superiors with rather more zeal than was usual. Yet within a few months the sermon acquired major political importance. It was instrumental in the fall of George Abbot, Archbishop of Canterbury. According to his own account, he was asked to license the sermon for the press, but refused to do so, since he believed that its absolutism was too outspoken. Charles I had himself read – and very much approved of – Sibthorp's work. He disliked Abbot's attitude, and deprived the prelate of the powers, though not the name, of an archbishop. In Abbot's view, the whole affair had been engineered by his enemies, the Duke of Buckingham and William Laud. This may be true, but even so the project would have come to nothing if it had not been for one crucial fact. Charles liked Sibthorp's ideas.[40]

Abbot's refusal to license Sibthorp's book was overridden by a panel of bishops – Neile, Howson, Montaigne, Buckeridge and Laud himself. Plainly, Sibthorp had strong ecclesiastical support. Perhaps – as Abbot suspected – Laud was the moving force behind the book's publication. The same was certainly not true of Roger Maynwaring's two sermons. Maynwaring – a royal chaplain – preached twice before the king in July 1627, on both occasions setting forth doctrines that were uncompromisingly absolutist. Charles was very struck by his arguments, and the sermons were soon published 'by his Majesties speciall command'. These were not empty words. Even Laud – who probably agreed with Maynwaring's opinions, and who was not usually over-sensitive towards popular feeling – noticed that the sermons contained material which many might find objectionable. He attempted to dissuade the king from having the work printed, pointing out that 'there were many things therein which would be very distasteful to the people'. Whether from sheer pig-headedness, or through a delusion that if once his loyal subjects read the truth they could not fail to recognise it, Charles ignored the bishop's counsels. Again, there can be no doubt whatever that Charles agreed with Maynwaring's ideas.[41]

Maynwaring's political arguments were largely derived from the works of such theorists as De Dominis, Saravia, Buckeridge and Andrewes. He

---

40 Robert Sibthorp, *Apostolike obedience. Shewing the duty of subjects to pay tribute and taxes* (1627) title page, dedication; *ST*, ɪɪ, 1458–9, 1457, 1462–4, 1451–3.
41 William Laud, *Works*, eds W. Scott and J. Bliss, 7 vols (Oxford 1847–60) vɪɪ, 7; Roger Maynwaring, *Religion and alegiance: in two sermons* (1627) title page; *PP 28*, v, 642.

displayed a wide knowledge of recent absolutist literature, from which he straightforwardly deduced the consequence that kings should be obeyed unless their commands conflicted with 'the originall Lawes of God, Nature and the Gospell'. The Forced Loan did not violate any of these laws, and so, in Maynwaring's opinion, it did not matter that it infringed the laws of the land. It is unclear that Maynwaring had any developed conception of what these laws were. Steeped in the learning of the neo-scholastics and of recent English churchmen, he cared little for the ideology of Coke and his colleagues. He did indeed recognise that there was an alternative to natural law absolutism, namely contractual theory. But he attempted to show that even contractualists – such as Suarez – gave the sovereign the power to tax his subjects without their consent.[42]

Sibthorp adopted a similar technique, drawing on Catholic and Calvinist resistance theorists to show that even these enemies of kings acknowledged that the Prince had the right to levy taxes. He repeatedly cited the Calvinist Paraeus, and 'Bucanus (who is no Royalist)', as well as Jesuits, and declared that it was his intention 'especially to make use of Anti-royalists, because they cannot be excepted against in this point'. Like Maynwaring, Sibthorp does not appear to have believed that there was any alternative to 'royalism' – that is to say, royal absolutism – except contractual resistance theory. In his view, the doctrine that the king's power was limited implied the notion that kings were subject to the people. He inveighed against 'that factious fraternitie' who 'make the Law above the King, and the people above the Law, and so depose Princes, by their Tumults, and Insurrections'.[43]

As academic exercises in the application of absolutist theory to a concrete case, the sermons of Sibthorp and Maynwaring were competent pieces of work. As propaganda they were ill-judged and probably ineffective. Sibthorp's observation that people might as well pay the Loan voluntarily, since otherwise they would be compelled to do so, was particularly tactless.[44] Nevertheless, it was as propaganda that they were published. Within a few months, however, Charles decided to abandon the Loan and resort once more to Parliament.

Parliament met on 17 March 1628 and a week later complaint was made against Sibthorp and Maynwaring in the House of Commons. In the end Maynwaring alone was impeached. The fact that he delivered another two absolutist sermons while Parliament was sitting may well have increased hostility to him. The Commons' formal declaration against him was read out at a conference between committees of both Houses on 4 June. When summoned before the Lords, Maynwaring vainly asked that his case be judged by the bishops alone, since only they were competent to understand the nuances of theological argument. He found few defenders in the Upper House, though Carleton argued that the book should not be burned since this would offend the king, and John Williams, Bishop of Lincoln, had the honesty to admit that

42 Maynwaring, *Religion and alegiance*, I, 11, 13, 19, 20, 26, 27; II, 46.
43 Sibthorp, *Apostolike obedience*, 11, 13, 15, 16, 23.
44 *ST*, II, 1465; Sibthorp, *Apostolike obedience*, 36.

Maynwaring 'was invited to speake what he sayed originally by Letters from us [sc. the bishops]'. On 14 June the Lords sentenced Maynwaring. Among other things, he was to be imprisoned at the House's pleasure, to be barred from the ministry for three years, and to be disabled for ever from holding any 'ecclesiastical dignity or secular office'. They also asked the king to suppress the book by proclamation.[45]

In 1628 majorities in both Houses of Parliament believed that the king's recent conduct, and in particular the Loan, was ill-advised, unnecessary and unorthodox. The king himself had for the moment abandoned his earlier policies and was willing to allow Maynwaring to act as a scapegoat. Of course, many people believed that what was wrong with Maynwaring's book was that it supported absolutism, not just that it defended a particular royal policy. Pym's speeches against Maynwaring were vigorous indictments of absolutist theory, and no doubt he and others hoped to elicit a condemnation of such ideas from the king. Charles failed to oblige. On 24 June he issued a proclamation suppressing Maynwaring's book. 'The grounds thereof', he declared, 'were rightly laid, to perswade obedience from the Subjects to their Sovereigne, and that for conscience sake.' So Maynwaring's theory was correct. 'Yet', the proclamation continued, with studious obscurity, 'in divers passages, inferences, and applications thereof, trenching upon the laws of this land, and proceedings of parliaments, whereof he was ignorant, he so far erred, that he had drawn upon himself the just Censure and Sentence of the high Court of Parliament.' Desiring 'to take away all occasions of scandall or offence', Charles therefore suppressed the book. Though vague on what exactly Maynwaring had done wrong, this proclamation made it clear that the fundamentals of his theory were right. Absolutism was true. Charles wrote to Attorney-General Heath telling him to prepare a pardon for Maynwaring. The king had decided not to punish but reward his chaplain. On 18 July he was presented to the rectory of Stanford Rivers. In 1636 he was promoted to the bishopric of St Davids.[46]

The cases of Cowell and Maynwaring did not, then, witness the universal condemnation of absolutism. Society did not ritually purge itself of ideas which everyone found objectionable. Yet, in both cases an absolutist king was willing to compromise with the House of Commons. This was not altogether surprising. Parliament served functions which both kings found useful. That is to say, it supplied money and advice. In 1610 and 1628 the Stuarts were anxious to work with Parliament for financial reasons. The condemnation of a book was a small price to pay for the subject's love – and generosity. It is worth pointing out that in 1628 the subsidy bill was not sent up to the House of Lords until 16 June – two days *after* the Lords had condemned Maynwaring.[47]

The kings' needs led them to compromise, but their patience was not inexhaustible. If the Commons trenched too far upon the royal prerogative, the

45 *PP 28*, ɪɪ, 86, ɪv, 101–3, v, 619, 636, 644, 647–8.
46 *SRP*, ɪɪ, 197–8; *CSPD 1628–29*, 196, 217.
47 *PP 28*, ɪv, 340.

king could always prorogue or dissolve Parliament. Finding the Lower House intractable, James resorted to this expedient in 1614 and 1621, and his son did the same thing in 1626, 1628, 1629 and 1640. The possibility of dissolution drove the Commons towards compromise. In these circumstances a rhetoric of reconciliation was developed by people of all ideological complexions. The main ideas involved in this kind of thinking were three. Firstly, absolutists and their opponents were willing to agree that kings *ought* ordinarily to rule according to the law. Secondly, they held that the king's prerogative and the liberty of the subject were intimately linked. To attack one was necessarily to assault the other. Thirdly, they maintained that it was wrong for a subject to divide the king from his people. In other words, it was objectionable to put unpopular ideas into the king's head, or, for that matter, to distribute anti-monarchical propaganda among the people. These ideas provided verbal formulae to which everyone could assent, but, as we shall see, they did little to reconcile underlying disagreements.

JAMES I'S SPEECH OF 21 MARCH 1610

On 8 March 1610 James I took the case of Cowell out of the hands of Parliament. On 11 March Samuel Harsnett, Bishop of Chichester, delivered a sermon at Whitehall in which he claimed that subsidies were not free gifts since the king had the right to levy taxes even without the consent of his subjects. This sermon was noticed unfavourably in the Commons. On 21 March James I decided to pour oil on troubled waters by treating Parliament to a two-hour oration on the subject of political authority and obligation. In this speech James distinguished between the first kingdoms – in which kings ruled by mere natural justice – and later 'settled' states in which various laws and constitutional procedures had been established. It was obviously in the public interest that people be ruled by known laws and procedures. So the king's duty to rule in the public interest entailed a further duty to abide by the constitution. The king was bound to maintain the laws 'by a double oath' – firstly in virtue of the duties of kingship itself, and secondly because he swore to do so at his coronation. 'A king governing in a settled kingdom', said James, 'leaves to be a king and degenerates into a tyrant as soon as he leaves off to rule according to his laws.' Whatever the powers of monarchs considered abstractly might be, any good king was obliged to act within the law. 'Therefore all kings that are not tyrants or perjured will be glad to bound themselves within the limits of their laws, and they that persuade them the contrary are vipers and pests, both against them and the commonwealth.' With characteristic boastfulness, he added that 'I am sure to go to my grave with that reputation and comfort, that never king was in all his time more careful to have his laws duly executed, and himself to govern thereafter, than I.'[48]

---

48 *PP 10*, II, 59–60; *ST*, II, 1463; James I, *Political writings*, ed. Johann P. Sommerville (Cambridge 1994) 183–4.

Of James's political writings, this speech was easily the most often quoted. Three days after it was delivered, a letter-writer reported that it had won 'the great Contentment of all Parties'. It was subsequently cited or paraphrased by thinkers of every shade of opinion. The important point is that these thinkers invariably used the king's remarks to confirm their own political prejudices. In 1621 Sir Robert Phelips told the Commons that the king was bound to abide by the laws – including the privileges of the Lower House – and quoted his majesty's own words to prove the point. In 1628 Henry Sherfield drew on the speech to show that the prerogative was under the law, while Pym applied the royal remarks on 'vipers and pests' to Roger Maynwaring, and Sir Nathaniel Rich used the same words to describe 'the projectors of the Loan'. On the other hand, Secretary Coke quoted from the speech in order to lend credibility to Charles's assurances that he would rule according to the law: 'It is to be assumed that his government will be according to the law. We cannot but remember what his father said, "He is no king, but a tyrant, that governs not by law." But this kingdom is to be governed by the common law and his Majesty assures us so much.' Coke was arguing that there was no need for the Petition of Right, since the king could be trusted to rule well. He also believed that the Petition was pointless, since in the final analysis subjects had no choice but to trust their sovereign.[49]

In the 1630s the speech was quoted by such writers as Burton and Bastwick to establish two points – firstly, that the bishops were vipers and pests, and secondly that the king was not responsible for their actions. Both took it for granted that the liberties of the subject were being subverted and that true religion was being overthrown. In his speech, James had undertaken to act legally, and it would ill become a loyal subject to doubt the royal word. Moreover, Charles had given the same assurance in assenting to the Petition of Right, in this showing himself 'a Peereles Sonne to his Peerelesse Father'. So the king could be exonerated from blame for the actions of Laud and his colleagues, who were, in consequence, the vipers of whom James had spoken. The Scotsman Robert Baillie took the same line in 1641, using the speech to convict 'Bishop Lad' and 'the Canterburians' of undermining the liberties of English and Scots alike. It is certain that Charles did not see eye to eye with Baillie on this matter, and his father would probably have been less than delighted to see his words put to such a purpose.[50]

If James had hoped to forge an ideology which would be acceptable to all, allowing people to bury their old differences, his speech was a failure. Everyone could, indeed, agree that the king was bound to rule according to the law. But this proposition was doubly ambiguous. Firstly, there was disagreement on what was law. If God's law of nature gave the king sovereign power, and

---

49 Sawyer, ed., *Memorials of . . . Winwood*, III, 141; *CD 21*, VI, 245, 340; *PP 28*, II, 189, IV, 108, 164, III, 126.
50 Henry Burton, *For God and the king* (1636) 39, 96; John Bastwick, *The answer of Iohn Bastwick* (1637) 26; Robert Baillie, 'A postscript for the personate Iesuite Lysimachus Nicanor', 9, in *Ladensium AYTOKATAKPIΣIS, The Canterburians self-conviction*, 3rd edn (1641).

human laws were valid only inasmuch as they cohered with divine law, it followed that there could be no valid law against absolute monarchy. So, to admit that the king was bound by the law was to concede precisely nothing. Secondly, there were two senses in which the king could be said to be *bound*. He might have a moral obligation not to change the laws, or, on the other hand, he might be bound in the much stronger sense that the laws would remain in force even if he attempted to abrogate them. Plainly, James and Charles believed that their duty to abide by the laws was of the first variety. A king who flouted the law of the land sinned, they held, and was a tyrant, but he could validly enforce his decrees by coercive measures. James's speech of 21 March 1610 should be compared with another of 21 May in the same year, in which he declared that 'what a king will do upon bargain is one thing and what his prerogative is is another thing'. The royal prerogative could not be limited by human law. It was papists and puritans, not true Christians, who wished to reduce monarchs to cyphers. The king's own goodness, and not the law, was the only safeguard against tyranny: 'if a king be resolute to be a tyrant, all you can do will not hinder him. You may pray to God that he may be good and thank God if he be.' Others believed that the law was superior to the king and sufficient to prevent tyranny, since it would adjudge void whatever the king might illegally command. As Pym argued in 1628, there was little point in talking about limitations upon royal power unless such limitations could be enforced at law: otherwise 'they are limitations in show, not in substance'. In short, James's speech did not bridge the ideological gulf between absolutists and their opponents.[51]

On close analysis, the speech dissolves into little more than pleasantries. Perhaps the king hoped to conciliate moderate or uncommitted opinion by promising to govern according to law. Doubtless, the same objective underlay the rhetoric of such men as Pym and Burton who used James's words to free the king from blame for his own policies. As long as men retained any respect for the king's wishes, it was clearly worth alleging that his majesty did not really favour the evil policies which had been foisted on him by wicked vipers. So James's speech lived on in the history of propaganda. But its effects in reconciling differences of opinion were nugatory. The same was true of the frequently voiced notion that the royal prerogative and the subject's liberties were indissolubly linked.

THE MARRIAGE OF PREROGATIVE AND LIBERTY

Just as the king ought to abide by the laws, it was agreed, so his prerogative could not be separated from his subjects' rights. As Cecil put it, speaking on behalf of James I, 'the marriage between law and prerogative is inseparable and like twins they must joy and mourn together, live and die together, the separation of the one is the ruin of the other'. Charles I said much the same

51 *PP 10*, ii, 103; *PP 28*, iv, 107.

thing: 'my maxim is', he told Parliament in 1628, 'that the people's liberties strengthen the King's prerogative, and the King's prerogative is to defend the people's liberties'. Underlying this idea was the obvious truth that a people would be better able to provide the king with money for the defence of the realm if they were rich than if they were poor. Without security in their property, argued Hedley in 1610, the king's subjects would 'use little care or industry to get that which they cannot keep and so will grow both poor and base-minded like to the peasants in other countries, which be no soldiers nor will be ever made any, whereas every Englishman is as fit for a soldier as the gentlemen elsewhere'. Conversely, if the powers of the king were too stringently limited, he would be unable to defend his subjects. As Edward Hyde later wrote, 'if the least branch of the prerogative was torn off, or parted with, the subject suffered by it, and . . . his right was impaired'.[52]

People had little difficulty in agreeing that it would be a good idea to have a just balance between prerogative and liberty. In the same way modern politicians are united in holding that we should strive for a just solution to the problems created by discrimination – but they differ drastically on what the problems are, and how we should solve them. Provided that a proposition is sufficiently vague or vacuous, everyone may be willing to endorse it. This is no indication whatever of substantive agreement. How, then, was the notion of a balanced constitution used? The answer is that people of all opinions appealed to the concept, but used it to mean just what they chose. In other words, devotees of the rule of law argued that since prerogative was indissolubly linked to the liberty of the subject, the king could never infringe the rights which the law guaranteed. Absolutists, on the other hand, drew on the same idea to show that the prerogative was ultimately illimitable, since the prosperity of the governed could not be secured if the authority of the governor were undermined.

It was all very well to assert a link between law and prerogative, but the question remained: which took precedence, or, to use a seventeenth-century idiom, which was the substantive and which the adjective? In the fifteenth century, Fortescue had dealt with this point, preferring the liberty of the subject to royal power, and pointing out that not only the subject but also the king himself would profit if this liberty were inviolable. The same notion informed the thinking of many a seventeenth-century lawyer and Parliamentarian. In 1610 Hedley appealed to the concept of the balanced constitution, or, as he put it, 'this so ancient, honourable and happy state, so prudently compact of the sovereignty of the king and the liberty of the subject'. But he made it plain that the subject's property rights were superior to royal power. Wealthy subjects made for a powerful king. If it were 'in the king's absolute power' to take his subjects' property, they would have no incentive to gather wealth. So royal power depended on the inviolability of private property. 'This ancient liberty of the subject in England is that which doth and always hath maintained and

---

52 *PP 10*, ii, 50, 194–5; *PP 28*, vi, 182; Clarendon, *The life of Edward Earl of Clarendon*, 2 vols (Oxford 1857) i, 89.

upholden the sovereignty of the king.' 'The riches of the subject', argued Fuller in the same Parliament, 'is the best treasure of the king', and he cited James's *Basilicon Doron* to confirm the point. So the individual had 'an absolute property in his goods by the rule of law'. Sir Edward Coke appealed to this set of ideas in 1621, stressing the importance of restoring 'the subjects libertie, which is the Kings wealth. For nothing can be good for the Kinge that is ill for the subject.'[53]

In 1628 the House of Commons embodied the same principles in its reply to the king of 14 April: 'The preserving of those fundamental liberties which concern the freedom of our persons, and propriety of our goods and estates, is an essential means to establish the true glory of a monarchy.' Royal absolutism was self-defeating, since it served only to deprive the king of his greatest source of might – the people's wealth: 'for rich and free subjects as they are best governed, so they are best able to do your Majesty service either in peace or war'. Equally partisan was Henry Burton's use of the concept of a balanced polity in 1636. Burton declared that 'the Kings Prerogative, his just lawes, and the Peoples liberties, are so combined together, that they must be altogether preserved intire'. Unpacking this idea, he argued that just as no one could be 'for God' unless he was 'also for the true Religion', so it was impossible to be 'for the King' unless one was also 'for his lawes, and his peoples rights and liberties'. So the only genuine supporters of the royal prerogative were those who subjected that prerogative to the law and the liberty of the subject. Anything else was disloyalty towards the king.[54]

Burton quoted Charles's own words on the bond between liberty and prerogative to substantiate his views. In similar fashion, Henry Parker drew upon another royal statement in which his majesty had declared that he held 'no King so great as he that was King of a rich and free people, and if they had not property of goods, and liberty of persons, they would be neither rich nor free'. Charles was arguing that the king possessed power to take Ship Money, though Parliament had not consented to it, since its purpose was 'to preserve the Dominion of the Seas, which was so necessary, that without it the Kingdom could not subsist'. His point was that a king might take his subjects' property without their consent in what he deemed to be emergencies, but should not do so otherwise. So the general rule that property was inviolable stood, though in marginal cases it gave way to the demands of public necessity. Parker used the royal words to prove a rather different case. 'Here we see', he wrote,

> that the liberty of the subject is a thing which makes a King great; and that the Kings prerogative hath only for its ends to maintaine the peoples liberty. Wherefore it is manifest, that in nature there is more favour due to the liberty of the subject, then to the Prerogative of the King, since the one is ordained onely for the preservation of the other.

53 Sir John Fortescue, *De laudibus legum Angliae* (1616) f. 78a; in Fortescue, *On the laws and governance of England* (Cambridge 1997) 49; *PP 10*, ıı, 197, 194–5, 157; *PD 10*, 10; *CD 21*, ıv, 158.
54 *PP 28*, ıı, 450; cf. Eliot in *CD 29*, 260–1; Burton, *An apology of an appeale* (1636) 28; cf. Glanville in *PSP 40*, 127.

Parker's idea of a just balance between prerogative and liberty was to give everything to the latter and nothing to the former.[55]

Other people were equally unbalanced about the balanced constitution, though in the opposite direction. For Charles Merbury, writing in 1581, the prince's prosperity was not dependent upon that of his subjects but vice versa: 'the prosperous estate of the subjectes, is derived from the prosperitie of the Prince, their honour from his honour, their estimation from his estimation'. A king who lacked power would be powerless to defend his subjects. As Archbishop Bancroft told Parliament in 1610, the king's 'strength is the ground of our stability and if he fails 'tis our ruin'. To question the king's power, Secretary Coke told the Commons in 1628, was to strike not only at the king but also at his subjects, 'who are supported by that power'. Sir Thomas Wentworth appealed to the rhetoric of a balanced constitution in a famous speech delivered later in the same year. 'The authority of the king', he declared, 'is the keystone which closeth up the arch of order and government.' Royal authority took precedence over the liberties of the subject, for unless protected by authority the liberties would dissolve.[56]

Wentworth's speech has been compared with another made by John Pym in 1640. The rhetoric of both speeches was in some respects similar, but the fundamental ideas of the speakers were very different. While Wentworth looked to the king's authority as the guardian of order, Pym believed that order might be maintained only by preserving the 'ancient laws and liberties of the kingdom'.[57] In the early seventeenth century there were, indeed, a number of ideas to which everyone appealed. Of these, the notion of a balanced polity was one. Another was order. Two points are worth making about these concepts. Firstly, almost all political theorists from Plato to the present day have been willing to argue for order and a balanced polity. Only rarely have disorder and imbalance been favoured. Yet political theorists have disagreed fundamentally with each other.

Secondly, the contents which people in early Stuart England gave to their concepts of order and balance were derived from other principles on which they were far from unanimous. It was these other principles which determined their actions. Of course most people did not want political conflict, far less civil war. Platitudes and pious hopes about balance were useful in disguising the reality of disagreement on matters of substance.[58] In a similar fashion, the rhetoric of godly reformation and of building the Temple helped to unite the Parliamentarians in the early 1640s, but did not prevent the development of a widening rift on religious matters after 1644. The concept of a balanced polity could also serve as a handy piece of propaganda. There was a certain

55 Burton, *Apology*, 29; Charles I, *His maiesties declaration to all his loving subiects of the causes which moved him to dissolve the last Parliament* (1640) 19; Parker, *The case of shipmony*, 4–5.
56 Charles Merbury, *A briefe discourse of royall monarchie* (1581) 2; *PP 10*, ii, 79; *PP 28*, ii, 430; Kenyon, *Stuart constitution*, 18.
57 Pym quoted in Kenyon, *Stuart constitution*, 17.
58 A different interpretation is in M.A. Judson, *The crisis of the constitution: an essay in constitutional and political thought in England* (New Brunswick 1949) 66.

plausibility in both the argument that wealthy subjects rendered a king powerful, and that a powerful king would secure and enrich his subjects. Either argument might convince moderates. Moreover, for the king to assert an intimate link between prerogative and liberty was to demonstrate a tender regard for the rights of his subjects, even if prerogative won out in the end. In the same way, the Commons were able to manifest their scrupulous care for kingly power while simultaneously subjecting that power to rigorous limitations.

If it was wrong to alter the balance of the constitution – whatever that meant – then it was also wrong to persuade the king (or the people) to effect imbalance. Anyone who did so might well be a viper and pest. For everyone agreed that no one should make a division between the king and his people.

MAKING A DIFFERENCE BETWEEN THE KING AND THE PEOPLE

It was a truism of early Stuart political thinking that disunity weakened the state. As the much-quoted adage had it, 'a kingdom divided cannot stand'.[59] Political or religious disagreement, it was believed, hindered the pursuit of co-operative enterprises, and, at its worst, threatened military destruction. Disaffected factions would take up arms against their opponents, or ally with foreign powers, inviting invasion. There was plenty of Continental evidence that ideological conflict did lead to civil war and invasion. In England, a prime reason for fear and hatred of popery was the belief that papists were liable to rebel as soon as they had an opportunity. Catholic political writings did little to discourage this belief.

Since disunity spelled disaster, it was wrong to foment discord. The exact legal nature of the offence was debatable, but the general rule was endorsed by all. In 1610 Cecil told Parliament that if, in making his financial proposals, he 'had moved a thing not fit for the people but such a one as was fit for the King and so made a separation betwixt the King and the subject, I were unworthy to sit here'. In 1621 Lionel Cranfield informed the House of Commons that 'it first came from traitors' hearts to make a difference between the King and his subjects'. In the same session Secretary Calvert declared that 'there hath been this parliament an uniting of the King's heart to the subjects, and the subjects to the King and woe be to him that would make a separation'. By 1628 many of the Commons believed that such a separation had been made, and wished woe upon its perpetrators. Rous asserted that Maynwaring 'goes about to divide the King from the body and the body from the head', and the House included this charge in its declaration against the clergyman. There was talk in this session of attainting Maynwaring – an indication that some, at least, believed that it was treason to divide the king from his subjects. In 1629 Phelips inveighed against innovating clerics who had 'set dissension betwixt

---

59 *The practise of Princes. Published by A.Ar* (1630) 8; *CD 21*, III, 167; William Chillingworth, *Works*, 3 vols (Oxford 1838) III, 32. The source is biblical: Matthew 12:25; Mark 3:24; Luke 11:17.

the King and us'. In 1640 Sir John Glanville resorted to generalities in replying to his confirmation as Speaker of the House of Commons: 'It was wont to be and I hope ever will be the tenet and position of our house of Commons That the good of the king and his people cannot bee severed. And cursed bee everyone that shall goe about to divide it.'[60]

Though there was agreement on the evil of creating division between king and subject, there was no unanimity on what actions counted as creating division. In general, the rule was that only wicked ideas, or evil actions could be divisive. No one thought that it would be wrong for good and righteous folk to disagree with and avoid bad people. John Hales decried schism in religious matters and its secular equivalent, sedition, but pointed out that 'when either false or uncertain Conclusions are obtruded for truth, and Acts either unlawfull, or ministring just scruple are required of us to be perform'd, in these cases consent were conspiracy, and open contestation is not faction or Schisme, but due Christian animosity'.[61] No one (except Catholics) believed that Protestants were at fault for dividing themselves from papists, for Protestantism was true; it was Catholics who erred by not recognising this. Similarly, loyal subjects had no obligation to unite themselves with traitors or rebels. Disunion, in this case, was wholly admirable.

The argument that those who divided the king from his subjects deserved condign punishment was most frequently voiced by anti-absolutists, especially in the years after 1627. In their view, absolutism was a false and dangerous doctrine which should be concealed from the king. Pym attacked Maynwaring because the cleric 'went about to infuse into his Majesty that which was most unfit for his royal breast – an absolute power not bounded by law'. In 1629 Grosvenor and Eliot focused attention on a particularly insidious consequence of the king's seduction by wrong-headed clergymen, namely his majesty's disaffection with Parliaments. The notions that the king had been misled by absolutist clerics and that his failure to call Parliament was a consequence of this soon became staple elements in the propaganda of those who opposed royal policy. In its full-blown version, the theory blamed everything on the papists. At first, the argument ran, papists had tried to encourage the subject to rebel. But the loyalty of the English proved unconquerable. So the papists now decided to change their tactics and destroy England by polluting the mind of the king against his people. Unless Charles's loyal subjects acted quickly to save his majesty from popish indoctrination, the plan would succeed.[62]

---

60 *PP 10*, II, 114; *CD 21*, II, 90, 408; *PP 28*, III, 261, IV, 102. Moves to attaint Maynwaring are mentioned in ibid., III, 262, 405; VI, 115. *CD 29*, 178; *PSP 40*, 130. A valuable discussion of the connection between ideas of division and treason is Conrad Russell, 'The theory of treason in the trial of Strafford', *EHR* 80 (1965) 30–50.
61 John Hales, *A tract concerning schisme and schismatiques* (Oxford 1642) 2.
62 *The practise of Princes. Published by A.Ar*, 7; Burton, *Apology*, 28–9; Parker, *The case of shipmony*, 32, 37; Burton, *Lord bishops, none of the Lords bishops* (1640) sig. L1b; *PSP 40*, 258–9; *PP 28*, III, 408; *CD 29*, 68–9, 259; Calybute Downing, *A sermon preached to the renowned company of the artillery, 1 September 1640* (1641) 27–9.

One implication of this kind of propaganda was that the king's mental abilities were those of a child. As long as it remained unrealistic to advocate active resistance, this was perhaps inevitable. If the king could do no wrong it was necessarily true that whatever was wrongly done was the responsibility of evil ministers. But the crucial point is that these thinkers approached the notion of the division of the king from his subjects in a wholly partisan fashion. The essential contention was that the king's policies were wrong because they were illegal. It was only at a secondary level that the concept of division was called into play. Maynwaring and Strafford were absolutists – the one in theory, the other in practice. So they deserved punishment. The added argument that preaching or practising false doctrine caused disaffection between king and people was hardly fundamental, though it might serve a useful purpose in convincing moderates, or, especially, in making it easier for the king to assent to the condemnation of his allies.

Equally partisan was the king's own use of the conventional idea that no one should make a difference between a Prince and his subjects. Of course, Charles did not think that there was anything wrong with putting absolutist ideas into the king's head, or with encouraging subjects to render due obedience towards their sovereign. But he did maintain that a few 'ill affected persons of the House of Commons' persistently polluted the minds of the loyal majority against the king. These men acted 'for private and personal ends, ill beseeming publike persons trusted by their Countrey'. It was their 'disobedient and seditious carriage' which forced him, much against his will, to dissolve Parliament. Their objective was 'to cast Our affairs into a desperate condition, to abate the powers of Our Crowne, and to bring Our government into obloquie; that, in the end, all things may bee overwhelmed with anarchie and confusion'. Ultimately they aimed at 'nothing more then to bring into contempt and disorder all Government and Magistracy'. Just as his opponents emphasised that the king himself was not responsible for actions carried out in his name by a small but potent faction of crypto-Catholic bishops and courtiers, so Charles exonerated the majority of the House of Commons from blame for what had really been done by 'some few Vipers amongst them, that did cast this mist of undutifulnesse over most of their eyes'.[63]

The king claimed that disobedience was responsible for the divisions which troubled the commonwealth. In 1637 Christopher Dow similarly blamed the dissolution of the last Parliament upon the 'seditious carriage of those ill-affected persons of the house of Commons' who 'raised so much heat and distemper, upon causelesse jealousies'. It was, he declared, the continued existence of the same attitude, 'fomented by turbulent and malevolent spirits', which prevented the king from summoning Parliament again. In 1639 Henry

---

63 Charles I, *A declaration of the true causes which moved his maiestie . . . to dissolve the two last meetings in Parliament* (1626) 19–20; *His maiesties declaration . . . of the causes which moved him to dissolve the last Parliament* (1628) 3, 41; *His maiesties declaration . . . of the causes* (1640) 3, 6.

Peacham affirmed that 'all disobedient subjects' deserved 'to be severely punished' because they endangered that 'unity and peace' which should prevail 'between all Christian Princes and their Subjects'. Disobedience was particularly inexcusable since 'we now live under a most gracious, mild and mercifull Prince as ever reigned in England'.[64]

The rhetoric of division was manipulated to partisan ends by men of all political persuasions. Some thought that it was seditious subjects who divided the commonwealth by disobedience. Others believed that the threat came from a misguided king who demanded obedience against the laws and interests of the land. As long as a violent solution to the conflict remained impossible, it was perhaps inevitable that people resorted to the rhetoric, which at times wore pretty thin. The reality of ideological conflict is a blindingly obvious feature of early Stuart history. The Commons howled for the blood of Cowell and Maynwaring because they knew that these men disagreed radically with their own political ideas. In this chapter we have seen that fundamental differences of opinion on political matters not only existed, but were recognised to exist. To understand why ideological dissension led, as it did, to political and finally military conflict, it is necessary to look at the practical issues which troubled people in early Stuart England.

---

64 Christopher Dow, *Innovations unjustly charged upon the present church and state* (1637) 62; Henry Peacham, *The duty of all true subjects to their king: as also to their native countrey* (1639) 22–3.

CHAPTER 5

The Liberty of the Subject

Cowell and Maynwaring annoyed the Commons by expressing absolutist views. But far more serious grievances arose when the king himself acted in ways that appeared to flout the law of the land and undermine the liberties which that law guaranteed. The main liberties in question were freedom from taxation and legislation except with your own consent. Immunity from arbitrary imprisonment became an issue in 1627. Charles arrested at least a hundred refusers of the Forced Loan, but was reluctant to bring them to trial. He did not want the legality of the Loan to be tested in court. So he let the prisoners languish in jail. The issue of arbitrary imprisonment, then, followed in the wake of the Loan – which itself raised the question of property. Property lay at the centre of debate on the liberties of the subject. The individual's property rights were the most closely defended of these liberties. If these rights were broken, the other liberties might prove indefensible. A king who could tax at will would have the financial resources to disregard the rights of his subjects. In particular, he could rule without ever calling Parliament or heeding its counsels. When the abstract political theories of absolutism and its rivals were brought to bear upon the concrete case of the English constitution, dispute focused on the issues of imprisonment, Parliament and especially property. Of course, the concept of property is familiar enough today. But people in the early seventeenth century brought to its analysis a set of assumptions and attitudes which we no longer share. To ignore these assumptions is to miss not just the flavour but the substance of early-seventeenth-century political thinking.

PROPERTY

God, it was agreed, had given the earth and its fruits to humans. God created the world for the benefit of people. Without material goods the human race would be in no position to fulfil the purposes for which God had placed it on earth. Starving individuals would be unable to do God's work. So our right to use the land and its products was derived from the will of God, expressed most clearly in the first chapter of Genesis. God's will conferred not only the right to use lands and goods, but also restrictions upon such use. Strictly speaking, God alone held full dominion over the earth: 'God hath *dominium merum, immediatum, et liberum*: he hath absolute, free or immediate dominion over the creatures. Man had onely but *dominium conditionatum*, such a dominion that was not an absolute and simple dominion to use them at his pleasure.' Our right to use material goods was circumscribed by limitations. Goods could not justly be used against God's will, and, in particular, against the welfare of humanity – for it was to promote this welfare that God had given the earth to the human race. Supreme dominion – *dominium altum* – was God's alone. Adam, the first man, had possessed 'not this supreame dominion, but subordinate to God'.[1]

Of course, the fact that God had given the earth to humans did not serve to show who now possessed which parts of it, or even how it should be possessed. Both private and communal ownership were recognised as valid. The majority of thinkers believed that communism had originally prevailed. They claimed that the earth had at first been held in common, but that pure reason – the law of nature – did not prescribe that it should always be held in this way. 'Nature creating man gave unto him those worldly blessings to use well, with warrant either to hold them in Common, or in Proper, as reason from tyme to tyme could best perswade his will.' Though communism might have been the original form of ownership, it had no eternal validity. Private property had long ago been found convenient, possibly as a consequence of sin. Communism was acceptable in the Garden of Eden, but among fallen humans it was subject to abuses, 'whereupon naturall reason perswaded, that all things being divided, everie man should knowe his owne: otherwise no peace or concord could be maintayned in humane society'.[2]

Some authors, indeed, asserted that private property had existed from the very beginning. This was Selden's view, and George Saltern specifically denied that nature had at first established communism: 'I cannot agree . . . that al thinges by the Lawe of nature were common; but as I take it the distinction of properties was enacted by Almighty God in the beginning, and by him imprinted with other Lawes, in nature.'[3] So there were differences of opinion on the origins and early history of property. But these were of little practical consequence. Everyone agreed that whatever the earliest form of ownership had been, private property was now the norm, and that it was fully justified. Indeed, private property was commonly held to be the prescription of the law of nations, though not perhaps of the original law of nature.

The law of nations was construed either as a set of deductions from the first principles of natural law, or else as those practices which were common to

---

1 John Weemse, *The portraiture of the image of God in Man* (1627) 280, 282.
2 Ap-Robert, *The younger brother his apology by it selfe* (St Omer 1618) 9, 8.
3 John Selden, *Of the dominion, or ownership of the sea* (1652) 19–20; George Saltern, *Of the antient lawes of Great Britaine* (1605) sig. F3a. According to John Cotton, nature gives rights of property to whoever labours on vacant soil: *Gods promise to his plantation* (1630) 5.

most human societies. In any event, its prescriptions – including private property – were held to be binding. As Sir John Davies put it, 'by the Law of Nature all things were common', but 'then came in the Law of Nations, which did limit the Law of Nature, and brought in property'. John Donne remarked that 'all mankind is naturally one flock feeding upon one Common', but pointed out that 'for society and peace' private property was 'reasonably induc'd'. According to the Elizabethan Civil lawyer Richard Cosin, 'common dominion of all lands and goods' might have prevailed in the first days of human history on earth, when 'scarcitie of men' ensured that there was 'innough, and more than sufficient for everie one'. Later, however, when population increased and contention arose 'it was thought meet by generall good liking of all nations to bound out the dominions of everie man in severall proprietie: which course all the civill nations in the world doo inviolablie and lawfullie practise, notwithstanding the first law of nature was to the contrarie', Whatever had happened in remote antiquity, it was now possible for all men to unite in condemning what Pym called 'that error that all things ought to be in comon'.[4]

In modern usage, communal ownership is contrasted with private property. In the early seventeenth century, property, or propriety, was by definition private. A second feature of property was that it could not justly be taken away from its owner without his consent. To say that something was a man's property, or – and this was by far the commoner usage – that he had property in something, was precisely to say that the thing in question could not be taken from him without his consent. To take property without consent was to steal, and thus to break the Eighth Commandment. So private property was a prescription of the law of nations, while the ban on stealing was a precept of the moral law. These laws did not show who in particular held what property in England. Nature had laid down no detailed rules on the transference of property, and nations differed in their practices.

It was, in consequence, human positive law which determined who held property in what. 'Though the distinction of demesnes and the propertie of goods be parcel of the law of nations', said Fulbecke, 'yet the meanes whereby they are acquired are prescribed by the civill and common law.' The law of nations might demand that there be property, but the particular rules governing such matters as inheritance varied from nation to nation: 'the right of demesne and property is not alike in all nations, but is moderated, and ordered by the lawes of particular common weales'.[5] The question of what lands and goods constituted someone's property was answered 'by the municipal law of that kingdom, wherein he liveth or was born'.[6] This principle had the following important implication. If the king had power to make law without

4 Sir John Davies, *The question concerning impositions* (1656) 29; John Donne, *Essays in divinity*, ed. E.M. Simpson (Oxford 1952) 7; Richard Cosin, *An answer to the two first and principall treatises of a certaine factious libell* (1584) 255; Pym in *CD 21*, ɪɪ, 462.
5 William Fulbecke, *The pandectes of the law of nations* (1602) ff. 12b, 13a.
6 Hedley in *PP10*, ɪɪ, 189.

the consent of his subjects, he could alter established regulations on ownership, and, in effect, take property without consent. Anyone who wanted to
defend individual property rights against royal encroachment had therefore to
deny that the king could legislate without consent. The questions of lawmaking and property were logically linked.

The law of nations instituted private property. But it did not follow that the
lands or goods which any particular man happened to be using constituted his
property. The laws of nature and nations were held to permit slavery or, in its
English.form, villeinage. The king's villeins might occupy and use land, but
their right to do so could be cancelled at the king's whim. They held no
property. 'There is great difference betwixt the kings free subjects and bondmen', said Hedley in 1610, 'for the king may by commission at his pleasure
seize the lands or goods of his villeins (*villani*), but so can he not of his free
subjects.'[7] Although the laws of nature and nations allowed slavery, they did
not spell out who in particular was enslaved. Human law defined who was
free and who was a slave.

The law of nations preferred private property to communism. It also permitted slavery. So, if all the lands and goods in the kingdom belonged to the
king, the law of nations would have been upheld, for private property would
prevail though one man owned everything. Nor would the law of nations be
breached if English subjects were villeins, for it allowed villeinage. To prove
that Englishmen were free and that they held property it was therefore necessary to turn to the laws of the realm. The laws of nature and nations might
create a general presumption in favour of the thesis that subjects possess liberty and property. But as long as villeinage remained a theoretical possibility,
the essence of the anti-absolutist case rested upon the law of the land. This law
gave the vast majority of the king's subjects free status. To strike at their
property was to deprive them of this status. Liberty depended upon property
in the literal sense that to deprive a man of property in his goods was to
reduce him to villeinage.

In 1610 Nicholas Fuller told the House of Commons that the English subject had 'an absolute property in his goods by the rule of law'. In the Short
Parliament of 1640 Harbottle Grimston invited the House to consider the
question of property before it debated ways of assisting the king in his war
with the Scots: 'Let therefore first our propertye be settled; and all', he said,
'would serve the Kinge for the preservation of the kingdome.'[8] Anti-absolutist
arguments on property had changed little in the intervening period. The king,
so the case ran, was subject to the common law, with which he could never
dispense. By the common law, the English possessed property in their lands

---

7 Hedley, ibid., 192. According to Giles Jacob, *A new law-dictionary* (1729) sig. 5B2b, 'he was
properly a pure Villain . . . whom the Lord might put out of his Lands and Tenements, Goods
and Chattels at his will'. Whether the seventeenth-century conception of what villeinage had been
corresponds with medieval reality is dubious: cf. Alan Macfarlane, *The origins of English individu-
alism: the family, property and social transition* (Oxford 1978).
8 Fuller in *PP 10*, ɪɪ, 157; Grimston in *PSP 40*, 178.

and goods. This property was absolute. That is to say, it did not give way before any powers which the king might claim. If the king had extra-legal powers to take property, subjects would be no better off than villeins, or beggarly foreigners. They would have no incentive to work, since they could not call the products of their labour their own. Moreover, extra-legal royal powers rendered Parliament powerless. If subjects had no property, the voting of subsidies was a pure and needless formality.

All these arguments were repeatedly expressed throughout the early seventeenth century. Anti-absolutist principles underwent little change, though they were applied more rigidly in the face of royal attack or circumvention. A case in point is the question of benevolences, by which the king invited his wealthier subjects to contribute to his finances, under pain of royal displeasure. Payment was, in theory, voluntary, since refusers incurred no legal penalties. When James I failed to raise money from Parliament in 1614, he levied a benevolence, which Oliver St John, a Wiltshire gentleman, refused to pay. St John was so incensed that he wrote to the mayor of Marlborough exposing the iniquities of benevolences, which, he said, were 'against law, reason and religion'. In essence, he objected to them because they infringed the principle that taxation requires consent, and in spirit if not letter he was right. St John was prosecuted in Star Chamber, and his case certainly attracted sympathy. To say that taxation required the consent of the taxed was an insufficient defence against absolutism as long as the king possessed the means of compelling the individual's consent. So some claimed that taxation required not mere consent, but consent in Parliament. 'The goods of the subject are his own', said Phelips in 1628, 'and cannot be taken lawfully from him, though he consent, without Parliament.' In 1628 benevolences were condemned by the Petition of Right.[9]

Once anti-absolutists had shown that subjects possessed property in their goods by the law of the land, they were able to argue that taxation without consent was nothing more than theft. Absolutists rejected this argument. They held that subjects did indeed have property in their goods, but denied that property was absolute. In a case of public necessity individual property rights gave way to the common good. The king alone could decide what constituted public necessity. The subordination of property to necessity was one instance of the general theme that the higher laws of God and nature circumscribed property rights.

God's law gave the earth to mankind, the law of nations set up private property, and human law fleshed out the details. God's gift, however, had

9 *ST*, ıı, 900. Further examples of principled opposition to the benevolences of 1614, 1622 and 1626 are discussed in Richard Cust, *The Forced Loan and English politics 1626–1628* (Oxford 1987) 156–64; Sir Walter Raleigh, *The prerogative of parliaments in England* (1628) takes St John's case as its starting-point: p. 1; Phelips in *PP 28*, ıı, 130, cf. 124. On Phelips's attitude towards benevolences cf. Conrad Russell, *Parliaments and English politics 1621–1629* (Oxford 1979) 55. Petition of Right in S.R. Gardiner, *The constitutional documents of the puritan revolution* (Oxford 1906) 66–7. Benevolences had already been condemned by statute in 1484.

been conditional. The earth could justly be used only to promote and not to subvert God's purposes, and these included people's temporal welfare. It was incumbent upon property-owners to use their wealth in a way which would further this primary goal. 'No man', pronounced Ap-Robert, 'may give, or lend his goods to any one who will in all men's judgments assuredly abuse them.' Again, it was held to be wrong to give away so much of your property that you became a burden on others. 'If one shall give all he hath', declared Walter Balcanquall, Dean of Rochester, 'knowing that he must become chargeable to others, it is sinne.'[10]

On some occasions, by contrast, people had a duty not to keep but to part with their goods. For example, Christians had an obligation to give alms to the poor. Indeed, rights of property dissolved altogether in the face of extreme poverty. God gave us all a duty to preserve our own lives, and in consequence to use material goods such as food and shelter. So the duty of self-preservation entailed a duty to take other people's goods whenever this was necessary for continued existence. In conditions of famine, wrote John Donne, 'one may lawfully steal' since 'all things return to their primitive community'. Famine, he said, 'defeats . . . all Propriety'.[11]

If private necessity undermined rights of property, the same was *a fortiori* true of public necessity. In natural law thinking, the sovereign decided what constituted public necessity. He possessed the authority to take goods without consent if he deemed that the public interest required such a course. In absolutist theory it was the king who possessed sovereignty, for he derived his power from God alone. In the radical version of natural law theory, the king's power arose from a grant of the people, and they, not he, were the ultimate arbiters of the public interest. Royal power was limited by the conditions on which it had been granted to the king, and these could include the provision that he tax only with the people's consent. The plea of necessity could be invoked against the king. Thirdly, it was possible to argue that necessity gave the king no warrant to break the law. The law provided sufficiently for all emergencies. Moreover, to flout property rights for the sake of promoting the public good was bound to prove a self-defeating enterprise. The public good required that property be inviolable, for only thus would the English remain free and prosperous.

Opponents of absolutism agreed that subjects had an obligation to contribute to the welfare of the kingdom. The old notion persisted that in normal circumstances the king should make do with his regular income. But everyone admitted that where the public good necessitated extraordinary royal expenditure the king's loving subjects should supply their royal master. Defenders of absolute property insisted that the law provided the mechanism by which the king could be supplied and the rights of his subjects maintained.

---

10 Ap-Robert, *The younger brother his apology*, 48; Walter Balcanquall, *The honour of Christian churches* (1634) 23.
11 Donne, *Essays in divinity*, 68.

This was Parliament. If the king believed that he needed money to defend the realm he could call Parliament. His subjects would happily supply him if they found that his case was justified. Defenders of absolute royal authority conceded that Parliament was the ordinary means by which the king could raise extraordinary revenue. But they denied that it was the only means. God had given the king authority to rule his subjects in their own interest, and, consequently, to do whatever was necessary to this end. So he could levy taxes outside Parliament in emergencies. Since this was an extraordinary power, it did not conflict with the ordinary property rights of the subject. Kings might, indeed, misuse their emergency powers to destroy rights of property. But this showed only that the subject's rights were incompatible with the misuse of royal powers, not that they were incompatible with the powers themselves. The argument that the king possessed no powers which he could misuse was bogus and anarchic. Without extra-legal powers of taxation the king would be unable to defend the realm in a crisis. There would be no remedy against such evils as invasion and rebellion, both of which threatened to deprive subjects of their property and of life itself. The paradoxical truth was that property could not be maintained unless the king held extra-legal powers which he could misuse to undermine property itself.

The first two Stuart kings levied a number of taxes without the consent of Parliament. Particular taxes attracted opposition for many reasons, of which some had little to do with constitutional principle. Impositions, for example, were commonly regarded as inflationary, and they discouraged trade. There were administrative problems connected with Ship Money, and the levy caused hardship because it fell upon an unusually high proportion of the population. But it would be mistaken to suppose that principled antagonism towards the crown's financial policies was merely a negligible afterthought, developed at a late date to provide a specious excuse for opposition. From the very beginning of James I's reign two separate accounts of the relationship between royal power and the subject's property were current in England. Absolute royal power faced absolute property. The result was conflict.

ABSOLUTE PROPERTY

Nicholas Fuller, as we have seen, told the House of Commons in 1610 that the subject possessed 'an absolute property in his goods by the rule of law'.[12] Fuller thought that it was timely to make this claim because he, like many other members of the Commons, believed that the king could not legally levy impositions – unaccustomed and extra-Parliamentary taxes on imports and exports. After 1608 impositions became a major source of royal revenue.

What paved the way for this was Bate's Case, or the case of currants, tried in the Exchequer in 1606. Whether this decision constituted a vindication of impositions in general or merely applied to Bate remained disputable. But the

12 Fuller in *PP 10*, ıı, 157.

reasoning employed by the judges could readily be extended to cover a wide range of extra-Parliamentary levies. Indeed, the arguments of Chief Baron Fleming came close to providing a justification of royal absolutism in the broadest sense. He distinguished between two forms of royal authority: 'The king's power is double, ordinary and absolute, and they have several lawes and ends.' His ordinary power applied in cases where the public interest was not involved, and here the monarch was bound by the common law. In other words, the common laws governed questions of private right, 'and these laws cannot be changed, without parliament'. But in matters which concerned 'the general benefit of the people' the king possessed an absolute power, subject only to the rules of 'Pollicy and Government'. The implications of these rules, said Fleming, were to be determined by 'the wisdome of the king, for the common good', and 'all things done within these rules are lawful'. If the king decided that something was in the public interest, it was not fit for subjects to question his judgment: 'the wisdome and providence of the king is not to be disputed by the subject'. Of course, the king might abuse his power, Fleming added, but to suppose that he would do so was 'no argument for a subject'.[13]

Armed with the precedent of Bate's Case, the king issued letters patent in 1608, authorising the collection of impositions on many commodities. Since the king spent money in protecting trade, it was reasonable that he be recompensed by those who profited from his efforts. The king was, in any case, desperately short of money, and the merchants could well afford to pay. These arguments did not convince those who believed that tonnage and poundage already paid for the king's protection of trade, and that royal financial problems were the consequence of James's extravagance, especially towards Scottish favourites. But the main reason why impositions attracted opposition was that they infringed the principle that taxation requires consent.

Of course, it was possible to argue that impositions were less a form of taxation than a means of regulating trade. Foreign sovereigns might impose duties on the importation of English goods. It was reasonable that the king of England be empowered to retaliate by raising levies on foreign commodities. This kind of argument was voiced as early as 1534 and was repeated by Coke and others in the opening decades of the seventeenth century (though Coke soon changed his mind). But in the years after 1608 it became increasingly obvious that the argument bore little relation to reality. The Stuarts used impositions not to regulate trade but to raise cash. Indeed, they derived more revenue from this source than from Parliamentary taxation – a fact which put the continued existence of Parliament in jeopardy. Moreover, the absolutist claims of Fleming made it plain that constitutional principles were at issue, and the commission of 1608 confirmed this. 'By the laws of all nations', it said, kings could 'raise to themselves such fit and competent means by levying of customs, and impositions upon merchandises . . . as to their wisdoms

13 Fleming in *ST*, ii, 389, 392.

and discretions may seem convenient'. This was a straightforward assertion of a royal right to extra-Parliamentary levies.[14]

On 23 May 1610 the House of Commons petitioned the king, informing him of 'the general Conceit' that the decision in Bate's Case could be 'extended much further, even to the utter Ruin of the ancient liberty of this Kingdom, and of your Subjects Right of Propriety of their Lands and Goods'. On 7 July the House petitioned the king once more. This time they declared that the 'law of propriety' was 'original' and an 'old fundamental right'. Impositions, they alleged, had caused 'a generall dearth and decay of wealth among your people, who will be no less discouraged, than disabled to supply your Majesty, when occasion shall require it'. If property were shaken, people would become idle and impoverished. 'The policy and constitution of this your Majesty's kingdom', they asserted, gave the king power to tax and legislate only 'with the assent of parliament'. Finally, on 17 July the Commons passed a bill affirming that 'without assent of parliament' impositions 'are and shall be adjudged in the law void and to none effect'.[15] Clearly, it was the settled and repeated opinion of the House that impositions were objectionable because they were levied without consent. The same opinion was commonly voiced by individual members.

If the king's 'right of imposition' were established, argued James Whitelocke on 22 May, 'the ancient frame of the commonwealth' would be 'much altered' and Parliament – 'the storehouse of our liberties' – would be endangered. On 23 June Nicholas Fuller claimed that the law gave the English property in their goods and concluded that the royal prerogative could not be extended 'to take away or prejudice the inheritance of the subject', for this would be contrary 'to reason and to the law of nations'. In other words, the law granted the subject rights of property, and the superior laws of nature and nations forbade the taking of property without consent – a point which Fuller documented with Scriptural citations. As Sir Roger Owen put it on 2 July, 'it is contrary to the law of nations to take away the property of man's goods'. The lawyer Thomas Wentworth preferred to deduce the illegality of impositions from the Ten Commandments themselves, asserting that the judgment in Bate's Case conflicted with the Decalogue.[16]

The two most famous speeches of 1610 against impositions were delivered by James Whitelocke and William Hakewill. Both were published in 1641 as propaganda justifying recent proceedings in the Long Parliament – another indication of how little the essentials of the anti-absolutist case had changed in

---

14 G.R. Elton, *The Tudor constitution*, 2nd edn (Cambridge 1982) 40–1; J.R. Tanner, ed., *Constitutional documents of the reign of James I* (Cambridge 1930) 264; G.W. Prothero, *Select statutes and other constitutional documents illustrative of the reigns of Elizabeth and James I*, 3rd edn (Oxford 1906) 354. Impositions are discussed in F.C. Dietz, *English public finance, 1558–1641* (1932) 362–6, 368–79. For Coke's later position see W.J. Jones, *Politics and the Bench: the judges and the origins of the English Civil War* (1971) 54 n. 3, and Glenn Burgess, *Absolute monarchy and the Stuart constitution* (New Haven 1996), 202.
15 *CJ* 431; *PP 10*, ɪɪ, 267, 411.
16 Whitelocke in *PP 10*, ɪɪ, 109; Fuller, ibid., 158–9; Owen in *PD 10*, 112; Wentworth, ibid., 61.

the course of the early seventeenth century. Hakewill stressed the certainty of the common law. In his view, it was important that 'certainty be set between the King and his poor subject', and the common law provided for just this. If the king could levy new taxes without the consent of Parliament, the law would have failed in its main purpose. The king had no power to tax without consent even in emergencies, since the common law provided sufficiently for all emergencies. So impositions were unjustified: 'these two Arguments used by me, that of Certainty, and this of the provision made by the Common-Law, are in my poor opinion, Arguments of direct proofs, that the King cannot impose'. Martin, like Hakewill, noticed that if the king possessed the authority to levy taxes without consent in emergencies, and if he was the sole judge of what constituted an emergency, his power would be absolute. He concluded that the king could not tax without consent, and, for this reason, condemned impositions.

Martin also enunciated the conventional common law principle that the king-in-Parliament was the supreme authority in the land: 'the King of England', he said, is 'the most absolute Kinge in his Parliament; but of hymself, his power is lymited by lawe'.[17] Precisely the same hackneyed maxim underlay the famous argument of James Whitelocke. 'In the king', he claimed, 'is a two-fold power; the one in parliament, as he is assisted with the consent of the whole state; the other out of parliament, as he is sole, and singular, guided merely by his own will.' The king-in-Parliament, he added, was superior to the king alone, and possessed '*suprema potestas*, the soveraigne power'. Since the principle that taxation required consent was one of the 'two maine fundamental points' of the law of England, any attempt by the king to levy taxes outside Parliament was *ipso facto* an attempt to change the law – and consequently an assault upon the other main fundamental point of the constitution, Parliament's monopoly of legislation. To permit impositions was, then, to undermine the authority of Parliament and, potentially, to threaten its very existence. A king who could tax and legislate by himself could not be trusted to summon Parliament or to take any notice of its advice.[18] In 1610 fears for the continued existence of Parliament were rife. Such fears were, indeed, a major reason for the failure of the Great Contract – which would have gone far towards making the king independent of Parliament.[19] They also fuelled opposition to impositions – and such opposition, in turn, made the king more reluctant to call Parliament.

In 1614 the Commons once more discussed a bill against impositions. Sir Herbert Crofts spoke in its favour, declaring that as long as impositions stood, no man was 'certain of the Property, but only of the Use, of his own Goods'.

17 William Hakewill, *The libertie of the subject: against the pretended power of impositions* (1641) 11, 24; Martin in *PD 10*, 89.
18 Yelverton (really Whitelocke) in *ST*, ii, 482–3.
19 A.G.R. Smith, 'Crown, Parliament and finance: the Great Contract of 1610', in Peter Clark, Alan G.R. Smith and Nicholas Tyacke, eds, *The English commonwealth 1547–1640*, 111–27, at 124–5.

By taking away rights of property, said Jones, impositions reduced free subjects to the status of 'the Kings Vilaynes'. To admit absolute royal power was to annihilate property. 'If the King may impose by his absolute Power', declared Brooke, no one would be 'certain what he hath; for it shall be subject to the King's Pleasure'. In the opinion of Sir Edwin Sandys the king's alleged power to levy impositions struck at 'the Foundation of all our Interests', and 'maketh us Bondmen'. 'Every man', he declared, 'hath a Propriety in his Goods, which will not suffer that to be transferred to another, without his own Consent.' Impositions might leave men the use of their goods, subject to the king's pleasure, but they destroyed property: 'We have no propriety in our goods as long as the king's prerogative is unlimited to impose as much upon us as he pleaseth.'[20]

The intransigence of the House's attitude towards impositions was one of the main reasons why the Parliament of 1614 was Addled. James dissolved it before any subsidies were voted or laws passed. When he summoned Parliament again in 1621 new issues forced the question of impositions into the background. England was afflicted by a deepening economic crisis, and events on the Continent made war likely. The prospect of war against foreign papists served to create an illusory unity, though ideological divisions prevented consensus on the form which such a war should take. In 1621 and 1624 people of all political persuasions strove to bury their constitutional differences. Impositions were not, indeed, forgotten. In 1624 Spencer told the House of Commons that 'He, that hath no Propriety in his Goods, is not free', and added that 'Allowance of Impositions takes away all Propriety.' Many no doubt agreed with him, but the House resolved to shelve the question of impositions in the face of more pressing business.[21]

Such business included monopolies which came under fire in the Commons in both 1621 and 1624. Monopolies, granted to courtiers who sold them to favoured merchants, aroused the resentment of others who were excluded from them. They also raised constitutional issues, and objections to them were often based on an extended version of the familiar principle that property could not be taken without consent. By issuing monopolies the king rewarded his servants, or made money, at public expense. For one thing, monopolies were inflationary. Again, to grant one man a monopoly was to exclude his rivals from a profitable enterprise. It deprived these rivals not of wealth but of the means of increasing their wealth. In a famous legal case of 1602 it was decided that 'all trades . . . which prevent idleness . . . and exercise men and youth in labour, for the maintenance of themselves and their families, and for the increase of their substance . . . are profitable for the commonwealth'. So to deprive a man of his trade by creating a monopoly was contrary

20 *CJ* 467 (Crofts), 493 (Jones), 467 (Brooke), 472, 484 (Sandys); Sandys in J.P. Cooper, ed., *Wentworth papers 1597–1628* (1973) 75. On impositions and the Addled Parliament cf. Clayton Roberts and Owen Duncan, 'The parliamentary undertaking of 1614', *EHR* 93 (1978) 481–98 at 496–7.
21 *CJ* 759, 760; cf. Russell, *Parliaments and English politics*, 199.

to the common interest. As so often, lawyers construed the public good as equivalent to, and not superior to, private rights.[22]

In 1610 Fuller employed a slightly different and stronger version of the argument. A royal order tending to prohibit subjects from labour, he claimed, would be 'unlawful and an absurd commandment because it is directly against the law of God, which saith six days thou shalt labour'. So, by extension, 'the grant and prohibition of any king tending to prohibit any of his subjects in his lawful calling or trade thereby to live, when he knoweth no other trade or living, is contrary to the law of God and therefore a void grant or prohibition'. A divine right to labour in one's calling was clearly incompatible with monopolies. Coke similarly affirmed that monopolies were wrong on principle, and merchants eagerly embraced his views. They did so because an appeal to principle was more persuasive than a mere assertion of narrow self-interest. The Act of 1624 declared that with a few exceptions monopolies were and always had been against the law.[23]

In 1625 the accession of Charles provided an opportunity for the question of impositions to be reopened by indirect means. Since the reign of Henry VI Parliament had voted each new monarch the subsidy of tonnage and poundage for life. This Parliamentary tax, together with certain levies which the king could make according to common law, constituted his legal customs revenues. In 1625 Sir Robert Phelips proposed that a saving clause be included in the bill for tonnage and poundage, spelling out 'that nothing in this Act may be passed against us, for Maintenance of Impositions'. It is possible that some members intended to go further, and make tonnage and poundage dependent on the abolition of impositions. Phelips also moved that the bill should be made temporary, ignoring Yorkist and Tudor precedents. This innovatory measure was bound to annoy the king – as Mallett pointed out. Nevertheless, the House decided to vote tonnage and poundage for one year only. The Lords refused to pass such a bill, but the king continued to collect both tonnage and poundage and impositions.[24] In the opinion of many members of the House of Commons, such action was wholly illegal.

In 1626 the Commons resolved that 'the taking of Tonnage and Poundage, without assent in Parliament' should be 'presented to his Majesty, as a Grievance', and decided to draw up a remonstrance to the king on the subject. The House's committee on grievances also suggested that the levying of impositions 'without common Assent in Parliament . . . should be again presented to his Majesty, as a great Grievance, under which the subject suffereth'.[25]

22 Sir Edward Coke, *The reports*, ed. G. Wilson (1776) 11, f, 86a.
23 Fuller in *PP 10*, ii, 160; Coke, *Reports*, 11, f. 53. On the adoption of Coke's views cf. Russell, *Parliaments and English politics*, 61–3.
24 *CJ* 813, 803; DHC 25, 12–13; *PP 25*, 313–14, 317, 430, 432–3, 511; Russell, *Parliaments and English politics*, 227–9. Russell convincingly argues that Phelips, Coke and Sandys may have intended to give impositions Parliamentary authority, not to deprive the king of them – another indication that it was constitutional principle and not mere money that was at issue in the debates on impositions.
25 *CJ* 863, 868; cf. 850. *PP 26*, iii, 320–1, 325–6, 392, 395, 398; cf. 83–6.

In 1628 the Commons passed a remonstrance which condemned 'the taking [of] tonnage and poundage without grant thereof by act of parliament ever since the beginning of your Majesty's reign'. This and other royal actions, they said, had made 'the hearts of your people . . . full of fear of innovation and change of government'. Later, a second remonstrance was prepared, declaring 'that the receiving of tonnage and poundage and other impositions not granted by parliament is a breach of the fundamental liberties of this kingdom'. The king should not 'take it in ill part', the remonstrance continued, if his 'loving subjects . . . shall refuse to make payment of any such charges without warrant of law demanded'.[26]

The king prorogued Parliament to forestall the passing of this remonstrance. But when they met again in 1629, the Commons soon reverted to the question of tonnage and poundage, which the king had continued to collect. Some merchants had refused to pay, on the grounds that the levy was extra-Parliamentary, and hence illegal. The customs officers confiscated the goods of a number of these men, including John Rolle. In 1629 the House proceeded against the officers, claiming that their action constituted a breach of Parliamentary privilege since Rolle was a member of the Commons. Of course, the officers had been acting on the king's command, but this cut little ice with many in the Lower House. They relied on the principle that illegal royal orders were void, and that anyone who obeyed them was punishable at law. The consequence of this was to separate the king from his ministers, and, in effect, to permit active resistance to royal commands. When the Speaker, obeying the king's orders, attempted to adjourn the House on 2 March, he was forcibly kept in his chair while a declaration was read which condemned as enemies of the commonwealth anyone who paid, or advised payment, 'of the subsidies of Tonnage and Poundage, not being granted by Parliament'.[27]

The king's collection of tonnage and poundage attracted hostility in the Commons during 1628–29. But in the session of 1628 it was another measure – the Forced Loan – which won most attention. The main thrust of the arguments voiced on this subject was once more directed against the *illegality* of the levy, not against its inexpediency. The same ideas which were used to condemn impositions and the collection of tonnage and poundage were likewise employed to condemn the Loan.

On 26 March the House resolved that 'it is the undoubted right of the subjects of England that they have such a propriety in their goods that they are not to be taken from them, nor to have levies, taxes, and loans set upon them without assent of parliament'. On 3 April a still clearer resolution was passed in a grand committee. 'The ancient and undoubted right of every free man', it declared, 'is that he hath a full and absolute property in his goods and

26 *PP 28*, IV, 315, 471.
27 Protestation of 2 March in Gardiner, *Constitutional documents of the puritan revolution*, 82–3. A valuable discussion of the Parliamentary session of 1629 is C. Thompson, 'The divided leadership of the House of Commons', in Kevin Sharpe, ed., *Faction and Parliament: essays on early Stuart history* (Oxford 1978) 246–84.

estate, and that no tax, tallage, loan, benevolence, or other like charge ought to be commanded or levied by the King, or any of his ministers, without common assent by act of parliament.' What was wrong with the Forced Loan was not that it was inexpedient, or hard to administer, but that it struck at the property rights of the subject, infringing what Digges called 'an undoubted and fundamental point of this so ancient common law of England, that the subject hath a true property in his goods and possessions'.[28]

The king had claimed that public necessity justified the Loan. The point of asserting that the subject had a 'full', or 'true' or 'absolute' property was to contest this claim. Sir John Eliot told the Commons that he was concerned 'not for monies, or the manner how to be levied', but for 'the propriety of goods'. In other words, he was willing to contribute money to measures dictated by the public good, but was unwilling to have money taken from him without his consent in Parliament. To admit that the king possessed extra-legal powers to take goods in emergencies was to undermine the law, and 'that ceasing, all propriety ceaseth'. The king's recent exactions had served to destroy the rule of law and bring in 'the chaos of a higher power'. Extra-Parliamentary taxation subverted the constitution by making it possible for the king 'to annihilate acts of parliament, and parliaments themselves'.[29]

Later, when he had been imprisoned in the Tower for seditious conduct in the Parliamentary session of 1629, Eliot wrote two works of political theory. In one of these – the *De jure majestatis* – he argued that the king *did* possess extra-legal powers which he could use to defend the public interest in emergencies. This treatise is largely an English summary of a Latin work by the Continental absolutist Arnisaeus. It is far from clear that it represents Eliot's own views. In the other book – *The monarchie of man* – Eliot took a markedly different line. He quoted Cicero to show 'that nothing should be taken either of the goods or person of a subject without a judgement of the Senate (who are the makers of the Lawes)'. He argued, on the basis of 'the use and practise of all times from the moderne to the ancient', that '*de iure*, and in right . . . Princes are to be regulated by the lawes, and the lawes have an operation on the Prince'. Reverting to the classics, he asserted that 'the law is *Rex omnium*, as Pindarus saies, the king and governour of all kings'. Writing in the Tower, Eliot was aware that it would be unwise for him to handle the question of royal power 'with any roughnesse, lest it reflect some new beame of terrour on our selves'. Yet in *The monarchie of man*, as in his Parliamentary speeches, he maintained that the law, which protected property, was superior to the king and limited his powers. His views were unchanged, though a new note of pessimism had crept into their expression: 'there is such a confluence of flatterie conducing to our prejudice, such labour to make Monarchie unlimited, an absoluteness of government without rule . . . as to attempt against it is

28 *PP 28*, ii, 125, 276, 334.
29 Eliot in *PP 28*, ii, 57. The king's position on the Loan is made clear in the commission for Middlesex – *PP 28*, vi, 27 – and in the printed instructions to commissioners – ibid., 30.

now to ride against the tide'. After 1629 Eliot saw little prospect of preventing the victory of absolutism in England.[30]

In 1628 it still seemed possible that this outcome could be averted by legal means. This was the point of the Petition of Right. The Petition acknowledged no emergency royal powers of taxation. The claim of necessity, in short, did not justify the king in flouting the law. It was, in any case, self-contradictory to infringe the liberties of the subject for the sake of promoting the public good. Sir Francis Seymour confessed that 'he is no good subject nor well affected to his Majesty and the state that will not willingly and freely lay down his life, when the end may be the service of his Majesty and the good of the commonwealth'. A subject, then, should be prepared to sacrifice life itself for the public good. 'But on the contrary', he asked rhetorically, 'when against a parliament law the subject shall have taken from him his goods against his will . . . shall it be accounted want of duty in us to stand upon our privileges hereditary to us, and confirmed by so many acts of parliament?' In Seymour's view, it could never be in the public interest to deprive the subject of his goods without the consent of Parliament. He defused the absolutist argument for extra-Parliamentary levies – which claimed that private property rights were subordinate to the public interest – by identifying the public interest with the preservation of property. In defending their property, he claimed, the English would 'but tread the steps of our forefathers who ever preferred the public interest before their own right, nay, before their lives'. His argument is a neat illustration of the way in which the rhetoric of the public good was used by anti-absolutists to defend private rights.[31]

In the 1630s Charles again appealed to necessity to justify extra-Parliamentary levies, of which the most notorious was Ship Money. When the Short Parliament met in 1640, Ship Money soon came under attack in the House of Commons. Once again, objections to it centred on the principle that taxation requires consent. On 4 May the Speaker, John Glanville, told the House that 'in his conscience shipmoney was not legall'. Many agreed with him. Harbottle Grimston argued that as long as Ship Money stood, there was no point in voting subsidies – for the subject possessed no property, and evidently no one could give what he did not have ('*nemo potest dare quod non habet*'). The abolition of Ship Money, and of all other extra-Parliamentary levies, was the logical prerequisite to the voting of subsidies by Parliament. Of course, Ship Money did not literally deprive subjects of all their goods. But it did deprive them of property in those goods. In the words of Falkland, 'though our goods

---

30 Sir John Eliot, *De jure majestatis*, ed. A.B. Grosart (1882) 165, 175; *The monarchie of man*, ed. A.B. Grosart, 2 vols (1879) II, 49, 52, 45. Different interpretations are in C.H. McIlwain, *Constitutionalism and the changing world* (Cambridge 1939) 78–9; R.W.K. Hinton, 'Government and liberty under James I', *The Cambridge Historical Journal* 11 (1953) 48–64, at 49; J.N. Ball, 'The Parliamentary career of Sir John Eliot', unpublished Cambridge University Ph.D. dissertation, 1953, 278–9; cf. Ball, 'Sir John Eliot and Parliament, 1624–1629', in Sharpe, ed., *Faction and Parliament*, 173–208, at 175. Ball's contention that Eliot granted the crown a 'discretionary power' is certainly correct, but Eliot subordinated such power to the law of the land.
31 *PP 28*, II, 56–7.

were not taken away yet the property was'. If the king could tax without
consent in a case of necessity, and if he alone could decide what constituted
such a case, then he could deprive his subjects of their goods at pleasure. 'If
the king be judge of the necessitye', said Sir John Strangeways, 'wee have
nothing and are but Tennants at will.'[32]

In the Short Parliament the condemnation of Ship Money was a major goal
of many members of the House of Commons. A wider objective was to rule
out extra-Parliamentary taxation of all kinds. To take away Ship Money, said
Edward Kirton, 'was not enough; for others could invent as well as Mr Noye
and wee must expect new oppressions' (Attorney-General Noy was widely
held responsible for Ship Money). Pym argued in much the same way, and
wished to 'have it published that no charges should bee laid upon the people
without consent in parliament'. Of course, the Petition of Right had already
gone some way towards meeting Pym's demand. It had asked 'that no man
hereafter be compelled to make or yield any gift, loan, benevolence, tax, or
such like charge without common consent by Act of Parliament'. These words
could easily be construed as ruling out Ship Money. St John, for example,
claimed that the question of the legality of Ship Money had long since been
decided, for 'in the matter of [the] Loane, this of ship money was likewise
Judged'. The condemnation of the Forced Loan by the Petition of Right suf-
ficed to make all extra-Parliamentary taxation illegal. In spirit St John was
certainly correct.[33]

There was nothing particularly novel about the arguments used against
Ship Money in the Short Parliament. The same arguments – often expressed
in strikingly similar words – had been voiced against impositions, the Forced
Loan, and Charles's collection of tonnage and poundage. From the very beginning of the period the idea of absolute property was commonplace among
members of the House of Commons and those whom they represented.[34]
Indeed, it is so easy to find statements of this idea that it is tempting to assume
this was the *only* view of property current in England. Such an assumption
would be mistaken, for there were English absolutists.

ABSOLUTISTS ON PROPERTY

In his *True law of free monarchies*, James I declared that all kings possess
supreme power over the lands and goods of their subjects. By this he meant
not that they actually own all the material wealth in their kingdoms, but that
they could use this wealth in their God-given task of ruling. Of course, the

32 *PSP 40*, 195 (Glanville), 178 (Grimston), 191 (Falkland), 159 (Strangeways).
33 Ibid., 190 (Kirton, Pym), 185 (St John). Kirton's claim that Noy invented Ship Money was
commonplace but mistaken: Noy's role, and earlier Ship Money schemes, are discussed in R.J.W.
Swales, 'The Ship Money levy of 1628', *Bulletin of the Institute of Historical Research* 50 (1977) 164–
76, especially 165.
34 The idea outside Parliament is discussed in Derek Hirst, *The representative of the people?* (Cambridge 1975) 176; Clive Holmes, 'The county community in Stuart historiography', *Journal of
British Studies* 19 (1980) 54–73, at 64–9; Richard Cust, *Forced Loan* 150–85.

king ought to abide by settled laws wherever his higher obligations made this possible. So he should respect property rights. Nevertheless, James held, kings had power to levy at least some taxes even without the consent of their subjects. 'All kings', he told Parliament in 1610, 'have power to lay impositions.' James was fully aware that a king could misuse his power: 'if he might impose he might bring in all the money of the kingdom'. This, he thought, was no argument against the power. 'I am sure none of you', he told Parliament, 'when you have advised wisely and considered, but will cross his mouth and deny that to be a reason, that because a king may do in excessive manner, therefore he shall not do it at all . . . Because he may be good or ill, should we have power to set him limits? Beware of such arguments.'[35]

As we have seen, many of his loving subjects failed to take their monarch's advice. Yet even in the House of Commons, views similar to the king's were occasionally expressed. In 1610 Attorney-General Hobart declared that the king 'may by common law impose', and added that even if 'he might not by law, yet sure he may by reason of state'. In the same year Henry Yelverton told his fellow members that by the law of nations the king could levy impositions. He denied that this power could be taken from the king by Act of Parliament, for the right of imposing 'concernes the King in his prerogative and government'. This argument, which was practically identical with that voiced by Fleming in Bate's Case, aroused the ire of other members. Richard Martin, for instance, pointed out that it gave the king 'an arbitrary, irregular, unlimited and transcendent power', and others joined in the attack on Yelverton for the 'tyrannical positions, that he was bold to bluster out'. Again, in 1628 Sir Francis Nethersole argued that just as 'a private man in his necessity may preserve his life with that which is another man's', so the king could preserve the kingdom by similar means. His opinions were ignored by his fellow members in the Lower House.[36]

Among the clergy, ideas of this kind were far more common, as we have already seen. People such as Bancroft, Harsnett, Maynwaring and Sibthorp believed that the king possessed extra-legal powers of taxation. So, too, did the Civil lawyer Cowell. Another civilian, William Fulbecke, claimed that 'in the law of tributes, subsidies, and prerogatives royal, all Nations have consented'. Like James I, he thought that by the law of nations every monarch had the right to levy taxes, even against the wishes of his subjects. For 'speciall causes', he argued, kings had 'free disposall' of the 'landes and goods' of their subjects. But 'they may not without cause bereave them of their goods'. So it remained true that subjects held property in their goods. The clergy's *Constitutions and canons* of 1640 took much the same line. Customs, subsidies and 'all manner of necessary support and supply', they stated, were 'due to Kings from their subjects by the Law of God, Nature, and Nations, for the publike

35 James I, *Trew law, Political writings* ed. Sommerville (Cambridge 1994) 74; *PP 10*, ii, 102.
36 *PP 10*, ii, 199 (Hobart); *PD 10*, 89, 88 (Yelverton, Martin); Carleton to Edmondes in R.F. Williams, ed., *The court and times of James the First*, 2 vols (1848) i, 121 (on Yelverton); *PP 28*, ii, 125, cf. 132 (Nethersole).

defence, care and protection of them'. Taxes, then, were not gifts freely given, but debts owed to the king. This, however, did not diminish the subjects' 'propertie . . . in all their goods and estates', for it was 'part of the Kingly office to support his subjects in the propriety and freedom of their estates'. Similarly, Charles I justified the Forced Loan and Ship Money by appealing to necessity – and thus effectively claiming extra-legal emergency powers – and yet assured his subjects that he 'ever intended' them to enjoy 'property of goods'.[37]

It was one thing for kings or clerics to assert a royal right to make extra-Parliamentary levies, and quite another for such levies to become effective at law. What put the seal of legal approval upon impositions and Ship Money were the decisions in Bate's Case and Hampden's Case. Did the judges in these cases base their verdicts on a narrow and precedent-bound construction of the law, or did they adopt the full apparatus of absolutist theory? Of course, it is no part of the function of a judge, giving judgment in a court of law, to spell out a whole theory of the state. It is true, but hardly surprising, that judges often appealed to legal concepts and precedents rather than to any abstract philosophy of politics.[38] Some judges – for instance Bramston and Davenport in Hampden's Case – avoided the wider theoretical issues altogether.[39] Others, however, did not. A case in point is Fleming in Bate's Case. All power is from God, he said, and added that 'To the King is committed the government of the realm and his people.' In his opinion 'the power to govern' included an 'absolute power', not regulated by the law, to rule in the public interest. So the king could levy impositions, and could also 'impose any quantity he pleases'. The quantity, he declared, 'is to be referred to the wisdom of the King, who guideth all under God by his wisdom, and this is not to be disputed by a subject'.[40]

Sir Robert Berkeley, giving judgment on Hampden's Case in 1638, was equally willing to face the theoretical issues. In a case of necessity, he said, the king had 'regal power' to make extra-Parliamentary levies 'for the preservation of the safety of the commonwealth' (*salus reipublicae*). Without this power, he continued, 'I do not understand how the King's Majesty may be said to have the majestical right and power of a free monarch'. Berkeley specifically denied that the king could take his subjects' goods only 'upon a common consent in Parliament'. He asserted, however, that royal power was congruent with the subject's rights of property. This was, of course, conventional

37 Fulbecke, *The pandectes of the law of nations*, ff. 68a, 12b; *Constitutions and canons ecclesiasticall* (1640) sig. C1b; Charles I, *His maiesties declaration to all his loving subjects, of the causes which moved him to dissolve the last Parliament* (1640) 19, cf. 46–7. That kings have the power to tax without consent was stated by Thomas Bilson as early as 1603: *A sermon preached at Westminster before the King and Queens maiesty* (1603) sig. C2a–b.
38 A slightly different interpretation is in M.A. Judson, *Crisis of the constitution: an essay in constitutional and political thought in England* (New Brunswick 1949) 141, 349.
39 Russell, 'The Ship Money judgments of Bramston and Davenport', *EHR* 77 (1962) 312–18, revises the traditional view that the judgments were narrowly technical, but shows that they avoided the constitutional commitment of Berkeley and Croke.
40 Fleming quoted in J.P. Kenyon, *The Stuart constitution* (Cambridge 1966) 62–4.

among absolutists, and Berkeley was able to quote the king's own words on the point. Virtually the only absolutist to deny that subjects have rights of property against the crown was Thomas Hobbes.[41]

In 1610 Lord Chancellor Ellesmere himself attacked the Commons' bill against impositions, asserting that it was 'so strange both in form and matter as in former times have not been seen'. He inveighed against its preamble, which had asserted 'that the propriety of any man's goods or chattles cannot nor ought not to be altered or changed, nor any way charged, by any absolute authority of the King's Majesty, without common consent in Parliament'. This principle, he believed, was mistaken. Later in James's reign Sir John Davies wrote a defence of impositions in which he drew on a variety of arguments, and not least upon the theory of royal absolutism. 'The Law of Nature or Nations', he said, 'is nothing else but that which common reason hath establisht amongst all men for the common good of all men.' This law, he claimed, 'is of equal force in all Kingdoms, for all Kingdoms had their beginning by the Law of Nations'. Davies proceeded to argue that 'by the same Law of Nations, Tributes and Customes became due to the King or Prince to maintain him in his place of Government'. The king might have agreed to abide by settled laws in ordinary cases. But he still retained prerogatives 'in point of Government' which 'cannot be restrained or bound by Act of Parliament'. By the law of nations kings possessed the power to rule and defend their kingdoms. No inferior law could deprive them of it.[42]

Some people, Davies knew, had argued that 'the King hath no such Prerogative . . . whereby he may take away the Lands or Goods of a Subject without his consent'. He neatly drew the sting from this contention. Consent, he argued, could take two forms – express and tacit (or implicit). If the king should take my goods in a case of necessity 'he doth me no wrong, though he doth it without my consent, for my implicit consent doth concur with it, for that I being a member of the Common-weal, cannot but consent to all Acts of necessity tending to the preservation of the Commonwealth'. The law of nations was common reason. To deny the powers which it guaranteed was therefore irrational. So all rational people consented to them.[43]

Davies believed that the king had the power to levy impositions. This prerogative was derived from the law of nations, not from the common law: 'the Kings Prerogative is more ancient than the customary Law of the Realm'. In Davies's view the question of the king's 'Prerogative in laying Impositions upon Merchandizes, ought not to have been made or moved at all'. No one

41 Berkeley quoted in Gardiner, ed., *Constitutional documents of the puritan revolution*, 122. Hobbes's views on property are discussed in Johann P. Sommerville, *Thomas Hobbes: political ideas in historical context* (1992) 48–51, 89–85, 163–5. In Hampden's Case, Sir Francis Crawley employed arguments very like those of Berkeley: *ST* III, 1083. Crawley is also briefly discussed in Glenn Burgess, *The politics of the ancient constitution: an introduction to English political thought, 1603–1642* (1992) at 205–7, though he is there called Sir Edward (205), and later he appears as Sir Edmund (288).
42 *PP 10*, I, 281 (Ellesmere); Davies, *The question concerning impositions*, 7–8, 4, 29–30, 131.
43 Davies, *The question concerning impositions*, 97–8.

should have been allowed to discuss it. On 21 May 1610 James himself reprimanded members of the House of Commons for disputing his power to impose. The following day Thomas Wentworth told the Lower House that if, as the king supposed, it was sedition to debate the king's prerogative, then 'all our law books are seditious, for they have ever done it'. He suggested that the House should 'make some answer to the King'. They should tell him the truth about his prerogative, and thereby discharge the trust reposed in them by their 'country in preserving their liberties which they have lost'. On 23 May the Commons addressed a remonstrance to James, affirming the 'ancient, general, and undoubted Right of Parliament to debate freely, all Matters which do properly concern the Subject, and his Right or State', and, in particular, to discuss impositions.[44]

Differences of opinion on questions of abstract political theory spilled over into attitudes on the relationship between royal power and the subject's property. Some people claimed that the law, which guaranteed rights of property, was superior to royal power, and denied that the king possessed any extra-legal authority to take a subject's goods. Others claimed that the king's supreme power to provide for the public good entailed rights of extra-Parliamentary taxation. Did a similar analysis apply to other constitutional questions – for example to the problem of imprisonment without cause shown, which attracted particular attention in 1627–28?

IMPRISONMENT WITHOUT CAUSE SHOWN, AND THE PETITION OF RIGHT

In a treatise of 1557, the lawyer William Stanford permitted the monarch to imprison without showing cause. In some cases it would be contrary to the public interest for criminals to be charged as soon as they are arrested. For example, to charge suspected traitors with treason is to warn their fellow-conspirators that the game is up. 'Were it otherwise', said Raleigh, 'the King should never come to the knowledge of any conspiracy or treason against his Person or state.'[45] Under James I, few people questioned the right of the king, acting through the Privy Council, to suppress the cause of imprisonment in such circumstances. There was little complaint about this royal prerogative as long as it was exercised in a way that was compatible with the general principles of the common law. This changed when Charles I misused his power by imprisoning more than a hundred refusers of the Forced Loan, whom many thought were not criminals at all.

When Thomas Hedley attacked impositions in the Parliament of 1610, he denied that the king could ever tax without consent, but confessed that for 'matter of state' his majesty might imprison people without showing cause. The House itself admitted as much in its petition of temporal grievances,

---

44 Ibid., 33, sig. A2a; *PP 10*, II, 102 (James I), 108 (Wentworth); *CJ* 431.
45 William Stanford, *Les plees del coron* (1557) ff. 72b–73b; Raleigh, *The prerogative of parliaments*, 6.

presented to the king on 7 July. In 1621 Sir William Fleetwood introduced a bill into the Commons 'for the better Securing of the Subjects from wrongful Imprisonment, and Deprivation of Trades and Occupations'. This measure was primarily directed against the powers of monopolists to imprison. But in the course of debate the issue of the king's prerogative was raised once more. Again, few speakers questioned it. True, Alford argued that if the king could imprison without showing cause for 'matters of state', it was essential that this term 'matters of state' be defined – else 'lett us be Villaines'. If the king alone decided what constituted 'matters of state', then he could, in effect, imprison anyone for anything, and bring no charge. Alford's point fell on deaf ears. 'Matter of state' was not subjected to legal definition, and the king's power to suppress the cause of commitment was acknowledged. Sir Edward Coke himself spoke in favour of the conventional view, and justified his opinion with legal precedent. On this question he was no leader of radical opposition to the crown in 1621. Indeed, he was more conservative than many in the House. Coke held that by law as few as two Privy Councillors could commit without showing cause. In 1621 he was himself a Privy Councillor. The bill, which was passed by the House, required that at least six Councillors authorise the commitment. In 1624, when the bill was reintroduced, a further restriction on the exercise of the king's authority was added, limiting the maximum period of imprisonment to ten days. After ten days, a charge had to be brought. Even this bill, which never became law, left the power itself intact.[46]

Until the reign of Charles I, then, there was wide agreement that the king possessed the prerogative of imprisonment, though the grounds of this prerogative were debated. Stanford and Coke held that the royal power was granted to the king by common law. The Elizabethan antiquary Lambarde, by contrast, dated this prerogative to the Conquest. William of Normandy had 'governed by a meere and absolute power, as in a Realme obtained by Conquest'. Later, Magna Carta had re-established the rule of the common law in many areas, but kings retained the old 'absolute Authoritie' in 'a few rare and singular Cases'. The royal prerogative of imprisonment, then, was derived not from the common law, but from the absolute authority of a conqueror. In 1613 the Privy Council itself declared that this royal right was one part of his majesty's 'absolute power incident to his sovereignty'.[47] From the practical point of view, however, it did not matter whether the prerogative of imprisonment was construed as an aspect of the king's sovereignty – which was above the law – or as a power guaranteed to the monarch solely by the

46 *PP 10*, II, 185, cf. 191–2 (Hedley); 259–60 (petition); *CJ* 596 (Fleetwood); *CD 21*, III, 324 (Alford), V, 180 (Coke); cf. III, 172, 323–4; V, 226; VI, 213; Russell, *Parliaments and English politics*, 57–8.
47 William Lambarde, *Archeion, or, a discourse upon the high courts of justice*, eds C.H. McIlwain and P.L. Ward (Cambridge, Mass. 1957) 17, 62; *APC, 1613–14*, 211. Lambarde's views are discussed in W.H. Dunham, 'Regal power and the rule of law: a Tudor paradox', *Journal of British Studies* 3 (1964) 24–56, at 53–5, and in Elton, 'The rule of law in sixteenth-century England', in *Studies in Tudor and Stuart politics and government: papers and reviews 1946–1972*, 4 vols (Cambridge 1974–92) I, 266.

common law. While people agreed in substance, theoretical tensions aroused little conflict.

This picture changed drastically in 1627. Alford had warned the Commons that as long as 'matters of state' remained undefined the royal power was subject to abuse. Charles proved the truth of Alford's words by deeds. As all were well aware, the refusers of the Loan had not been guilty of treason. Indeed, it was doubtful that they were guilty of anything at all. To cite 'matter of state' for their commitment was to rely on a hollow pretext. But it was a legal pretext. In 1628, many members of the House of Commons were anxious to condemn his majesty's recent proceedings, including the Loan and the imprisonment of refusers. Imprisonment without cause shown was therefore declared illegal. Coke now announced that he had been misled by Stanford's opinion.[48] But it would be wrong to suppose that what made Coke, or others, change their minds on the king's power of imprisonment was a new and more accurate reading of English legal sources. The royal prerogative of imprisonment without cause shown attracted opposition because it was regarded as a tool in the enforcement of absolutism, and not because of any sudden discovery of precedents reposing in some dusty manuscript.[49] Again, those who denied the Commons' claims did not rest their case upon any narrow construction of legal precedent. Many were willing to appeal to the central doctrine of the theory of royal absolutism in order to justify their position: without extra-legal emergency powers the king could not perform his God-given task of governing the realm. So the law could not possibly deprive the king of this power.

The Parliament of 1628 assembled on 17 March. By 3 April the Commons had resolved 'that no free man ought to be committed, or detained in prison, or otherwise restrained by the command of the King, or the Privy Council, or any other, unless some cause of the commitment, detainer, or restraint be expressed, for which by law he ought to be committed, detained, or restrained'. In other words, imprisonment was not lawful unless cause was shown. The position of 1610 and 1621 had been abandoned. The subject's liberty from imprisonment – except according to due legal process – was elevated to an absolute principle, fully equivalent to his right of property in lands and goods. 'It is a fundamental right of the kingdom', said Digges on 26 March, and on the following day Selden told the Commons that the

48 Stephen D. White, *Sir Edward Coke and 'the grievances of the commonwealth', 1621–1628* (Chapel Hill 1979) 233.
49 J.A. Guy, 'The origins of the Petition of Right reconsidered', *HJ* 25 (1982) 289–312, at 296–8, quite plausibly emphasises the part played by the discovery of the king's attempt to tamper with the record of Sir John Heveningham's case in hardening attitudes towards the prerogative of imprisonment. The literature on the Petition of Right and the 1628 Parliament is vast. Two discussions are Russell, *Parliaments and English politics*, 323–89, and L.J. Reeve, 'The legal status of the Petition of Right', *HJ* 29 (1986) 257–77. Reeve discusses Charles's later attempts to evade the implications of the Petition in the cases of Selden and others in 'The arguments in the King's Bench in 1629 concerning the imprisonment of John Selden and other members of the House of Commons', *Journal of British Studies* 25 (1986) 264–87. See also Reeve's *Charles I and the road to personal rule* (Cambridge 1989).

distinguishing mark of 'freemen' was 'that they cannot be imprisoned at pleasure'. By ancient custom, he said, 'only Jews and villeins' could be committed
without cause shown. If the king could deprive subjects of liberty – or of
property – without their consent, then their status was no better than villeinage. Sir Edward Coke appealed to grounds even higher than fundamental law:
'I will conclude with the chiefest authority, the Acts of the Apostles, 25 cap.
verse the last: It is against reason to send a man to prison and not to show
the cause.'[50]

   The point of basing the liberty of the subject's person upon fundamental
law was to trump any royal claims to a power by which this liberty could be
infringed. The argument worked only on the assumption that royal power
was subordinate to the laws of the land. 'Our laws', said Richard Cresheld,
'are the *ne plus ultra* both to the King and the subject, and as they are Hercules's
pillars, so are they the pillars to every Hercules, to every prince, which he
must not pass.' Imprisonment 'without any declaration of the cause', he
claimed, 'is against the fundamental laws and liberties of this realm'.[51] Cresheld's

---

50 *PP 28*, II, 276, cf. 231; ibid., 129 (Digges), 151 (Selden), 102 (Coke). Pym also claimed that
commitment without cause shown was against God's law: ibid., III, 162. Members of Parliament
in the reigns of James I and Charles I often argued that if English liberties were undermined,
people would be reduced to the status of slaves or villeins: see pp. 97, 111, 137–8, 143–4, 154
above. As we have seen, the liberties in question included freedom from imprisonment without
cause shown, from legislation and taxation without consent, and from extra-legal discretionary
royal powers in general. In an excellent recent work – *Liberty before liberalism* (Cambridge 1998) –
Quentin Skinner has shown that a number of writers in the 1640s–1650s and later also argued that
individual liberty is possible only in a state where the consent of the people's representatives is
essential to lawmaking (49). Skinner locates these writers within a 'neo-roman' tradition which drew
on the thinking of ancient Roman authors (and perhaps especially Sallust: see ibid., 139–42). The
English neo-romans, he tells us, included John Milton, Marchamont Nedham, James Harrington
and Algernon Sidney. According to Skinner, other people said that even if rulers possess discretionary extra-legal powers, we can still be free, for they may exercise their powers in a benevolent
way that is compatible with our liberty; but the neo-romans mounted the distinctive argument
that as long as rulers have discretionary powers, we are *not* free – since the 'continued enjoyment'
of our 'civil liberty remains at all times dependent on their goodwill' (70).
   This 'neo-roman' theory is strikingly similar to the position commonly voiced in the early
Stuart Commons, that if the king has the power to imprison without showing cause, or to
perform other discretionary acts outside the law, we are villeins. As the present chapter indicates,
absolutists argued that the king's discretionary powers did not undermine liberty or property,
since the king could be trusted to respect his subject's rights although he was empowered to
undermine them; anti-absolutists denied that the king had any power of arbitrary imprisonment,
or of taxing or legislating without consent, arguing that subjects were not free if kings had such
authority. According to Skinner, 'the most basic contention' of 'neo-roman ideology' was that 'it
is only possible to escape from personal servitude if you live as an active citizen under a representative form of government' (77). He notes that the neo-romans 'generally agree' that 'the mass
of the people' should not themselves actively participate in political decision-making, but should
be represented by 'an assembly chosen by the people to legislate on their behalf' (32). These
positions are again close to views that were widespread in the Commons before 1640, though
arguably before the Civil War the House was keener to widen the franchise than it later became –
Derek Hirst, *The representative of the people? Voters and voting in England under the early Stuarts*
(Cambridge 1975) 63–84; David Underdown, *A freeborn people: politics and the nation in seventeenth-
century England* (Oxford 1996) 54, 89. A number of the neo-romans were eager to exclude from
political participation – including voting – all who had sided with the king and all who dissented
from godly puritan religious opinions.
51 Ibid., II, 146, 147.

analogy between the laws and the pillars of Hercules – the straits of Gibraltar – was somewhat unfortunate since, whatever classical mythology might say, it was evidently possible to sail beyond them. But his central message was clear: the laws of the land limited the king's power. He did not specify whether these limitations were contractual in origin, or arose from ancient and rational custom.

In England, said many of the Commons, royal power was limited by law, and a major function of the law was to protect the subject's liberty: 'the liberty of the subject is one of the great favorites of the law that would free any man from bondage'. If the king possessed extra-legal emergency powers which he could exercise for reason of state, then the subject's liberty would be undermined. So *all* royal power was subordinate to the common law. 'I deny that distinction of the absolute and legal power', said Browne, and added that 'reason of state is a meere chimera'. In his opinion, there were no circumstances in which a king could flout the law, or infringe the liberties which that law guaranteed. The law provided for all emergencies: 'there is no danger but the law hath made provision for it'. England, said Phelips, was a 'limited monarchy' in which royal power was 'restrained for the good of the subject'. 'The condition of a free man', he declared, 'is to live where there is not *dominium regale*, but *dominium regale politicum*, and this is the state of England.' The idea – derived from Fortescue – was old. The application to imprisonment was new but, in view of Charles's actions in 1627, predictable.[52]

'Even in 1628', it has been said, 'the opposition leadership carefully avoided any proposals which could be read as an invasion of prerogative rights.'[53] From the perspective of anti-absolutist theory this notion has something to commend it. The prerogative was a department of law. The resolutions of the House of Commons, and the Petition of Right itself, were purportedly nothing but declarations of old law. So they did not invade the prerogative, but merely spelled out its true nature. From the perspective of absolutist ideas, however, the case was rather different. It is manifest that a good many people believed that the Petition of Right *did* infringe the royal prerogative, and did so not for the purely empirical reason that it incorporated bad law (since legal precedent was in favour of royal power to imprison without cause shown) but for a much more drastic reason: the Petition undermined the king's God-given power to govern England. *All* attempts to subject the prerogative to legal definition struck at royal power.

The Commons' proposition, said the Earl of Banbury in the House of Lords on 22 April, 'does upon the matter take away all prerogative'. 'The Petition of the Commons', claimed the Bishop of Exeter on 14 May, is 'incompatible with the King's prerogative'. 'This petition', declared the Earl of Dorset ten days later, 'will give the King and monarchy a greater blow than any power from beyond seas.'[54] On 12 May the king himself had sent a letter

52 Ibid., 189 (Sherfield); 173 (Browne), cf. 176; 109 (Phelips).
53 Elton, *Studies in Tudor and Stuart government and politics*, II, 160.
54 *PP 28*, V, 330 (Banbury), cf. 328; 424 (Bishop of Exeter); 522 (Dorset).

to the Lords in which he discussed the Commons' attitude to the prerogative. He had, he said, graciously permitted his subjects to 'debate the highest points of our prerogative royal which, in the times of our predecessors – kings and queens of this realm – were ever restrained as matters that they would not have disputed'. In other words, the prerogative could be debated only with the king's permission. Unfortunately, in the present instance the Commons had misused the freedom which his majesty granted them. They had denied him the power to imprison without cause shown. To do this, he said, was to 'dissolve the very foundation and frame of our monarchy'. Charles cited no legal precedents to confirm his prerogative. Instead, he struck a higher note: 'without overthrow of sovereignty we cannot suffer this power to be impeached'. In conclusion, he promised to exercise the power beneficently: 'it is not in our heart nor will we ever extend our royal power, lent unto us from God, beyond the just rule of moderation in anything which shall be contrary to our laws and customs wherein the safety of our peoples shall be our only aim'.[55] The king derived his authority from God alone. It was to God that he was accountable for its exercise. Being a good king, he would use his power for the common safety, and if this meant that he had to disregard established laws and customs he would do so moderately. Obviously, this idea was diametrically opposed to views expressed in the House of Commons. Equally obviously, it was no new opinion. Indeed, it added nothing to ideas long since propounded by James I and by churchmen. Nor was Charles the only person to voice such notions in the Parliament of 1628.

On 17 April Serjeant Ashley declared that kings rule not only by the common law but also by 'a law of state', and added that 'in the law of state their acts are bounded by the law of nature'. 'The common law', he said, 'doth not provide for matters of state.' Where such matters were at issue, the king was to govern by the law of state, and could ride roughshod over liberties guaranteed by the inferior and irrelevant common law. The king's power of imprisoning without cause shown was 'committed to him by God'. Of course he could suppress the cause, for 'every state hath *secreta regni*' (secrets of the kingdom – i.e. state secrets). Fearing a breach with the Lower House, the Lords made Ashley apologise for his words, which had been spoken at a conference between members of both Houses. But others said as much.[56]

Sir Robert Heath, the Attorney-General, affirmed 'that the resolutions of the House [of Commons] were incompatible with a monarch that must govern by rule of state'. 'God', he said, 'has trusted the King with the government of his kingdom. Yet God forbid he should do what he will. He is answerable for it, to give account for it. But not to his subjects.' In Heath's

---

55 Ibid., III, 372.
56 Ibid., II, 528–9; cf. V, 283, 293, 300, 303. Ashley believed that the Lords had called him to account in order 'to prevent further affliction intended towards me'; he also continued to maintain his earlier views – 'if I be in an error, surely I shall die a heretic': Ashley to Buckingham, ibid., VI, 217.

view, 'None can take account of him but God.' Of course, his majesty might misuse his royal prerogatives. He could, for instance, pardon all criminals, and then 'the bad will eat up the good'. But the fact that the king might misuse a power was no proof at all that he did not have that power. Again, there was nothing novel about this line, which had been used by James to justify impositions. In Heath's view, the king could imprison without cause shown. His argument in favour of this thesis was simple: 'The King', he said, 'is trusted by the King of Kings.'[57]

In the Commons, Sir Francis Nethersole claimed that for reason of state the king could imprison without showing cause. Nethersole had justified extra-Parliamentary taxation on similar grounds. In the Lords, Dorset adopted the same stance on imprisonment. Others agreed with him. Lord Keeper Coventry distinguished between the legal powers of the king – exercised by and under law – and his regal powers. If the Lords endorsed the Commons' propositions, he asked rhetorically, 'what latitude will be left for the regal part?' The idea that the king possessed a regal power separate from the law did not commend itself to everyone in the Commons. 'Some of late', said Sherfield in the Lower House, 'have found out a difference *inter legalem et regalem authoritatem regis* (between the legal and the regal authority of the king), and that both in church and pulpit. King James brands such with the name of vipers and pests to the commonwealth.' On this view, a sizeable proportion of the Lords were vipers. For they did distinguish between the two powers, and granted the king a regal power to imprison without cause shown. All the Lords, said Weston, agreed 'to allow a latitude herein to the power of the King', whatever the law might say.[58]

Weston proposed, and the Lords adopted, a clause to be added to the Petition of Right, declaring that the document left the sovereign power of the king untouched. The Commons refused to accept this. 'What is "sovereign power"?', asked Alford. He turned to Bodin for an answer: 'Bodin says it is that that is free from any condition.' Should the Commons recognise such a power in the king of England? Alford did not think so. 'By this', he observed, 'we shall acknowledge a regal as well as a legal power.' The king had no extra-legal power. So it would be wrong to acknowledge it. 'Let us give that to the king that the law gives him, and no more.' Others agreed with him. According to Glanville, 'it is not safe to acknowledge a power that is above the law'. '"Sovereign power"', said Coke, 'is no parliament word in my opinion.' To recognise any such power would be to 'weaken the foundations of law', since 'by implication' it would grant the king 'power above all these laws'. Speaking on behalf of the House of Commons, Glanville told the Lords that to admit a sovereign power would be to enable the king – or rather, a wicked successor – 'to alter the whole frame and fabric of the commonwealth,

57 Ibid., v, 203–4.
58 Ibid., iii, 107 (Nethersole); v, 324 (Dorset), 322 (Coventry); ii, 189 (Sherfield); v, 324 (Weston) – another version, at 329, says that all the Lords *who had spoken* agreed on this.

and to dissolve that government whereby this kingdom has flourished for so many years and ages'.[59]

At first glance, it looks as though the House of Lords disagreed radically with the House of Commons on the royal prerogative of imprisonment. In the Lords, a majority believed that the king held extra-legal powers, of which this prerogative was one. They also claimed that his majesty possessed sovereign power – by which they apparently meant sovereign power. In the Commons, a majority denied that the king held any extra-legal powers whatever, and concluded that he possessed no sovereign power. Yet, in the end, the Lords agreed to drop the clause saving sovereign power, and passed the Petition. It received the royal assent on 7 June, and thus acquired statutory force. What was the reason for this volte-face? Did the Lords change their minds when they began to appreciate the logical force of Coke's arguments? Or do the events bear another and entirely different significance?

At a committee of both Houses on 25 April, the Lords recognised that 'for reason of state' the king could imprison without showing cause. This power, they held, was part of the 'royal prerogative, intrinsical to his sovereignty and betrusted him withal from God'. They proposed that his majesty be invited to declare the cause of imprisonment 'within a convenient time'. The Commons found this proposal unacceptable. As Coke pointed out, if the king possessed an 'intrinsical prerogative . . . entrusted by God . . . then no law can take it away'. Human law could not abrogate divine law. So, if the king held a *jure divino* prerogative to imprison without showing cause, all Parliamentary measures to deprive him of it would be ineffective. When the Lords proposed their addition to the Petition of Right on 17 May, reserving the 'sovereign power' of the king, precisely the same reasoning led the Commons to reject the clause.[60]

The argument cuts two ways. If no human authority can deprive the king of powers which God has guaranteed to him, then it simply did not matter what the Petition of Right said. There was no need to reserve the king's sovereign power, since *nothing* could touch that power. Coke believed that the prerogative was a part of the common law. So, to define the common law was to define the prerogative. But suppose that Coke was mistaken. Suppose that the prerogative consisted of powers granted to the king not by the common law but by God alone for the good government of the realm. In this case the Petition of Right could readily be construed as a declaration of the common law which had absolutely no effect on the prerogative – since the prerogative was not defined by the common law.

This argument was frequently voiced in the Lords, and more rarely in the Commons. It explains the apparent revolution in the attitude of at least some of the Lords towards the Petition of Right. Of course, there were men in the Upper House who simply shared the views of Coke. Moreover, the Lords

59 Ibid., v, 463 (Weston's admission of authorship of the clause); iii, 452 (the clause), 494 (Alford), 527, 495 (Coke), 566 (Glanville).
60 Ibid., iii, 75 (Lords' first proposition), 95 (Coke), 452, 494–5, 529, 531–2, 563–5 (Lords' second proposal and reactions to it).

were under severe pressure to reach agreement with the Lower House. Without such agreement the Commons would vote no subsidies. The king desperately needed money to continue the war effort. England's military fortunes rested upon the Lords' decision. In the end, they endorsed the Petition. This does not prove that all or most of them no longer believed that the king still possessed an extra-legal power to imprison without cause shown, and sovereignty itself.

The prerogative, said Manchester – Lord President of the Council – on 17 May, cannot be infringed or abrogated by legislation. 'We agree tacit all', he told the Lords, 'that the King hath a prerogative; that though he made a law that he shall not commit without a cause expressed, yet such a cause may happen that he may.' Even those who most abhorred the king's recent conduct expressed similar opinions. John Williams, Bishop of Lincoln, held that it was necessary 'to provide for those inconveniences which no settled law can provide for' – an attitude alien to the lawyers' notion that the common law provided for all contingencies. Equally alien to Coke's thinking were the sentiments voiced by the Earl of Bristol on 20 May. The Petition, he said, contained a declaration of the rights of the subject. It was these rights which were at issue, he claimed, adding that 'the king's prerogative is not before us, but came to be named accidentally'. If the Petition contained an accurate description of the rights which the English possessed at law, then it could be endorsed without any additional clause saving his majesty's sovereign power, for it bore no relation to the prerogative. Law and prerogative were two separate things.[61]

The point was made still more clearly by the Earl of Clare on 24 May: 'neither can this petition, nor any thing else we shall do hurt that prerogative. In emergent occasions, no law can hinder what is necessary to be done for the safety of us all.' When Laud came to annotate his copy of the Lords' propositions of 25 April, he wrote these words upon it: 'Saving the right of our crown (*Salvo jure coronae nostrae*) is intended in all oaths and promises exacted from a soveraigne.' No saving clause was needed to safeguard the prerogative. The prerogative would save itself. In words, the Petition might seem to strike at royal power. In fact, it could not – and therefore did not. When Charles consulted the judges on the Petition, they gave him much the same answer. Even if the Petition became law, they told him, it would not abrogate his power to imprison without showing cause.[62]

In the Commons, the Privy Councillor Sir Humphrey May said much the same thing. The Lords' words asserting the sovereign power of the king were true, he claimed, and added that 'no act of parliament can alter these words'. In May's opinion, the resolutions of the Commons 'stretch very far on the King's power, and if they be kept punctually will give a blow to government'.

---

61 Ibid., v, 453 (Manchester), 454 (Bishop of Lincoln), 480 (Bristol); cf. 493 (Abbot).
62 Ibid., v. 524 (Clare); SP 16/102/14 (Laud); cf. Raleigh, *The prerogative of parliaments*, 15, which has an almost identical formula. The king's questions and the judges' answers are printed in *PP 28*, vi, 46–8.

The king, he reported, had 'said that if government is touched he should not be able to protect us'. In his majesty's opinion, the clause saving sovereignty 'added nothing to him'. It merely recorded what was true. May endorsed these sentiments. His colleague Sir John Coke took a more practical approach. Imprisonment without cause shown was necessary to good government. As a Privy Councillor he would continue to imprison people in this way when need arose: 'Make what law you will. If I discharge the place I bear, I must commit men and must not discover the cause to any jailer or judge.'[63]

Three separate questions troubled members of Parliament in 1628. The first was the *expediency* of the king's recent actions in levying the Forced Loan and imprisoning refusers without cause shown. No one defended these measures, which the king himself had abandoned. The second was the *legality* of such proceedings, and, in particular, of commitment without cause shown. The judges' decision – or failure to decide – in the Five Knights' Case appeared to indicate that the subject could expect no legal redress against arbitrary imprisonment. To combat this, a majority in the Commons argued that imprisonment without cause shown was always contrary to the common law. From the perspective of legal precedents this claim was dubious, and it was contested in both Houses. But the interesting point is that debate was by no means confined to the issue of legality. Underlying this issue was a third and far more fundamental question of constitutional principle, which threatened to bring the Parliamentary session of 1628, and England's intervention in Continental affairs, to a halt. This was: what is the relationship between royal power and the common law?

In the Commons a few members, including Sir Thomas Wentworth and the Civil lawyer Sir Henry Marten, regarded the resolutions of the House as declarations of the law bearing no relation to royal power. 'I hope it shall never be stirred here', said Wentworth on 26 April, 'whether the King be above the law or the law above the King.' But most followed the lead of Sir Edward Coke and John Selden who believed that the king possessed no extra-legal powers whatever. Pym recognised no royal authority 'distinct . . . from the power of the law'. In the House of Lords, where the bishops sat, a very different constitutional theory prevailed. The king, they said, did possess God-given authority to secure the public weal, and could rule outside the law if need arose. This was the point of the Lords' propositions of 25 April and 17 May, and of their declaration of 26 May.[64]

When Charles assented to the Petition on 7 June he solved the problem of the legality of imprisonment without cause shown. The Petition declared such

---

63 *PP 28*, III, 537, 560 (May), 189 (Coke).
64 Ibid., III, 98–9 (Wentworth), 578–9 (Marten). Marten acknowledged that the king possessed sovereign power but thought it inappropriate to mention such power in the Petition: 'sovereign power is then best worth when it is had in tacit veneration, not when it is profaned by vulgar hearings or examinations'. For reactions in the House of Lords to Marten's speech cf. ibid., v, 524, 527. A different interpretation of Marten's attitude is in B.P. Levack, *The Civil lawyers in England 1603–1641* (Oxford 1973) 118–20. *PP 28*, III, 494 (Pym); v, 532 (Lords' declaration of 26 May).

imprisonment illegal. But Charles did not end the underlying constitutional dispute, for he never renounced his claim to extra-legal powers. His actions in the 1630s violated what many regarded as law. In 1636 Henry Burton claimed that he had been imprisoned without cause shown. This, he observed, was contrary to the Petition of Right. In 1638 Sir George Croke drew attention to the king's commands to sheriffs, incorporated in the writ for the collection of Ship Money. The sheriffs were 'to commit to prison' all whom they found 'rebellious and contrary'. Moreover, said Charles, such people were to be left in jail 'until we shall give further order for their delivery'. Croke noted that 'this is against Magna Charta, by which every one is free from imprisonment unlesse it be done uppon indyctment or other legall processe'. In the Short Parliament Sir Francis Seymour inveighed – as others had so often inveighed before – against those 'bad people' who gave the king 'an unlimitted power' not only over his subjects' property, but also over the liberty of their persons.[65]

The Petition of Right did not dispel fears that the king's policies were undermining the traditional constitution. In fact, it is most unlikely that Charles had any intention of altering what he took to be the constitution of England. Problems arose because his view of the constitution differed drastically from that of a good many of his wealthiest and most influential subjects. The king believed that the Petition was a declaration of law which did not and could not impinge upon his sovereign authority. Anti-absolutists believed that it was a summary of old laws which always had bound and continued to bind royal power, though this fact had recently escaped notice. Doubtless, in the Parliament of 1628 some men who had previously been uncommitted or uninterested in constitutional questions came to adopt more definite views. But the opposing interpretations of the constitution had been developed long before. It was not pressure of circumstance but education which led Charles to take an elevated view of his own prerogative in the Parliament of 1628. He made his ideas plain on the very first day of the session when he told Parliament that 'great danger and a common danger is the cause of this parliament, and that supply is the chiefest end of it', adding that if they 'should not give that supply, which this kingdom and state requires at your hands . . . I must, according to my conscience, take those other courses, which God hath put into mine hands'.[66] If Parliament would not give him money, God had empowered him to raise it by other means. It is needless to dwell on the obvious fact that Sir Edward Coke and his fellows believed the king had no legal power – and therefore no power at all – to raise extra-Parliamentary levies. It is likely that they also resented the attitude towards the nature and functions of Parliament which his majesty's words implied.

65 Henry Burton, *For God and the king* (1636) 53; Gardiner, ed., *Notes of the judgment delivered by Sir George Croke in the case of ship money*, 16, in *The Camden Miscellany*, volume the seventh (1875); Gardiner, *Constitutional documents of the puritan revolution*, 107 (Ship Money writ); *PSP 40*, 253 (Seymour).
66 *PP 28*, ii, 3.

PARLIAMENT

It is a good idea for rulers to consult their subjects. Even despots find it useful to gain information on the attitudes of those whom they govern. In England, the institution in which the king and his subjects met to discuss 'arduous and urgent' affairs of state was Parliament. No one thought that the purpose of Parliament was to oppose the king. Rather, they believed that its function was to do the king's business and that of the commonwealth.[67] On this question, sweet harmony prevailed. But what was the king's business? Did it include the assertion of liberties which the king himself denied? And could members of Parliament continue to discuss such liberties even when the king wished them to turn to what he saw as more important matters? These were the divisive questions.

Viewing things from an absolutist perspective, James I and his son believed that it was the duty of their loyal subjects assembled in Parliament to discuss what the king told them to discuss. This usually meant supply. Both men were interested in Parliament primarily for financial reasons. Since they were good kings, at least according to their own lights, they recognised that the institution also had a role to play in recommending laws and in bringing legitimate grievances to the royal attention. When discussing grievances the two Houses might question the exercise of royal power. They might point out that in practice the uses to which the king's power was put were proving onerous to the subject, and ask his majesty to remedy the defects. But they ought not to dispute the power itself. Both kings recognised that the Houses possessed certain customary privileges. They held, however, that these privileges stemmed from the royal will, and not from any law that stood above the king. In particular, the Houses possessed no privilege to dispute or undermine the royal prerogative.

For anti-absolutists, by contrast, supply was only a minor function of Parliament. Another, and far more important purpose of the institution was to maintain the law, and the liberties which that law guaranteed. The law, of course, ought to have been preserved by the judges. But if they failed in their task, or if the king circumvented the law, it was the duty of Parliament to restore lost liberties. This would be impossible if the king could silence dissent. Parliamentary privilege – and in particular, freedom of speech and freedom from arrest – did not arise from royal grace but from the ancient fundamental law of the land. The privileges of a member of the House of Commons were absolute liberties, fully equivalent to the subject's property in his goods. Both rights existed by the same law – the common law – and for the same reason – to preserve England from absolute monarchy. It was nonsense to suppose that members of Parliament could not discuss the royal prerogative. If this were true, kings might extend their powers unchecked, and the place of Parliament as the guardian of English liberties would be destroyed at a stroke.

---

67 This point is well made in Mark Kishlansky, 'The emergence of adversary politics in the Long Parliament', *Journal of Modern History* 49 (1977) 617–40, at 619.

An obvious fact is that it was in the interests of both the king and anti-absolutist members of the House of Commons to bury their theoretical differences and co-operate in Parliament. Money supplied the king with an incentive for compromise. The preservation of Parliaments furnished anti-absolutists with an equally compelling reason to drop or tone down their theoretical claims. Evidently, Parliament could not preserve liberties if it did not exist. But it was the king who called and dissolved Parliament. So it was self-defeating to say or do things which annoyed the king. 'I was ever of opinion', Bacon told the Commons in 1610, 'that questions which concern the power of the king and the liberty of the subject should not be textual, positive and scholastical, but slide in practice silently and not be brought into position and order.' There was sense in this advice, and on occasion it was taken. In 1614 the king arrested some members of the Commons for things they had said in Parliament. When Parliament met again seven years later, the question of whether these arrests constituted an infringement of privilege was mooted in the Lower House. Sir Edward Coke successfully 'laboured to perswade that this poynt might be layd aside, not to urge the Kinge with the remembrance of what was done the last parliament'. Again, Charles I allowed the House of Commons to debate his prerogative in 1628. He did this in the hope that they would eventually vote him five subsidies. From his point of view it was a compromise made worthwhile by the prospect of cash.[68]

Yet despite the manifest merits of co-operation for all concerned, conflict between the king and his subjects did occur in Parliament. When this happened, theoretical tensions were usually involved. Such tensions focused on the questions of royal power and the subject's liberties. The problem of what Parliament itself was became contentious inasmuch, and only inasmuch, as it was connected with these questions. The debate on the nature of Parliament was subordinate to the more general dispute between absolutists and their opponents. On matters unaffected by this dispute agreement was widespread, though not universal. A case in point is the issue of the composition of Parliament.

We are sometimes told that Parliament was usually held to consist of three estates – the Lords spiritual, the Lords temporal and the Commons. It was only in 1642, it is said, that a new attitude gained ground. For in that year Charles's answer to Parliament's nineteen propositions suggested that the three estates included the king: they were king, Lords and Commons.[69] Did people in early Stuart England in fact deny that the king was a part of Parliament, or one of the three estates? Did it matter to them what the three estates were? The king was sometimes treated as a part of Parliament. On other occasions he was not. The concept of three estates was not recognised by law, and was

68 *PP 10*, ii, 98 (Bacon); *CD 21*, iv, 39–40 (Coke).
69 C.C. Weston, 'The theory of mixed monarchy under Charles I and after', *EHR* 75 (1960) 426–43, at 427, 429; Weston and J.R. Greenberg, *Subjects and sovereigns: the grand controversy over legal sovereignty in Stuart England* (Cambridge 1981) 3–5, 18, 43. A fundamental discussion of the idea of the three estates in political theory before the Civil War is Michael Mendle, *Dangerous positions: mixed government, the Estates of the Realm, and Answer to the xix Propositions* (University, Ala. 1985).

irrelevant to all the major political theories. In France the Estates General did meet as three estates – the clergy, the nobility and the third estate or commons. In England an Act of Parliament required the approval of the two Houses and the king. It mattered little whether the notion of three estates was used to describe the English scene. To say that the king was, or was not, one of the estates was to say precisely nothing about the nature and limitations of royal power.

Sir Edward Coke, who was no absolutist, held that the three estates were the Lords spiritual, the Lords temporal and the Commons. So too did Raleigh, and John Cowell said the same thing. On the other hand, Henry Peacham, whose general political position was close to Cowell's and very different from Coke's, treated the three estates as the king, Lords and Commons. The Elizabethan antiquary William Lambarde likewise regarded the king as one of the three estates, as did Lord Chancellor Ellesmere. James I claimed that Parliament consisted of the king and the three estates, agreeing in this with both Coke and Cowell. John Selden shifted ground on the question. At one time he argued that the king was one of the three estates. Later, he abandoned this position. The lesson of all this is that both absolutists and their opponents were happy to take either of the two possible lines on the question. The problem had few theoretical implications, and those which it did have were connected less with the rights of the king than with the position of the clergy.[70]

If the Lords spiritual were an estate of the realm, then it was possible to argue that Parliament had necessarily to include the bishops. Conversely, if they were not an estate, then it followed that Parliament could meet without the bishops. On the eve of the Civil War the bishops were excluded from Parliament, and debate on whether they were an estate assumed immediate practical significance. Before 1640 the issue was more academic, since no attempt was made to exclude them. In the Short Parliament Lord Saye and Sele did indeed assert that 'the High Court of Parliament could proceede without the Bishops', and he may already have had exclusion in mind. But earlier statements to the effect that the bishops sat in Parliament by virtue of their temporal baronies, and not as spiritual officers, reflected lay scepticism towards clerical claims rather than any deep-rooted aversion to the presence of bishops in the Upper House.[71]

70 Coke, *The fourth part of the institutes* (1644), 1; John Cowell, *The interpreter: or book containing the signification of words* (Cambridge 1607) sig. 3A3a; Raleigh, *The prerogative of parliaments*, 2, 57; Henry Peacham, *The duty of all true subiects to their king: as also to their native countrey* (1639) sig.* 3b; Lambarde, *Archeion*, 126, 128, 138; Ellesmere in Louis A. Knafla, *Law and politics in Jacobean England: the tracts of Lord Chancellor Ellesmere* (Cambridge 1977) 307; cf. *PP 10*, i, 276; James I, ibid., i, 31; *CD 21*, ii, 3; v, 425; John Selden, *Jani Anglorum facies altera* (1610) 123–6; *Table Talk of John Selden*, ed. Sir Frederick Pollock (1927) 64; cf. Elton, 'The English parliament in the sixteenth century: estates and statutes', in Art Cosgrove and J.I. McGuire, eds, *Parliament and community* (Dublin 1983) 69–95, especially 71–5.
71 *PSP 40*, 220 (Saye); cf. M.J. Mendle, 'Politics and political thought, 1640–2', in Russell, ed., *The origins of the English Civil War* (1973) 219–45, at 227–8; and Mendle, *Dangerous positions*, 126–7. Earlier statements to similar effect include Brooke in *CD 21*, ii, 370; Thomas Hearne, ed., *A*

In the face of lay apathy or hostility, the claims of clerics took on the aspect of laments at the ungodliness of the times, not serious calls for Parliamentary reform. Calybute Downing argued that Convocation – the representative body of the clergy – had been and should still be a part of Parliament, 'and the Parliament is not compleat without it, being one of the three Orders'. Richard Hooker famously but inaccurately asserted that 'the parliament of England together with the convocation annexed thereunto, is that whereupon the very essence of all government within this kingdom doth depend'. Convocation, however, was not in fact annexed to Parliament. Cowell claimed that proctors of the clergy should sit in the House of Commons. Downing agreed. But this was Utopianism. It mattered little that William Camden – one of the foremost historians of the age – endorsed the view that in early times the clergy 'had as much to do in parliament . . . as knights of shires and burgesses'. There was small likelihood that the clergy would ever be readmitted to the House of Commons.[72]

With hindsight it is easy to assume that those who denied that the Lords spiritual were an estate wished to exclude bishops from Parliament. They commonly did no such thing. Nor did people who argued that Parliament could meet without the Lords canvass the abolition of the Upper House. They were merely repeating a statement made in the medieval *Modus tenendi Parliamentum*, not advocating reform. The *Modus* and its followers claimed that the Commons but not the Lords were essential to Parliament. On the other hand, Sir Francis Kynaston in a manuscript treatise called 'A true presentation of forepast Parliaments' held that the king could exclude the Commons. Yet he made it clear that he hoped this would not happen: 'I pray God . . . I may never live to see a parliament wherein the loyall and loving commons shall be omitted.'[73] For most of the time most people were perfectly willing to accept the existing composition.

Another question on which agreement proved possible was this: did the king or Parliament make law? At first glance, it looks as though this question

---

collection of curious discourses, 2 vols (1771) I, 293, but cf. 294. Authors who canvassed the abolition of episcopacy on religious grounds sometimes pointed out that bishops were inessential in Parliament: William Stoughton, *An assertion for true and Christian church-policie* (1604) 174; David Calderwood, *Altare Damascenum* (1623) 395. Charles I already treated the bishops as an estate, and therefore an essential part of Parliament, at the time of the Scottish troubles: 'We cannot destroy Episcopall government without destroying one of the three estates of Parliament, which Wee will not doe': *A large declaration concerning the late tumults in Scotland* (1639) 425. But this refers to the Scottish Parliament.

72 Calybute Downing, *A discourse of the state ecclesiasticall*, 2nd edn (Oxford 1634) 76, 78; Richard Hooker, *The laws of ecclesiastical polity*, VIII, vi, 11; Cowell, *Interpreter*, sig. 3F3b; Camden in Hearne, ed., *A collection of curious discourses*, I, 306.

73 Nicholas Pronay and John Taylor, eds, *Parliamentary texts of the later Middle Ages* (Oxford 1980) 89–90; Dodderidge in Hearne, ed., *A collection of curious discourses*, I, 292; Selden, *Jani Anglorum facies altera*, 125; Sir Francis Kynaston, 'A true presentation of forepast Parliaments, to the view of present times and posteritie', BL Lansdowne Mss 213, ff. 146a–176b, at 158b. For the attribution to Kynaston, see Esther Cope, *Politics without Parliaments* (1987) 27–8, 40n., 122; Johann P. Sommerville, 'Ideology, property and the constitution', in Richard Cust and Ann Hughes, eds, *Conflict in early Stuart England: studies in religion and politics 1603–1642* (1989) 68 n. 9.

lies at the very heart of the controversy between absolutists and their opponents. Absolutists, we might suppose, ought to have said that the king made law. Anti-absolutists ought to have denied this. It is true that some critics of absolute monarchy did claim that laws were made by Parliament and not by the king.[74] But others – including Whitelocke in his famous speech on impositions of 1610, and St John when defending Hampden in 1637 – held that it was the king who made law, though admittedly he had to do so in Parliament. Of course, the absolutist John Cowell also believed that it was the king who made law. In 1621 James I lectured Parliament on the same theme. The king, he said, made law while Parliament merely advised. The fact of agreement on this point has been used to illustrate the general thesis that ideological unity prevailed in England before the Civil War.[75] This is unjustified. What anti-absolutists said was that by ancient custom, or by contract, new law could be made only with the consent of the two Houses of Parliament and the king. If these conditions were fulfilled, law was made. If not, then not. So law was made by fulfilling certain conditions, themselves specified by law. It did not matter in the least whether the king, or Parliament, or a particular member of Parliament, or anyone else whatever, was construed as the lawmaker. It was polite to his majesty to say that the king made law. Nothing was lost by this, for nothing was conceded. Absolutists, however, saw things differently. The king, they said, had been granted sovereign power over the land by God. As it happened, English kings had chosen to make law in Parliament. Good kings would abide by this settled custom. But it remained true that they could validly act otherwise. All constitutional provisions ultimately rested upon the king's will.

We moderns are obsessed with the lawmaking function of government for the simple reason that governments now rule by making law – or so we hope. This was not true in early Stuart England. Under James I virtually no new laws were made for fourteen years – from 1610 to 1624. Under Charles I there was no legislation between 1628 and 1640. Government operated not by making laws, but by applying – or circumventing – existing law. Given this, neither James nor Charles had any particular inclination to claim an extra-Parliamentary power of legislation. Of course, the distinction between law-making and executive action is not always easy to draw in practice. Did the collection of impositions without statutory authority constitute an act of legislation? Certainly, anti-absolutists believed that some of the king's deeds undermined the fundamental laws of the land, and that in effect they abrogated old law and created new. Parliament's monopoly of legislation was jealously guarded and violations were quickly detected. Everyone agreed that the king had a legal power to dispense individuals from the consequences of at least some statutes. For the public good, he could set aside a statute in

74 Lambarde, *Archeion*, 129; Selden, *Jani Anglorum facies altera*, 123–6.
75 *ST*, II, 483 (Whitelocke); Gardiner, *Constitutional documents of the puritan revolution*, 112 (St John); Cowell, *Interpreter*, sig. 2Qla; James I in *CD 21*, II, 4; Weston and Greenberg, *Subjects and sovereigns*, 19–20.

particular cases. But his right to set aside a statute in every case – and thus in effect to abolish it – was challenged. So too was his right to dispense anyone from the common law of the land, as distinct from statute. Finally, the king's power to make proclamations was carefully scrutinised. Professor Elton showed long ago that Henry VIII's famous Act of Proclamations 'did not enfranchise any personal legislative authority in the Crown'. The Tudors claimed no power to make law by proclamation.[76] The same goes for their Stuart successors. Yet anti-absolutists feared that James and Charles were aiming at just this – an indication of the deep distrust to which ideological divisions could lead.

In the eyes of anti-absolutists the royal dispensing power was an instrument of administrative inefficiency, not a token of the king's legislative sovereignty. A *non obstante*, by which the king dispensed an individual or group from the provisions of a statute, could never abrogate the liberties which English subjects held at common law. 'A *non obstante* in a patent or charter', said Coke, 'dispenseth with anything that concerneth the king's right but nothing can impeach the interest of a subject but an act of parliament.' 'The king', wrote Fuller, 'by a *non obstante* may dispence with a statute law, but not with the common law, nor alter the same.' In the opinion of John Glanville, the king had no power to dispense from the common law, or from statutes which declared that law. The English, he said, had a 'birthright and inheritance' in those statutes which confirmed their 'inherent right and interest of liberty and freedom'. He instanced 'the good old statute called Magna Carta'. Glanville believed that the king possessed only those powers which the common law granted to him. This was, of course, the central claim of Coke's constitutionalism. Since the common law gave the king no power to dispense with itself, he had no such power. The supremacy of the law was safeguarded.[77]

Absolutists, by contrast, believed that if he deemed it necessary the king could dispense with any human law whatsoever, including the common law. His power to do so was distinct from his legal dispensing power. By law, the king could only dispense from statute. By prerogative, he could dispense from the common law also. Despite the coronation oath, said Cowell, a king

76 Elton, *Studies in Tudor and Stuart politics and government*, ı, 271. Occasionally writers referred to proclamations as laws. William Pemble, *A summe of moral philosophy* (Oxford 1632) 73, divided public laws into those which were 'Endicted by the whole state, as Statutes', and those which proceeded 'from the King alone, as edicts, and Proclamations'. In *Leviathan*, Thomas Hobbes argued that the varieties of law were similar in both the Roman and English systems, and that 'the Proclamations of the Kings of *England*' corresponded to imperial edicts and constitutions: *Leviathan*, ed. C.B. Macpherson (Harmondsworth 1968) 329. Precisely the same claim occurs in 'A discourse of lawes', which was printed in *Horae subsecivae* (1620) and which has been attributed to Hobbes on the basis of statistical wordprinting. The 'Discourse' and two other essays from the *Horae* are reprinted in Hobbes, *Three discourses: a critical modern edition of newly identified work by the young Hobbes*, ed. Noel B. Reynolds and Arlene Saxonhouse (Chicago 1995), where the relevant passage is at p. 117.
77 Coke in *CD 21*, ıı, 387; Nicholas Fuller, *The argument of Master Nicholas Fuller, in the case of Thomas Lad, and Richard Maunsell* (1607) 18; Glanville in *PP 28*, ıı, 566, 565; cf. 527. A valuable discussion of the dispensing power is Paul Birdsall, '"Non obstante" – a study of the dispensing power of English kings', in *Essays in history and political theory in honor of Charles Howard McIlwain* (Cambridge, Mass. 1936) 37–76.

could 'alter or suspend any particular lawe that seemeth hurtfull to the publike estate'. No restrictions, said Davies, could be imposed upon 'a Prerogative in point of Government'. Even if the king consented to limitations upon his power to govern the realm, such limitations would not bind him. If 'any just or important occasion' arose, they would 'be as thred, and broken as easie as the bonds of Samson'.[78]

Since Charles and James claimed to possess an extra-legal prerogative by which they could rule the realm as they saw fit, they had no need to assert an ordinary right to legislate without Parliament. If an extraordinary power is exercised in ordinary circumstances it becomes indistinguishable from an ordinary power. Yet complaints against the uses to which royal proclamations were put reveal that some members of the House of Commons feared that the king was intent upon legislating by edict. In 1628 Coryton complained that proclamations were being used to suspend and abolish laws. Coke declared that 'proclamations come too high', and thought that this threatened to bring about 'alteration of government'. Selden agreed, remarking that 'nothing changes government more than proclamations'. Similar attitudes coloured the Commons' petition of temporal grievances of 1610. The petition informed James of the 'general fear conceived and spread amongst your Majesty's people, that proclamations will by degrees grow up and increase to the strength and nature of laws'. This, it continued, would greatly blemish the 'ancient happiness and freedom' of the English, and might also 'in process of time bring a new form of arbitrary government upon the realm'.[79]

This fear of arbitrary government was closely associated with the further fear that Parliament would cease to exist. In 1610 Sir Roger Owen warned the House of Commons against dealing too generously with the king on the matter of the Great Contract. If James had too large a regular revenue he could dispense with Parliament and rule by proclamation. This had happened in France: 'France by power of edicts never calleth parliaments.' Little was heard in early Stuart England of the common Tudor notion that Parliaments were a burden to the subject, to be called only when absolutely necessary. In 1610 Cecil was still able to tell the House of Lords that 'I hope we shall not need to have often parliaments, seeing that we enjoy so great privileges by his Majesty'. It is unlikely that these words would have gone down well in the Commons – precisely because a good number of them believed that their own privileges, and the liberties of all subjects, were under attack. Parliament – Whitelocke's 'storehouse of our liberties' – was needed more frequently than ever before because liberties were endangered. This notion lay behind the claim that Parliament should be held annually. It was expressed very clearly in the Commons' charges against Maynwaring in 1628. He had attempted, they

78 Cowell, *Interpreter*, sig. 2Qla; Davies, *The question concerning impositions*, 131–2.
79 *PP 28*, II, 90 (Coryton), IV, 243 (Coke), 244 (Selden); *PP 10*, II, 259; cf. Alford in 1607 in *CJ* 1035. Debate on proclamations is discussed in R.W. Heinze, 'Proclamations and parliamentary protest, 1539–1610', in D.J. Guth and J.W. McKenna, eds, *Tudor rule and revolution; essays for G.R. Elton from his American friends* (Cambridge 1982) 237–59.

said, to undermine 'the rights and liberties of the subjects', and in particular 'to avert his Majesty's mind from calling of parliaments'. What law Maynwaring had infringed by doing this was left obscure. By 1628 there were those in the Commons who believed that it was always a grievous offence to advise the king against summoning Parliament. By 1640 the idea had become commonplace. The king's failure to call Parliament, said Parker, was 'the grievance of all grievances'.[80]

From the point of view of anyone who thought that frequent Parliaments were necessary to the maintenance of the subject's liberty there existed one very awkward fact, namely that by custom Parliament was called and dissolved at the royal discretion. It might be true that the king *should* call Parliament often, but there was no mechanism to compel him to do so. Nor was there any legal means of preventing dissolution – though in 1621 Alford ineffectually claimed 'that the King could not dissolve a Parliament when we have things in the forge of moment till they were finished', and the puritan Alexander Leighton voiced a similar notion in 1628. The question of adjournment was, indeed, disputed. In the Commons, members said that the House could be adjourned only by itself. Charles, on the other hand, claimed that he could adjourn them.[81] But the king's powers of summoning, proroguing and dissolving Parliament remained uncontested. The king would never have parted with them without the threat of force. Until force, in the shape of a victorious Scottish army, was available, subtler means were needed to ensure that Parliaments remained in being, and continued to function as the guardian of liberty.

Of these means, the first was supply. Conrad Russell has argued that 'only once in the reign of James I, over the issue of impositions in 1614' did members of Parliament 'attempt to make supply conditional on the redress of grievances'. Yet the concepts of supply and redress were closely linked throughout the period. Sir Robert Cotton associated the two, but argued that supply should go first. Others agreed that contribution – the voting of subsidies – was dependent on retribution – the redress of grievances – but gave priority to the latter. The Commons, said Sir Julius Caesar in 1610 when speaking on their behalf in the Upper House, were very willing to contribute to the king's service, 'yet the demand is so great that without an exceeding noble

80 *PP 10*, I, 8 (Cecil), II, 109 (Whitelocke); *PP 28*, IV, 102 (charges against Maynwaring); Henry Parker, *The case of shipmony briefly discoursed* (1640) 39. Sir Roger Owen is discussed in William Klein, 'Ruling thoughts: the world of Sir Roger Owen of Condover', unpublished Johns Hopkins University Ph.D. dissertation, 1987; and more briefly in Klein, 'The ancient constitution revisited', in Nicholas Phillipson and Quentin Skinner, eds, *Political discourse in early modern Britain* (Cambridge 1993), 23–44, at 35–41. The history of Parliamentary privilege in the early Stuart period is surveyed in Johann P. Sommerville, 'Parliament, privilege, and the liberties of the subject', in J.H. Hexter, ed., *Parliament and liberty from the reign of Elizabeth to the English Civil War* (Stanford 1992) 56–84.
81 Alford in *CD 21*, III, 340; Alexander Leighton, *An appeal to the Parliament; or Sions plea against the prelacie* (1629) 337. The Commons resolved that they could adjourn themselves in 1604: *CJ* 150; cf. *CD 21*, III, 377–8, IV, 400, V, 194; *PP 28*, IV, 18, 40, 163, 220. Charles I asserts a royal power of adjournment in *His maiesties declaration to all his loving subjects, of the causes which moved him to dissolve the last Parliament* (1640) 1–2.

retribution, we cannot satisfy'. He asked their 'Lordships to declare what shall be given us'.[82] In 1626 the Commons voted no subsidies because Charles was unwilling to allow the impeachment of Buckingham. In 1628 they voted subsidies, but only after the king had given a favourable answer to the Petition of Right and after Maynwaring had been impeached. The Short Parliament of 1640 voted no subsidies because the king's attitude towards Ship Money had proved unsound.

In 1621–25 England faced the prospect, but not yet the reality of war. As so often, these circumstances had a unifying effect and a conspicuous feature of the Parliaments of 1621 and 1624 is the general reluctance of the House of Commons to discuss anything that the king might construe as trenching on his prerogative. Yet even in 1621 members recognised that it was unusual to vote subsidies before grievances had been discussed. 'It is the order of parliaments', said Thomas Crew, 'that grievances go first.' He held that it was only exceptional circumstances – 'the occasions of the time' – which warranted the immediate voting of subsidies. 'It hath never been seen', Caesar told the Lords in 1610, 'that subsidies have been moved in the beginning of a parliament', and the Commons' remonstrance of 5 April 1626 claimed that by ancient custom subsidies were voted only at the end of the session – that is to say, after grievances had been dealt with. Contribution and retribution were linked in theory. Moreover, the king did in fact pay for subsidies by remedying grievances. As Russell notes, subsidies lost their charm in the king's eyes 'because the gestures of goodwill Parliament requested in return for their subsidies also cost the King money'. He instances the Parliament of 1624. So even in 'the Prince's Parliament' subsidies were effectively conditional upon redress.[83]

The king called Parliament because he wanted money quickly and without fuss. In the Commons, members used this fact to preserve the liberties of the subject. The prospect of subsidies kept Parliament alive. But on its own this was not sufficient to maintain liberties. The Commons could buy liberty only if they could discuss it. This was why members of the Lower House insisted that they possessed freedom of speech and freedom from arrest for things said in Parliament. The second means of defending liberty, then, was by protecting Parliamentary privilege. On 22 May 1610 the Commons drew up a petition of right affirming 'the ancient and fundamental right of the liberty of parliament in point of exact discussing of all matters concerning them and their possessions, goods and rights whatsoever'. This was the liberty upon which all the others rested. If the king could punish members for words spoken in Parliament, said Phelips in 1621, if the privileges of the Commons

82 Russell, *Parliaments and English politics*, 49; Sir Robert Cotton, *The manner and means how the Kings of England have from time to time supported and repaired their estates*, in *Cottoni Posthuma*, 3rd edn (1679) 161–202, at 172–3; Cotton in *PD 10*, 57–8; Caesar in *PP 10*, I, 13–14.
83 *CD 21*, II, 24 (Crew); cf. Glanville in *DHC 25*, 114; *PP 10*, I, 14 (Caesar). Commons' remonstrance of 1626 cited in Clayton Roberts, *The growth of responsible government in Stuart England* (Cambridge 1966) 63; Russell, *Parliaments and English politics*, 52.

were mere graces dependent upon the royal will, if his majesty could command the House to discuss any particular item of business, then 'we are not freeholders but tenants at will'. His choice of words was significant. A king who could prevent Parliament from discussing liberties could destroy those same liberties, including property. The spectre of villeinage loomed again. The privileges of the House, declared Hakewill in the same session, 'are part of the law', held 'by inheritance'. 'We shall never sit here again', he said, 'if they be not maintained.' Unless privileges were preserved the king would be able to trample upon the property rights of the subject and dispense with Parliament. Phelips, too, insisted that the privileges of the Commons – 'our liberties' – were laws of the kingdom, and spelled out the underlying point that the king was bound by the law. 'The king', he said, was 'bound as well to his lawes by his oath as wee in our subjection to him.' Subjection was due only inasmuch as the king maintained law. On the same day the House approved a Protestation declaring that the Parliamentary freedoms of speech and from imprisonment were 'the ancient and undoubted birthright and inheritance of the subjects of England'.[84]

James had repeatedly warned the Commons that in his view their privileges were 'derived from the grace and permission of our ancestors'. 'We cannot', he said, 'endure our subjects to use such anti-monarchical words to us concerning their liberties.' It was for this reason that he tore the Protestation from the Commons' Journal. The two Houses, he held, derived their rights from the king, and these rights were subordinate to royal power. In particular, they ought not to be exercised in a way that conflicted with the purpose of Parliament. This purpose was to do the king's business. As James put it in 1610, 'the parliament is called by the king to treat of such things as he shall propound'. It is needless to dwell on the fact that the king's attitudes towards Parliament were wholly in conformity with his general political creed. The same goes for his son. In 1629 Charles told the Commons that Parliament met 'only by my power, and to treat of things that I propound unto you'. The king, he said, possessed a 'prerogative to command and offer any bill unto you'. He hoped that this assertion would encourage the Commons to vote tonnage and poundage. His hope went unfulfilled.[85]

It was safe for kings to make such assertions. For lesser people it could be dangerous to do so, as the cases of Cowell and Maynwaring illustrate. True, Bacon said in 1610 that it was customary for the Commons to desist from discussing the prerogative when the king told them to. But he refrained from spelling out the theoretical implications of this. A few were more forthright. Saravia claimed that Parliament derived its powers from the king, and that the liberties of the English were matters of grace, not right. David Owen bluntly declared that 'the Parliament in England possesses no power except from the

---

84 *PP 10*, ii, 110, 371 (petition of 1610); *CD 21*, vi, 245, v, 418 (Phelips); ii, 533 (Hakewill); Kenyon, *Stuart constitution*, 47 (Protestation).
85 Prothero, *Select statutes and other constitutional documents*, 312–13; *PP 10*, ii, 311; James I, *Political writings*, ed. Sommerville, 250–67 (James I); *CD 29*, 31 (Charles I).

king and under the king'. Both, of course, were absolutist clerics who wrote against Continental resistance theories. Both were willing to apply to English circumstances ideas which they had developed in a different context.

Owen wrote his treatise during the first months of the 1621 Parliament. At the command of his clerical superiors, he presented it to the king.[86] It was in the last months of 1621 that the famous row between James and the Commons over privilege arose. What happened was that the Commons debated foreign policy. The king told them that they had no right to do so. The Commons then responded by asserting their birthright to free speech. Conrad Russell has argued that the whole dispute blew up through a misunderstanding. The Commons believed that in discussing foreign policy they were merely following royal orders, since the debate was started by Sir George Goring, a client of the king's favourite, Buckingham. They met James's anger with genuine astonishment. All this may be true. Misunderstanding, and the machinations of Buckingham, doubtless played their part in wrecking the Parliament of 1621. But the important point is that the misunderstanding could easily have been cleared up if it had not been for the profound gulf which separated the king from many members of the House of Commons on fundamental issues of political and constitutional theory. 'Differences of opinion with which all parties could have lived quietly had been forced into the open', says Russell, 'and when they were forced into the open, all the traditional compromises and silences became impossible.'[87] These words may stand as the epitaph on Parliament not only in 1621, but also in 1610, 1614, 1629 and 1640.

Of course, an addled Parliament was not in the public interest. To trench on the king's prerogative was to invite dissolution and ultimately to jeopardise the very existence of Parliaments. Sir Benjamin Rudyerd was particularly

---

86 PD 10, 38 (Bacon); Hadrian Saravia, *De imperandi authoritate in Diversi tractatus theologici* (1611) 276; Owen, 'Detectio calumniarum sophismatum et imposturarum anonymi papistae', BL Royal Mss 10B.XIII, f. 11a: 'nullam esse potestatem Parliamenti in Anglia, nisi a Rege, et sub Rege'. Ibid., f. 2a (dedication to the Earl of Holderness): 'I am directed by my superiours, to give this booke unto the kinge, which I humblie desire your Lordship to doe for me.' The book is dated 21 July 1621 at f. 6a.
Owen went on to claim (ibid.) that 'the king and the king alone has supreme power in ecclesiastical matters and absolute power in political ones': 'potestatem habet, et solus habet, in ecclesiasticis supremam, in politicis absolutam'. Owen was an important member of an influential Arminian group in the diocese of Peterborough – a group which included John Buckeridge and the notorious absolutist Robert Sibthorp: John Fielding, 'Arminianism in the localities: Peterborough diocese, 1603–1642', in Kenneth Fincham, ed., *The early Stuart church, 1603–1642* (1993), 93–113, at 95–7. Conrad Russell has suggested that 'The statement by Owen . . . that "the Parliament of England possesses no power except from the King and under the King", is a plain and factual statement of the position in English law. It is still true today.' Now, it may be true that by a legal fiction Parliament today holds power not from the people but from and under the Queen. But there seems to be no evidence that Owen had any such fiction in mind. Elizabeth II does not hold absolute power. According to Owen, James I did. Members of the Commons derived their powers first and foremost from the law of the land. James, like Owen, derived them from the crown. See above, p. 173.
87 Russell, 'The foreign policy debate in the House of Commons in 1621', *HJ* 20 (1977) 289–309, at 290, 307; *Parliaments and English politics*, 133, 140; cf. R. Zaller, *The Parliament of 1621; a study in constitutional conflict* (Berkeley, Calif. 1971) 150ff.

fond of making this point, using it to support his case for moderation in 1628 and 1640. But there was a catch. Rudyerd might insist that as long as Parliaments 'be frequent there will be no irregular power'.[88] Others found the argument less convincing. Parliament could prevent the growth of irregular power only by undertaking actions which the king was likely to construe as inimical to the royal prerogative. That was the dilemma. Unfortunately, both the king and some influential members of the House of Commons were ideologues, for whom certain points were simply not negotiable. When these points arose, so did conflict.

In this chapter we have seen that attitudes towards royal government of the state were coloured by divergent political and constitutional theories. The same theories informed views on early Stuart rule of the church. But there was an added complexity to questions of church government. For whereas the state was a purely natural institution, the church had been set up by the law of grace, made manifest in Scripture.

---

88 *PP 28*, III, 129; *PSP 40*, 139–40, 178.

CHAPTER 6

The Church

In his *Utopia*, first published in 1516, Sir Thomas More described a hypothetical pagan society organised on rational principles, but lacking Christian revelation. The Utopians believe in God, and even accept the immortality of the soul. But reason proves insufficient to tell them much about God's nature or about how he ought to be worshipped. Recognising this, they tolerate a variety of religious practices. Yet, once they receive details of the Christian message, they soon embrace it. Reason, More is telling us, is compatible with the religious truths revealed in the Bible. Indeed, anyone who followed the precepts of reason closely would be happy to accept Christianity. But, on its own, reason was inadequate to achieve more than a glimmering of religious verity. The Utopians were tolerant – while More himself was not – because they had no certain guide in matters of faith – while he had the Scriptures and the traditions of the Catholic church.[1]

In early Stuart England, people similarly distinguished between knowledge which could be attained even by pagans, and the far more extensive knowledge available to Christians. Pagans could recognise the need for political society. Using reason, they could understand the duties of obedience which bound children to their fathers, and subjects to their magistrates. But they could discover little about Christ and his church. In order to grasp the truth on the nature of the church and on other religious matters it was necessary to turn to the Bible. The New Testament provided prime evidence on all religious questions, while the Old Testament was particularly valuable in delineating the relationship between the church and the commonwealth. In addition, the writings of the Fathers supplied information on the practices of early Christians which could be employed to flesh out the Bible's prescriptions.

Since grace and nature were compatible, what was true according to reason – the law of nature – remained true even after the addition of revelation (or grace). Christianity did not destroy natural rights and duties. Conversely, if a

---

1 St Thomas More, *Utopia*, ed. Edward Surtz, SJ (1964) 130–4; cf. ibid., 92 and Anthony Kenny, *Thomas More* (Oxford 1983) 37, 101–2.

practice was contrary to the Christian faith it could not in fact be rational, though it might seem so to the uninitiated. Now, by nature every common-wealth was an autonomous institution, possessing supreme temporal power over its own affairs. This doctrine was accepted by almost all theorists, of whatever religious complexion. Its corollary was that the church, or the clergy, could possess no powers which undermined the temporal autonomy of the civil magistrate.

The notion that the commonwealth was an autonomous institution, at any rate in the temporal sphere, can be traced back to Aquinas, and thence to Aristotle. Aquinas, in Christianising Aristotle, found it necessary to include a place for the church in his scheme of things. Indeed, he held that the pope, as the representative of the church, possessed supreme authority over Christen-dom, at least in spiritual matters. The exact nature of papal supremacy in Aquinas' theory remains debatable. But his followers in the sixteenth and early seventeenth centuries hammered out a clear doctrine on this question. Of these followers, the best known are the Jesuits Bellarmine and Suarez. Both argued that the pope could intervene in temporal affairs if the spiritual good of Christendom required such a course. Shorn of its niceties, and equi-vocations, this meant that the pope could depose a king whenever he happened to think that such action would be in the spiritual interest.

Jesuits such as Bellarmine and Suarez, it is sometimes said, and Presbyterian Calvinists such as Thomas Cartwright, believed in 'the separation of Church and State', while English conformist Protestants were 'Erastian' in outlook. These terms were rarely used by contemporaries and represent vast over-simplifications of complex issues. No Protestant – including Presbyterians – maintained that clerics could depose the king. Indeed, a major reason why sixteenth-century rulers found Protestantism attractive was that it deprived the clergy of their claims to temporal power and to exemption from the jurisdiction of the civil magistrate. Protestants argued that whatever temporal power a cleric happened to possess was derived solely from the civil authorit-ies, and a potent strand in Protestant thought held that the clergy should refuse to accept even delegated temporal jurisdiction: churchmen should keep out of politics. When Presbyterians adopted theories of legitimate resistance in the second half of the sixteenth century they drew on Catholic ideas to support their claims. But they steered well clear of the Catholic notion that the church could depose kings. 'New presbyter is but old priest' was not wholly true.

Though Presbyterians denied that the clergy could use the temporal sword, they granted the church a far wider measure of power than English monarchs found palatable. They argued that the Presbyterian form of church polity was the unalterable prescription of Christ, and that the church was a self-governing institution, independent of the civil magistrate in spiritual matters. The church was to be ruled not by bishops whom the king appointed, but by a hierarchy of assemblies, with elected pastors and lay elders at every level from the individual congregation to the national assembly. The function of these men was to impose true doctrine and moral discipline upon the population. In order to encourage the recalcitrant, the church might employ the spiritual censure of excommunication. This deprived sinners of the sacrament and publicised their unworthiness, but it carried with it no temporal penalties unless the civil magistrate chose to add them. The popish notion that excommunication automatically had temporal consequences was firmly rejected.

In Presbyterian theory, ecclesiastical assemblies could meet even without the king's permission. In 1605 an assembly of the kirk of Scotland met despite the king's prohibition.[2] Moreover, the king himself was subject to the church's spiritual censures which could be used against him if he failed in his duty of enforcing true religion. Although the church possessed no temporal power, it could use the threat of excommunication in order to persuade those who *did* possess such power to exercise it in a godly manner. One implication of this was that if someone – say the community – in fact had the authority to depose heretical or tyrannical rulers, churchmen could employ the spiritual sword to ensure that deposition took place. There is a clear affinity between this theory and the ideas of late-medieval French conciliarists. The continuity between the doctrines of the Sorbonnists and those of Scottish Presbyterians – between Almain and Samuel Rutherford – bears eloquent testimony to the strength of the 'auld alliance'.

In England, unlike France or Scotland, the Reformation was enforced by – and not in opposition to – the monarch. Bishops were retained, but their authority was subordinated to that of the crown. So one task of English theorists was to justify and explain the central position in ecclesiastical affairs which the civil magistrate in fact occupied. In the 1590s Richard Hooker grappled with this problem in the eighth book of his *Laws*. During the next two decades a series of confident and learned treatises spelled out a coherent doctrine on the question. Many of these works were specifically directed against Presbyterian and especially Catholic ideas. All rejected the papist claim that the clergy, acting independently of the king, could exercise temporal power to a spiritual end. All likewise rejected the Presbyterian, and popish, notion that the church could make binding ecclesiastical regulations without the assent of the civil magistrate. All asserted that Convocation – the clergy's representative body – could meet only when summoned by the king, and that his majesty might dissolve it whenever he pleased. Its decrees – canons – had no force without the royal assent, and this the king could withhold as he did in the case of the canons of 1606.

Bishops, the English churchmen continued, possessed a God-given power to oversee the religious affairs of their dioceses, but they could exercise this power only under royal supervision. The bishops, either singly or as a body, could do no more than remonstrate with his majesty if he slid into ungodly ways. No one could excommunicate the king. He, on the other hand, appointed bishops and could suspend or deprive them. Elizabeth suspended

2 S.R. Gardiner, *History of England from the accession of James I to the outbreak of the Civil War, 1603–42*, 10 vols (1883–84) I, 306.

Grindal, and Charles I suspended Abbot. Plainly, this theory gave the civil magistrate very wide control over the church. Who, however, *was* the civil magistrate? Was the king alone, or the king-in-Parliament supreme in England? Was the king bound by the law? These familiar questions took on new aspects when applied to ecclesiastical affairs.

Bishops deprived ministers who disobeyed the ecclesiastical canons of 1604. These canons had the royal assent but lacked the sanction of Parliament. If a minister's benefice is construed as his property, then deprivation constitutes an infringement of the fundamentals of the common law: the bishops were taking property without consent. The activities of the High Commission – the highest ecclesiastical court in the land – struck still more clearly at what many believed were the liberties of the subject. The Commission fined and imprisoned. Its statutory authority for doing so was dubious. Furthermore, it could impose the oath *ex officio* upon defendants. Those who took this oath obliged themselves to give truthful answers to all interrogatories which might be put to them. They could find themselves bound by oath not merely to betray their associates but also to confess their own guilt; so the oath contravened the principle that people should not be forced to accuse themselves. More generally, the ecclesiastical courts had the presumption to deal with cases which also fell under the cognisance of the common law – for example disputes over tithes, which clearly affected the subject's property rights. Finally, it was arguable that the religious practices which the bishops enforced, particularly under Charles I, were against the law.

It is easy to see why clerics often preferred tithe disputes to be tried in a church court. The ecclesiastical courts would understand. The jury in a common law court, on the other hand, would be as sure to decide 'against the Parson, as an old chimney is sure of blackness'.[3] The issues of clerical property and of control over the church at the local as well as national level attracted controversy throughout the early Stuart period. Disagreements on these points were reducible to wider constitutional disputes. But differences in religious belief added an extra dimension. Nicholas Fuller, for example, objected to proceedings in High Commission on religious as well as constitutional grounds. Fuller, who acted as counsel for Cartwright in 1591,[4] may well have favoured a Presbyterian form of church government. James, understandably, was no admirer of Fuller. In 1607 he wrote to Cecil reminding him of 'the evill deserts of the villain', whose ideas undermined royal government.[5] It is difficult to untangle the religious from the constitutional elements in Fuller's thought. He believed that anything unconstitutional was popish and vice versa. The same beliefs recurred in later thinkers.

Outspoken Presbyterianism died in England under the assault of Whitgift and Bancroft in the 1590s. But the notion that there was something wrong with 'lordly prelacy' persisted. A significant element in Protestant thinking deemed

3 William Fulbecke, *The second part of the parallele* (1602) sig. B1a.
4 Patrick Collinson, *The Elizabethan puritan movement* (1967) 419–21; cf. 425.
5 James I to Cecil, 19 October 1607, Hatfield Mss 134, f. 126b.

it wrong for any cleric to possess great wealth and worldly power. Such ideas commended themselves to those who resented episcopal power for constitutional reasons or for reasons of crude financial interest.[6] It was predictable that people who objected to the established church because it was an instrument of royal absolutism should make common cause with those who had religious scruples about its provisions. This fusion of religious and constitutional issues, already noticeable in Fuller, became much more prominent after 1625.

The Jacobean church was far from united. But it was far more united than the church under Charles. Anti-popery, which worked as a cohesive force while James ruled, divided the church under his son. Of course, there were disagreements in the Jacobean period on such matters as the ceremonies prescribed by the Prayer Book, and on the nature of Christ's descent into Hell. A small number of people separated from the church altogether, forming their own autonomous congregations. Others likewise set up gathered congregations, but admitted that communion with at least some members of the established church was licit. It was, indeed, in James's reign that Independency or Congregationalism first received coherent formulation – one of the few distinctively English contributions to the theory of church government. Yet a common hatred of popery allowed people to gloss over other issues. The king's own entry into controversy with Catholics had the effect of unifying Protestants, though this may not have been intended and though the anti-popery which English Protestants expressed took a variety of distinct forms.

In the 1620s the unity of the Jacobean church was shattered by the promotion of Laud and other clerics suspected of holding Arminian views. It is sometimes suggested that this development had major and lasting political effects, and, indeed, that religious doctrine lay at the heart of Charles I's disagreements with the Long Parliament.[7] Of course, it is true that orthodox Calvinists – the majority of English churchmen – resented Arminian doctrine,

6 There may be a connection between the idea that clerics should not hold temporal office and moves to exclude the clergy from commissions of the peace, but this is dubious since clerics of the rank of dean and above were exempted both in discussions of 1621 and in the bills of 1626 and 1628: *CD 21*, III, 111–112; cf. v, 124; *CJ* 832, 834, 841; Conrad Russell, *Parliaments and English politics 1621–1629* (Oxford 1979) 43, 277; *PP 28*, III, 437. Clearer evidence of such a connection is provided by a bill of spring 1640 to exclude clerics – except Privy Councillors – from temporal office: *PSP 40*, 273–4.

7 Nicholas Tyacke, 'Puritanism, Arminianism and counter-revolution', in Russell, ed., *The origins of the English Civil War* (1973) 119–43; Anthony Fletcher, *The outbreak of the English Civil War* (1981) pp. xxix–xxx; Tyacke, *Anti-Calvinists: the rise of English Arminianism c.1590–1640* (Oxford 1987); John Morrill, 'The religious context of the English Civil War', *TRHS* 5th series, 34 (1984) 155–78, reprinted in Morrill, *The nature of the English revolution* (1993) 45–68.

The question of just how united the Jacobean church was is addressed – from differing perspectives – in Patrick Collinson, *The religion of Protestants: the church in English society, 1559–1625* (Oxford 1982); Kenneth Fincham and Peter Lake, 'The ecclesiastical policies of James I and Charles I', in Fincham, ed., *The early Stuart church, 1603–1642* (1993) 23–49; and Fincham and Lake, 'The ecclesiastical policy of James I', *Journal of British Studies* 24 (1985) 169–207. Tyacke places the rise of Arminianism in the 1620s at the centre of his account of the religious history of the decades before the Civil War. His thesis has been attacked by Peter White, *Predestination, policy and polemic: conflict and consensus in the English church from the Reformation to the Civil War* (Cambridge 1992); Julian Davies, *The Caroline captivity of the church: Charles I and the remoulding of Anglicanism* which gave a place in the scheme of salvation to human free will. But it would be mistaken to suggest that most of the objections which were levelled against Laud were based on doctrinal misgivings. Accusations of Arminianism or popery rarely had a precise theological meaning, for these terms rapidly came to be used in a very wide and vague way. 'Wee charge the prelaticall Clergie with popery', said Selden, 'to make them odious though wee know they are guilty of no such thing.'[8] Several non-theological strands can be detected in the opposition to Laud. He and his clerical supporters defended royal absolutism. Again, they used the powers which the king had granted them in order to maintain and expand the church's property. Moreover, the religious 'innovations' which Laud effected were arguably illegal and implicitly challenged the supremacy of Parliament over religious affairs. Grievances on such counts often had little direct connection with doctrinal disputes, and owed much to long-standing constitutional controversies.

In his own eyes, Laud was no innovator. He believed that his opponents were factious folk who intended to undermine established authority in church and state. He, by contrast, wished only to remove the abuses which the indolence of his predecessor at Canterbury had encouraged. Laud was no papist. On 1 March 1627, he recorded, 'I dreamed that I was reconciled to the Church of Rome.' 'This', he added, 'troubled me much; and I wondered exceedingly, how it should happen. Nor was I aggrieved with myself only by reason of the errors of that Church, but also upon account of the scandal which from that my fall would be cast upon many eminent and learned men in the Church of England.'[9] One of Laud's fundamental problems was that he avoided the reality but not the scandal of popery.

On the question of the church's relationship to the state, Laud was as convinced an opponent of popery as any of his enemies. In Protestant theory, active resistance by the church or the clergy to the civil magistrate was always unlawful. This point deserves emphasis, since in recent years some commentators have stressed the religious elements in the opposition to Charles I, and have come close to suggesting that the Civil War began as a puritan revolution. It is not just that this approach overlooks the very large extent to which Charles attracted hostility because his actions – including his ecclesiastical

---

(Oxford 1992); and Kevin Sharpe, *The Personal Rule of Charles I* (1992). Tyacke has replied to his critics in 'Anglican attitudes: some recent writings on English religious history, from the Restoration to the Civil War', *Journal of British Studies* 35 (1996) 139–67. Other important contributions to the debate over the rise of Arminianism include Peter Lake, 'Calvinism and the English church, 1570–1635', *Past and Present* 114 (1987) 32–76; Lake, 'The Laudian style: order, uniformity and the pursuit of the beauty of holiness in the 1630s', in Fincham, ed., *The early Stuart church, 1603–1642*, 161–85; John Fielding, 'Arminianism in the localities: Peterborough diocese, 1603–1642', ibid., 93–113; Andrew Foster, 'Church policies of the 1630s', in Richard Cust and Ann Hughes, eds, *Conflict in early Stuart England: studies in religion and politics 1603–1642* (1989) 193–223. An outstanding book which casts a great deal of light on many questions connected with early Stuart religious history is Anthony Milton, *Catholic and Reformed: the Roman and Protestant churches in English Protestant thought, 1600–1640* (Cambridge 1995).
8 John Selden, *Table talk of John Selden*, ed. Sir Frederick Pollock (1927) 99.
9 William Laud, *Works*, eds W. Scott and J. Bliss, 7 vols (Oxford 1847–60) iii, 201.

policies – were held to be illegal rather than, or as well as, irreligious. More seriously, the idea that the war began as a revolt by the godly against popery misses the point that English Protestants condemned all resistance to the king (and all attempts to add new or declare old limitations to his powers) except by properly constituted authority. Absolutists, of course, thought that there was no such authority, while others looked to the law or Parliament to control the king. No one held that godliness conferred temporal authority upon people. So efforts to limit or resist the king had necessarily to take place through constitutional means, and in accordance with those constitutional theories – whether contractualist or Cokeian – which set such great store by the subject's liberties. The godly were private individuals with no public authority. They had no right of resistance and could use only prayers and tears to combat the evil edicts of those who *did* have authority. Anything else spelled anarchy and, worse still, popery. For it was papists who argued that the clergy, or even mere lay believers could resist the magistrate. Once again, English attitudes were defined by what the English opposed – the church of Rome.

PAPALIST THEORY

In the Middle Ages a number of Catholic theologians argued that the pope was lord of the world in both temporal and spiritual matters. For papalists this was a simple and convenient doctrine. In the early modern period the idea survived, particularly among Italian canon lawyers. Nevertheless, it came under heavy fire from within the Catholic camp.

Catholic monarchs did not take kindly to the claim that the pope was the supreme temporal ruler of the world or Christendom. The claim implied that kings were mere delegates of the pope who could remove them whenever he pleased. Philip II of Spain was happy enough to recognise the pope as a spiritual leader, but had no wish to encourage papal interference in the temporal affairs of his realms. He refused the pope's arbitration on the kingdom of Portugal, not wishing 'to acknowledge him to be the Judge of Kingdoms'. When the papalist Cardinal Baronius argued that Sicily was a possession of the Holy See, he came into serious conflict with Philip III. Philip banned Baronius' book, and its Neapolitan printer narrowly escaped life imprisonment. The English canons of 1606 related that Andrew Hoy, Professor of Greek at Douai, advocated a world empire under the pope, with the king of Spain as emperor. 'But what', the book asked, 'should we trouble ourselves with this point? The king of Spain, we suppose, will greatly scorn to be the pope's vassal; and the emperor that now is . . . as likewise all the kings and princes in the world, may see most evidently how grossly and shamefully they are abused.'[10]

10 John Donne, *Pseudo-Martyr* (1610) sig. C1b; Joseph de la Servière, *De Jacobo I Angliae rege cum Cardinali Roberto Bellarmino S.J. super potestate cum regia tum pontificia disputante (1607–1609)* (Paris 1900) 163; cf. on the Sicilian controversy William J. Bouwsma, *Venice and the defence of republican liberty* (Berkeley 1968) 310–13; *The convocation book of MDCVI. Commonly called Bishop Overall's convocation book* (Oxford 1844) 214.

Outside Rome, where popes were willing to listen to flattery, the notion that Christ's vicar was lord of the earth did not thrive. Catholic monarchs and natural law theory united in construing the commonwealth as an autonomous body exercising supreme power over its own temporal affairs. The Jesuits threw their weight behind this idea, which had a long history. The civil magistrate, they said, possessed full temporal power in his realm. But the pope was the spiritual sovereign of Christendom. Anyone who had been baptised was subject to him in spiritual matters. Since spiritual objectives were intrinsically preferable to merely temporal goals, the pope as custodian of the spiritual good could intervene in temporal affairs whenever he believed that this was necessary. In the later Middle Ages the notion that 'the pope has only spiritual jurisdiction, but yet is able to exercise a very full measure of temporal power'[11] was developed as a means of effecting a compromise between political Augustinians, who regarded the pope as the fountain of all legitimate authority, and extreme Aristotelians, who asserted that the secular power was wholly autonomous. The same notion became the orthodoxy of Catholic theorists in the late sixteenth and early seventeenth centuries.

The idea that the pope has only spiritual power but that he can use this power to effect temporal changes – for example by abolishing laws or deposing kings – has become known to posterity as the theory of the indirect deposing power. Adherents of the theory believed that the pope had no *direct* temporal power except in a small portion of Italy, but that the exercise of his spiritual power could have temporal consequences. In these cases, the power was *indirectly* temporal. 'By divine right', said Cardinal Bellarmine, 'the power attributed to Christ's Vicar is not properly temporal, but extends to temporal things.' Bellarmine believed that the great merit of this theory was that it kept the realms of grace and nature distinct, though compatible. By the law of nature, pagan Princes possessed supreme temporal authority over their subjects. The advent of Christianity – the law of grace – did not destroy this authority. It merely added a new power, namely the spiritual power of the pope, which by God's mercy ensured that Christian Princes and their subjects would not depart from the narrow road which led to godliness.[12]

This theory was supported by Scriptural quotations and by examples drawn from canon law and history. It was underpinned by a conception of the political universe as an ordered hierarchy of institutions, each of which was independent in its own sphere, but subordinate to the higher institutions in any matters which came within their competence. 'Human nature', said the Jesuit Thomas Fitzherbert,

> is led, as it were, by degrees and passeth from the lower, to the higher, or more worthy: as from the societie of the master, and the servant, to the

---

11 Michael Wilks, *The problem of sovereignty in the later Middle Ages* (Cambridge 1963) 315.
12 Robert Bellarmine, *De potestate summi pontificis*, in *Opera omnia* (Naples 1856–62) IV, pt 2, 295: 'Jure divino potestas in reges et principes Christianos non proprie temporalis sed quae se ad temporalia extendat, summo pontifici Christi vicario attributa est.' Ibid., 271.

familie: from the familie, to the towne, or corporation: and from thence, to some kind of common welth, as to the more perfect, for the more ease, and better commoditie of man: And therefore by the like reason, humane nature resteth not there, but tending ever to the best, and to her proper end, it passeth from all sortes of common welth, and civil societies, to the religious, or ecclesiasticall societie.

The law of nature showed that the church must have all the natural power over inferior societies which it needed to promote the spiritual welfare of its members. The law of grace identified the church as the Christian church, whose representative was the pope. 'It cannot be doubted, but that our Christian Church . . . is that religious, and ecclesiastical society, whereto all other societies are by the law, and course of nature subordinat, and subject.'[13]

Christ, said the Catholics, had gone to the trouble of setting up a church. He did so for a purpose, namely to further the spiritual good of humanity. So the church possessed whatever powers were necessary to secure this goal. Clearly, it would be very useful if clerics could inflict temporal penalties upon those who were heretics or otherwise obstructed God's cause. Indeed, a church which could not do these things would be severely handicapped in its fight against Satan and all his works. Manifestly, Christ would not have instituted a handicapped, imperfect church. It was absurd, said the Jesuit Suarez, to suggest that Christ had granted the pope power to direct Christians but not to coerce them, if necessary by temporal means. Such a grant would have been 'imperfect and ineffective'. 'If bad Princes could not be temporally chastised by their Pastour', wrote Thomas Fitzherbert, 'when they contemne the spiritual rod of Ecclesiasticall censure (as wicked Princes commonly do) Christ had not provided sufficiently for the government of his Church.' Without the indirect deposing power, argued Parsons, God's Providence 'might seem to be defectuous'. The church could use the temporal sword in self-defence, said Matthew Kellison, for if 'the Church could not do this in such case of necessitie, Christ had not sufficiently provided for her'.[14]

The theory of the indirect deposing power was endorsed by many Catholic theologians, both English and Continental. In 1606 an Act of Parliament prescribed that Catholic recusants could be made to take an oath abjuring the doctrine. The penalty for a second refusal was praemunire. A number of English Catholics refused it and took the consequences. Some priests suffered a traitor's death rather than swear what they held to be an unlawful oath. Since no pope was ever again to depose an English monarch, this attitude might seem to witness the strange dominance of tradition over realism. The priests died for a doctrine which was in fact outdated. There is some truth in

---

13 Thomas Fitzherbert, *The second part of a treatise concerning policy and religion* (Douai 1615) 37–8, 42.

14 Francisco Suarez, *Defensio fidei Catholicae*, in *Opera*, XXIV, 315: 'imperfecta et inefficax'; Fitzherbert, *A supplement to the discussion of M.D. Barlowes answere* (St Omer 1613) 35; Robert Parsons, *A discussion of the answere of M. William Barlow* (St Omer 1612) 109; Matthew Kellison, *The right and iurisdiction of the prelate and the prince*, 2nd edn (Douai 1621) 217.

this approach – since traditions were and are persistent, and frequently outlive their usefulness. But, in the early seventeenth century, it was far from clear that the deposing power was outmoded.

After dinner on 31 December 1605 James I announced that he had despatches from Rome informing him that the pope intended to excommunicate him and that Catholics threatened to kill him unless he granted them liberty of conscience. As a matter of stark reality, the papal Secretary Cardinal Borghese advised the nuncio in Flanders in November 1605 that he might profitably keep alive the king's fears of excommunication, and ten years later the Spanish ambassador Gondomar wrote to Philip III suggesting that in view of James's persistently heretical conduct it would be well for 'his Holiness to rebuke him so that after a failure to improve he might start to invoke against him the penalties and censures by law established'. There were English people who thought that deposition, and Spanish invasion, were good ideas. In 1606 the Jesuit Joseph Creswell lamented the fact that Spain was 'governed at this present by half a dozen of Fooles', since he felt that otherwise 'such were their Power and Abilitie as they might cast England into the Sea with their Shovells'.[15]

Reality was sufficient to give James cause for concern about his Catholic subjects, and to underline the wisdom of John Rawlinson's advice that 'our only safe course shall be, never to thinke ourselves safe, so long as this Trojan Horse is among us'. Rumour was worse. In 1608 Cecil received word that some Jesuits were planning to send five members of the Society to England to kill the king and Prince Henry. In 1610 Sir Edwin Rich reported from Naples that a leading English Jesuit intended to assassinate the king by sending him a poisoned suit of clothes. The king's fears of assassination were particularly acute in the months after the murder of Henry IV of France. Reports circulated that James had been excommunicated, and even killed. In 1612 George Abbot, Archbishop of Canterbury, wrote to the king relating the rumour that Prince Maurice of Nassau had been murdered and expressing the fear that there was some great conspiracy afoot. Two years later Abbot himself was attacked by a mad Catholic with a knife. The king suspected that this was part of a wider plot against himself.[16]

An act of papal deposition absolved subjects from their civil allegiance. A king who continued to exercise power after deposition was nothing more than a usurping tyrant, and could be assassinated by anyone. The connection

15 *CSPV, 1603–1607*, 308; Ottavio Mirto Frangipani, *Correspondance*, III, ed. A. Louant (Brussels 1942) 746; A.J. Loomie, ed., *Spain and the Jacobean Catholics*, 2 vols (1973–78) II, 56 (Gondomar); Creswell as reported by Cornwallis to the Privy Council, 7 October 1606, in E. Sawyer, ed., *Memorials of affairs of state . . . collected chiefly from the original papers of Sir Ralph Winwood*, 3 vols (1725) II, 376. For a statement similar to Creswell's cf. Henry Foley, *Records of the English province of the Society of Jesus*, 7 vols in 8 (1882) IV, 376.
16 John Rawlinson, *The Romish Iudas* (1611) 32–3; *CSPD, 1603–1610*, 636; Bilderbeck to Trumbull, 27 May 1610, in *HMC Downshire*, II, 297; Beaulieu to Trumbull, 7 January 1611, ibid., III, 9; *CSPV, 1607–1610*, 511; Abbot to the king, 17 August 1612, in *CSPD, 1611–1618*, 144; Abbot to Trumbull, in *HMC Downshire*, IV, 512–13; R.F. Williams, ed., *The Court and times of James the First*, 2 vols (1848) II, 227.

between deposition and assassination was close, especially in the mind of James I, who wrote vigorously against the doctrine. His writings helped to convince people that he was a zealous opponent of popery. By 1625, however, the dangers of deposition and assassination had receded. Charles did not share his father's fears. Some leading clerics came to abandon the Jacobean doctrine that popery is a rebellious religion. This made them seem more popish than their predecessors, though they were in fact as rigid in their rejection of the indirect deposing power.

Protestants denied that there were Scriptural precedents for clerics exercising temporal power over princes. King Uzziah, they said, had not been deposed by the high priest, but voluntarily withdrew from public affairs when he contracted leprosy. On the other hand Scripture gave a clear instance of the deposition of a high priest by a king in the story of Solomon and Abiathar.[17] Such texts, and examples drawn from history, were used to support the Protestant position. The essence of their case, however, rested on the contention that states are autonomous in civil matters. The indirect deposing power destroyed this autonomy, whatever Catholics might say to the contrary.

It was all very well to argue that the church could use temporal coercion only when the spiritual good was at stake. The truth was that as long as the pope decided what constituted the spiritual good, he could depose civil magistrates at will. Catholic protestations that the pope could depose only those princes who were obstinate heretics and who led their subjects into heresy were frivolous, since the pope decided what was heresy. Andrewes admitted that Bellarmine 'sometimes seems to restrict this power to driving out heretical Princes', but added that 'this restriction is meaningless where the pope alone judges what doctrine is heretical and who is a heretic'. The distinction between direct and indirect power was a mere 'May-game', and 'nothing but a Miste to dazzle the eyes of men wherein there is no simplicity or truth'. 'Power', said Thomas Hobbes, 'is as really divided and as dangerously to all purposes, by sharing with another Indirect power, as with a Direct one.'[18]

Like Hobbes, English divines were perfectly familiar with the concept of indivisible sovereignty, which underlay their argument. The clergy, they said, possessed no powers which impinged on the temporal sovereignty of the civil magistrate. Unlike Hobbes, they believed that clerics possess some powers. These were purely spiritual. They had been granted by God to ecclesiastics for the promotion of true religion. Such religion was defined by Scripture and

17 Pierre Du Moulin, *A defence of the Catholicke faith* (1610) 77; *De monarchia temporali pontificis Romani* (1614) 133; Richard Field, *Of the church, five books*, 4 vols (Cambridge 1847–52) III, 522; Leonel Sharpe, *A looking-glasse for the Pope* (1616) 197; William Tooker, *Duellum sive singulare certamen cum Martino Becano Iesuita* (1611) 154–5; John Buckeridge, *De potestate papae in rebus temporalibus* (1614) 517–23, 567; Richard Thomson, *Elenchus refutationis Torturae Torti* (1611) 37–8.
18 Lancelot Andrewes, *Responsio ad apologiam Cardinalis Bellarmini* (1851), p. xviii: 'Ad Reges Haereticos statu suo movendos alicubi videri vult Cardinalis potestatem hanc restringere: (quanquam parum adjuvaret haec restrictio, ubi idem ipse Papa solus judicat, quod dogma haereticum, quis haereticus).' Du Moulin, *A defence of the Catholicke faith*, 61; George Carleton, *Iurisdiction regall, episcopall, papall* (1610) 244; Thomas Hobbes, *Leviathan*, ed. C.B. Macpherson (Harmondsworth 1968) 600.

not by the mere whim of the sovereign. Protestants were agreed that the clergy held not temporal but only spiritual powers. They diverged on the nature of these powers. Their problem was to construct a theory which would avoid the papalist notion of clerical sovereignty while simultaneously safeguarding the clergy's spiritual authority and thus preserving the interests of Christ's immortal kingdom against incursions by the civil magistrate – Hobbes's mortal God.

ANTI-PAPALIST CLERICALISM

'The civill power', said the Scottish Presbyterian Samuel Rutherford in 1644, 'is above the Church-men as they are . . . members of a Christian Commonwealth, and the Church power is above the Magistrate as he is a member of the Church and to be edified to salvation, or censured for scandals.' In the opinion of Rutherford and other Presbyterians, the relationship between the prince and churchmen (including lay elders) was one of 'mutual subordination'. Civil and ecclesiastical authority were 'two parallel supreme powers on earth'. The civil magistrate was supreme in secular affairs and could promote the good of the state by using temporal coercion. Churchmen, on the other hand, were the ultimate arbiters on earth of the ecclesiastical good, and could use spiritual sanctions to back up their decisions. Church assemblies were the final human interpreters of God's word: 'though Synods may erre, yet are they of themselves Christs lawfull way to preserve veritie and charity and unity'. Rutherford cited the scholastics Jean Gerson and Jacques Almain to confirm his theory and concluded that the government of the church was no part of the civil magistrate's office.[19]

According to the Elizabethan Presbyterian Thomas Cartwright, the prince's office was to ensure that 'nothing in the churches be disorderly or wickedly done'. In performing this office he had to abide by ecclesiastical decrees. The civil magistrate was obliged 'to see that the lawes of God touching his worship and touching all matters and orders of the church be executed and duly observed'. But it was churchmen who made the orders: 'the making of the orders and ceremonies of the church . . . does . . . pertain unto the ministers of the church and to the ecclesiastical governors'. The 'civil magistrate', said Cartwright, had no power 'to ordain ceremonies pertaining to the church'. Princes were 'servants unto the church'. They should use the civil sword on behalf of true religion, but should always 'remember to subject themselves unto the church, to submit their sceptres, to throw down their crowns, before the church: yea as the Prophet speaketh, to lick the dust off the feet of the church'.[20]

Commenting on the church of England in the 1620s, the Scotsman David Calderwood took much the same line. The English, he argued, erred by failing to oust bishops and introduce presbyteries. They also took a misguided

19 Samuel Rutherford, *The due right of presbyteries or, a peaceable plea, for the government of the Church of Scotland* (1644) second count, 406–7, 309, 332–3, 425–47.
20 Thomas Cartwright, *A replye to an answer made by M. Doctor Whitgifte* (1574) 33, 154, 144.

view of the relations between civil and ecclesiastical power. In his opinion, the function of Parliament, the supreme temporal authority in the land, was to make laws concerning civil and criminal matters, but not to interfere in the government of the church. Ecclesiastics should, indeed, consult the prince before they summoned synods, but if the church's danger were great and the prince refused to help, synods might meet without his permission. It was the church, and not the prince, which possessed the power to dissolve as well as convoke synods. Nor could the prince deprive the clergy of the right to exercise their powers within his dominions. Such deprivation was a spiritual act, and therefore beyond the competence of the civil magistrate. Though churchmen had no power 'to appoint other things in the worship of God, than are appointed already by Christ', they had full authority 'to set down canons and constitutions about things before-appointed, and to dispose the circumstances of order and decency that are equally necessary in civil and religious actions'. The civil magistrate had no legislative authority in ecclesiastical affairs, and could not veto the church's canons. Conversely, clerics were obliged to steer clear of politics. The good pastor, in Calderwood's view, 'keepeth himself within the bounds of his own place and calling, and neither meddleth with civil causes, nor taketh upon him civil offices, nor seeketh after civil honour'.[21]

Presbyterians such as Cartwright and Calderwood rejected the theory of the indirect deposing power, but granted churchmen autonomy in ecclesiastical matters. The same basic scheme featured in the writings of a number of Catholics who opposed the papalism of Bellarmine. William Barclay, a Scotsman who taught Civil Law in France and Lorraine, argued that in any Christian commonwealth there were 'two powers' – temporal and spiritual – 'whereof neither is subject to the other'. Clerics, as much as laymen, were bound to abide by the temporal laws of the state in which they lived, for they were subject to the king in all secular affairs. The king, however, was subject to the clergy – represented by the pope – in ecclesiastical matters. So, 'Emperors and Kings are both over and under the Popes.' Neither power, he declared, 'should be Master over the other'. Nothing had done the cause of Catholicism more harm than the efforts of 'certain Popes' to 'annex and adjoin a sovereign temporal government to that spiritual sovereignty which they had'. Barclay's book was published posthumously at London in 1609, and his son John defended its contents against Bellarmine himself a few years later. In 1608 George Blackwell, leader of the Catholic secular priests in England, likewise abjured the theory of the indirect deposing power. In doing so he drew upon the sixteenth-century theorists Almain – a Frenchman – and Major – a Scot who taught in France. Their writings on this question, together with the works of Gerson, had been republished at Paris in 1606.[22]

21 David Calderwood, *Altare Damascenum* (1623) 394, 15, 16, 23, 32; *The pastor and the prelate; or reformation and conformity shortly compared* (Edinburgh 1843) 15, 33.
22 William Barclay, *De potestate papae*, translated as *Of the authoritie of the Pope* (1611) 96, 88, 69, 92; *A large examination taken at Lambeth of M.G. Blackwell* (1607) 63–4.

The Protestant authorities in England welcomed Catholic denunciations of the papal deposing power. But they found papist and Presbyterian ideas on the church's autonomy almost equally unacceptable. In Presbyterian theory, the church's officers were appointed by election, not by royal decree. Cartwright inveighed against 'forced elections without the consent of the people'. This idea struck not only at the rights of patrons – including the king – to present clerics to benefices, but also at the royal power of nominating bishops to oversee the church. Of course, the Presbyterian system of church government by a hierarchy of elected assemblies undermined episcopacy. Presbyterians regarded episcopacy as a popish institution. But in condemning it they drew on the arguments of Catholic conciliarists. Robert Parker, a Jacobean divine whose ideas on church government fell between Presbyterianism and Independency, quoted extensively from the works of Gerson and other French conciliarists in his *De Politeia Ecclesiastica* (On Ecclesiastical Polity), published in 1616. Cartwright believed that a General Council – 'if any be' – was the supreme human authority in ecclesiastical matters. Rutherford cited Gerson and Almain to confirm his opinion that the church should be ruled by elected assemblies.[23]

According to Rutherford, 'the God of nature for conserving human societies, hath given the power of government originally, not to one, but to a multitude'. In just the same way, he added, 'the God of Grace must have given a power of government to a society and multitude of little churches'. God gave civil power to the whole community, and spiritual power to the whole church, consisting of a society of congregations. The implication was that just as a single congregation was accountable to an assembly which represented a number of congregations, so the king was accountable to the whole commonwealth. Rutherford spelled this out in his *Lex Rex*, which took issue with the absolutist ideas of such writers as Buckeridge and De Dominis. The community, he argued, could remove a tyrannical ruler. One way in which a king might prove to be a tyrant was by persecuting the true religion, or by failing to heed the pious exhortations of the church. It was the office of churchmen to decide whether or not the king had erred in these ways. Churchmen could not themselves depose Princes: 'presbyteries never dethroned kings'. But they could exclude them from the church, for 'Kings are under the co-active power of Christ's Keys of discipline', and clerics had 'the Keys of the Kingdom of God, to open and let in believing princes, and also to shut them out, if they rebel against Christ'. A Prince who was sufficiently irreligious to merit excommunication was likely to turn out to be a tyrant. So the church could mark out candidates fit for deposition even if it could not itself depose. The theory was distinct from Bellarmine's indirect deposing power. But from the point of view of Princes the distinction mattered little,

23 Cartwright, *Replye*, 39, sig. A1b; Robert Parker, *De politeia ecclesiastica libri tres* (Frankfurt am Main 1616) e.g. lib. 3, 11, 26–9, 31, 41–2, 77, 80, 87, 104, 113, 161; Rutherford, *The due right of presbyteries*, second count, 332–3.

and anti-Presbyterian propagandists made much of the affinities between popery and Presbyterianism.[24]

It might be thought that Rutherford and earlier Presbyterian resistance theorists took their ideas on the state from their theories of ecclesiastical government. This is dubious. Cartwright, indeed, believed that the form of government in the commonwealth 'must be fashioned and made suitable unto the church'. The English constitution, which he took to be mixed, was peculiarly well adapted to Presbyterianism since it was also mixed: Christ ruled as a monarch, the pastors and elders governed as aristocrats, and heads of households, who elected, provided the democratic element. But Presbyterians borrowed their notions on the accountability of kings to their subjects, and on the legitimacy of active resistance, from Catholic natural law theory. Rutherford was quite candid about this. He admitted that the Jesuits shared many of his own views on civil government. His accidental agreement with them on these points did not prove that he was a Jesuit. In fact, the idea of original popular sovereignty was widely accepted 'before any Jesuit was whelped'. Indeed, said Rutherford, it dated back to Gerson, Almain and the Sorbonnists. He was indebted to Catholic conciliarists for his ideas not only on church government but also on civil authority. The same holds good of his intellectual ancestors, the Huguenot resistance theorists.[25]

In England, Presbyterianism was, to some extent, an indigenous movement. Godly Elizabethan clerics found that their bishops were insufficiently favourable to the cause of further reformation, and lamentably lacking in zeal for the goal of a learned preaching ministry. They felt that such objectives might best be achieved through the introduction of Presbyterian discipline. They did not necessarily endorse the ideas of clerical autonomy and of legitimate resistance which characterised the Presbyterian tradition from Beza to Rutherford. Such English Presbyterians as Cartwright and Stoughton were extremely and understandably coy on the subject of resistance. But the equation of Presbyterianism, clericalism and resistance was hard to live down. Bancroft saw to that.

There are many reasons why English clerics rejected the theories of Presbyterians on the relations between church and state. For one thing, the statutes which declared Elizabeth and the first two Stuarts to be Supreme Governors of the church were hard to reconcile with Presbyterian ideas. Secondly, and crudely, English monarchs were not in the habit of promoting Presbyterians to high ecclesiastical office. Thirdly, the abolition of episcopal power was an immediate goal of the Presbyterians. Anyone who hoped for elevation to the

---

24 Rutherford, *The due right of presbyteries*, first count, 340–1; *Lex Rex, or the law and the Prince* (Edinburgh 1843) p. xxi. Similarities between Presbyterian and papist doctrines on resistance are exposed in e.g. David Owen, *Herod and Pilate reconciled* (Cambridge 1610) *passim*; John Corbet, *The epistle congratulatorie of Lysimachus Nicanor of the societie of Jesu, to the Covenanters in Scotland* (1640) *passim*; Henry Leslie, *A speech, delivered at the visitation of Downe and Conner* (1639) 15–16; Charles I, *A large declaration concerning the late tumults in Scotland* (1639) 3–4.
25 Cartwright, *Replye*, 144, 35; Rutherford, *Lex Rex*, 206, 208.

episcopate, or who looked to the bishops for favours, had a vested interest in rejecting Presbyterianism. Fourthly, the English clergy developed their own individual theory of church government. This theory acquired momentum in the later sixteenth and early seventeenth centuries. It thrived when George Abbot was Archbishop of Canterbury, and when it looked as though a good many of the bishops themselves were amenable to godly reformation.

THE ROYAL SUPREMACY

Bellarmine held that the pope was empowered to procure the spiritual welfare of Christians. When necessary, he could use the temporal sword. Cartwright believed that it was the business of churchmen to govern ecclesiastical affairs. In these matters the Prince was the church's servant and not its master. Clerics, he claimed, could never use temporal weapons. The civil magistrate, on the other hand, had no authority to meddle in spiritual questions. Any other system confused the offices of pastor and Prince.

English Protestants kept the two offices distinct. Clerics alone, they said, could preach God's word and administer the sacraments. They alone could inflict spiritual censures upon sinners – and judge who was worthy to receive such censures. It belonged to the office of the pastor and not the Prince to interpret God's word and to admonish those who strayed from righteousness. But it was the Prince's office to rule the church. God had ordained civil power for spiritual as well as temporal ends. Of course, the magistrate ought to heed the advice of pious clerics: but it was only advice. The final human authority on ecclesiastical questions lay with the Prince. 'Papists and Puritans', said William Barlow, 'will have the King but an honourable member, not a chiefe Governor in the churches of his own Dominions.' English Protestants, by contrast, recognised his ecclesiastical Supremacy.[26]

The basis of the Supremacy was the law of nature. Nature instituted magistracy. Magistracy included power in ecclesiasticals. According to Sir John Hayward, the king's 'supreme authoritie under God in Ecclesiasticall affaires' was 'a principall point of Regalitie, and therefore necessarily annexed to the sovereign majesty of every state'. The law of nature, said the canons of 1606, gave parents and magistrates the duty 'to bring up their Children and Subjects, in the service and worship of God'. Preaching in 1606, John King – later Bishop of London – deduced the Supremacy from the concept of indivisible sovereignty; it was, he said, 'no more possible there should be two authentic authorities within one kingdom, than that one and the same body can bear two heads'. So, since the king was supreme in temporals he must also be supreme in ecclesiasticals.[27]

26 William Barlow, *The first of the foure sermons preached before the kings maiestie at Hampton Court* (1607) sig. A4a.
27 Sir John Hayward, *A reporte of a discourse concerning supreme power in affaires of religion* (1606) 3; *The convocation book of MDCVI*, 29; John King, *The fourth sermon preached at Hampton Court* (Oxford 1607) 25.

The king's duty to provide for the good of the church was regarded as an aspect of his more general duty to promote the welfare of his subjects. 'The Commonwealth', said Laud, 'can have no blessed and happy being, but by the Church.' Religion, in the words of Pemberton, was 'the basis and foundation of a truly-prosperous polity'. Christopher Lever's *Heaven and earth* was a disquisition on the theme that 'the best Policy is Religion'. But the prince's duty to further the cause of godliness was not merely an oblique consequence of his obligation to maintain the temporal welfare of his people. There was a higher goal than temporal felicity, namely the spiritual good. Princes were bound to do what they could to secure this goal for their subjects. Thomas Jackson rejected the Catholic claim that 'power regal procures only temporal good'. The ends of magistracy, wrote John Donne, were not only peace, but 'Peace and Religion'. The title page of King James's *Workes* displayed personifications of 'Pax' and 'Religio' beneath the royal crown.[28]

Since natural law, and not revelation, was the basis of the Supremacy it followed that heathen as well as Christian kings were supreme heads of the church within their realms. This implication, which seemed absurd to Catholics and Presbyterians, was accepted by English Protestants. Richard Thomson, defending Andrewes against popish attack in 1611, declared that heathen and Christian kings both had precisely the same powers over the church, though pagans were likely to exercise them badly if they bothered to exercise them at all. 'Princes not baptized, nay nor so much as godly minded', said Samuel Collins in 1617, 'have the same supreme right to govern the Church that Christian Kings and professing the faith have, though by error and transportation they either neglect it and perish it, or perhaps evil employ it.'[29]

Natural law gave ecclesiastical Supremacy to all sovereign magistrates, including pagans. Of what powers did the Supremacy consist? No one thought that a pagan or even a Christian king was authorised to prescribe false doctrine to the church. Indeed, it was no part of the royal office to interpret doctrine at all. Nor could the king perform the other functions which were proper to clerics. He could not preach, or administer the sacraments, or inflict spiritual censures. But he could make laws and use coercion to ensure that clerics did all these things adequately. He did not possess the powers of clerics, but he did possess an overarching, 'architectonic'[30] power to see that the clergy acted well.

'The first work of this supremacy', said John Buckeridge in 1606, 'is *reformatio Ecclesiae*, the reformation of the Church, by abolishing Idolatrie, superstition and heresy, and placing of true Religion.' One important way in which reformation might be effected was by 'calling of Councels and Synods'. English

---

28 Laud, *Works*, I, 6; William Pemberton, *The charge of God and the king* (1619) sig. A4b; Christopher Lever, *Heaven and earth, religion and policy* (1608) 1; Thomas Jackson, *A treatise of Christian obedience*, in *Works*, 12 vols (Oxford 1844) XII, 192; Donne, *Pseudo-Martyr*, 168.

29 Thomson, *Elenchus refutationis Torturae Torti*, 94; Samuel Collins, *Epphata to F. T.* (Cambridge 1617) 534; cf. *Increpatio Andreae Eudaemono-Iohannis Iesuitae* (Cambridge 1612) 409.

30 James Cooke, *Iuridica trium quaestionum ad maiestatem pertinentium determinatio* (Oxford 1608) 28; Thomson, *Elenchus refutationis Torturae Torti*, 79–80.

Protestants granted the Prince the right to convoke and dissolve church councils. Richard Harris, writing against papists at James's behest, held that the king could 'call Councells of Synods by his authority' and claimed that the first six General Councils of the early Christian church had been convoked by emperors. The king, he asserted, could summon provincial as well as national synods; bishops were empowered to call provincial synods only by delegation from the civil magistrate. In 1606 Andrewes vindicated the royal power to call clerical assemblies in a sermon directed against both Presbyterians and papists. Defending Andrewes against the papists five years later, Robert Burhill argued that the king could not only convoke and dissolve councils, but also watch over their proceedings. Moreover, the canons on which the councils resolved acquired the force of law only with the king's consent. Clerics, said Edward Boughen in 1637, 'made no canons without the assent, and consent, and confirmation of Christian Kings'.[31]

The king's legislative power in church affairs was, indeed, a straightforward consequence of his duty to cause religion 'to be planted and advanced in his dominion'. Harris granted the Prince 'the right and power by Regal authority, to make church laws', and added that he could 'delegate such as should judge of the laws so made'. The king's lack of skill in church matters was no bar to his legislative supremacy: though not as skilled as lawyers in civil affairs, said Jackson, he was nevertheless supreme in temporals. The king was 'the fountain of all civil Justice under God in this Kingdom', and he appointed judges to try cases in accordance with his laws. But it was no part of his office to act as a judge himself. Similarly, argued Harris, 'it pertaineth not to his Majesty, to exercise all inferior acts of Ecclesiastical government, though he be supreme Ecclesiastical Governor'. The judges judged particular cases, but the king judged the judges. A ruler, said Collins, could be supreme even though he could not himself exercise the powers of his subordinates: 'Else how shall a woman be Queen over soldiers . . . and yet no soldier, nor fit to bear arms?'[32]

There was, of course, an important difference between the cases of civil judges and soldiers on the one hand, and clerics on the other. Judges and soldiers derived their powers from his majesty. Clerics, by contrast, drew their spiritual powers from God alone by means of ordination or consecration. Since these powers came from God, it was not within the province of the Prince to take them away. At first glance, it looks as though this idea imposed a stringent limitation on the Royal Supremacy. How could the Prince reform the church if he had no power to deprive ungodly bishops? English Protestants circumvented this point by arguing that although the king could

31 Buckeridge, *A sermon preached at Hampton Court* (1606) sig. E1a; Richard Harris, *English concord* (1614), 97, 165, 158; Robert Burhill, *Pro Tortura Torti* (1611), 106; Edward Boughen, *A sermon concerning decencie and order* (1638) 18–19; cf. Andrewes, *Responsio ad apologiam*, 446; Collins, *Epphata*, 520.
32 Robert Pricke, *The doctrine of superioritie, and of subiection* (1609) sig. C7b; Harris, *English concord*, 97; Jackson, *Treatise of Christian obedience*, 225–6; Collins, *Epphata*, 519–20, 517.

not deprive a bishop of his episcopal powers, he could deprive him of the right to *exercise* these powers. 'The secular powers', wrote Francis Mason, 'doe not depose a Bishop by degradation, nor by utterly debarring him from his Episcopall function: but only by excluding him from the exercise of Episcopal acts upon their subjects, and within their dominions.'[33]

Kings could forbid obnoxious clerics to perform their spiritual functions. They could also ensure that these functions were exercised in particular ways. For instance, the king might set down rules defining the circumstances in which sinners should be excommunicated. Although the Prince himself had no power to excommunicate, he could make laws, said Harris, 'by force and virtue whereof this or that obstinate subject ought to be excommunicated'. Moreover, he added, 'it is in the Kings absolute power, to command any Bishop within his dominion, to absolve any man whom by appeal he shall find to be unjustly excommunicated'.[34]

The king could hear appeals against unjust excommunications. He was himself immune from excommunication. According to Collins, 'a multitude is inexcommunicable, by the verdict of the School'. The point of excommunication was to cut off an individual from spiritual communion with his fellows. It made no sense to excommunicate a whole society. Collins extended the idea, drawing on the absolutist equation between the king and the state: 'every Prince is virtually a whole Kingdom'. So Princes could not be excommunicated. Saint Ambrose's action in excluding the Roman emperor Theodosius from the sacrament, he held, was 'not rashly to be imitated'. David Owen denied that Ambrose had excommunicated Theodosius. Harris and Burhill took the same line. So too did the Caroline Arminian Thomas Jackson, asserting that 'the supreme majesty is not excommunicable'. The jurisdiction of the clergy was subordinate to that of the Prince. As the much quoted adage had it, 'the Church is in the commonwealth, but the commonwealth is not in the Church'.[35]

Manifestly, the theory of the Royal Supremacy gave the Prince very wide powers over ecclesiastical affairs. He could not exercise the functions of a churchman in person, and to this extent the integrity of the pastor's office was safeguarded. But he could control the conduct of his clergy. The theory had virtues. It served to explain how the Reformation had happened in England. By legislation and coercive action godly Princes had ousted wicked and promoted pious clerics, who preached the Lord's pure word. As long as kings used the Supremacy in ways which seemed to further the cause of true religion, the theory worked well enough. Trouble arose when the Prince employed his

33 Francis Mason, *Of the consecration of the bishops in the Church of England* (1613) 113.
34 Harris, *English concord*, 216.
35 Collins, *Epphata*, 531–2; Owen, *Anti-Paraeus* (Cambridge 1622) 12–14; Harris, *English concord*, 218; Burhill, *De potestate regia* (Oxford 1613) 285–6; Jackson, *Treatise of Christian obedience*, 237; cf. John Hacket, *Scrinia reserata* (1693), I, 33; 'Ecclesia est in republica sed respublica non est in ecclesia': John Panke, *Eclogarius, or briefe summe of the truth of that title of supreame governour* (Oxford 1612) 12; Buckeridge, *Sermon*, sig. D2b; Cooke, *Iuridica trium quaestionum*, 29; cf. Laud, *Works*, I, 6: 'the Church can have no being but in the Commonwealth'.

powers to encourage false doctrine and popish ceremonies. The theory provided no effective checks to such action. Divines might remonstrate with his
majesty when they discovered that he was slipping into irreligion. But they
had no recourse if he chose to silence them by suspension, deprivation or
cruder temporal means. Papists argued that this was the crucial defect of the
Royal Supremacy. It allowed the king to introduce heresy. In substance the
charge was correct as strict Calvinists discovered when Charles I countenanced
the proceedings of Laud and his cronies. English Protestants explored two
ways of meeting this difficulty.

The first was to resort to Providence. God in his mercy would protect
commonwealths from the evils of tyranny by cutting short the lives of
tyrants. He was still more merciful towards the church, which Christ had
undertaken never to desert. True religion was bound to survive, though heresy
might thrive for a while. So good Christians should put their trust in Providence. The Catholic argument, which looked for human means – in the shape
of the indirect deposing power – to preserve the church, was both blasphemous and muddle-headed. 'It is in effect as much . . . as to deny God's providence', said Thomas Jackson. Yet Catholics themselves were forced to rely on
Providence to protect the church against an evil pope. So their reasoning was
confused.[36]

Reliance on Providence came easily as long as Princes were godly. Many
churchmen found it more difficult when in the 1630s the king instituted what
they took to be irreligious policies. In these circumstances it was tempting
to argue that the king's ecclesiastical prerogative was, like his other prerogatives, subordinate to the supreme legislative authority of Parliament and limited by the common law. Statutes had set up true religion in England. Attempts
by the king to alter religion would contravene not only the higher law of
God, but also statute, and would be invalid on both counts. Royal agents
who enforced ungodly and illegal policies would be responsible for their own
actions, since the king could do no wrong. Such agents were usurpers of
authority that properly belonged to Parliament. If they were bishops they might
also turn out to be usurpers in another sense, for clerics had a duty not to
meddle in affairs of state. These arguments were nothing more than an extension of anti-absolutist constitutional ideas to the ecclesiastical sphere. In the
House of Commons they were voiced by people who believed that royal
ecclesiastical policies were undermining the liberties of the subject. There was
often an anti-clerical edge to this notion. The bishops, acting under the king,
enforced clerical claims in a way which was incompatible with lay interests.
When clerics, disillusioned by the activities of the bishops and the king, expressed similar views, they played into the hands of the House of Commons.
In the 1640s anti-clericalist laymen and clericalist anti-Laudians made common
cause. The alliance triumphed. The laymen proved the senior partners.

36 Jackson, *Treatise of Christian obedience*, 211–12; Thomas Preston, *Last reioynder to Mr. Thomas
Fitzherberts reply concerning the oath of allegiance* (1619) 214; Marc'Antonio De Dominis, *De republica
ecclesiastica pars secunda* (1620) 795.

Under James I such developments lay in the future. The king staunchly opposed popery, as his writings proved. Tensions within the clergy did not prevent a broad consensus on questions of church government. His majesty, they agreed, ruled the church through the bishops and Convocation. Many critics of the Elizabethan church abandoned aggressive Presbyterianism when they came to think that their ideal of an orthodox preaching ministry was available under the rule of the bishops.[37] The tendency continued while James was king. Royal absolutism in church affairs, and episcopalianism became orthodox tenets. Indeed, many clerics who adopted Calvinist ideas on doctrine entirely rejected the views on church government of their Continental co-religionists. They held that episcopacy was not only permitted but also prescribed, or at least highly recommended by God's word.

EPISCOPACY BY DIVINE RIGHT

The Royal Supremacy and *jure divino* episcopacy were integral aspects of the outlook on church government of many Jacobean divines. Proponents of the *jure divino* theory included Neile, Andrewes and De Dominis among those who were hostile to the Calvinist theology of grace; George Abbot, Carleton and Downame among Calvinists. John Bridges, Dean of Salisbury and later Bishop of Oxford, gave unequivocal support to the theory in 1587,[38] and it was endorsed by such influential thinkers as Hooker, Bilson and Saravia during the next decade. It acquired very wide adherence from clerical writers under James I. Essentially, the theory consisted of two propositions. Firstly, episcopacy had been set up by Christ as the best, if not the only possible form of church government. Secondly, the powers of bishops – except, of course, any temporal power which the civil magistrate chose to delegate to them – were derived from God alone. By divine law, bishops were distinct from other clerics, and had authority over them. This authority came from God and not from the king. In his officially commissioned *English concord* Richard Harris explained to the papists that English churchmen did not derive purely episcopal powers from the king: 'All English Academicks would detest such descending of our Bishops from the King; who giveth unto our Bishops chosen and consecrated, their Baronies, and Jurisdiction coactive by corporall or temporall mulcts . . . but not Jurisdiction meerely sacerdotall or Episcopall; viz. to excommunicate, to give Orders, to confirme & c.'[39] James I placed the seal of royal approval upon such ideas:

---

37 Peter Lake, *Moderate puritans and the Elizabethan church* (Cambridge 1982) *passim*.
38 John Bridges, *A defence of the government established in the Church of England* (1587) sig. S4a–5b, S8b.
39 Harris, *English concord*, 129. The history of the theory of *jure divino* episcopacy is discussed in M.R. Sommerville, 'Richard Hooker and his contemporaries on episcopacy: an Elizabethan consensus', *JEH* 35 (1984) 177–87; Johann P. Sommerville, 'The Royal Supremacy and episcopacy "jure divino", 1603–40', *JEH* 34 (1983) 548–58; Anthony Milton, *Catholic and Reformed*, esp. 454–61; Peter Lake, *Anglicans and Puritans? Presbyterianism and English Conformist thought from Whitgift to Hooker* (1988), esp. 88–97, 215–22.

That Bishops ought to be in the Church, I ever maintained it, as an Apostolike institution, and so the ordinance of God; contrary to the Puritanes, and likewise to Bellarmine; who denies that Bishops have their Jurisdiction immediately from God (But it is no wonder he takes the Puritanes part, since Jesuits are nothing but Puritan-Papists).[40]

According to James, bishops derived their jurisdiction immediately from God. But the Elizabethan Act of Supremacy insisted that all authority within the realm was derived from the monarch. Was there a contradiction here? Did the theory of *jure divino* episcopacy represent a clericalist assault upon the Royal Supremacy? It is often claimed that it did but this is dubious. Two points are crucial. Firstly, though episcopal power did not stem from the king, the right to exercise such power did. The king could silence bishops by taking this right away from them. Moreover, he could ensure that episcopal authority was exercised in a way that was compatible with his own laws. Clerical freedom of action was ultimately limited to prayers and tears. Secondly, the *jure divino* jurisdiction claimed by bishops was purely spiritual. They claimed that according to God's law the power to excommunicate – and, consequently, to judge who was worthy of excommunication – was held by bishops alone and not by all ministers. This claim did not derogate from the Royal Supremacy for English monarchs had not asserted a power to excommunicate, or to do anything else that belonged to the ministerial function of clerics. The target of *jure divino* episcopalians was Presbyterianism – which asserted the equality of ministers and thus rejected episcopacy – and to a lesser extent Catholicism – for many Catholics asserted that the jurisdictional powers of bishops were derived not from God but from the pope. English churchmen believed that ecclesiastical affairs could best be governed by bishops acting *under* the king. The only sense in which their theory limited the king's power to rule the church was that in normal circumstances he was required to admit episcopacy. Since the early Stuart kings were fond of episcopacy this caused no problems. In any case, the limitation was not very strong, for most theorists agreed that in a time of necessity the civil magistrate could introduce some other form of church government – and it was the magistrate who decided what constituted a time of necessity.

The idea that Laudians were clericalist in the sense that they granted the clergy powers which could be exercised against the king's will does not stand up to scrutiny. Laud was quite explicit on this point:

40 James I, *Premonition*, 44, in *An apologie for the oath of allegiance . . . together with a premonition of his maiesties*, 2nd issue (1609). There are contrasting views of James I's attitudes towards episcopacy in Maurice Lee, Jr., *Great Britain's Solomon: King James VI and I in his three kingdoms* (Urbana, Ill. 1980) 167–71 (an account which doubts the extent of James's commitment to *jure divino* episcopacy), and Milton, *Catholic and Reformed*, 454–61, esp. 456 (which argues that James gave the doctrine his 'full support'). A recent survey of James's thought is J.H. Burns, *The true law of kingship: concepts of monarchy in early modern Scotland* (Oxford 1996) 222–81; at 270 Burns speaks of the king's 'uncertainty as to *jure divino* episcopacy', and states that James 'at one point professed to believe' that episcopacy was an Apostolic institution, implying that he held different views on other occasions. But James tells us that he 'ever maintained' this position, and Burns does not provide evidence why we should doubt the king's word or see him as uncertain about episcopacy.

our being Bishops, *Jure divino*, by Divine Right, takes nothing from the Kings Right or power over us. For though our Office be from God and Christ immediately, yet may wee not exercise that power, either of Order or Jurisdiction, but as God hath appointed us, that is, not in his Majesties, or any Christian Kings Kingdomes, but by and under the power of the King given us so to doe.

Bishops were bound to obey the king's laws. Of course, there were disputes on what the law was, and many people did not share Laud's views on this question. But it was Laud, and not his opponents, who looked to the king as the final interpreter of human law. Laudians may have been clericalist in that they asserted clerical liberties against lay interference, but they had royal backing in this and did not attack the king's Supremacy. John Cosin, prebendary and later Bishop of Durham, was accused of saying that the king had no more power to excommunicate than the man who rubbed the heels of Cosin's horse. It is often overlooked that even if he did say this, his position was in full accordance with the doctrine of the Royal Supremacy. Kings had no power to excommunicate. 'Our Church disclaimeth it', said Cosin, quite correctly, 'and . . . it is a slander laid upon us by the papists.' His doctrine on excommunication was orthodox: 'the exercise thereof was under the king, but the power of it only from Christ'. Princes, he added, were 'supreme governors both of Church and State; and . . . by this supreme dominion they might command churchmen at any time to do their office, or punish them for neglect of it'.[41]

Presbyterians objected to episcopacy and therefore, *a fortiori*, to episcopacy *jure divino*. Some alleged that any claim by one churchman to *jure divino* authority over another was incompatible with the Royal Supremacy.[42] In effect, this was to say that the theory of the Royal Supremacy demanded the equality of ministers – a ludicrous thesis. The campaigns of Whitgift and Bancroft, the canons of 1604, and the Hampton Court Conference had the effect of crushing active Presbyterianism in England. A number of clerics who were dissatisfied with the established church but who saw no prospect of replacing it with a Presbyterian system now turned to Congregationalism or Independency. The basic tenets on church government of these men were that each individual church was autonomous and that ultimate ecclesiastical power lay with the congregation as a whole. Unlike Separatists, the Independents were willing to recognise at least some of the English parochial congregations as true churches. In the years after 1604 Henry Jacob and William Bradshaw spelled out these ideas in a series of pamphlets. Both men shared the Presbyterians'

---

41 Laud, *A speech delivered in the Starre-chamber, on Wednesday, the XIVth of Iune* (1637) 7; John Cosin, *Works*, 5 vols (Oxford 1843–55) IV, 371–2. The accusation against Cosin is discussed in W.M. Lamont, *Godly rule: politics and religion 1603–60* (1969) 61; but there are significant variations in contemporary accounts: *CD 29*, 36–7, 44, 174.
42 *Informations, or a protestation, and a treatise from Scotland* (1608) 82, 89, 92; Alexander Leighton, *An appeal to the Parliament; or Sions plea against the prelacie* (1629) 25, 39–40; cf. William Bradshaw, *A protestation of the Kings supremacie* (1605) 12.

belief in the equality of ministers, and Independents, like Presbyterians, sometimes argued that *jure divino* episcopacy was incompatible with the Royal Supremacy.

William Ames, one of the most influential of English divines, subscribed to Independency, and it is possible that some English gentlemen found the scheme appealing – a congregation could more easily be controlled by a local landowner if it was exempt from outside interference, whether by bishops or by Presbyterian synods. Viscount Saye and Sele sent his sons to study under Ames at Franeker,[43] and during the 1640s proved a staunch champion of Independency. But Congregationalists formed an insignificant minority in Jacobean England. The argument that *jure divino* episcopacy struck at traditional ideas about the Royal Supremacy did not catch on. It was first voiced in Parliament only in 1640 – by Pym.[44] With the exception of committed Presbyterians and Independents, few Jacobeans were hostile to the *jure divino* theory. It was what the bishops did that counted, and under James there was a broad consensus that most of them were doing acceptable things.

This is not to say that perfect unity reigned in James's church. Laud's religious views attracted hostility while he was still at Oxford. One of his enemies, Robert Abbot, took issue with the Arminian ideas of Richard Thomson in a treatise which was published in 1618.[45] Significantly, both Abbot and Thomson defended the Royal Supremacy against papist attack. Jurisdictional questions led to little controversy among conformist churchmen. It is difficult to detect a characteristically puritan, or Anglican, theory of the state in Jacobean England. It is equally difficult to find such a theory of church government. There were, indeed, disputes over ecclesiastical jurisdiction. But these divided the laity from the clergy, and absolutists from their opponents, rather than puritans from Anglicans.

THE CHURCH, THE LAW AND THE LAITY

In 1605 Archbishop Bancroft, acting in the name of the clergy, presented articles of complaint against the common law judges to the Privy Council. The articles claimed that the ecclesiastical and common law jurisdictions were independent, though both were under the king. His majesty, they said, had 'sufficient authority in himself, with the assistance of his council, to judge what is amiss in either of his said jurisdictions, and to have reformed the same accordingly'. The point of these remarks was to show that the king and not the common law set the boundaries between the two jurisdictions. So

43 K.L. Sprunger, *The learned Doctor William Ames* (Urbana, Ill. 1972) 80, 237. The Independent and separatist congregations in England are discussed in Murray Tolmie, *The triumph of the saints: the separate churches in London 1616–1649* (Cambridge 1977). A valuable discussion of Independent thought is M.R. Sommerville, 'Independent thought, 1603–1649', unpublished Cambridge University Ph.D. dissertation, 1982.
44 *PSP 40*, 152.
45 *In Richardi Thomsonis . . . animadversio brevis* is appended to Abbot's *De gratia, et perseverantia sanctorum* (1618).

prohibitions, which took cases out of the ecclesiastical and into the common law courts, were permissible only when the king allowed them. The judges replied by agreeing that if there were any abuses in the jurisdictions, they ought to be reformed. But they held that the law defined the limits. So a prohibition according to law was no abuse. Moreover, the law could be changed only by Parliament, not by the king alone: 'what the law doth warrant in cases of prohibitions to keep every jurisdiction in his true limits, is not to be said an abuse, nor can be altered but by parliament'.[46] At this point the controversy dissolved into the wider question of whether the king was an absolute ruler, or a constitutional monarch bound by a law which Parliament alone could amend.

The judges believed that the king's ecclesiastical jurisdiction was subordinate to the common law and statutes. The idea had a long history. Under Henry VIII, Lord Chancellor Audley told Bishop Gardiner that by statute 'it is provided that no spiritual law shall have place contrary to a Common law or act of Parliament'. Were this not so, he added, 'you Bishops would enter in with the King, and, by means of his supremacy, order the laity as you listed'. Thankfully, however, the church was under the law, and 'so we laymen shall be sure to enjoy our inheritance by the Common laws and acts of Parliament'.[47] Similar notions informed the attitudes of many early Stuart lawyers and gentry towards the pretensions of the clergy.

Of course, there were cross-currents. One was the anti-clericalism so common in post-Reformation England. Many people resented the claims to wealth, status and power of the clergy. They disliked the interference in their private lives of the church courts. Such sentiments were not confined to those who took a low view of the royal prerogative. Thomas Hobbes opposed clerical claims while arguing for royal absolutism. Conversely, it was possible to defend ecclesiastical jurisdiction while at the same time opposing high claims for the prerogative. Sir Dudley Digges did this – but then he was a close friend of Archbishop Abbot, and a member of the most powerful ecclesiastical court, the High Commission. Again, there was a crude financial aspect to jurisdictional disputes. Prohibitions brought business, and fees, into the hands of the common lawyers. But it would be overly cynical to suppose that Coke, the great champion of prohibitions, was motivated by mere filthy lucre. Ambitious though he was, he knew how to subordinate profit to principle. When Thomas Sutton, perhaps the richest commoner in England, died in 1611 James I was eager to overturn his will and lay hands on his wealth. Coke thwarted him and received grudging praise for this from the Laudian absolutist Peter Heylin. The judge, said Heylin, 'stood stoutly to his trust' 'by which though he got the Kings displeasure, yet amongst others he preserved the reputation of an honest man'.[48] Later, Coke risked and underwent dismissal for his beliefs. When due account is taken of lawyers' special pleading, and of

46 *ST*, ɪɪ, 134.
47 J.A. Muller, *The letters of Stephen Gardiner* (Cambridge 1933) 390–2.
48 Peter Heylin, *Cyprianus Anglicus*, 2nd edn (1671) 119.

naked anti-clericalism, it remains true that much lay criticism of the church courts was based upon constitutional principle.

The court of High Commission fined and imprisoned. Its powers to do so were derived from the king as Supreme Governor of the church. The judges' decision in Cawdrey's Case of 1591 spelled out what was already implicit in the Elizabethan Act of Supremacy – that Parliament had restored old but not added new jurisdiction in ecclesiastical matters to the crown. So, did the ancient common laws of the land give the king power to fine and imprison? These things, said Nicholas Fuller in a pamphlet published in 1607 and reprinted in 1641, could be done only 'according to the due course of the lawes of the Realme' – that is to say, by the common law courts – unless statute provided otherwise. In matters affecting the liberty and property of the subject the common law was supreme. Fuller drew on Magna Carta to confirm his position, in this following such Elizabethan critics of the High Commission as Morice and Beale. The common law protected the subject's liberty and property. It did not permit the king to take them arbitrarily. In particular, the king had no ancient prerogative to fine and imprison for ecclesiastical offences. Any such power which he held, and could delegate, was therefore statutory, and so based on the consent of the realm. Which statutes gave ecclesiastics the power to fine and imprison? The earliest, said Fuller, was 2 Hen. 4, c.15, which 'was procured by the Popish Prelates in the time of darkness'. The power was a popish innovation and no part of the crown's ancient jurisdiction. In restoring that jurisdiction, the Elizabethan Act of Supremacy had abolished Henry IV's statute.[49]

Fuller's argument was questionable, and depended on a tendentious reading of the Act of Supremacy. But his basic idea was simple and influential. By using fines and imprisonment the Commission infringed the liberties of the subject. In their petition of 7 July 1610 the House of Commons complained that the Commission was exceeding the bounds laid down by Elizabeth's statute, for 'commissioners do fine and imprison and exercise other authority not belonging to the ecclesiastical jurisdiction restored by that statute, which we conceive to be a great wrong to the subject'. Coke held that the Commission had no power to fine or imprison except in a few cases which he thought had been set down by Act of Parliament. In 1611 when new letters patent were issued defining the Commission's functions, but leaving the disputed powers intact, Coke detected in them 'divers points against the laws and statutes of England', and he, along with the other judges who had been appointed to the Commission, refused to sit. Coke objected not only to fines and imprisonment

---

49 Nicholas Fuller, *The argument of Master Nicholas Fuller in the case of Thomas Lad, and Richard Maunsell* (1607) 3, 4, 25; cf. Fuller's arguments in the parliamentary session of 1606–7 in D.H. Willson, ed., *The parliamentary diary of Robert Bowyer, 1606–1607* (Minneapolis 1931) 344–9. The constitutional implications of debates on ecclesiastical jurisdiction are discussed in R.G. Usher, *The rise and fall of the High Commission* (Oxford 1913) 222–6; R.A. Marchant, *The church under the law: justice, administration and discipline in the diocese of York 1560–1640* (Cambridge 1969) 239–40. The use of Magna Carta by Morice and Beale is discussed in Faith Thompson, *Magna Carta: its role in the making of the English constitution 1300–1629* (Minneapolis 1948) 216–28.

but also to the wide use of the oath *ex officio*. He thought it could licitly be tendered in only a limited range of cases: 'to administer it generally is against Lawe'. Earlier, Cartwright had argued that the oath was contrary to the law of God, and in the case of Maunsell and Ladd in 1607 – a test case on the Commisssion's powers – Fuller claimed that it conflicted with Magna Carta, while Henry Finch argued that it was against the law of nature.[50]

After 1616, when Coke was dismissed, controversy over the High Commission declined in both volume and intensity – perhaps because Coke's fate served as a warning to other judges, or perhaps because the court under Abbot exercised its powers with increasing moderation. But the old arguments lived on. Christopher Sherland attacked the Commission's authority in the House of Commons of 1626. In 1628 Alexander Leighton complained of the power of imprisonment and the oath *ex officio* which were, he thought, 'against the Law of God, the Honour of the King, the law of the Land, the nature of Ecclesiasticke jurisdiction, and the right of the Subject'. In the Short Parliament Pym listed encroachments of the church courts, drawing attention to the High Commission's powers 'to fine and imprison, to administer the oath *ex officio*, with many the like usurpations'. Sir John Eliot – son of the more famous Sir John – likewise denounced the oath as unjust, and Speaker Glanville agreed.[51]

In 1629 the publisher and bookseller Michael Sparke argued that the Commission's jurisdiction over unlicensed printing conflicted with 'the hereditary liberty of the subjects' persons and goods'. He appealed to Magna Carta and the Petition of Right. In 1637 John Bastwick discovered yet another liberty which had been infringed by the bishops acting through the Commission: 'yea nobody without penalty may pisse within the compasse of their yards and Courts'. Perhaps he was thinking of the case of Francis Litton who was 'apprehended in Paule's for pissing against a pillar in the Church', and imprisoned by the High Commission, despite his rather implausible claim that he did not know St Paul's was a church.[52]

The Commission, some said, undermined the liberty and especially property of the subject. So too did the deprivation of ministers. A benefice was freehold property. Bishops deprived clerics of their benefices according to canons which had not received the assent of Parliament. To do this was

---

50 *PP 10*, ii, 263; Usher, *The rise and fall of the High Commission*, 199–200, 219–20; J.R. Tanner, ed., *Constitutional documents of the reign of James I* (Cambridge 1930) 156–63; M.H. Maguire, 'Attack of the common lawyers on the oath *ex officio* as administered in the ecclesiastical courts in England', in *Essays in history and political theory in honor of Charles Howard McIlwain* (Cambridge, Mass. 1936) 199–229, at 222–3, 226; C.M. Gray, 'Prohibitions and the privilege against self-incrimination', in D.J. Guth and J.W. McKenna, eds, *Tudor rule and revolution: essays for G.R. Elton from his American friends* (Cambridge 1982) 345–67, at 362. A bill against the oath *ex officio* was twice read in the House of Commons in 1614: *CJ*, 493, 503.
51 CUL Mss Dd.12.20, f. 68a (Sherland); Leighton, *An appeal to the Parliament*, 33; *PSP 40*, 151 (Pym), 225–6 (Eliot, Glanville).
52 Sparke quoted in F.S. Siebert, *Freedom of the press in England, 1476–1776* (Urbana, Ill. 1952), 140; John Bastwick, *The letany of John Bastwick* (1637) 5; Gardiner, ed., *Reports of cases in the courts of Star Chamber and High Commission* (1886) 280–1, cf. 298.

arguably to infringe the basic principle that property may never be taken without the consent of the subject in Parliament. In Cawdrey's Case the judges rejected the argument on the grounds that the right of deprivation was part of the crown's ancient ecclesiastical jurisdiction. But the idea continued to attract devotees. The canons of 1604, said one member of the Commons in 1610, were 'not enjoined by statute'. So refusal by the clergy to subscribe to them was no ground for deprivation. The House's petition of ecclesiastical grievances complained that clerics who were 'ever ready to perform the legal subscription appointed by the statute of 13° Elizabeth' had been deprived of 'their ecclesiastical livings (being their freehold)'. Sir Nathaniel Rich took the same line on deprived ministers in 1625. 'They refuse not', he declared, 'to subscribe to the articles according to the statute. But another subscription is required by canon; and no canon can compel a man under penalty to lose his freehold.' Rich reverted to the same theme in the Parliament of 1628. Sherland agreed with him, asserting that 'there is nothing to enjoin subscription'. 'To subscribe to a canon not confirmed by act of parliament', said Selden, 'was like giving way to the destruction of ourselves in our freeholds.'[53]

Canons, then, could not abrogate rights of property. Nor could they alter any other provision of common or statute law. 'The English customes', declared Selden in 1610, 'never permitted themselves to be subjected to . . . Clergy-canons; alwaies (under parliament correction) retaining . . . whatsoever they have by long use or allowance approved.' In the same year the Commons discussed 'a bill against canons ecclesiastical not confirmed by parliament'. Cecil detected its wider implications: 'I will say no more but that I have, ever since this parliament began, observed that the Lower House have very much called the King's prerogative in question.'[54] To say that a canon could not bind – or at least, could not bind the laity[55] – without Parliament's consent was to strike at the royal prerogative. Rights of property, and freedom from legislation without consent, were entwined in the ecclesiastical as in the civil sphere.

In depriving clerics of their benefices, bishops interfered with the interests of lay patrons. People who had gone to the trouble and perhaps expense of securing a congenial minister for a benefice within their gift were unlikely to take kindly to the deprivation of their nominee. 'Our right of presentation', Pym told the Commons in 1628, is 'our inheritance'. It was undermined by episcopal interference. Again, lay patrons sometimes grew tired of ministers. As things stood they could do little to remove them. A bill which had wide lay support throughout the period would have remedied this state of affairs by giving Justices of the Peace jurisdiction over 'scandalous and unworthy' ministers. It passed the Commons in 1604 and was revived in 1610, 1614, 1621, 1624, 1626 and 1628. The bishops were less than delighted by the idea. In 1610

---

53 *PP 10*, i, 126; ii, 256; *DHC 25*, 26; *PP 28*, iii, 514 (Rich, Sherland), 515 (Selden).
54 Selden, *The duello or single combat* (1610) 21; *PP 10*, i, 100; ibid., 103 (Cecil). Fuller's views on the bill contrast strongly with Cecil's: ibid., ii, 406.
55 This was the point insisted on by Pym and St John in the Short Parliament: *PSP 40*, 168, 201.

George Abbot thought it 'no marvel' that the Commons 'speak against the church' since in other matters they were equally willing to 'touch the King's prerogative'. He attacked the proposal in trenchant terms: 'this bill', he told the Lords, 'is so vile that I think your Lordships shall do well to cast it out of the House'. If they passed it, 'you shall leave the church in worse estate than in the time of the persecuting emperors'. In 1621 and 1628 Digges spoke against the measure. Not surprisingly, Civil lawyers joined him. Sir Henry Marten noted that by this bill 'we shall at one blow take away Magna Carta from the clergy. Since there was a clergy they ever had this privilege to be tried before themselves.' Others accepted his history but denied the theory. The clergy had forfeited their right to Magna Carta, said Wilde, while Selden pointed out that clerical liberties 'by many acts of parliament are lessened and varied'.[56]

Selden, whose motto was 'liberty above all things', was one of the most outspoken opponents of royal absolutism in the Parliament of 1628–29. He was also a persistent critic of high clerical claims, or, to put it in Richard Montagu's words, 'the most pernicious underminer of the Church, and of Religion in the Church, that the Prince of darknes hath set on worke to do mischiefe many yeeres'. In his notorious *Historie of tithes* he argued that they had always been subject to the civil jurisdiction of the state. Though he avoided any direct denial of their *jure divino* status, the implications of his argument were obvious. Tithes, like any other form of property, were regulated by statute and common law. The claim that divine law entitled clerics to a set amount of their parishioners' wealth struck at the subject's rights of property. Absolute property was incompatible with *jure divino* tithes. The line of reasoning which was brought into play to vindicate property against royal encroachment worked equally well against clerical pretensions.[57]

Selden was no puritan. Nor was Coke. Others were, but used constitutional as well as religious principles to criticise the government of the church. In 1604 the Presbyterian William Stoughton argued that tithes, wills and matrimony were temporal matters; so they should be dealt with by the common law courts. He asserted that tithes were not prescribed by God, concluding that they could be replaced with some other form of maintenance for ministers. Such claims were doubtless intended to sugar the pill of Presbyterianism for popular consumption. Since the king was hostile to the discipline, it was only natural that its advocates turned to his majesty's ideological opponents for support, and argued that the established church infringed the subject's liberties while Presbyterianism guaranteed them. Laud's critics drew on the same ideas. 'Alter our religion without act of parliament', said Rich in 1628, 'and alter our liberties.'[58]

---

56 *PP 28*, III, 520 (Pym); *CJ* 237, 466, 818; *CD 21*, II, 439–40 (the bill); *PP 10*, I, 128 (Abbot); *CD 21*, II, 439–40; *PP 28*, III, 430–2 (Digges *et al.*).
57 Richard Montagu, *Diatribae upon the first part of the late history of tithes* (1621) 20; Selden, *Historie of tithes* (1618) passim.
58 William Stoughton, *The assertion for true and Christian church-policie (1604)* 91, 116, 127; Rich in *PP 28*, III, 514.

During the 1630s the puritan triumvirate – Bastwick, Burton and Prynne – said much against the Laudian church. All three objected to the popery and Arminianism they thought it promoted. They also objected to the unconstitutional and downright illegal nature of its activities. Professor Lamont has argued that Prynne was a champion of the Royal Supremacy against clerical tyranny. This is true if by the Royal Supremacy we mean the supremacy of king-in-Parliament. It was the business of Parliament, Prynne said in 1629, and not of the king and the bishops, 'to settle, protect, define, declare and ratifie the proper sense and meaning of our Articles, and the undoubted Doctrines of our Church'. Prynne had no time for a personal, extra-Parliamentary Supremacy. Neither did Burton or Bastwick. The claim that the king was 'not tyed to any Lawes', said Bastwick, was 'damnable doctrine'. Burton looked to Parliament – the 'body representative' of the church of England – to reverse Laudian innovations. He claimed that the laity had as much part to play as the clergy in managing religious affairs, else 'what should become of our Parliamentary Lawes, by which our Religion hath been established, and the Popish abolished?' What Parliament set up the bishops had subverted, 'stopping the ordinary course of Law, that the Kings people may bee cut off from all benefit of the Kings good Lawes, and of their native ancient liberties'.[59]

Though their essential grievances were religious, radicals such as Burton and Bastwick courted popularity by larding their pamphlets with talk of the subject's liberty. In this they appealed to a sizeable body of the laity who disliked the activities of the church courts for reasons which had little to do with religious doctrine. If the Commons in say 1610 or 1628 had had their way, the government of the church might well have been altered and the balance of power tipped away from king and bishops and towards Parliament and the laity. After 1640 the Commons did get their way and the church was not merely altered but radically transformed. The High Commission and later episcopacy itself were abolished. Few contemplated such extreme steps in 1629. What happened in the intervening period to change things so drastically? The answer can be given in one word – Laud – or in four – the rise of Arminianism.

LAUD AND ARMINIANISM

Backed by Charles I, Laud ruled the church from 1633, when he became Archbishop of Canterbury, and dominated it for several years before that. The king clearly liked his divinity, but many found it less appealing. There were four reasons for this. Firstly, his attitude towards the church of Rome was too friendly, and he refused to condemn popery as Antichristian. Secondly, he promoted 'Arminians' – clerics who opposed the orthodox Calvinist theology

---

59 Lamont, *Godly rule*, 46–7; William Prynne, *The church of Englands old antithesis to new Arminianisme* (1629) sig. a1a; Bastwick, *The answer of Iohn Bastwick* (1637) 26; Henry Burton, *A tryall of private devotions* (1628) sig. M3b; *An apology of an appeale* (1636) sig. C3a; *For God and the king* (1636) 69.

of grace. Thirdly, he introduced religious practices which were unusual if not unprecedented. Finally, he made efforts to protect and increase the wealth of the clergy, displaying little regard for the interests of the gentry or – as some saw it – the liberties of the subject. In all these areas Laud continued tendencies present in James's reign, but with new zeal and tactlessness.

When James defended the oath of allegiance against Catholics in his *Premonition* of 1609, he included a long section arguing that the pope was Antichrist. The proto-Arminian Lancelot Andrewes supported the royal point of view in the following year. Robert Abbot, a rigorous Calvinist, made the same claim in *Antichristi Demonstratio*. Dedicated to the king, it was published by the royal printer in 1603 and again in 1608. The idea was utterly conventional in Jacobean England. It attracted little opposition, except of course from Catholics. But verbal agreement on the Antichristian nature of popery disguised fundamental differences of attitude towards the church of Rome. Essentially, some thought that popery was the quintessence of evil, a mocking parody of Christ's true church, or, to use the contemporary term, the mystery of iniquity; others, by contrast, held that the Roman church was a true church despite its many corruptions, and treated the equation of the pope with Antichrist as a tentative hypothesis rather than a dogmatic truth.[60]

James himself subscribed to this second approach. He was, it is true, the most commonly quoted of those authors who identified the pope as Antichrist. But in the royal hands this identification was treated rather eccentrically, as Richard Montagu spotted in 1626. James's primary grievance with Catholicism was the pope's claim to be able to depose civil magistrates. True, it was not his only grievance. He made clear his doctrinal objections in the *Premonition* of 1609 and later in a polite controversy with the French Cardinal Du Perron. The king believed that popish teaching on such points as transubstantiation and the invocation of saints was mistaken, but he thought that disagreement on these matters might be ironed out by discussion. The main stumbling-block to reunification of the churches was papal power, especially in temporals. James was willing to recognise the pope as Patriarch of the West if he dropped his pretensions and exercised only the authority which St Peter had possessed. 'I acknowledge the Romane Church to be our Mother Church', he said in 1604, 'although defiled with some infirmities and corruptions.' In 1609 he suggested that the pope was Antichrist, but did not want to 'urge so obscure a point, as a matter of Faith to be necessarily beleeved of all Christians'. Indeed, he implied that he would recant his position as soon as the pope abandoned his temporal claims. The king hoped for the religious unification of Christendom which, he thought, could be brought about by a General

---

60 James I, *Premonition*, 51–108, in *An apologie for the oath of allegiance . . . together with a Premonition*; Andrewes, *Tortura Torti*, ed. J. Bliss (Oxford 1851) 304–11; *Responsio ad apologiam*, 21–3, 307–20; Abbot, *Antichristi demonstratio, passim*. Other examples are discussed in Christopher Hill, *Antichrist in seventeenth-century England* (1971) 19–33. Two excellent works on attitudes towards Roman Catholicism are Peter Lake, 'Anti-popery: the structure of a prejudice', in Richard Cust and Ann Hughes, eds, *Conflict in early Stuart England: studies in religion and politics 1603–1642* (1989) 72–106, and Milton, *Catholic and Reformed*, 31–373.

Council from which Jesuits and puritans – Presbyterians – were excluded. Once political radicals had been eliminated, people of goodwill would soon be able to reach agreement on doctrine.[61]

The king's attitude to Rome was coolly rational, and based largely on his own high views of royal power. Others were much more passionately opposed to popery in all its aspects, and saw little to be gained from discussions with Antichrist and his minions. Reunification, they said, was impossible. In 1621 Thomas Clarke, a layman, noted that some foolish people had imagined that 'there might well be an union between us and them to make one and the same Universall Church'. The idea, he thought, was execrable: 'I trust through the helpe of Gods spirit, it shall be made manifest to the whole Church of God, that it is no more possible, than by mixing with the puritie of the Gospell, the Abomination of desolation . . . there can bee made one and the same true Christian religion.' Popery, then, was the abomination of desolation. True believers should shun or exterminate it, but never compromise with it.[62]

Under James, divisions on the nature of popery became apparent in the field of foreign policy. The king's pacific stance towards Catholic aggression on the Continent – particularly after the outbreak of the Thirty Years War – and, worse still, his moves to marry his son to a Spanish princess, were greeted with puzzlement by those who saw international affairs in terms of a perpetual struggle between Antichrist and the forces of righteousness. Since James had shown himself a vigorous opponent of popery in the controversy over the oath of allegiance, his foreign policy seemed difficult to explain. Some thought that he was playing a deep and devious game, lulling Antichrist into false security by dissimulation. Another notion was that the king had been duped by Antichrist's agent, the Spanish ambassador Gondomar. Such ideas retained some plausibility until the equation of the pope with Antichrist came under open attack from divines who were known to possess royal favour. The crucial event here was the publication of Richard Montagu's *New Gagg* in 1624. Thereafter, divisions of opinion on the nature of popery became increasingly difficult to ignore.[63]

Montagu was not a particularly original thinker. His divinity resembled that of such eirenic Jacobean churchmen as Andrewes and Casaubon. But whereas they avoided religious controversy whenever possible, Montagu relished a fight. In his *New Gagg* and again in his *Appello Caesarem* of 1625 he went out of his way to attack beliefs which were commonplace among a wide section of the population. He minimised the number of points on which the

61 Montagu quoted in John Cosin, *Works*, III, 80–1; James I, *Premonition*, 33–50, in *An apologie for the oath of allegience . . . together with a Premonition*; Isaac Casaubon, *Ad epistolam illustr. et reverendiss. Cardinalis Perronii responsio* (1612) *passim*; James I, *Premonition*, 46 (Patriarch of the West), 51 (obscure point), 107–8 (possibility of recantation), 112–13 (General Council); Speech of 1604 in *Political writings*, ed. Sommerville, 139 (Mother Church).
62 Thomas Clarke, *The popes deadly wound* (1621) 1–2.
63 Attitudes towards James's foreign policy are discussed in S.L. Adams, 'Foreign policy and the Parliaments of 1621 and 1624', in K. Sharpe, ed., *Faction and Parliament: essays on early Stuart history* (Oxford 1978) 139–72, especially 148.

English church differed from Rome, and claimed that the question of Anti-christ was unresolved. Unlike Montagu, Joseph Hall was a man of peace. Like Montagu, he held that Rome was a true though corrupted church. He was answered by Henry Burton and a clerical war of words resulted. To many, the softening of the official line on popery in the early years of Charles I's reign seemed to presage some more dramatic shift towards Rome. As Thomas Spencer noted in 1629, the admission that Rome was a true church could be used to mount a potent case in favour of popery. If the English church admitted that salvation was possible for Catholics, and if Catholics denied that salvation was possible in the English church, then the sensible course for any individual was to become a papist at once. The religion of Protestants was no safe way to salvation.[64]

Laud himself argued that the problem of Antichrist was unsolved. In the 1630s he discouraged the publication of books which made the conventional equation, but allowed attacks on it, including a treatise by Robert Shelford which claimed that 'the great Antichrist is not yet come'. At Oxford, Gilbert Sheldon (the future Archbishop of Canterbury) publicly denied that the pope was Antichrist. There were other straws in the wind. The missions of the papal agents Panzani and Con suggested that work was afoot to reconcile England with Rome, and conversions at Court confirmed this impression. Papists holding high offices of state included Portland (Lord Treasurer), Cottington (Chancellor of the Exchequer and Master of the Court of Wards) and Secretary Windebank. In 1635 the assertion that popery was a rebellious religion was excised from the Prayer Book. All this outraged anti-papist sentiment and lent credibility to the notion that Laud, in league with Rome, planned to subvert English religion and liberties.[65]

Montagu's opinions on grace, like his attitudes towards popery, had Jacobean and indeed Elizabethan precedent. Under James, such eminent divines as Bishops Andrewes and Overall disagreed with the Calvinist doctrine of predestination but made little effort to force their views on others. Calvinism remained the orthodox though not quite the official creed of the English. Montagu deliberately attempted to change this state of affairs. He denied that Calvinism was any part of the doctrine of the church of England. His ideas were attacked not only by clerics – including Bishop Carleton – but also by laymen. In 1626 Francis Rous published a pamphlet showing that James I had been an orthodox Calvinist. In the House of Commons Rous and his stepbrother John Pym were among the most vocal critics of Arminianism. Their efforts came to nothing. Montagu was made Bishop of Chichester on the death of Carleton in 1628. True, the king issued a declaration in the

---

64 Thomas Spencer, *Maschil unmasked* (1629) sig. A1b–A2a.
65 Robert Shelford, *Five pious and learned discourses* (Cambridge 1635) 300; cf. 274, 284; Hill, *Antichrist*, 37–9; G.E. Aylmer, *The king's servants* (1961) 357; Heylin, *A briefe and moderate answer to the seditious and scandalous challenges of Henry Burton* (1637) 150–7. The reality behind rumours of Charles's negotiations with papists is discussed in G. Albion, *Charles I and the court of Rome* (Louvain 1935), and C.M. Hibbard, *Charles I and the popish plot* (Chapel Hill 1983).

same year, ordering his subjects to cease debating the disputed points, and a few months later he suppressed Montagu's book. These conciliatory steps did not appease orthodox Calvinists – for good reason. The declaration was used to prevent the publication of predestinarian writings, while the spread of Arminianism went unchecked. In 1629 a number of booksellers petitioned the House of Commons 'in complaint of the restraint of books written against Popery and Arminianism and the contrary allowed of by the only means of the Bishop of London'. The Bishop of London was Laud.[66]

It is unclear to what extent there was an internal, logical connection between Arminian doctrine on the one hand and Laud's ceremonial innovations on the other. Arguably, Arminian ideas encouraged an emphasis on ceremonies and sacraments at the expense of preaching. Alternatively, it is possible that the connection was arbitrary: Laud defined his position by opposing Calvinism rather than by working out his own systematic philosophy. He liked what Wren called the 'beauty of holiness' because it symbolised things that he believed Calvinists hated, and took a liberal stance on the church of Rome for similar reasons. Finally, it may be that Charles and not Laud was responsible for the ceremonial changes of the 1630s. There is evidence that this was so in the famous St Gregory's case of 1633 when the king decided that communion tables should be placed 'altar-wise' at the east end of churches. This was as flagrantly innovatory a measure as Laud's enforcement of ceremonial conformity. The railing in of the altar at the east end was a change obvious to all, including those who knew little and cared less about the theological subtleties which divided Arminians from orthodox Calvinists. It also arguably violated the provisions of the Prayer Book, and offended people who liked the book and its ceremonies as well as those such as Bastwick who believed that the church is 'as full of ceremonies, as a dog is full of fleas'. It divided moderate churchmen from Laud and his supporters. Bishop Williams, the epitome of Jacobean moderation and no Presbyterian revolutionary, himself published a treatise against the practice in 1636.[67]

Laudian ceremonies cost money and the parishioners paid. There were other ways in which Laud's policies struck at lay property rights and at the provincial gentry's control over the affairs of his own locality. In 1629 the king issued instructions ordering the bishops to ensure that 'none under Noblemen, and men qualified by the Law . . . have any private Chaplain in his

66 Carleton, *An examination of those things wherein the author of the late appeale holdeth the doctrines of the Pelagians and Arminians, to be the doctrines of the church of England* (1626); Francis Rous, *Testis veritatis. The doctrine of King Iames our late soueraigne of famous memory. Of the Church of England. Of the Catholicke Church. Plainly shewed to bee one in the points of predestination, Free-will, certaintie of saluation* (1626). Charles's declaration in Gardiner, *Constitutional documents of the puritan revolution* (Oxford 1906) 75–6; Proclamation suppressing Montagu's *Appello Caesarem* in *SRP*, II, 218–20; *CD 29*, 58. See also the works mentioned in n. 7 above.
67 Matthew Wren, *A sermon preached before the kings maiestie* (Cambridge 1627) 16; Kevin Sharpe, 'The personal rule of Charles I', in H.C. Tomlinson, ed., *Before the English Civil War: essays on early Stuart politics and government* (1983) 53–78, at 62–3 (St Gregory's); Bastwick, *Letany*, 17; John Williams, *The holy table, name and thing* (1636). Williams was a personal as well as a principled enemy of Laud.

house'. As Heylin observed, 'the Country Gentlemen took it ill to be deprived of the liberty of keeping Chaplains in their houses'. John Davenport thought that 'the right and power of entertaining chaplains' had been 'settled upon the nobility and others by Magna Carta' – another example of the fusion of religious grievances with the rhetoric of liberty. Notoriously, Laud's actions towards the Feoffees for Impropriations raised constitutional issues. These men – including Davenport and Christopher Sherland – amassed funds to buy up impropriated tithes for the support of godly preaching ministers of their own choice. In doing so they effectively 'usurped upon the king's regality', challenging his majesty's right to rule the church through his bishops. But when the Feoffees' assets were confiscated, Charles equally effectively challenged his subjects' right to use their property as they saw fit. The question of who was to control the church – king and bishops, or local gentry – also underlay the case of Henry Sherfield who as Recorder of Salisbury attempted to introduce a radical programme of social reform combined with godliness. In 1633 he was censured as a contemner of authority by Star Chamber, for, as Heylin put it, 'what Security could be hoped for in Church or State, if every man should be a Sherfield, and without asking leave of the Prince or Prelate, proceed to such a Reformation as best pleased his Phansie?'[68]

Prohibitions, which protected the subject's liberties against clerical encroachment, did not thrive under Laud. 'They have sued out a Prohibition against Prohibitions', said Prynne of the bishops in 1637, 'that they may play *Rex* [King], and doe what they list without controll.' The archbishop avowedly followed a policy of recovering property for the church, and though his success was limited he stepped on lay toes in his efforts. In London he attempted to secure full tithes for the clergy. The appointment of his friend William Juxon, Bishop of London, to the high secular office of Lord Treasurer in 1636 may have been connected with this programme. It was also a symbol of clerical pretensions. No cleric had been Treasurer since before the Reformation. The thesis that Laud, unlike Abbot, encouraged the clergy to flout the gentry's will at every turn relies on impressionistic evidence. But the charge was included in the Root and Branch Petition of 1640 which complained of 'the encouragement of ministers to despise the temporal magistracy, the nobles and gentry of the land . . . knowing that they, being the bishops' creatures, shall be supported'. In passing, it is interesting to note that the Petition did not here count the king as a temporal magistrate.[69]

68 Charles I's instructions in Heylin, *Cyprianus Anglicus*, 189; Heylin's comments, ibid., 190; John Davenport, *Letters of John Davenport, puritan divine*, ed. I.M. Calder (New Haven 1937) 40; Hill, *Economic problems of the church*, paperback edn (1971) 262; cf. on the Feoffees R. O'Day, *The English clergy: the emergence and consolidation of a profession 1558–1642* (Leicester 1979) 92ff; Heylin on Sherfield in *Cyprianus Anglicus*, 216. On Sherfield cf. Paul Slack, 'Religious protest and urban authority: the case of Henry Sherfield, iconoclast, 1633', in Derek Baker, ed., *Schism, heresy and religious protest* (Cambridge 1972) 295–302.
69 Prynne, *A breviate of the prelates intolerable usurpations* (Amsterdam 1637) 73; cf. Hill, *Economic problems of the church*, 330, and on the tithes of London, ibid., 275–88, especially 281–2. Root and Branch Petition in Gardiner, ed., *Constitutional documents of the puritan revolution*, 138.

This reference to the Petition brings us back to our problem: on what grounds were Laud's actions condemned? Or which of the four reasons took precedence – popery, Arminianism, ceremonial innovations or constitutional impropriety? There is a certain artificiality to the question, since in the minds of many all four were inextricably linked. Arminianism, people thought, was bound to lead to popery. In the words of the Earl of Bedford, it was 'the little thief put into the window of the church to unlock the door'. Arminian errors, said Prynne, 'are in truth meere Popery'. Few had the theological subtlety of John Prideaux, who noticed that semi-Pelagian ideas held no monopoly even among papists.[70] Again, Laudian ceremonies looked popish and they, like popery, were arguably against the law, while Arminian doctrine was clearly contrary to the wishes of a majority in Parliament. Such people as Sherland and Sherfield combined religious hostility to Arminian innovations with political hostility to royal absolutism. But others distinguished between the issues. There is little evidence that Selden or Coke was particularly excited by doctrinal matters, though they had much to say on constitutional questions. Conversely, deep-rooted religious grievances just tipped Rudyerd into the Parliamentary camp at the outset of the Civil War, despite his customary moderation. So our question is legitimate. Was opposition to Laud's policies essentially religious or constitutional in character?

A common modern view is that Arminianism explains everything. If, by Arminianism we mean a narrow theological code, this notion does not have much to recommend it. It is intrinsically implausible that the exceedingly subtle theological distinctions which were debated at the Synod of Dort led hard-headed English gentry into mortal conflict during the 1640s. More to the point, the thesis has little empirical justification. True, Conrad Russell has argued an eloquent case in favour of the idea that it was the rise of doctrinal Arminianism which led Pym, in the Parliament of 1628, to acquire 'an intense concern with questions of law and liberties, on which his previous silence had been so complete as to be deafening'. Russell stresses 'the priority' of 'religious over constitutional issues in Pym's intellectual make-up', and it is incontestable that Pym *was* a dogmatic proponent of certain religious opinions. Yet religion was not his only concern, and in 1628 he had a great deal to say about purely constitutional questions: the Forced Loan and imprisonment. 'It would seem clear', says Russell, 'on chronology alone, even without the aid of logic, that it was the rise of Arminianism which first persuaded Pym that the rule of law was in danger.'[71] This argument is suspect; 1628 came after 1626–27 and those years witnessed not only the rise of Arminianism but also the most flagrant violations of English liberties perpetrated by a monarch in over a century. Chronology is compatible with the idea that these liberties were Pym's major concern.

70 Bedford quoted in Tyacke, 'Puritanism, Arminianism and counter-revolution', 136; Prynne, *The church of Englands old antithesis to new Arminianisme*, sig. 2 π 3a; John Prideaux, *Lectiones decem* (Oxford 1626) 144.
71 Russell, 'The parliamentary career of John Pym, 1621–9', in Peter Clark, Alan G.R. Smith and Nicholas Tyacke, eds, *The English commonwealth 1547–1640* (Leicester 1979) 161, 164, 162.

Extending our horizons beyond Pym to his fellow members of the House of Commons, doctrinal Arminianism seems even less important. On 24 March 1628 Sir Robert Harley complained against the writings of various clergymen – Montagu, Jackson, Cosin, Sibthorp and Maynwaring. 'They would introduce popery', he said. Popery, indeed, was the main grievance against Cosin: his *Private Devotions*, wrote Prynne, 'smells, nay, stinckes of Poperie'. Of the five clerics, Thomas Jackson was the clearest theological Arminian. When Harley and Sherfield attacked him, Sir Edward Coke rose in his defence, describing him as learned and honest.[72] Thereafter, little was heard against him. The only cleric impeached in 1628 was Maynwaring. There is little evidence that he was an Arminian, and less that his Arminianism accounted for his impeachment.

In 1629 Arminianism was, indeed, a dominant issue in the House of Commons. Yet even in that year it gave way to what Tyacke calls 'the more mundane subject of tunnage and poundage'. Very little was said against Arminian theology in the Short Parliament. Later in 1640, the Root and Branch Petition exposed the iniquities of Laud's misgovernment in twenty-eight articles. Of these, only one had any direct connection with doctrinal Arminianism. Others decried the oath *ex officio*, monopolies, Ship Money, trial by ecclesiastical courts of cases 'determinable of right at Common Law', and the publication of the dangerous tenet 'that subjects have no propriety in their estates', as well as 'many other outrages' perpetrated by the bishops 'to the utter infringing the laws of the realm and the subjects' liberties'. The Petition strongly suggests that what annoyed people most about Laud was the fact that his actions affected them in this life, not that he held unorthodox views about how to get to the next. This is confirmed by provincial protests. Anthony Fletcher argues that the provincial campaign against episcopacy in the early days of the Long Parliament was 'essentially an anti-Arminian one'. On a wide definition of Arminianism this is certainly correct. But the evidence he presents suggests that the theology of grace played only a very minor role in turning people against Laud. Of far more importance was the drive for conformity which undermined the gentry's control over the religious life of their own locality.[73]

Of course, Laud aroused resentment for religious reasons. But these reasons were tied to constitutional grievances, and that in two senses. Firstly, and crudely, much of what the archbishop did was arguably illegal and inimical to the liberties of the subject. It is very difficult to show that purely theological

---

72 *PP 28*, ıı, 86. Harley's remark was directed particularly against Montagu and Jackson. Prynne, *A briefe survay and censure of Mr Cozens his couzening devotions* (1628) 98–9; Russell, *Parliaments and English politics*, 345. A fine account of Harley and his family is Jacqueline Eales, *Puritans and Roundheads: the Harleys of Brampton Bryan and the outbreak of the English Civil War* (Cambridge 1990). Very important on Arminianism at the local level is John Fielding's 'Arminianism in the localities: Peterborough diocese, 1603–1642'.

73 Tyacke, 'Puritanism, Arminianism and counter-revolution', 135; Root and Branch Petition in Gardiner, ed., *Constitutional documents of the puritan revolution*, 137–44; Fletcher, *The outbreak of the English Civil War*, 94–5, 108, 109.

questions took precedence over such liberties in the minds of most of his opponents. Even doctrinal and ceremonial changes annoyed people at least in part because they were changes, and thus against the settled customs of the land. Other Laudian policies trenched still more directly upon English liberties.

Secondly, religious zeal did not automatically lead to political opposition. In a post-Marxist age it is easy to assume that certain godly Protestants, or puritans, were so convinced of the truth of their religious views, and so sure that God intended them to set up his kingdom on earth, that they were willing to flout established laws and rebel against authority. Just as for Marxists the dialectic foreordains revolution and the dictatorship of the proletariat, we might argue, so, for the puritan, God and the whole scheme of history rendered revolution and the triumph of the saints inevitable. What this argument overlooks is the central place given to civil authority in the religion of Protestants. The duty of subjection was fundamental, even for the saints. Henry Burton – not noted for his moderation in opposing Laudianism – inveighed in the strongest terms against the 'new sprung-up opinion' of those who denied that 'the morall law' applied 'after that a man is once brought to be a beleever in Christ'. The moral law, he emphasised, included the Fifth Commandment, and this required subjection to the civil magistrate. Such subjection was a religious duty, binding upon all.[74]

Anti-popery reinforced the point. Catholics confused the realms of grace and nature in the theory of the indirect deposing power. Protestants, on the other hand, denied that the elect had any political authority. Subjection to the civil magistrate was a Christian duty, even if he was a heathen or a heretic. Doubtless, many Protestants held millenarian views, and hoped or expected that Christ would soon reappear to rule with the godly. But few were antinomians, for few argued that the elect were entitled to break human or divine law. Confidence that the saints would one day win did not imply that they had any right to usher in their victory by force.

There remained the constitutional questions. Was the king accountable to his subjects in Parliament? Was he bound by the laws of the land? Protestantism (or puritanism) was inert on these matters. The questions were answered by reference to constitutional theories which themselves had no dependence upon theological doctrine. It was perfectly possible for a staunch anti-Laudian to adopt absolutist ideas and conclude that the king alone held ultimate human authority in ecclesiasticals. If protest did not dissuade him from his iniquities, prayer and tears were the only remedies. Such zealous critics of Laudianism as Thomas Morton maintained absolutist views on civil government and sided

74 Burton, *The law and the gospell reconciled* (1631) sig. B2a, 31; cf. William Hinde, *The office and use of the morall law of God in the dayes of the gospell* (1623) 117. Puritanism, as distinct from anti-Arminianism, rather unjustifiably went out of fashion as a putative cause of the Civil War during the past couple of decades. But interest in puritanism is reviving. A good recent collection of essays is Christopher Durston and Jacqueline Eales, eds, *The culture of English puritanism, 1560–1700* (1996).

with the king when war began. It was equally possible for a friend of Laud to side against Charles for constitutional reasons. Selden did this.

Hostility towards the king's ecclesiastical policies was grounded partly in theological convictions and partly in fears for liberty. *Resistance* to Laud against the king's will was based upon constitutional theory. Had all puritans followed Morton's example, Laud and his royal master would have had fewer troubles. Religious resistance *was* constitutional resistance.

Conclusion

The story so far has been a plain and simple tale of principled conflict. Two absolutist monarchs carried out measures which many of their subjects took to infringe the fundamental liberties of the English people. Impositions, the Forced Loan, the collection of tonnage and poundage without Parliamentary consent, royal ecclesiastical policies – all these things struck at rights of property and at the legislative supremacy of Parliament. Conversely, attempts by members of the House of Commons to defend liberties were construed by James and Charles as assaults on the royal prerogative. Neither king had any deep-rooted hostility to the idea of Parliaments; indeed, they liked pleasant, co-operative Parliaments; the trouble was that Parliaments so often turned out to be unpleasant and uncooperative.

This story should not be mistaken for a full account of English politics before 1640. Patently, ideological differences would have created few difficulties if kings had not chosen to put their views into practice. The king's personality counted, and in particular Charles's political ineptitude counted for a great deal. In 1628 a gentleman named Hugh Pyne was accused of saying that Charles was no more fit to govern England than a half-witted shepherd of his acquaintance.[1] Pyne had a point. Of course, his majesty's cavalier disregard for the feelings of his subjects was connected with his own high opinion of royal power. But Charles's political incompetence cannot be fully explained in terms of his absolutist ideas. His father and his eldest son held similar ideas but managed to die peacefully in their beds.

Again, factions existed at Court. People jockeyed for place and power. Clients defended the interests of their patrons in return for protection and promotion. On occasion, the conflicts between court factions were played out in Parliament. It is arguable that the impeachments of the 1620s had more to do with such struggles than with any disputes about principle. In the counties, likewise, personal ambitions and crude material interests featured prominently in politics. Some people cared little about high questions of constitutional

1 *ST*, ɪɪɪ, 359–68.

principle. The Cheshire gentleman William Davenport is one example, and the famous antiquary Sir Robert Cotton may be a second.[2] Others paid lip-service to principles, but changed their tune when it suited them. It is tempting to believe that self-interest underlay all talk about principles. Factional strife and bread-and-butter local issues, we might conclude, were the real moving forces in English politics. There are two problems with this kind of approach – one theoretical, the other empirical. If we distinguish too rigidly between ideas and interests we are in danger of missing the point that interests themselves are shaped by ideas. People have divergent ideas about what things are in their interest. So we can always ask what principles underlay self-interest.

Empirically, the emphasis on faction and localism at the expense of constitutional conflict is open to a whole series of objections. For one thing, local comments on such measures as the Forced Loan or Ship Money often survive in fragmentary form. It is difficult to tell much about what locals were thinking from a mere sentence or two. Calendars of manuscript collections – such as the State Papers – are even less helpful.

There are other pitfalls. The people of early Stuart England were capable of considerable subtlety in their use of political concepts, and this deserves to be recognised. For instance, many writers claimed that royal power came from God. Some modern commentators have concluded that they therefore endorsed the theory of the Divine Right of Kings. This does not follow. The important questions were: did royal power come *directly* from God or from the people, and was it circumscribed by ancient custom? If these questions are ignored it is easy to find agreement where none existed.

Distortions may also arise from an overly literal approach to the sources. Dietz argued that 'no very high constitutional principles can be found inherent in the attitude of the counties' towards the Forced Loan of 1626–27. More recently, John Morrill has made similar claims about Ship Money: 'The constitutional propriety of ship money was not the main reason for opposition to it.' Relying, as it does, on State Papers, this thesis is suspect. State Papers reflect what the king or his ministers were told and this is not always synonymous with what was true. There were good reasons why people should conceal their constitutional misgivings from his majesty. When Richard Legge refused to pay Ship Money because it was extra-Parliamentary, Baron Davenport imprisoned him – without cause shown. Both Ship Money and the Loan were highly efficient taxes. This does not mean that they were approved by the individuals who paid them. Some, no doubt, disbursed cash willingly. Others dragged their heels for reasons which had little to do with constitutional

2 J.S. Morrill, 'William Davenport and the "silent majority" of early Stuart England', *Journal of the Chester Archaeological Society* 58 (1975) 115–29. Cotton's political ideas are discussed in K. Sharpe, *Sir Robert Cotton, 1586–1631: history and politics in early modern England* (Oxford 1979) 223–47. Cotton managed to keep on good terms with both Selden – who dedicated his *Historie of tithes* to him – and Selden's arch-enemy Richard Montagu, who referred to Cotton as 'that Noble and worthy Gentleman, my ever honoured friend', in *Diatribae upon the first part of the late history of tithes* (1621) 111.

theory. But a good many had constitutional objections, and paid only to save their skins. Thomas Scot forked out £8 on the Loan in 1627. 'Neither', he commented, 'did I lend it willingly, or in hope to have it again out of the subsidies, but, as I told the mayor and aldermen, to escape imprisonment and death.'[3] Such threats can lead people to disguise their real views. Moreover, in early Stuart thought the appropriate institution to raise constitutional grievances was Parliament, not the individual. Individuals obeyed, or took the consequences – a point on which everyone was agreed. If we look to the Parliaments which met after the Loan and after the levying of Ship Money we find that much was said about the illegality of these taxes. Had Charles wished to enforce absolutism, he should have avoided calling Parliament in 1628 and especially in 1640. But then his hand was forced.

People did in fact use constitutional arguments against royal policies – even outside Parliament. It was on such grounds that the Justices of the Peace of three counties objected to the benevolence of 1614. At least one man refused to pay the benevolence of 1622 for constitutional reasons and was imprisoned as a result – Lord Saye and Sele. The subsidymen of Bedfordshire declined to pay the benevolence of 1626 because it was extra-Parliamentary, and Sir Edward Rodney reported that the people of Somerset had similar misgivings. The ideological implications of the Forced Loan, says Richard Cust – the Loan's most recent historian – 'were so familiar and so widely discussed that few of those involved could have been entirely ignorant of them'.[4]

Thomas Scot wrote a vigorous denunciation of the Loan, taking issue with a sermon by the absolutist cleric Isaac Bargrave. Going further than most, Scot countenanced active resistance to the king himself on the grounds that Charles had oppressed the people 'with loans & impositions & exacted services contrarie to right and libertie'.[5] Later, Scot refused to allow soldiers to be billeted in his home and was called to account for this by the Privy Council. Though he sat as a member for Canterbury in the Parliament of 1628, he spoke little and we might conclude that he was uninterested in central politics. Certainly, the focus of his political activities was his own locality. But his writings reveal that he was fully aware of the wider ramifications of local issues. When men who were not resident freemen of the city stood for election to Parliament in 1628, Scot believed that not only local customs but also the liberties of all English people were under attack: 'if free parliaments be gone, all is lost; and free parliaments cannot long continue if the freedom and right of elections be violently and deceitfully taken from us, or we fetched about to resign it out of our hands'. Free elections, he held, were 'the liberty, honor, and happiness of England if duly observed; and the only way to prevent slavery and ruin'. In

3 F.C. Dietz, *English public finance 1558–1641* (1932) 236; Morrill, *The revolt of the provinces: conservatives and radicals in the English Civil War 1630–50*, 2nd edn (1980) 28; Clive Holmes, 'The county community in Stuart historiography', *Journal of British Studies* 19 (1980) 64–5; J.S. Cockburn, *A history of English assizes, 1558–1714* (Cambridge 1972) 235. Scot in *PP 28*, vi, 222–3.
4 Richard Cust, *The Forced Loan and English politics 1626–1628* (Oxford 1987) 153, 157, 160–1, 186.
5 Ibid., 176, 179.

his view, the billeting of troops in the city was objectionable not so much because of its local effects, but because it was part of a deep conspiracy by the 'popish and Arminian and Maynwarian faction' to subvert 'the liberty of a free Englishman'. Headed by Buckingham, Scot thought, these men planned to use the soldiers 'to cut some of our throats and to settle the excise and mass'. Was Scot, rather than William Davenport, typical of the silent majority in early Stuart England?[6]

In Scot's mind, constitutional fused with religious grievances, local with national. Yet he was no member of what John Morrill has called the '"official" country' – vocal Parliamentary critics of royal policy. His case serves to confirm Morrill's dictum that 'the "pure" and "official" country labels should be seen as the two extreme ends of a political continuum or spectrum'.[7] In other words, there was no rigid distinction between two groups of gentlemen, one concerned exclusively with local and the other with national or constitutional matters. Indeed, we could argue that the 'official' country ideology – the ideology of liberty – survived and flourished precisely because it bound together a diversity of local and indeed personal interests. It was when the king conceded ideological ground in 1640–42 that the 'country' opposition split and that its localist roots were fully revealed.

Factional struggles could cut across disputes of principle. But factions could also represent ideological stances. Patrons often adopted particular clients – and vice versa – because they found their views congenial. Clients could be men with active minds, not mere cyphers of their lords. Take the example of John Pym. 'Though it is possible to show many instances of common action between two like-minded people', argues Conrad Russell, 'it is surprisingly hard to show any case of Pym accepting a "line" either from Bedford, or from his other noble patron, the Earl of Warwick.' Such people acted in concert because they shared similar political ideas. Again the third Earl of Pembroke stood for a distinctive political position: constitutional moderation combined with orthodox Calvinism and hostility to Spain. His adherents believed in the same broad principles. Buckingham's clientage, on the other hand, was too large to correspond to any single ideological flavour, and though the duke's policies were increasingly identified with Arminianism as well as arbitrary government in the years 1626–28 his supporters continued to include the staunch anti-Arminian Sir Robert Harley. Loyalty to a patron on some questions did not imply loyalty on all. Buckingham's following can best be regarded as a number of distinct factions, each with its own particular platform. All they had in common was that they looked to the duke to lead them.[8]

6 *PP 28*, vi, 218–43, 128, 127, 220, 232. Scot is discussed in P. Clark, 'Thomas Scot and the growth of urban opposition to the early Stuart regime', *HJ* 21 (1978) 1–26 and in Cust, *Forced Loan*, esp. 175–85.
7 Morrill, *Revolt of the provinces*, p. x.
8 Conrad Russell, 'The parliamentary career of John Pym, 1621–9', in Peter Clark, Alan G.R. Smith and Nicholas Tyacke, eds, *The English commonwealth 1547–1640* (Leicester 1979) 151. Pembroke's clientage is discussed in V.A. Rowe, 'The influence of the Earls of Pembroke on parliamentary elections, 1625–41', *EHR* 50 (1935) 242–56, and its ideological coherence is noted

Some issues transcended faction. The attempted impeachment of Buckingham in 1626 may indeed have been engineered by his rival at Court, Pembroke; it may have had little to do with constitutional disputes. The same does not hold good of the impeachment of Maynwaring, which was patently motivated by ideological concerns. Again, opposition to impositions, benevolences, the Forced Loan, Ship Money, imprisonment without cause shown, and royal ecclesiastical policy, owed as much to ideas which were common – though not universal – among the English gentry as it did to manoeuvres at Court. Divisions of opinion did indeed exist at Court. Some people were too well connected and powerful to be ignored by the king, and held high office under him though they did not share his views. So opponents of royal policy who were not themselves courtiers could often find support at Court. This does not mean that they took their ideas from there. Nor does it indicate that principled opposition was somehow less divisive than it would otherwise have been.

Faction and localism, though they existed, did not render ideas insignificant. Did ideological disagreements make the Civil War inevitable? In a sense, the question is misguided. Had England been invaded by papists who advocated the deposition of the king and social revolution it is likely that the English would have buried their differences and united against a common enemy in 1640, or 1642 or later. More realistically, had the Irish taken up arms against Charles before the Scots did so, events could have been altered drastically in England. None of the long series of voluntary actions which culminated in civil war was inevitable – or predetermined – and the war itself was not inevitable. But it is reasonable to ask how far the war may be explained by reference to ideological divisions.

Firstly, if the king's subjects had swallowed absolutist claims they would have used only prayers and tears against his majesty, however deplorable they found his actions. Conversely, if Charles had been a strict devotee of Coke's theory of the ancient constitution it is difficult to believe that he would have pursued his more contentious policies. The king was no respecter of legalities as understood by a high proportion of his subjects. Among much else, his attempt to tamper with the record on the Five Knights' Case makes this plain. The fact that he held such high views of his own powers was of central significance not only in 1628 but also in 1640–42, for it raised the crucial question of whether he could be trusted to abide by his word. A number of people rightly thought that he could not, and feared that when opportunity arose he would negotiate for a papist army to overthrow the Parliament. Their problem was that in binding the king they were themselves forced to act illegally, thus making plausible the king's own claims to stand for legality.

in Russell, *Parliaments and English politics 1621–1629* (Oxford 1979) 12–13; S.L. Adams, 'Foreign policy and the Parliaments of 1621 and 1624', in K. Sharpe, ed., *Faction and Parliament: essays on early Stuart history* (Oxford 1978) 142–4. On Buckingham cf. Roger Lockyer, *Buckingham: the life and political career of George Villiers, first Duke of Buckingham 1592–1628* (1981) *passim*, and on Sir Robert Harley's Protestant zeal, Patrick Collinson, *The religion of Protestants: the church in English society 1559–1625* (Oxford 1982) 164–70.

Few people desire war if they can achieve their objectives peaceably. There was no revolutionary party, bent on overthrowing monarchy and wresting sovereign authority for the House of Commons, in any Jacobean Parliament, nor indeed in any Parliament before the Civil War. This does not show that the war was an accident resulting from a sudden and inexplicable breakdown in 1642 or a little earlier. Ideological divisions did exist in James's reign, and assumed immense political importance under his son, though they were not divisions between progressives anxious to usher in Parliamentary democracy and conservatives eager to maintain the status quo. No one wanted to alter the English constitution – the ancient frame of government – but there were profound disagreements on what that constitution was. The extent to which these mattered at any time depended upon many things and not least upon recent royal actions. When absolutism was put into practice, anti-absolutists grew irritated. That is why Charles I attracted more hostility than his father. Yet as long as kings held absolutist views, and as long as their financial needs made it tempting to act on such views, the danger of conflict was great.

Financial needs became especially acute when England was at war. The pressures of war, we might argue, and not high-flown ideas, explain the disagreements between Charles I and his Parliaments in 1628 and 1640. England's administrative structure was not geared to war. So when it came a 'functional breakdown' occurred.[9] In the longer term, the declining value of the subsidy put pressure on the crown and led the king's servants to explore alternative ways of raising revenue. Parliament lost its former importance not because kings were hostile to it, but because it had ceased to be an efficient instrument of business. Administrative structure, functional breakdown, the declining value of the subsidy, the pressures of war – all these may be useful illustrative devices, but all are metaphorical locutions, not reasons for action. To say that functional breakdown occurred in 1626–28 is, on its own, to say nothing about why particular individuals acted as they did. The evidence of the Parliament of 1628 suggests that hostility towards the king's recent policies was rooted not in distress at functional breakdown but in the conviction that his majesty had flouted the law of the land. English institutions, we are sometimes told, were unable to cope with war against the Scots in 1638–40. This is a sad comment indeed upon the country's administrative structure. It also stretches credulity. England had a long history of war with the Scots, and, indeed, of victory over that 'beggarly nation'. Moreover, the English soon managed to find the administrative resources to fight a civil war, and, a few years later, to inflict resounding defeat upon Scotland. The suspicion remains that Charles failed to vanquish the Scots because his English subjects were disaffected. Disaffection led to administrative breakdown, not vice versa.

In an inflationary age the king had financial problems and extravagance did not help to solve them. The crown's difficulties were well understood by at least some members of the House of Commons. Pym, Digges, Rich and

9 Russell, *Parliaments and English politics*, 64–70.

Rudyerd were all in favour of augmenting the king's *legal* revenues. Rudyerd, the quintessence of moderation, was particularly anxious to increase Parliamentary grants and thereby lead his majesty to love Parliaments.[10] Why did such schemes come to nothing? One reason, of course, is that people do not like paying taxes. But there is more to it than that. The subsidy did not decline in value miraculously. Charles thought he knew what lay behind the low returns of 1628–29 – the seditious spirit of an anti-monarchical minority in the House of Commons: 'their spirit infused into many of the Commissioners and Assessors in the Countrey, hath returned up the Subsidies in such a scantie proportion, as is infinitely short, not onely of our great occasions, but of the precedents of former Subsidies, and of the intentions of all well affected men in that House'.[11] Conversely, fears that a wealthy king, infected with absolutist ideas, would trample on English liberties made people reluctant to relieve the crown's necessities. Royal financial problems were objectively soluble. It was ideology which made them so intractable. Very similar ideological divisions survived to trouble the reigns of Charles's sons.

It is a commonplace that the Civil War and the Interregnum were periods of great fertility in English political thought. Winstanley, Hobbes, Harrington – all were unquestionably original thinkers. But it would be unwise to overemphasise the innovatory nature of the bulk of what was produced in those years. The Levellers owed a great deal to both Coke and the natural law tradition, though they put their sources to uses which earlier writers would have found surprising. The famous argument that allegiance should be given to any government which actually holds possession – common in the midcentury Engagement controversy, and voiced by Hobbes among others – had roots in Coke and in traditional attitudes towards God's Providence.[12] Again, royalist doctrine in the Civil War and beyond was heavily indebted to what had gone before. David Owen's *Herod and Pilate reconciled* of 1610 was republished in 1642, 1643, 1652 and 1663. The same author's *Anti-Paraeus* appeared in English translation in 1642. The dialogue *God and the king*, published in 1615, was reprinted in 1663. Filmer's *Patriarcha* first came out in 1680.

There was equal continuity among anti-absolutists. The final three parts of Coke's *Institutes* were published only in 1642–44; the last two parts of the *Reports* in 1656 and 1659. The speeches of Hakewill and Whitelocke on impositions, delivered in the Parliament of 1610, were printed in 1641, and Fuller's *Argument* of 1607 reappeared in the same year. Royalists in the Civil War and

10 Russell, 'The parliamentary career of John Pym', 151; 'Parliament and the King's finances', in Russell, ed., *The origins of the English Civil War* (1973) 91–116, at 106–7.
11 Charles I, *His maiesties declaration to all his loving subiects, of the causes which moved him to dissolve the last Parliament* (1628) 12–13.
12 Robert Austine, *Allegiance not impeached: viz by the Parliaments taking up of arms* (1644) 1–4, draws on the judgment in Calvin's Case to confirm the thesis of a reciprocal link between protection and obedience. On Hobbes and the Engagement controversy cf. Quentin Skinner, 'Conquest and consent: Thomas Hobbes and the Engagement controversy', in G.E. Aylmer, ed., *The Interregnum: the quest for a settlement* (1972) 79–98. See also Johann P. Sommerville, *Thomas Hobbes: political ideas in historical context* (1992) 67–70.

Tories at the time of the Exclusion Crisis accused their opponents of borrowing ideas from Jesuit resistance theorists. There was justice in the charge. In 1643 the Parliamentarian pamphleteer William Bridge cited several papists to vindicate his contractualist theory of the origins of government, and drew on Molina to refute patriarchalism. The puritan John Canne turned to the notorious Mariana to justify the execution of Charles I in 1649.[13] Parsons's *Conference about the next succession* was republished as an antidote to royalism in 1648, 1655 and again at the time of the Exclusion Crisis. In 1679 Suarez's *De legibus* was printed at London. Rutherford, himself indebted to papists, replied to the Jacobeans Marc'Antonio De Dominis and John Buckeridge – among others – in his *Lex Rex* of 1644. Buckeridge had written against Bellarmine in 1614, De Dominis against Suarez in 1620. Another anti-Catholic work of political theory, the abortive canons of 1606, appeared in print only in 1690 – as a contribution to the controversy over the propriety of swearing allegiance to William and Mary. John Locke, whose *Two treatises* was published as part of the same debate, drew on the writings of Hooker and William Barclay. Indeed, what is most striking about the arguments used in this controversy is not their novelty but their antiquity.[14]

The Civil War was no great watershed in English political thinking. It did not mark the advent of a new age of secular thought. God bulks large in the writings of John Locke and his Tory adversaries as He did in those of Jacobean and Caroline thinkers. The law of nature was God's law. God was the author of nature, and reason the instrument by which people could understand his handiwork, though reason was prone to falter when not accompanied by the light of grace. Agreement on these points was commonplace throughout the century. The thesis that the war secularised thinking overlooks the extent to which pre-war attitudes were already secular – in the sense that reason and not grace was held to be the source of political truths, and that these truths were independent of theological dogmas.

Yet in one area attitudes did change. Political science – prudential calculation of interest – was not at first inimical to old ways of thinking, for Machiavelli was moralised, and prudence subordinated to justice. But the growth of science diminished the area over which Providence reigned. Providence, as we have seen, propped up the old theories at crucial points. It was Providence which guarded the state against tyranny and the church against heresy. The decline of faith in Providence is one reason why absolutism fell into disfavour – why passive obedience became a joke and non-resistance a jest. Constitutional checks, and not mere reliance on an unpredictable divinity,

13 William Bridge, *The truth of the times vindicated* (1643) 2, 4, 7, 11; John Canne, *The golden rule, or justice advanced* (1649) 11. Further examples of citations of Mariana by Civil War pamphleteers are discussed in G. Lewy, *Constitutionalism and statecraft during the golden age of Spain: a study of the political philosophy of Juan de Mariana, SJ* (Geneva 1960) 156–7.
14 The arguments are succinctly summarised in Mark Goldie, 'The Revolution of 1689 and the structure of political argument: an essay and an annotated bibliography of pamphlets on the Allegiance controversy', *Bulletin of Research in the Humanities* 83 (1980) 473–564, at 529.

now seemed the only reliable safeguard against tyranny. J.S. Mill expressed the conviction neatly in the nineteenth century. 'Leaving things to the government', he said, 'like leaving them to Providence, is synonymous with caring nothing about them, and accepting their results, when disagreeable, as visitations of Nature.'[15] So representative democracy was the only appropriate form of government for a civilised nation. The theory of royal absolutism, of the Divine Right of Kings, was exploded. But a new problem had arisen: what can be done when the people's representative is a tyrant?

---

15 J.S. Mill, *Considerations on representative government*, in Marshall Cohen, ed., *The philosophy of John Stuart Mill* (New York 1961) 404.

Revisionism Revisited: A Retrospect

One purpose of the first edition of this book was to 'reawaken interest in the ideological dimension' of early modern English politics.[1] A second and connected aim was to challenge the widespread 'revisionist' view that the English Civil War had few long-term origins. From the 1970s onwards, an influential group of so-called 'revisionist' historians argued that early-seventeenth-century English society was harmonious and cohesive. England, they said, was a peaceful place, and there was very little sign that civil war was going to break out until quite soon before 1642, when it actually did so. In the words of one leading revisionist, there was no 'high road to civil war'.[2] Another has written of the 'Unrevolutionary England' that existed until the 1640s.[3] They all agreed that the war was not a result of long-standing divisions on

---

1 J.P. Sommerville, *Politics and ideology in England 1603–1640* (1986) 5.

2 G.R. Elton, 'A high road to civil war?', in Elton, *Studies in Tudor and Stuart politics and government*, II (Cambridge 1974) 164–82, and in C.H. Carter, ed., *From the Renaissance to the Counter-Reformation: essays in honor of Garrett Mattingly* (New York 1965) 325–47. Elton's article answers the question in its title with a resounding 'No': there was no high road to civil war. Though the bulk of revisionist scholarship dates from the mid-1970s onwards, Elton's article first appeared in 1965, and Elton perhaps deserves the credit – or blame – for pioneering the whole revisionist movement. Elton was primarily a historian of the Tudor period and especially of the 1530s. He was usually a vigorous advocate of the idea that historians ought to base their conclusions on a mass of primary evidence, but in his own forays into the Stuart period he sometimes grounded very wide generalisations on somewhat slender archival foundations. For example, he asserted that the English in early Stuart times held 'fundamentally identical views' on the constitution (Elton, 'The unexplained revolution', in *Studies in Tudor and Stuart politics and government*, II, 183–9, at 183), but devoted remarkably little space to analysing any of the books or pamphlets in which contemporaries discussed constitutional questions. Elton's convictions that the Civil War had few long-term origins and that there were no major ideological or social conflicts in the early seventeenth century may not have been supported with many references to primary sources, but they did sit very well with his views on the 1530s. In that decade, he believed, Thomas Cromwell had effected profound and lasting administrative changes which amounted to a 'Revolution in Government'. Since Cromwell did his work well, England could not have been a divided and unstable place in the early 1600s. Since the conflict of the 1640s was not about deep divisions but about mundane conflicts of personality and Court faction, it could not properly be called a revolution, and the status of the sixteenth – rather than the seventeenth – century as England's revolutionary age was preserved.

3 Conrad Russell, *Unrevolutionary England* (1990).

constitutional questions, and they all argued that consensus prevailed on such matters until a short time before the shooting started.

Most revisionists said rather little about the actual contents of the constitutional theories which people expressed in the decades before 1642. This was understandable, since if everyone agreed, it did not matter much just what it was they agreed on. Revisionists took early Stuart political consensus to be an established fact which scarcely needed proving. A key point of *Politics and Ideology* was to show that it was not a fact, and that it should be disestablished, since it could be disproved. If we investigate the books, speeches and pamphlets of early-seventeenth-century people, it argued, we find that they held sharply differing ideas on politics and the constitution. If we look at political practice, it continued, we discover that these differences in ideas fuelled conflict and that conflict culminated in civil war.

Since 1986 – when the first edition of this book was published – the revisionist line has come under fire from many directions, and there is now an excellent and growing literature of 'post-revisionist' scholarship.[4] There have also, however, been some fine attempts to defend revisionist thinking. Revisionist scholars have begun to take ideas far more seriously than they used to. Formerly, they were content simply to tell us that a single shared ideology prevailed in England before the Civil War, without going into detail on the precise nature of that ideology. But now they venture more frequently into the realm of political theory, and some of them have constructed a complex case for reaffirming their earlier revisionist views, despite the evidence presented by *Politics and Ideology*.

The most prominent of all the revisionist historians is unquestionably Conrad Russell. In a number of essays and lectures he has argued that nearly everyone of any importance in early Stuart times endorsed a single political philosophy which combined the idea that kings rule by divine right with an emphasis on their duty to abide by the law of the land. Central to Russell's position is his claim that there were few if any absolutists amongst the English laity. Practically the only absolutists in England were a handful of eccentric and disregarded clerics, he argues, and he concludes that the vast bulk of the country's political élite united in rejecting absolutism. The English, in his opinion,

---

4 Outstanding examples are Richard Cust, *The Forced Loan and English politics 1626–1628* (Oxford 1987); Ann Hughes, *Politics, society and civil war in Warwickshire, 1620–1660* (Cambridge 1987); Richard Cust and Ann Hughes, eds, *Conflict in early Stuart England: studies in religion and politics 1603–1642* (1989); Thomas Cogswell, *The Blessed Revolution: English politics and the coming of war, 1621–1624* (Cambridge 1989); Ann Hughes, *The causes of the English Civil War* (1991); David Underdown, *A freeborn people: politics and the nation in seventeenth-century England* (Oxford 1996). Three recent articles which survey important aspects of the debate between the revisionists and their opponents are Johann P. Sommerville, 'English and European political ideas in the early seventeenth century: revisionism and the case of absolutism', *Journal of British Studies* 35 (1996) 168–94; Sommerville, 'The ancient constitution reassessed: the common law, the Court and the languages of politics in early modern England', in Malcolm Smuts, ed., *The Stuart Court and Europe: essays in politics and political culture* (Cambridge 1996) 39–64; and Nicholas Tyacke, 'Anglican attitudes: some recent writings on English religious history, from the Reformation to the Civil War', *Journal of British Studies* 35 (1996) 139–67.

shared a single political outlook. In so far as it was ideas which came to divide them, he asserts, it was *religious* ideas.[5] On political questions, they steered a middle course between theories of royal absolutism and notions of legitimate resistance – according to which the people is empowered to discipline wicked kings. Since virtually everyone shared the same middle-of-the-road outlook on politics, the Civil War manifestly did not spring from dissension on matters of political principle. Various aspects of this basic case have been developed by Russell's allies, who include Paul Christianson, Glenn Burgess, Kevin Sharpe and John Morrill.[6] Burgess, in particular, has put forward a series of claims which challenge the general arguments and many of the details of *Politics and Ideology*.

The paragraphs that follow survey the evidence for and against the arguments of Russell and his supporters, concluding that their efforts to revive revisionism have been unsuccessful, though valiant. Key issues in the debate are absolutism, resistance, the languages of politics, and consensus. They are discussed in turn below.

ABSOLUTISM

A major claim of Russell and his allies is that there were hardly any absolutists in early Stuart England, especially amongst the laity. Since there were almost no absolutists, they argue, it is most implausible to suggest that the Civil War arose from fears of absolutism, or that Parliamentarians took up arms to prevent the king from establishing a style of government which neither he nor his supporters – except for a few crazed clerics – had any intention of introducing. Revisionists admit that people often made high-sounding remarks on the divine origins of royal power, but assert that such talk about divine right was mostly vague chatter, or else that it was directed against Roman Catholic claims that kings are subordinate to popes. Talk of divine right was not absolutism, they insist, for to be an absolutist you have to argue (amongst other things) that kings make law on their own and not in Parliament. Few people claimed that kings could and should make law by proclamation; so, few were absolutists. This line of reasoning is faulty. There *were* absolutists, and they included powerful and important political figures.

5 Russell's works include *Unrevolutionary England* (see n. 3 above); *Parliaments and English politics 1621–1629* (Oxford 1979); *The causes of the English Civil War* (Oxford 1990); and *The fall of the British monarchies 1637–1642* (Oxford 1991). His views on early Stuart political thinking are well expressed in *The causes of the English Civil War* 131–60; see also *The Fall of the British Monarchies* 144, 461.
6 See especially Paul Christianson, 'Royal and Parliamentary voices on the ancient constitution, *c.*1604–1621', in Linda Levy Peck, ed., *The mental world of the Jacobean Court* (Cambridge 1991) 71–95; Christianson, *Discourse on history, law, and governance in the public career of John Selden, 1610–1635* (Toronto 1996); Glenn Burgess, *Absolute monarchy and the Stuart constitution* (New Haven 1996); Burgess, *The politics of the ancient constitution: an introduction to English political thought 1603–1642* (1992); Kevin Sharpe, *The personal rule of Charles I* (1992); Sharpe, *Politics and ideas in early Stuart England: essays and studies* (1989); and John Morrill, *The nature of the English revolution* (1993).

Revisionists try to erase early Stuart absolutism by redefining the term in such a way that we will not be able to find any thinkers whose views were extreme enough to qualify them as absolutists. One problem with this approach is that it abolishes Continental as well as English absolutism: on the revisionist definition, thinkers like Bodin and Bossuet – two of the most famous French absolutists – become constitutionalists, hard to distinguish from writers like Coke; which is absurd.[7] Another difficulty is that even if most people around 1600 did firmly reject what *revisionists* call absolutism (though revisionists themselves do not see eye to eye on what it was),[8] this does not demonstrate that they agreed in rejecting (or accepting) anything else. Nor does it show that they rejected absolutism defined in a more traditional way. That people in the past did not adopt some modern definition or theory does nothing to prove that they all agreed with each other. People in the seventeenth century did not hold modern ideas on physics. We could say that they all united in rejecting modern ideas on the stars (for instance), and conclude that they therefore agreed with each other: Galileo and the Catholic church said essentially the same things, since they both disagreed with Einstein and Stephen Hawking. This kind of claim has little point except to define into existence a happy harmony that never existed.

A good starting point is the thinking of James VI and I. The king was a layman, and an exceptionally important political figure. He was not an ignored eccentric, living on the margins of society. If James turns out to have been an absolutist, then we have discovered one highly significant exception to the revisionist rule. Until very recently, there was wide agreement that the king was in fact an absolutist. Paul-Alexandre Janet's best-selling old French manual on the history of political thought declared that James defended the 'divine right' and 'absolute power' of kings.[9] In his survey of early modern history, the eminent Italian scholar Giorgio Spini affirmed that the king's political writings expounded 'the most extremist absolutist doctrines'.[10] R.W. and A.J. Carlyle, in their authoritative multi-volume study of medieval and sixteenth-century political thought, likewise portrayed James as a straightforward absolutist. Discussing James in their chapter on 'The theory of the absolute monarchy', they declared that he had united 'the secular theory of the absolute king and the theological theory of his absolute authority as being by divine right'.[11] C.H. McIlwain was one of the most eminent of twentieth-century

7 This is the central argument of Sommerville, 'English and European political ideas in the early seventeenth century: revisionism and the case of absolutism'.

8 It is unclear that revisionists agree on what absolutism was; Christianson sees the doctrines expressed by James VI and I in the *True law of free monarchies* as absolutist ('Royal and Parliamentary voices on the ancient constitution', 77–8) while Burgess affirms that they were anti-absolutist (*Absolute monarchy and the Stuart constitution*, 40–3).

9 Paul-Alexandre Janet, *Histoire de la science politique dans ses rapports avec la morale*, 5th edn, 2 vols (Paris 1913) II, 144: 'droit divin'; 'pouvoir absolu'.

10 Giorgio Spini, *Storia dell'età moderna*, 3 vols (Turin 1965) II, 511: 'le piú estremistiche dottrine assolutiste'.

11 R.W. Carlyle and A.J. Carlyle, *A history of medieval political theory in the West*, 6 vols (1903–36) VI, 437.

scholars of Jacobean political theory. In 1918 he edited James's political writings, analysing his majesty's ideas in the course of a long introduction. McIlwain thought that the king had adopted 'absolutist doctrines' and he asserted that to 'anyone with even the slightest knowledge of the constitutional history' of the period it would be 'obvious how utterly inconsistent' James's ideas were with the views of lawyers and members of Parliament.[12] Elsewhere, he discussed the king's famous speech of 21 March 1610, concluding that 'the theory here laid down is plain absolutism'.[13] Such fine scholars as W.H. Greenleaf and George Mosse took exactly the same line.[14] The best recent guide to early modern political ideas is undoubtedly *The Cambridge History of Political Thought 1450–1700*, published in 1991. In John Salmon's excellent contribution to that volume, James once more appears as an absolutist.[15] Examples could easily be multiplied.

Despite all this, however, revisionists have recently looked again at James and discovered that he 'was no absolutist'.[16] They have not found any new writings by the king, but have used the same texts as everyone else. So why the difference of opinion? Is it that McIlwain and the rest did not properly understand James, and that the revisionists have for the first time grasped the king's true meaning? The answer is less startling. Revisionist writers use a new definition of absolutism. In this book, James's ideas have been portrayed in time-honoured fashion as absolutist; and absolutism has been described as the theory that the ruler in any state holds sovereign authority, cannot be actively resisted, can change existing constitutional arrangements in a case of necessity (though he ought otherwise to maintain them), and should be obeyed by his subjects provided that his commands are not contrary to those of God and nature. Revisionists, however, employ a very different concept of absolutism.

Revisionist definitions, or the strange case of the disappearing absolutists

According to Glenn Burgess, to 'qualify as a theorist of "absolutism" an English thinker would need to make the claim that the king could give laws to his subjects, without consultation'. In practice, he continues, this 'amounts to the claim that proclamations should have a force superior to that of statute or common law'.[17] Absolutists, in short, are people who believe that kings can make law by edict or proclamation, and that they have no need to consult

12 Charles Howard McIlwain, ed., *The political works of James I* (Cambridge, Mass. 1918) p. xl.
13 C.H. McIlwain, *The High Court of Parliament and its supremacy* (New Haven 1910) 348.
14 W.H. Greenleaf, *Order, empiricism and politics: two traditions of English political thought 1500–1700* (Oxford 1964) 66. George L. Mosse, *The struggle for sovereignty in England, from the reign of Queen Elizabeth to the Petition of Right* (East Lansing 1950) 58.
15 J.H.M. Salmon, 'Catholic resistance theory, Ultramontanism, and the royalist response, 1580–1620', in J.H. Burns and Mark Goldie, eds, *The Cambridge history of political thought 1450–1700* (Cambridge 1991) 219–53, at 247–9; see also 679–80. James also appears as an absolutist in Johann P. Sommerville, 'Absolutism and royalism', ibid., 347–73, at 365.
16 Burgess, *Absolute monarchy and the Stuart constitution* 40.
17 Ibid., 98.

their subjects. On the revisionist account, people like James I who argued for 'the iniquity of resistance and the inviolability of the duty of allegiance' were not absolutists, since their arguments 'entailed no commitment to any particular view of the king's authority to make law, or the ways in which such authority should be exercised'.[18] To be an absolutist (revisionists tell us) you must assert that the king alone makes law, and that he exercises his legislative power on his own, and not in consultation with his subjects. So absolutism is not just a theory about where power ultimately resides in a country, but also an account of how it is to be exercised. Absolutists (say the revisionists) hold that kings make law on their own, not in Parliament. Perhaps kings might from time to time call Parliaments, but they are under no obligation to do so, and could just as well legislate without them if they pleased.

On the revisionist view, then, absolutists are people who claim that kings may make law by proclamation whenever they please. If you encounter someone who thinks kings ought to consult their subjects before legislating, you have not discovered an absolutist; and anyone who says that monarchs ought ordinarily to abide by settled constitutional procedures is also no absolutist. Perhaps the largest problem with this approach is that it disqualifies more or less all the most famous of Continental absolutists from claiming the title. For instance, Jean Bodin – the best-known French absolutist – thought that an absolute king possessed the authority to legislate but that he should ordinarily exercise it only with the advice of his subjects. Bodin was a firm believer in representative institutions like the French Estates General and the English Parliament. He and others held that monarchs ought to depart from established law only in emergencies. Absolutists (say the revisionists) want kings to rule by proclamation, and free them from any obligation to consult their subjects or uphold old constitutional arrangements. Moreover, Burgess tells us (and other revisionists seem to agree), absolutists hold that monarchs are in no sense bound by their own laws. In absolutist theory, Burgess suggests, kings alone make law and if they later find that they do not like what they made, they can simply unmake it. Kings are under no moral obligation to obey their own laws. Furthermore, Burgess continues, the absolutist sovereign has no need to appeal to *necessity* to justify altering the law. The idea that necessity validates breaches of established law was characteristic not of absolutism but of the English common law: 'one should hesitate before arguing that theories built on "necessity" were theories of absolutism', since the 'idea that necessity could justify the abandonment of law, even the destruction of property rights, was a central principle of English common law'.[19] So, if we find someone saying that kings ought to depart from settled laws only in emergencies we have a common law thinker, not an absolutist. And the same holds good if we encounter a writer who argues that kings ought ordinarily to obey their own laws, or that they should abide by customary constitutional procedures. The

18 Ibid., 99.
19 Ibid., 50.

English constitutional tradition, says Burgess, stressed the duty of kings to rule 'by and through known and declared laws', while absolutists held that sovereigns are under no obligation to govern 'through defined constitutional channels'. Absolutists (so the revisionist case runs) thought that kings were perfectly entitled to break the law of the land, and claimed that a tyrant was not a king who flouted the laws of his realm (even good kings could do that), but one who governed wickedly, subordinating the public good to his private whims. On the other hand (proceeds the revisionist line), English constitutionalists maintained that tyrants are rulers who refuse to obey the law, while good monarchs abide by it.[20] Equipped with these revisionist definitions, Burgess has a relatively easy time demonstrating – to his own satisfaction, at least – that James I was no absolutist.[21] His task is easy, because it is exceedingly difficult to find *any* thinker – in England or elsewhere – who will pass his rigorous tests for absolutism.

In a moment, we shall turn to the question of how useful the revisionist idea of absolutism is in describing what early Stuart people actually said. But first it might be worth reflecting briefly on some of the definition's implications. One interesting feature of it is that it makes it impossible for any government to be absolutist unless it claims and exercises the right to legislate without consent. It is, Conrad Russell tell us, 'a rather poor sort of absolutist who does not believe that the King by himself can make law'.[22] A ruler who did not make any laws could not possibly be an absolutist. He could tax without consent, imprison without cause shown, and torture at will, and yet he would still not be an absolutist since he did not assert the authority to make law by proclamation. Charles I ruled without Parliament between 1629 and 1640, and in those years he made no laws. On the revisionist definition of absolutism, it therefore follows that literally *whatever* he did then, he could not have been an absolutist. To take the most extreme case, he might have illegally taxed, imprisoned, and even executed the entire population of the country, but he would still not have been an absolutist. And since he was no absolutist, they could not have objected to his absolutism. So they and he were united in political outlook – or would have been if he had not killed them. Clearly, there is something odd about this kind of definition of absolutism.

Revisionists say that anyone who appeals to necessity to justify conduct that would otherwise be illegal is not really an absolutist. Absolutism, they tell us, is 'a system of ordinary, normal or perpetual government', and is not about extraordinary powers which rulers might have in emergencies.[23] So Continental rulers like Louis XIV turn out to be absolutists only if they claimed the power to flout law in *ordinary* circumstances and not just in a case of necessity.

20 Ibid., 105–6.
21 Ibid., 40–3.
22 Russell, *Causes of the English Civil War*, 150.
23 Burgess, *Absolute monarchy*, 50 n. 129, quoting J.G.A. Pocock, 'A discourse of sovereignty', in Nicholas Phillipson and Quentin Skinner, eds, *Political discourse in early modern Britain* (Cambridge 1993) 388–9.

One problem here is that few if any rulers made such a claim. The French kings and their propagandists insisted that monarchs ought to abide by settled laws except when necessity required them to act otherwise. Pamphleteers working for Richelieu, Mazarin and Louis XIV appealed to reason of state to justify questionable royal actions. Their claim was that kings ought ordinarily to keep established law, but that necessity, or reason of state, justified them in breaking it. There would have been no point in appealing to necessity, if kings were empowered to change old laws whenever they pleased. So, on the revisionist definition, French seventeenth-century reason of state theorists must join the swelling ranks of non-absolutists.[24]

Another problem with the revisionist concept of absolutism is that it is hard to see why any rational person in early modern times would have bothered to adopt it. In England, the revisionists tell us, people found absolutism objectionable. If an English king embraced it, he was asking for trouble. Suppose a king wanted to break an established law. He could justify doing so by claiming that he was entitled to change the laws whenever he liked, and this would qualify him (in revisionist terms) as an absolutist. Or he could justify precisely the same actions by asserting that there was an emergency – and thus avoid the unpopularity connected with absolutism. Obviously, it would make sense for the king to argue that he was employing emergency powers. Quite why this would have satisfied anybody is, perhaps, difficult to say. If I tell you that I have the power to torture you whenever I want, you are not likely to be pleased. But you may be no happier if I inform you that I can torture you only when I think necessity requires me to – and not when I think it unnecessary. Either way, I alone decide whether you are tortured. In both cases, you may well find my power over you rather worrying.

So there are some problems with the revisionist definition of absolutism. Nevertheless, we should employ that definition if the English used it in the early seventeenth century. Of course, people then did not often use words ending in '-ism', and did not talk about 'absolutism' or 'constitutionalism'. But they did use the term 'absolute power', and did grow concerned that the king was trying to introduce it, or that wicked counsellors were attempting to persuade him that he had it. For instance, in 1628 Pym told the House of Commons that the evil clergyman Roger Maynwaring had erred by going 'about to infuse into his Majesty that which was most unfit for his royal breast – an absolute power not bounded by law'.[25] What the cleric had done, of course, was to publish sermons justifying the Forced Loan of 1626–27. We are fortunate in having both the text of what Maynwaring wrote, and full records of the proceedings connected with his case, which tell us exactly why people objected to his ideas, and why Parliament impeached him. This evidence makes it clear that Maynwaring said nothing at all to suggest that the king

24 A good analysis of French thinking on reason of state is W.F. Church, *Richelieu and reason of state* (Princeton 1972).
25 *PP 28*, iii, 408.

should henceforth legislate by proclamation; nor did members of Parliament take him to be arguing in favour of the notion that monarchs should in ordinary circumstances make laws by decree. It is true that one of the charges against him was connected with his 'undermining of parliaments'.[26] But Maynwaring nowhere argued that the king should abolish Parliament and legislate by edict. He called Parliaments 'most *Sacred* and *honourable*' and 'the *Highest*, and *greatest Representations* of a *Kingdome*', but argued that the king was empowered to tax even without Parliamentary consent in a case of '*Necessity*, extreame and urgent'. The 'urgent and pressing *Necessities* of State', he said, could not always wait for the 'long and pawsing *Deliberations*' of 'so great and vast a body, as such *Assemblies* are'.[27]

Quite clearly, then, Maynwaring was no absolutist on the revisionist definition of the term. He said nothing at all to suggest 'that proclamations should have a force superior to that of statute or common law',[28] and he granted Charles I the authority to override established arrangements only in emergencies and not in ordinary circumstances. Yet members of Parliament evidently regarded his views as so objectionable that they impeached him, and the committee which reported on his case wanted him to be attainted as a traitor.[29] Ideas which fell well short of what revisionists now call absolutism attracted outspoken hostility in the House of Commons. So ideological conflict was possible even amongst non-absolutists – or at least, among people whose views were less extreme than the revisionist ideal of an absolutist. Even if England had been entirely free of absolutists on the revisionist model, harmony would not have reigned there.

Pym took Maynwaring to be an advocate of 'absolute power not bounded by law'. He and other members of the Commons were worried that ideas like Maynwaring's were becoming widespread, and influencing the king. The 'absolute power' which Pym feared was not, then, the 'absolutism' that revisionists describe – though it corresponded rather closely to traditional ideas about absolutism. Revisionists themselves affirm that very few people in England adopted the views which they style absolutist – and it is doubtful that even those few really did so. Burgess calls Maynwaring and Filmer absolutists, but neither suggested that the king should abolish Parliament and make law by proclamation.[30] If no one in the early seventeenth century argued either for

<hr>

26 Ibid., 416.
27 Roger Maynwaring, *Religion and alegiance* (1627) I, 26–7.
28 Burgess, *Absolute monarchy*, 98.
29 *PP 28*, III, 412.
30 Burgess, *Absolute monarchy*, 218–19. Burgess states that Filmer 'got closer . . . than anyone else in early Stuart England to saying' 'that royal proclamations had the force of common or statute law', and he affirms that to count as an "absolutist"' 'in English terms' you must say precisely that. This appears to entail that although Filmer got closer to being an absolutist than anyone else, he was not in fact one, and therefore that there were none at all. In order to support his claim that Filmer got close to saying that proclamations have the force of statute, Burgess quotes him as asserting that 'originally the difference was not great between a proclamation and a statute': *Patriarcha and other writings*, ed. Johann P. Sommerville (Cambridge 1991) 59. But this quite evidently does not amount to saying that there is little difference between the two now, or that

or against the revisionist concept of absolutism, there is no reason why we should employ it. Surely it is preferable to discuss what Pym and his contemporaries meant by 'absolute power', rather than what Russell and his allies understand by the term.

At times, though, revisionists hint that their concept of absolutism *was* widely used in the early modern period – but not in England. On the continent of Europe, the argument runs, people like the Frenchmen Bodin and Bossuet put forward absolutist ideas, and kings like Louis XIV enforced them; but in England everyone rejected absolutism and lived happily together in ideological harmony until shortly before the Civil War. The English – we are told – emphasised that monarchs ought to rule 'by and through known and declared laws', and 'through defined constitutional channels'. Absolutists, however, thought that the sovereign had no duty at all to govern by settled laws or known procedures; the king's only obligation was to govern well, but it was completely up to him how he did this. According to Continental absolutists – the revisionist case proceeds – a tyrant was a king who did not govern well; according to the English constitutional tradition, on the other hand, tyrants were monarchs who failed to rule by established laws. James I undertook to 'rule my actions according to my Lawes', and argued that 'all Kings that are not tyrants . . . will be glad to bound themselves within the limits of their Lawes'. Therefore – the revisionist analysis concludes – he was no absolutist but a good English constitutionalist.[31] Once again, the problem here is that no one anywhere seems to have adopted the views which revisionists call absolutist. In particular, Bodin and Bossuet took exactly the same line as James I, recommending that the king rule in a law-abiding manner. In the words of Bodin, a good king 'measureth his manners, according unto his lawes', while a tyrant 'measureth his lawes, according to his own disposition and pleasure'.[32] Evidently, Bodin shared the English opinion that kings should rule 'by and through known and declared laws', and 'through defined constitutional channels'.[33] The same was true of Bossuet, the most famous apologist for Louis XIV's absolutism. He vigorously criticised forms of government in which there was no law apart from the king's will, insisting that monarchs

---

the king can legislate by proclamation if he pleases. Filmer's basic objective (as Burgess himself notes: *Absolute monarchy*, 219) was to show that in England law was made by 'the sole authority of the king'. In early times, he argued, kings had made law on their own, and though they now legislated in Parliament it was still royal authority alone which created law in England: 'in parliament all statutes or laws are properly made by the king alone at the rogation of the people' (Filmer, *Patriarcha*, 57). Filmer was here largely quoting James I, who adopted precisely the same position on this point: King James VI and I, *Political writings*, ed. Johann P. Sommerville (Cambridge 1994) 74, 183. If his views on this issue made Filmer something like an absolutist, then James must have been like one too.

31 Burgess, *Absolute monarchy*, 105–6. The quotations from James are in King James VI and I, *Political writings*, 184.
32 Jean Bodin, *The six bookes of a commonweale*, translated by Richard Knolles, ed. Kenneth Douglas McRae (Cambridge, Mass. 1962) 212 (this translation was first published in 1606); Bodin, *Les six livres de la république* (Paris 1583) 290.
33 Burgess, *Absolute monarchy*, 105–6.

ought to respect settled constitutional arrangements and be careful not to infringe their subjects' legally guaranteed rights of property. In his opinion, kings ought to preserve 'ancient laws' and 'praiseworthy customs', not subvert them.[34]

It seems, indeed, that every absolutist – in England and elsewhere – argued that kings ought to rule through known and declared laws. So too did virtually all other European political theorists. A moment's reflection shows that this is not all that surprising. Subjects would have been very confused if kings had attempted to govern by unknown laws, or by ones they failed to declare. And if they had tried to rule without laws at all, life would have been completely bewildering. Laws define crime and how it should be punished. Virtually all of the most tyrannical regimes in history have ruled by and through known laws and procedures in most circumstances, flouting law only in necessity. Mussolini made the trains run on time, but that does not mean he was a constitutional ruler. The revisionist definition of absolutism was asserted by no one in early modern times, and contradicts many fundamental claims made by thinkers like Bodin and Bossuet – who are standardly described as absolutists. In England, like everywhere else in Europe, there were no absolutists – on the revisionist model. But in England there were quite a number of people who agreed with such theorists as Bodin and Bossuet on key points. The next section is about them.

Reappearing absolutists

In his excellent book *Anglicans and Puritans?*, Peter Lake proposed a definition of absolutism which contrasts with the revisionist account, but conforms to more traditional usage, and – in particular – to the way in which people saw things in the seventeenth century. Lake employed the

> term 'absolutist' . . . to refer to accounts of political power which derive the ruler's authority either from a direct divine gift or an irreversible grant from the people. While under a moral obligation to obey the laws of the land, such rulers were theoretically unbound by human law and certainly free to override any of the legal rights of their subjects in case of necessity. Such a view of power thus rendered illegitimate any and every attempt to limit or resist the ruler.[35]

This concept of absolutism was what Pym had in mind when he attacked Maynwaring for advocating 'an absolute power not bounded by law'.[36] Pym was annoyed that Maynwaring granted the king the authority to override individuals' legal rights of property in what he took to be emergencies.

34 Jacques-Bénigne Bossuet, *Politics drawn from Holy Scripture*, translated by Patrick Riley (Cambridge 1990) 263–4, 269.
35 Peter Lake, *Anglicans and Puritans? Presbyterianism and English Conformist thought from Whitgift to Hooker* (1988) 7.
36 *PP 28*, III, 408.

Maynwaring did indeed think that Charles could disregard established customs in a case of necessity, and he argued that the king's powers are derived directly from God, and not from the law or the people. Bodin and Bossuet likewise held that kings are not accountable to the people over whom they rule, that law takes its authority from the sovereign (not vice versa), and that (despite their general obligation to govern in a law-abiding manner) kings are empowered to set aside particular laws in emergencies. Bodin and Bossuet, like Maynwaring, said nothing at all to suggest that monarchs ought always to make laws by proclamation, or that they should not rule by and through known and declared laws. They were not absolutists on the revisionist definition. But they have normally been classed as absolutists by modern writers on political theory, and in the seventeenth century theories like theirs were recognised as very different from the constitutionalist ideas which prevailed in the House of Commons (and this is a major reason why in 1628 the Commons impeached Maynwaring, rejected a Bodinian account of royal sovereignty, and insisted that the king was under the law). In brief, there were people in early modern Europe who adopted the ideas that Professor Lake describes as absolutist, and there were others who expressed fear and distaste at those same ideas. But there was no one who advocated what revisionists describe as absolutism. It makes sense, then, to abandon the revisionist paradigm, and to use Lake's definition – which is substantially that employed in this book, and by most commentators on early modern political ideas. Were there English absolutists on this model? The answer is a resounding yes, as we shall see in what follows.

All this talk of definitions might sound overly semantic. Certainly, we should not lose sight of things in our concern with words. In particular, we ought not to forget that the main point at issue in the debate over revisionism is whether people held markedly different views on political and constitutional questions before the Civil War, or (alternatively) agreed on fundamentals and diverged only on the occasional minor point. So in the paragraphs below we will look not just at whether people really were absolutists (on whatever definition), but also at whether they agreed with each other.

Sir Francis Kynaston was a courtier who served Charles I as an esquire of the king's body (another of the esquires was Edward Filmer, brother of the more famous Sir Robert). Kynaston wrote 'A True Presentation of Forepast Parliaments', which was never printed but circulated widely in manuscript, and survives in a number of copies. Amongst those who read it was the king's secretary Windebank.[37] According to Kevin Sharpe, 'this long and fascinating' work is a prime example of middle-of-the-road political theorising. He tells us that the 'True Presentation' suggested that the honourable achievements

---

37 Esther Cope, *Politics without Parliaments* (1987) 27–8, 40n., 122; Johann P. Sommerville, 'Ideology, property and the constitution', in Richard Cust and Ann Hughes, eds, *Conflict in early Stuart England*, 68 n. 9; Kevin Sharpe, 'Introduction: Parliamentary history 1603–1629: in or out of perspective', in Sharpe, ed., *Faction and Parliament: essays on early Stuart history* (Oxford 1978) 1–42, at 14–15.

which were sometimes attributed to Parliament ought really to be ascribed to kings. But 'rival claims to credit for the honourable actions of a parliament which consisted of King, Lords, and Commons scarcely constitute a conflict of authority'.[38] So Kynaston's general political theory falls well within the mainstream of English thinking – thinking which (on the revisionist view) emphasised consensus and harmony, and stoutly rejected absolutism. Burgess adopts a similar approach. He admits that Kynaston occasionally said things which the unwary might misinterpret as absolutist. But when the courtier made high-sounding assertions, he tells us, he was writing in 'a *defensive* rather than an *aggressive*' mode, and did not intend 'to mount innovatory claims on the king's behalf'. Kynaston, he states, 'was *not* suggesting that kings had the power to give laws to their subjects without seeking their consent', and so he was no absolutist. Though he enunciated some principles which 'in the abstract can sound absolutist', 'upon close examination' he turns out to have endorsed 'customary legal and constitutional practices'.[39] For both Burgess and Sharpe, then, Kynaston was an ideological ally of the likes of Pym and Coke, who also defended the ancient constitution, and who rejected the absolutism of Maynwaring. On practical matters, their case goes, he agreed with the standard anti-absolutist theory of the constitution, though occasionally and for defensive reasons he made the odd flattering general statement about royal power.

There are major problems with this account of Kynaston, and Conrad Russell himself simply – and rightly – classes the knight amongst absolutists, though more dubiously insisting that they were a rare breed.[40] Whether we see his tone as 'aggressive' rather than 'defensive' (it is both by turns) is largely irrelevant to deciding if his ideas are absolutist, since manifestly it is possible to put forward absolutist theory both defensively (as Bodin did) and aggressively (like Bossuet). Whether or not we call Sir Francis an absolutist is itself mainly a matter of terminology (he was one on Lake's definition, but not on that of the revisionists). But Kynaston's treatise makes it abundantly clear that he was a vigorous ideological opponent of Coke and his supporters. Certainly, only an extremely broad conception of consensus could turn Coke and Kynaston into allies. With friends like that, Coke would scarcely have needed enemies. Kynaston lost few opportunities for sneering at the judge, and, indeed, at lawyers in general. Coke, he declared, was styled 'The Father of the Law' by many members of the House of Commons, and he 'too vaingloriously affected and assum'd' that title. In fact, though, he better deserved to be called the son of the law, since just as sons often get their wealth from their fathers, so Coke derived 'his Estate and great Inheritance' from his legal practice.[41] Lawyers in general were greedy and grasping, and they commonly

38 Sharpe, 'Introduction: Parliamentary history 1603–1629: in or out of perspective', 14–15.
39 Burgess, *Absolute monarchy*, 39–40.
40 Russell, *Causes of the English Civil War*, 152.
41 [Sir Francis Kynaston], 'A True presentation of forepast Parliaments', BL Lansdowne Mss 213, ff. 146a–176b, at 149b.

took large fees for worthless advice.[42] It would be no bad thing for Parliament to meet without them.[43] The king could, in any case, exclude the entire Commons from Parliament if he pleased: early Parliaments had often met without the Lower House, and no English monarchs 'did ever necessitate themselves' 'to summon the Commons'.[44] When Parliaments assembled, their duty was to attend first of all to the business which the king placed before them: 'such matters are only (or at leastwise first & principally) to be treated on by the Parliament, which the King shall please to propose to the Parliament'.[45] Kings alone made law, and they could not share this power, for sovereignty is indivisible: 'Soveraignty, and Subjection' 'cannot be in one & the same' person at one time.[46] True, English monarchs had decided to legislate in Parliament, but 'a wise and just King may do all that a Parliament man can do, without a Parliament'.[47] In particular, the monarch was perfectly entitled to levy taxes 'without a Parliament'.[48] Kings were accountable only to God, and subjects had a duty to obey them provided that their commands did not contradict His. If the king ordered you to do something that was not against divine law but was 'contrary to the Laws of the Kingdom, or directly against the Libertie of the People', you would be obliged to obey. If officials carried out the sovereign's illegal orders, the king took responsibility and would be called to account by God, 'the King of Kings, to whom all Kings are onely accountable'. It was not for Parliament to attempt to discipline such officials. They had no authority to do so, and it was also extremely imprudent to annoy the king by impeaching his ministers. The chances were that he would simply rule without Parliament and tax without consent, as he was fully entitled to do.[49]

Kynaston held that people should obey the king's illegal orders. In the House of Commons in 1628–29 many members argued that no one had any obligation to obey unlawful royal commands – such as those requiring payment of the Forced Loan and tonnage and poundage. Kynaston affirmed that Parliament should discuss what the monarch told it to discuss. In 1629 the Commons refused to comply with the king's request that they draw up legislation on tonnage and poundage, and instead debated grievances. Kynaston condemned impeachments, and the Parliaments of the 1620s justified them, impeaching Bacon, Cranfield and others. Kynaston claimed that Parliament could not call royal officials to account for doing the king's bidding, and in 1629 the Commons began proceedings against the customs officers for obeying royal orders to collect tonnage and poundage. Kynaston argued that the king was perfectly justified in ruling without Parliament and in taxing without

42 Ibid., 163a.
43 Ibid., 152a.
44 Ibid., 158b.
45 Ibid., 163a.
46 Ibid., 159a.
47 Ibid., 147b.
48 Ibid., 172b.
49 Ibid., 171a–2b.

consent. Many people took a very different view, and two of the main complaints against the king's regime in 1640 were that Charles had not summoned Parliament for eleven years and that he had raised extra-Parliamentary levies such as Ship Money. Kynaston thought the king could call Parliament without the Commons. Most members of the Lower House resoundingly disagreed. On major political questions, then, Kynaston's thinking was very different from that of many in the Commons, but rather similar to the ideas of other theorists with Court connections – like Maynwaring, Hobbes and Sir Robert Filmer – the brother of Kynaston's colleague. If the relationship between Kynaston's thought and Coke's is to be described as one of consensus – as Burgess contends – then it would be interesting to know what would count as conflict.

Kevin Sharpe has told us about another political treatise which he also portrays as standing squarely in the mainstream of the English tradition of consensus politics. In this work – Ralph Starkey's *The Priviledges and Practice of Parliaments* of 1628 – we may hear the authentic voice of moderates who 'clung to the ideal of harmony and order when it was breaking down around them' – or so Sharpe informs us. The book, Sharpe proceeds, asserted that 'it was desirable to make laws by the consent of the whole realm' but that '"simply to binde the King to or by those Lawes were repugnant to the nature of an absolute Monarchy"'.[50] Kynaston and Hobbes would doubtless have agreed with this sentiment, and so too would Filmer, who argued that kings are above the laws, though good kings ruled in a law-abiding manner.[51] Filmer closely followed James I on this as on many other questions. According to James, 'the King is above the law', though good monarchs would conform their actions to their laws, thus setting an example to their subjects.[52] Ideas like this were not popular in the Commons, however. Although Sharpe does not note it, the claim that it would be 'repugnant to the nature of an absolute Monarchy' simply to 'binde the Kinge' to obey the laws was not original with Starkey, but was in fact taken by him (without attribution) from an earlier work – John Cowell's notorious *Interpreter*.[53] In 1610, the Commons called Cowell into question for things he had said in his book, and many wanted him severely punished. Of course, the fact that they disliked the book is no indication that they objected to this particular passage. If, as Sharpe suggests, Cowell's words about absolute monarchy really did represent the consensus view – on which practically everyone agreed until the Civil War began – then we would expect that the Commons would have had nothing to say against them, and might perhaps even have seen them as mitigating the offences that Cowell committed elsewhere in the book. In fact, however, the Lower House

50 Sharpe, 'Introduction: Parliamentary history 1603–1629: in or out of perspective', 14–15. The quotation from Starkey is from *The priviledges and practice of parliaments in England* (1628) 41.
51 Filmer, *Patriarcha and other writings*, 41–2.
52 King James VI and I, *Political writings*, 75.
53 John Cowell, *The interpreter: or booke containing the signification of words* (Cambridge 1607) sig. 3A3b.

objected very strongly indeed to the words, quoting them to confirm its first charge against Cowell – that he placed the king above the law.[54] Manifestly, if there was ideological harmony in 1610, it did not centre – as Sharpe suggests – on Cowell's views.

One revisionist idea about Cowell is that he was indeed an absolutist, but that he was practically alone in this, and that the king and the two Houses of Parliament therefore agreed readily in condemning him. As we have seen, this claim is open to the objections that the Lords did not condemn him, and that it does not seem to have been his absolutism that James I found objectionable.[55] A more recent notion is that Cowell was not in fact 'an absolutist' but was 'simply careless in discussing politically sensitive matters'.[56] Cowell, on this account, displayed 'carelessness' and 'ham-fistedness' in talking about the king's powers, and by so doing 'infringed the unspoken conventions structuring consensus'. What Cowell did, the argument runs, was to misuse terminology in talking about kingship, employing words in contexts that people found inappropriate.[57] It was not his ideas, but his insensitive use of language that got him into trouble. But if Cowell was called to account not for the things he said but for carelessness in how he said them, it is hard to see why he did not simply come forward and admit his mistake. In an atmosphere of broad ideological agreement, surely the Commons would have forgiven a few small slips. Again, there is no evidence that he was attacked for infringing unspoken conventions about the use of language, and doing so was not an offence in English law, nor did Parliament punish it on other occasions. Until the advent of revisionism, no one made any comment on Cowell's ham-fistedness or carelessness.

In 1628, Pym presented the House of Commons' charge against Maynwaring to the Lords. Amongst precedents justifying the cleric's punishment, he cited Cowell's case.[58] When the Lords delivered judgment against Maynwaring, Attorney-General Heath declared that 'Dr. Cowell's errors' are 'yours, Mr. Dr. Maynwaring'.[59] Whether Heath really thought they were errors is questionable, since he soon drew up a pardon for Maynwaring – on the orders of the king himself.[60] But both he and Pym clearly believed that Cowell and Maynwaring held essentially the same views. Yet on the revisionist account, Maynwaring was a genuine absolutist while Cowell was guilty only of insensitive speech. The two said much the same things and elicited similar reactions from Parliament. It looks as though both were absolutists. Of course, we may speculate that only one meant what he said, and that everyone else who said similar things was just 'careless'. In this way, we can suggest that there were very few absolutists, and that there was little conflict over absolutist ideas.

54 *PP 10*, ɪɪ, 38.
55 See above, pp. 113–19.
56 Burgess, *Absolute monarchy*, 78 n. 74.
57 Burgess, *Politics of the ancient constitution*, 149–50.
58 *PP 28*, ɪᴠ, 109–10.
59 *PP 28*, ᴠ, 623.
60 See above, p. 123.

Similarly, we could claim that at Edgehill only one royalist really meant to shoot at the roundheads, while the rest were just careless and ham-fisted. Cowell said that 'the king of England is an absolute king', and that he 'is above the Law by his absolute power'. The Commons proceeded against him because he said these things.[61] The simplest interpretation of these events is that he believed that the king was an absolute ruler, while they did not.

As we saw, James I's chaplain William Wilkes declared that the 'law is the worke of the King, to whose regall dignitie it appertaines to make Lawes'.[62] Revisionists stress that absolutists gave the king legislative power. Wilkes did this. We might expect that revisionists would grant that he was an absolutist. But Glenn Burgess has questioned this. His argument is instructive. 'It is possible', he tells us,

> that Wilkes meant by this that the king outside of parliament could make laws superior to statute and common law. Possible, but extremely unlikely. A few pages earlier he had cited Fortescue as authority for the claim 'that the *King* cannot alter and change the lawes of this *Realm* at his pleasure, because the rule of his government is not onlie royall, but pollitick'.[63]

Certainly, it seems odd to find an absolutist supporting Fortescue's ideas on limited monarchy. It would be equally strange if a modern conservative endorsed Karl Marx's views on class struggle and revolution. But there would be nothing at all unusual in a conservative quoting Marx, either to refute him, or to show that he contradicts his present-day followers. A common technique in early-modern religious controversy was to quote your opponents' favourite texts against them. Wilkes's book was directed against puritans, who argued that the godly are entitled to disobey the king's laws on religious ceremonies. If we look at the whole passage from which Burgess quotes, and not just at edited highlights, we find that Wilkes did *not* endorse Fortescue's ideas. Addressing the puritans, who want to break the law, he told them that 'Your Fathers at the Lawe' 'with grave *resolution* assure, that the *King* cannot alter and change the lawes of this *Realme* at his pleasure', and he cites Fortescue as an example of one of these 'Fathers at the Lawe'; if the puritans' lawyer allies were right, he proceeded, and even the king must obey the law, then surely individual subjects ought to obey it too. So by the standards of their friends the lawyers, the puritans should stop disobeying.[64] By suppressing the words 'Your Fathers at the Lawe . . . assure', it is possible to make it look as though Wilkes himself adopted ideas which he in fact attributed to common lawyers. The same technique could be adapted easily enough to turn Catholics into Protestants, the left into the right, and day into night.

Burgess compares Wilkes's views with those of Peter Heylin, whom he portrays as another constitutional moderate. Heylin, he tells us, made the

---

61 Cowell, *Interpreter* sig. 3D4a, 2Q1a. *PP 10*, ii, 38.
62 William Wilkes, *A second memento for magistrates* (1608) 56, quoted above at p. 39.
63 Burgess, *Absolute monarchy*, 102–3.
64 Wilkes, *Second memento*, 49.

occasional high-sounding remark about divine right, but much more important-
ly he affirmed 'the king's duty to govern lawfully', and he was, indeed,
'primarily a theorist of obedience to law', who advocated the 'rule of law'.[65]
Heylin was a royal chaplain and a close associate of William Laud, whose
biographer he became. He was also a good friend of Sir Robert Filmer, and
was to lament the fact that the knight's *Patriarcha* had not been printed.[66]
Heylin was 'commanded by authority' to reply to recent writings by Henry
Burton, in which the puritan had attacked the Laudian regime.[67] The result
was his *Briefe and Moderate Answer* of 1637, and it is this work which Burgess
cites to demonstrate Heylin's anti-absolutism and his devotion to the English
constitutionalist tradition. Although Burgess's account is somewhat vague on
exactly what Heylin found objectionable about Burton's views, it leaves the
reader with the distinct impression that Burton must have been advocating
disobedience to the law, and that Heylin – 'primarily a theorist of obedience
to law' – was taking him to task for this, and defending 'the rule of law'
against his criticisms. If this were so, we would expect that Heylin's political
doctrines would have made him popular, and that when the Long Parliament
met in 1640 it would have congratulated him on the stand he had taken in
defence of 'the rule of law' – which it held so dear. We would also expect that
they might have upbraided Burton for attacking the rule of law. But events
turned out very differently. Imprisoned by the Laudians in 1637, Burton was
released when the Long Parliament met and treated as a hero. In the Civil
War, Heylin became a royalist, and was declared a delinquent by Parliament,
which confiscated his property. Laud was arrested in 1640 and later tried and
executed. One of the charges which faced him at his trial was that he had
commanded Heylin to write against Burton, and that in the *Briefe and Moderate Answer* 'an unlimited power was pressed very far'.[68]

The House of Commons, which brought the charges, did not view Heylin
as 'primarily a theorist of obedience to law'. They regarded him as an advocate of unlimited royal power. Of course, it is possible that they were simply
mistaken, and that if they had been as perceptive as modern revisionists they
would have dropped the accusation against Laud, and embraced the Archbishop and the chaplain as their ideological allies. Yet they were not alone in
failing to spot Heylin's constitutionalism. Algernon Sidney, who was executed for his anti-absolutist deeds and doctrines in 1683, similarly saw Heylin
as a proponent of unlimited monarchy. Sidney grouped Heylin with Laud,
Maynwaring, Sibthorp and Hobbes as people who had adopted the same
execrable principles as Filmer. Sidney's modern editor calls these writers the
'leading 17th-century defenders of absolute monarchy'. Sidney himself wrote

65 Burgess, *Absolute monarchy*, 103, 104.
66 Peter Heylin, *Certamen epistolare: or, the letter-combate* (1659) '387' = 208. See also Heylin,
Historical and miscellaneous tracts (1681), p. xiv, which shows that Filmer was associated with
Heylin before the Civil War.
67 Heylin, *A briefe and moderate answer, to the seditious and scandalous challenges of Henry Burton*
(1637) sig. d1b.
68 William Laud, *Works*, ed. W. Scott and J. Bliss, 7 vols (Oxford 1847–60) IV, 84–5.

primarily against Filmer, but also referred frequently to Heylin – more frequently than to any of the others. He claimed that Filmer was Heylin's disciple.[69] Who understood Heylin's ideas better, the Long Parliament and Sidney,
or recent revisionists?

In 1632, Heylin published *Augustus. Or an Essay of those Meanes and Counsels, Whereby the Commonwealth of Rome was altered and reduced unto a Monarchy.*
This book had been written long before, but it had obvious relevance to
England after 1629, when Charles I embarked on his Personal Rule. Heylin
described the devious and dissembling means by which Augustus had ended
the republican government of ancient Rome and taken 'absolute Majesty' for
himself. The Roman emperor had been careful to retain old constitutional
forms, while ensuring that he alone wielded real power. For example, he had
permitted criticisms of his rule, knowing that 'as long as the *Common-people*
reteined *Liberty of speech*, they were lesse sencible of the losse of *Liberty in
State*'.[70] Throughout, Heylin's tone was one of approval for how Augustus
had acted, and it is easy to read the work as political advice from Charles's
chaplain to the king. Indeed, it has been asserted that the book 'offers perhaps
the most unadulterated commendation of Machiavellian ethics and absolute
rule to be found anywhere in early Stuart historiography'.[71]

But maybe Heylin had changed his mind by the time that he wrote the
Briefe and Moderate Answer against Burton – and it was, after all, upon that
work that the revisionist view of Heylin as a defender of the rule of law was
based. In fairness, therefore, we should examine it in a little detail. Heylin
claimed that Burton was not an isolated fanatic, but a member of a dangerous
faction in the church – the puritans. These people argued 'that Kings are but
the Ministers of the Common-wealth, and that they have no more authority
then what is given them by the people'. Moreover, he said, they vigorously
rejected the idea that kings have 'unlimited power' and that subjects owe them
'absolute obedience'.[72] According to Burton and his fellow-puritans, Heylin
proceeded, subjects are obliged to obey the monarch only if he commands
things which accord with the law of the land: 'Then for the obedience of the
Subject, you limit it to positive lawes; the King to be no more obeyed then
there is speciall Law or Statute for it.' This looks very much as though Heylin
is saying that *Burton and the puritans* are theorists of 'obedience to law' and that
they advocate the 'rule of law'. He spelled out that he himself took a very
different line on the subject's duty of obedience. Though the puritans yielded
the king only 'this poore obedience', obliging people to obey his majesty no

69 Algernon Sidney, *Discourses concerning government*, ed. Thomas G. West (Indianapolis 1990) 11
(Laud, Heylin etc.); 11 n. 7 (editor's comment); 123, 134, 284 (Filmer as Heylin's disciple).
70 Heylin, *Augustus. Or an essay of those meanes and counsels, whereby the Commonwealth of Rome
was altered and reduced unto a monarchy* (1632) sig. A3a (the book was written 'long since' but is
now first published, with the author's permission); '120'=122–3 (Augustus imitated Lycurgus'
Sparta, where kings had 'absolute Majesty'); 124 (old forms); 150 (liberty).
71 D.R. Woolf, *The idea of history in early Stuart England: erudition, ideology, and 'the light of truth'
from the accession of James I to the Civil War* (Toronto 1990) 185.
72 Heylin, *Briefe and moderate answer*, 26.

'further then warranted by Law', Heylin granted Charles unlimited power and required subjects to give him absolute obedience.[73] He castigated Burton for taking a different line: 'And you Master *Burton* have condemned that absolute obedience unto Kings and Princes which is due to them from their subjects; and that unlimited power which is ascribed unto them, because theirs of right.'[74]

Heylin was, it is true, a theorist of obedience – but of obedience to the king rather than to the law. He held that rulers get their power from God alone, and not from the people, arguing that they are therefore accountable only to the deity, and subject only to limitations imposed by His laws. Kings had, indeed, graciously permitted their subjects various liberties over the years, and good kings would respect these and rule in a generally law-abiding manner. But if kings decided that it was necessary to order their subjects to break the law of the land they were fully entitled to do so, and subjects were bound to obey. The only circumstance in which people were justified in disobeying the king was if he required them to infringe the law of God Himself. 'It's true indeed', Heylin said, 'in things that are directly contrary to the law of God, & such as carry in them a plaine and manifest impietie, there is no question to be made, but it is *better to obey God then man.*' But if the king commanded you to do things that were not against God's law, it was your duty to obey. It was no good arguing that his orders conflicted with the laws of the realm, even if they were of the most sacrosanct and fundamental kind. If individuals could refuse to obey the king any time some puritan politician told them that his commands broke fundamental law, the monarch would be unable to govern the country properly, and the individual would suffer. 'For put the case', he told Burton, 'the King in necessary and emergent causes, touching the safety of the kingdome, demand the present ayd of all his subjects; and any *Tribunitian* spirit should informe them, that this demand is contrary unto the *fundamentall lawes of state*: according to your rule, the subject is not bound to obey the King, nay he might refuse it, although the businesse doth concern especially his owne preservation.'[75] Heylin believed that kings ought to abide by law in ordinary circumstances but were justified in breaking it if they thought that necessity demanded such a course, and subjects were obliged to obey their commands unless they infringed God's law. This was the same theory as Maynwaring's, and like his it legitimated such extra-Parliamentary levies as impositions, the Forced Loan and Ship Money.

Though Heylin placed obedience to the king above obedience to the law, he did not advise Charles to make a habit of ruling lawlessly, or to abolish all the laws of the land on a whim. He was not an advocate of the rule of anarchy, and therefore we could in some sense style him a proponent of the rule of law. The same goes for Bodin, Bossuet and virtually every other early modern absolutist, since they too were not anarchists. This does *not* show that Heylin

73 Ibid., 179.
74 Ibid., 156.
75 Ibid., 32.

shared the principles of Burton, or the House of Commons, or Algernon Sidney. They said that subjects had no obligation to obey royal commands or pay the king's financial exactions except if they were warranted by law. He said that they ought to do what the king ordered unless it conflicted with divine law – which was silent on things like the Forced Loan and Ship Money. They were opponents of absolutism. He was an absolutist – in the traditional sense, though not in the new revisionist sense which has turned absolutists into an exceedingly (indeed utterly) exclusive club.

Others who like Heylin argued that subjects ought to obey the king rather than the law of the land include James I and Thomas Jackson, Dean of Peterborough. Like Maynwaring and Sibthorp, they claimed that people should obey the Prince provided that his commands did not conflict with those of God. The king, said James, was God's deputy, and the people's 'obedience, I say, ought to be to him, as to Gods Lieutenant in earth, obeying his commands in all things, except directly against God, as the commands of Gods Minister'.[76] The king was no anarchist, and never suggested that monarchs should embark on a systematic policy of subverting law. He recommended that they govern through law, and advised his son to manage kingly authority 'boldly, and yet temperately, not stretching his royall Prerogative but where necessitie shall require it'.[77] Subjects, however, were obliged to obey the king even if he ruled intemperately. They could never actively resist him, and they could disobey him only if he commanded 'directly against God'. Thomas Jackson similarly required subjects to obey their sovereigns in things which were not 'apparently repugnant to the laws of Christ'.[78] It has been suggested that he was 'no absolutist' on the grounds that 'his chief concern' was 'with resistance theory rather than with extending the scope of royal authority'.[79] But absolutists commonly believed that the king's power was absolute, and hence that it did not need to be extended; and Bodin, Bossuet, Hobbes and virtually all other absolutists were concerned with resistance theory.

If subjects have a duty to obey extra-legal royal commands, then they must pay when the king asks for cash, whether or not his levies accord in all respects with the law of the land. Charles I took Ship Money, the Forced Loan, and tonnage and poundage, though all lacked parliamentary consent and were widely regarded as illegal. Both he and his father levied impositions

---

76 King James VI and I, *Political writings* 72.
77 Ibid., 249.
78 Thomas Jackson, *A treatise of Christian obedience*, in *The Works of Thomas Jackson, DD*, 12 vols (Oxford 1844) xii, 185–343, at 256.
79 Burgess, *Absolute monarchy*, 40. Burgess (ibid.) also argues that Jackson (in *Treatise of Christian obedience*, 330) could not have been an absolutist since 'he seems also to have believed that royal authority in England was most supreme or sovereign when exercised through "the highest court of this kingdom", parliament'; in a footnote Burgess states that this is 'admittedly a trifle ambiguous' (40 n. 98). Jackson did indeed call Parliament 'the highest court of this kingdom', but it is unclear why doing so, or saying that people ought to give especial weight to things the king did in the full formality of a Parliament – the representative body of the kingdom – should count as evidence that he was no absolutist. In France, royal edicts were registered in the Parlement of Paris, but French kings are and were commonly regarded as absolute monarchs.

on merchandise, again without obtaining Parliament's consent. From 1608, impositions were collected on a wide range of commodities, bringing in around £70,000 a year to begin with, and something near £250,000 by 1640. Since a parliamentary subsidy was worth not much more than £70,000 at the start of James's reign, and less later, it is understandable (as Russell observes) that the crown was tempted to hang on to impositions unless Parliament offered very convincing reasons why it should abandon them.[80] It never did, and both James and Charles got far more from impositions than they did from Parliament – raising a distinct question mark over the usefulness of that institution. In this book, we have seen evidence that the debate on impositions involved conflicts of political and constitutional principle, and that absolutists and their opponents brought different viewpoints to bear on the nature of the relationship between royal authority and individual rights of property. For instance, Sir John Davies used absolutist ideas to justify impositions, while many anti-absolutists argued that the duties infringed the subject's rights of property, and the fundamental rule that taxation requires Parliamentary consent. According to recent revisionist work, however, the debate on impositions involved no conflict on issues of principle, and neither Davies nor the others who sided with the king were absolutists.

The king's case on impositions – the revisionist argument runs – did not in any way impinge on the property rights of English subjects. Both in 1606 – when Bate's Case was tried – and in 1610 – when impositions were debated in Parliament – 'the crown's case clearly rested on the argument that impositions on imports were not a threat to the property rights of the king's subjects. Indeed, they had nothing to do with English property rights, which *were* protected by the common law.'[81] Those who defended extra-Parliamentary impositions were careful to argue that they 'were not a threat to common law because they were only applied in areas beyond the territorial jurisdiction of English common law' – namely 'the high seas'. So between 'the competing sides in the imposition debate there was substantial *theoretical* agreement. Everyone agreed that the common law protected property, within England at least, and that the king could not infringe upon property rights without his subjects' consent.' The king, said the Jacobean consensus – or so revisionists contend – had some rights of extra-Parliamentary action 'in areas where the common law had no force' like 'the high seas'. But in England monarchs could not tax without consent.[82] Davies endorsed this 'consensual position'. 'The essential point of this consensus', we are told, 'was that *domestic* property rights were within the sphere of the common law, and could not be infringed by the absolute prerogative'. According to the revisionist line, Davies emphatically

---

80 Russell, *Causes of the English Civil War*, 179–80. David Harris Sacks, 'The paradox of taxation: fiscal crises, Parliament, and liberty in England, 1450–1640', in Philip T. Hoffman and Kathryn Norberg, eds, *Fiscal crises, liberty, and representative government 1450–1789* (Stanford 1994) 8–66, at 44 (£250,000).
81 Burgess, *Politics of the ancient constitution*, 141.
82 Ibid., 141–2.

did *not* 'attempt to give the king an absolute prerogative of a sort that would enable him to override the requirements of the common law'.[83] In summary, the revisionist account states that impositions were levied only on imports, and only on the high seas. English writers who supported impositions, we are informed, defended them on the grounds that they had nothing to do with domestic property rights.

There is, at first sight, a certain oddity in the revisionist view that harmony reigned on the question of impositions. Back in the nineteenth century, in his classic Victorian account of early Stuart England, S.R. Gardiner declared that the crown's arguments for levying impositions – as presented in the judgments on Bate's Case of 1606 – were 'based on principles which would lead to the extinction of English liberty'. He claimed that the crown's position was subjected to a thorough examination in the Parliament of 1610, and that 'the superiority in argument was decidedly on the side of those who took the popular view of the subject'.[84] So Gardiner thought that two different sets of principles had been brought to bear on the question of impositions, and that one protected the subject's liberties, while the other threatened to undermine them. Burgess has rejected Gardiner's interpretation, arguing that he did not really understand what the debate was about. In Burgess's opinion, the crown and the Commons shared the same basic view. Yet if we glance at the records of the 1610 Parliament we find much evidence that is at odds with Burgess's account but close to Gardiner's. For instance, on 23 May the Commons formally petitioned the king about impositions. James had forbidden them to debate 'your Majesty's Right of Imposing upon your Subjects Goods exported or imported' (note, in passing, that they mentioned *exports* as well as imports), and in response they asserted the 'ancient, general, and undoubted Right of Parliament, to debate freely, all Matters which do properly concern the Subject, and his Right or State'. They went on to talk about the judgment in Bate's Case, which had vindicated the king's power to collect impositions. Far from endorsing the principles underlying that judgment, they informed the king that 'a general Conceit is had' that the 'Reasons of that Judgment may be extended much farther, even to the utter Ruin of the ancient Liberty of this Kingdom, and of your Subjects Right of Propriety of their Lands and Goods'.[85] So they saw the king's case on impositions as a threat to rights of property in general. On 7 July they petitioned the king once more, condemning impositions on the grounds that subjects 'have such a propriety, as may not without their consent be altered or charged'.[86] But Burgess tells us that impositions did not threaten property. Perhaps the Commons were simply too dull-witted to perceive this. Or perhaps they knew what they were talking about. The evidence supports the latter interpretation.

83 Ibid., 147.
84 S.R. Gardiner, *History of England from the accession of James I to the outbreak of the Civil War 1603–1642*, 10 vols (1883) II, 6.
85 *CJ* 431.
86 *PP 10*, II, 266.

The early Stuart kings got very large sums of money from impositions, so it would seem on the face of it that they *did* affect people's property. Burgess suggests that they did not threaten *domestic* property rights, since they were levied on *imports* as they crossed the high seas. The goods in question – so his case runs – belonged to *foreigners*, not to English people. 'When Bate's goods were taxed', he informs us, 'they were Venetian not English'.[87] So impositions did not endanger English property rights. This argument is open to the decisive objection that from 1608 impositions were in fact levied on *exports* as well as imports, and on goods belonging to English as well as foreign merchants. Merchants passed on the cost to the consumer at large, who therefore paid more. Manifestly, they affected English property.

Moreover, the principles enunciated by Chief Baron Fleming in Bate's Case suggested that the king could levy duties not just on exports and imports but (as Kenyon says) 'on any commodity at any time'.[88] Fleming argued that in addition to his ordinary legal powers the king also had an 'absolute power' to govern for 'the general benefit of the people'. The king, he said, used his ordinary power when he dealt with matters that related to people's private rights. His absolute power, on the other hand, concerned *salus populi* – the public good. This absolute power was to be exercised 'according to the wisdom of the King for the common good' and 'all things done within these rules are lawful'. These words could easily be read as empowering the king to levy any extra-Parliamentary tax that he happened to think was in the public interest. It is difficult to read them in any other way. True, Fleming pointed out that the goods which Bate imported had belonged to Venetians, and not to the king's English subjects. In giving judgment on Bate's Case, he specifically refrained from spelling out whether James could impose duties on an English subject or English goods: 'That the king may impose upon a subject I omit; for it is not here the question if the king may impose upon the subject or his goods.'[89] Yet his general principles provided no grounds at all for denying the king a right to tax English goods, and in 1608 the king did just that, imposing duties on English merchants and their goods. In 1610, James and his supporters were eager to get cash from Parliament, and they assured the Commons that his majesty would not extend impositions to internal trade. On 22 May Sir Julius Caesar, the Chancellor of the Exchequer, told them that 'there was never thought in his Majesty nor any his counsel that he might impose upon land commodities'. In the Commons, many were unimpressed, and on the following day the House approved the petition against impositions

87 Burgess, *Politics of the ancient constitution*, 141. There is much useful information on impositions in Menna Prestwich, *Cranfield: politics and profit under the early Stuarts: the career of Lionel Cranfield Earl of Middlesex* (Oxford 1966), esp. 30–1, 119–20, 147–8, 178–80, 186–90.
88 J.P. Kenyon, *The Stuart constitution 1603–1688: documents and commentary* (Cambridge 1966) 55. On Fleming, see also G.R. Elton, *Studies in Tudor and Stuart politics and government*, I (Cambridge 1974) 269. Elton and Kenyon both adopt an interpretation of Fleming's judgment in Bate's Case which differs sharply from that of Burgess, suggesting that there is no consensus on this point amongst revisionists.
89 Kenyon, ed., *Stuart Constitution*, 62–3.

– the petition which claimed that the judgment in Bate's Case undermined rights of property in general. Individual members spoke to the same effect. The lawyer Thomas Wentworth was unhappy with James's stance because he thought that it permitted the king and not the law to decide on the validity of taxes, and that it justified taxation without consent. As he read the royal case, it said that kings are empowered to levy extra-Parliamentary taxes, but that good kings will mercifully refrain from doing so. Whitelocke similarly argued that the royal position threatened to overthrow 'the ancient frame of the commonwealth'.[90] Burgess has suggested that Fleming's principles ruled out all extra-Parliamentary levies except on the import of goods belonging to foreigners. Fleming and the Commons, he claims, shared the same principles. There is no evidence for this.

According to Burgess, Sir John Davies was yet another devotee of the consensual anti-absolutist view on impositions. Davies was a common lawyer and judge who wrote a book about impositions late in the reign of James I. In 1626 Charles introduced the Forced Loan, which was widely regarded as illegal. Later, of course, Maynwaring was impeached for preaching in its favour. Sir Randal Crew – Chief Justice of the King's Bench – had doubts about the Loan. So Charles sacked him, and gave his job to Davies.[91] This seems a little odd if Davies really did endorse the view that '*domestic* property rights' 'could not be infringed by the absolute prerogative' – as Burgess claims.[92] But Davies said no such thing. Far from arguing that English kings have no power to tax without consent, he strongly affirmed that they have every right to do so. The king of England, he declared, 'hath and ever had as absolute a Prerogative *Imponere vectigalia*, or to lay Impositions, as the Emperor of *Rome* or *Germany*, or any other King, Prince, or State in the world, now have, or ever had'.[93] So if you found evidence that a Roman emperor or any other ruler had possessed the power to impose taxes on some commodity, you could be sure that the king of England held the same power. Davies helpfully listed some of the things that the Roman emperors and others had used their absolute power to tax, including marriages, lawsuits, urine, prostitution, windows, salt, and innumerable other domestic goods and services.[94] Davies observed that the king of England levied impositions only on 'Merchandizes crossing the Seas', and that he did not tax domestic products 'by his absolute power alone'.[95] Did this mean that he believed '*domestic* property rights' 'could not be infringed by the absolute prerogative', as Burgess suggests? Emphatically not. Having listed the various exactions imposed by foreign sovereigns, Davies addressed the question of why English kings did not introduce similar

---

90 *PP 10*, ii, 108–9.
91 Gardiner, *History of England*, vi, 149. Hans S. Pawlisch, *Sir John Davies and the conquest of Ireland: a study in legal imperialism* (Cambridge 1985) 32.
92 Burgess, *Politics of the ancient constitution*, 147.
93 Sir John Davies, *The question concerning impositions* (1656), 148.
94 Ibid., 148–61.
95 Ibid., 148.

taxes: 'what is the reason of this difference? from whence commeth it? assuredly not from a different Power or Prerogative, for the King of *England* is as absolute a Monarch, as any Emperor or King in the world, and hath as many Prerogatives incident to his Crown'.[96] English kings were fully empowered to take domestic property without consent, but avoided doing so because of their 'bounty and noble nature', and because they owned enough land to refrain from burdening their subjects.[97] It was not the law but the king's goodness which protected English property rights. Like other absolutists, Davies did not recommend that James rule lawlessly. But he made it clear that in his opinion it was ultimately the king rather than the law that ruled in England.

We are sometimes told that practically the only absolutists in early Stuart England were a few eccentric and marginal clerics. Figures like Laud, Heylin, Saravia and Sibthorp were clerics but they were not marginal, and there were quite a few lay absolutists, often with powerful court connections. Some of them not only believed in absolutist theory, but also went to the trouble of writing books in which they expressed their views – though writing is a time-consuming and often thankless task, and it is unlikely that more than a tiny percentage of people who hold any particular political position write a book about it. Under James, lay absolutist writers included the king himself, the Regius Professor of Civil Law at Oxford (Gentili), the Regius Professor at Cambridge (Cowell), and the king's Attorney-General for Ireland, Sir John Davies – none of them minor or marginal figures. Under Charles, absolutist works were written by Sir Francis Kynaston, Sir Robert Filmer, and Thomas Hobbes, the friend and adviser of the leading courtier William Cavendish, Earl (and later Marquess and Duke) of Newcastle. Hobbes was a trenchant absolutist who wrote two classic works of political theory before the Civil War (*The Elements of Law* and *De Cive*).[98] Probably the most widely read early Stuart political writings nowadays are those of James I, Filmer and Hobbes. It is odd that they were all absolutist laymen and that revisionists tell us that there were virtually no absolutist laymen.

Contemporaries seem to have been unaware that the absolutist layman was an endangered species. Before the end of James's reign, one political commentator observed that the land was divided into 'regians & Republicans'. The former held that the king's 'absolute will' was 'the principall rule of all proceedings & obedience in the Commonwealth', while the latter argued that 'the peoples good is the chiefe end of all civill proceedings, and the rule of all such proceedings to be only the lawe of the land'.[99] This may well be an accurate depiction of things in about 1624. But by 1642 the king had the support of a great many moderates, who rejected absolutism. The absolutist inclinations of

---

96 Ibid., 161.
97 Ibid., 162–3.
98 Hobbes and his context are discussed in Johann P. Sommerville, 'Lofty science and local politics', in Tom Sorell, ed., *The Cambridge companion to Hobbes* (Cambridge 1996) 246–73.
99 Folger Mss V.a.24, 27–8.

Charles I helped to bring about a political crisis in 1640–42, when a number of constitutional moderates came to side with the king, often for social and religious reasons, and because the king ceded constitutional ground in 1641 – for instance agreeing to the Triennial Act and to the abolition of Ship Money, Star Chamber and High Commission. No historian seems ever to have suggested that all the royalists in the Civil War were absolutists. Yet the leading revisionist argues that the war could not have involved issues of political or constitutional principle since the king's supporters did not all stand for absolute – indeed, arbitrary – power, and the Parliamentarians did not promulgate a philosophy of resistance.

RESISTANCE

According to revisionists, the Civil War was not about differences of political or constitutional principle, for just as 'the spokesmen for Royalism in 1642 were not champions of arbitrary government', 'so those who spoke for the Parliamentarians were not, in the main, principled defenders of resistance', instead insisting that 'they were fighting in self-defence – the one ground on which prevailing theory regularly recognized resistance to be lawful'.[100] There are a number of problems with this interpretation. Firstly, it has the awkward implication that French absolutists and resistance theorists in fact agreed with one another. In France, people like Bodin and Bossuet put forward views which are usually seen as absolutist, but they were careful to stress that they did *not* advocate arbitrary government. Rabid anti-absolutists – such as Hotman, Beza and the author of the *Vindiciae contra Tyrannos* – permitted active resistance to tyrants, but emphasised that it had to be in self-defence. On the revisionist account, there was therefore no disagreement between people who adopted Bodin's views and those who followed the *Vindiciae*. Yet the two groups did argue against one another, and there *were* French Wars of Religion – just as there *was* an English Civil War.

Secondly, it is simply false to claim that people in early-seventeenth-century England agreed that self-defence is a legitimate reason for resisting kings. Parliamentarian pamphleteers in the Civil War, and later John Locke, were extremely keen to discover earlier authors whose general political position favoured strong monarchical power but who allowed resistance in a few exceptional circumstances. Just as the absolutist William Wilkes found it inviting to cite Fortescue against the puritans, so the anti-absolutist Locke cited William Barclay – 'the great Champion of Absolute Monarchy' – and the Elizabethan Bishop Thomas Bilson – 'a great Stickler for the Power and Prerogative of Princes' – as admitting that in extreme cases the people *could* defend itself against its ruler. Indeed, Locke quoted at some length from a passage in which Barclay allowed resistance if the ruler planned 'to ruine the Kingdome and Commonwealth', as when the Roman emperor Nero had 'resolved' to lay

100 Russell, *Causes of the English Civil War*, 132–3.

Rome waste 'with Fire and Sword', or when Caligula had expressed the wish that the Roman people 'had but one Neck, that he might dispatch them all at a blow'.[101] Of course, neither Charles I nor his sons went quite that far, and it is doubtful that people like Barclay and Bilson would have condoned resistance to them. Certainly, it was not wholly convincing to imply that such writers would have been Parliamentarians or Whigs if they had lived at the right time. Still, it was good propaganda to quote them, and if Locke had found more champions of 'Absolute Monarchy' who said such things he would doubtless have drawn on them too. Bilson and Barclay were repeatedly quoted by anti-absolutists because they were two of the very few sticklers for the royal prerogative who allowed resistance, albeit only in the most extreme circumstances. Bilson's book was published in 1585, and Barclay's in 1600. Later absolutists denied that kings could ever be resisted. James I, Saravia, Buckeridge, Filmer and like-minded writers emphatically did *not* permit people to take up arms against the king in self-defence. If kings ruled tyrannically, they said, prayers and tears were the people's only resort.

The German resistance theorist David Paraeus did indeed allow violent self-defence against rulers: 'in a case of necessity', he declared, 'it is lawful to defend yourself' by force even against the Prince. On the revisionist view, we might expect that his book would therefore have been welcomed by the English establishment. After all, revisionists assure us, talk about necessity was typical of common law discourse, and everyone agreed that people could fight against their ruler in self-defence.[112] In fact, the book was publicly burned

101 John Locke, *Two treatises of government*, ed. Peter Laslett (Cambridge 1988) 419–25 (second treatise, sections 232–9). The use of Bilson and Barclay in the Civil War and again in the 1680s is discussed in J.H.M. Salmon, *The French wars of religion in English political thought* (Oxford 1959) 82, 85, 154–7.

102 David Owen, *Anti-Paraeus* (Cambridge 1622) 74–80; 'in casu necessitatis licita est defensio' (76; quoting Paraeus). Although Russell (*Causes of the English Civil War*, 133) affirms that 'prevailing theory regularly recognized' self-defence as a ground for resistance, it seems that this position is not endorsed by all revisionists. For Burgess argues that justifications of resistance on the grounds of self-defence were very rare. Discussing the Jacobean cleric Andrew Willet, Burgess informs us that 'he was one of the very few explicit resistance theorists to be found in Jacobean England', and that 'he gave an extremely cautious vote of approval for a limited theory of resistance – or, more properly of self-defence' (Burgess, *Absolute monarchy*, 10–11). Burgess portrays Willet as a follower of Paraeus on the question of resistance, but notes that he added a number of qualifications to Paraeus' theory. Arguably, these qualifications are so stringent that they virtually destroy the theory, and he might better be described as a critic rather than a follower of the German. Willet distinguished between resistance to tyrannical rulers by 'the Civil state' on the one hand, and by private individuals on the other. In the first case, he declared, resistance is lawful only in a few special circumstances – for instance, if 'the land is oppressed by foreign invaders' or 'where the government is altogether elective, as the Empire of Germany'. Secondly, private individuals are authorised to resist the Prince only in a few rare cases, which Willet specified: for instance, they could not resist to defend property but only life itself, and they could not make any 'assault upon the person of their Prince, to put his life in danger': Andrew Willet, *Hexapla: that is, a six-fold commentarie upon . . . Paul to the Romanes* (1620) 592–4. Burgess (*Absolute monarchy*, 11) argues that Willet was most unusual in giving cautious approval to a theory of resistance in self-defence, and this is correct, though it contradicts Russell's thesis. However, Burgess is less convincing in arguing that because Willet 'suffered no trouble for expressing these ideas' it was perfectly safe to voice theories of resistance (ibid.). For Willet's ideas scarcely amount to a theory of resistance. See also pp. 253–4 below.

at Oxford, Cambridge and London, and the University Press of Cambridge brought out a detailed refutation of it – David Owen's *Anti-Paraeus*, dedicated to James I. Far from endorsing the German's ideas about self-defence, Owen utterly condemned them, insisting that the only remedies for persecuted subjects were 'flight, endurance, prayers, and tears'.[103] Thomas Hobbes was just about alone amongst early-seventeenth-century absolutists in permitting people to defend themselves by resisting the king – and this was one of the doctrines that royalists most strongly objected to in his theory.[104]

A third objection to the revisionists' case on resistance is that they usually talk about resisting the king's person, but ignore the fact that resistance can also mean fighting against his supporters. Their argument runs more or less like this: if the Civil War had ideological origins, we would expect there to have been deep-rooted disagreements between people who wanted arbitrary government and others who justified taking up arms against the king. But there were few advocates either of arbitrary rule or of employing force to depose or injure the monarch. Therefore, the Civil War did not have ideological origins.[105] Unfortunately, revisionists do not make clear just why ideological division should have taken that particular form, rather than focusing on, say, property rights, or royal powers of imprisonment. Another problem is that it proves very little indeed to show that before 1642 few people advocated employing force against the monarch's person. In the early years of the Civil War Parliamentarians said that they were fighting not against the king's person, but against his evil advisers, and it is likely that many of them believed what they said. So they went to war because they thought that it was justifiable or even obligatory to take up arms against the monarch's wicked counsellors, not against the monarch himself. If we want to trace the history of the ideas that led them into war, therefore, we should look at the development of the notion that people may use force not against the person of the king but against evil advisers. At least some members of Parliament do seem to have adopted that notion quite clearly by 2 March 1629, when the Speaker was held down in his chair while Sir John Eliot's resolutions were read denouncing as enemies of the kingdom those who favoured Arminianism and extra-Parliamentary taxation. Arguably the idea's roots stretched far further back, influencing the Commons' actions towards Cowell in 1610 and the impeachments of the 1620s. Initially, people tried to use the law to counter absolutist ideas and policies. When that failed, they resorted to force.

In the Civil War, royalists *denied* that subjects are justified in fighting against the king's servants. This idea, too, had earlier origins. While some held the Speaker in his chair in 1629, others moved to free him. There was, indeed, something slightly ludicrous about the claim that using violence against a royal official who was carrying out royal orders was not resisting the king himself. As Henry Ferne observed in 1643, it was ridiculous to draw too fine

103 Owen, *Anti-Paraeus*, 80: 'fuga, patientia, preces, & lachrymae'.
104 Jean Hampton, *Hobbes and the social contract tradition* (Cambridge 1986) 197–207.
105 A very fine statement of this position is in Russell, *Causes of the English Civil War*, 131–5.

a distinction between resisting the king's servants and resisting the king himself. Even the most energetic ruler had to employ subordinates to carry out his orders, and if you permitted active resistance to them you effectively allowed people to thwart the king's own policies by force. It was absurd to suggest that 'the Soveraigne could by himselfe execute his Commands without under Ministers of power; so that the resisting of them, acting by the power which he has committed to them, is a resisting of him'.[106] In the words of the Elizabethan cleric John Bridges, it was 'the common practise of the arrantest rebels' to pretend that their quarrel was not 'directlie against the *prince*' but against counsellors who had abused him.[107] Like Civil War royalists, Bridges granted subjects no right of resistance to so-called wicked counsellors. The same was true of many others. James I and like-minded writers certainly did not allow subjects to assault officials engaged in carrying out the king's orders.

A fourth objection to the revisionist thesis is that resisting the person of the ruler had long been equated with popery. In post-Reformation English polemic, it was papists who deposed and assassinated kings, while good Protestants fought against wicked and rebellious Catholics, not against godly rulers. Parliamentarians denied that they were resisting the king because they wanted to distance themselves from activities traditionally considered popish – and not because ideological harmony reigned between them and Laud or Strafford, whose heads they cut off.

Fifthly, it could be dangerous to assert the legitimacy of resisting tyrants. The Oxford cleric John Knight followed Paraeus' theory on resistance, and was imprisoned for his pains although he kept his remarks at a theoretical level and did not apply the theory to English practice. The Cambridge lecturer Isaac Dorislaus was silenced for arguing that subjects may sometimes resist their sovereigns, though he avowedly intended only to justify the Dutch Revolt against Spain – a revolt which English governments had themselves supported.[108] One recent revisionist notion – advanced by Glenn Burgess – is that it was perfectly fine to put forward theories of resistance provided that you did not say things which 'produced seditious or treasonable *action*'.[109] The expression of abstract *theories* on resistance, he informs us, was unproblematical. The cases of Knight, Dorislaus and others do not confirm this, and Burgess is able to cite just a single example to support his viewpoint – the cleric Andrew Willet. In one work, says Burgess, Willet set out what was 'at best a hesitant and heavily qualified endorsement of resistance theory', but in another 'he closely followed' the ideas of 'the notorious David Paraeus'. However, Burgess proceeds, Willet 'did not follow Paraeus blindly or slavishly', for the German asserted that the church can excommunicate kings and Willet denied

106 Henry Ferne, *A reply unto severall treatises pleading for the armes now taken up by subjects* (1643) 85–6.
107 John Bridges, *A defence of the government established in the Church of Englande for ecclesiastical matters* (1587) 114.
108 See above, pp. 72, 74, 79.
109 Burgess, *Absolute monarchy*, 10.

it. Moreover, Paraeus said that kings may be coerced while Willet argued that
'"assaulting the Prince by force"' is '"most unlawfull"'. Burgess concludes
that 'Willet gave an extremely cautious vote of approval for a limited theory
of resistance'. On Burgess's own account, then, there was just one English
pre-Civil War writer who voiced resistance theory in a book that was openly
published in England and not suppressed by the authorities.[110] And that writer
found it expedient to be 'extremely cautious' in expressing a very much
diluted version of resistance thinking. This does not suggest that it was a good
idea to advocate resistance theory before 1640.[111]

A sixth and final objection to revisionist arguments on resistance is that calls
for violent revolution tend to be made when conflict moves from the intellectual to the military arena. People justify resistance when they are thinking of
taking up arms to attain their goals. As long as they believe they can get their
way by non-violent means – for instance, through the law courts – they are
likely to keep quiet about rights of resistance. To tell a king that if he does not
give me what I want I have the authority to use force against him, is an
excellent way of inviting retaliation. The absence of calls for armed resistance
is no indication whatever that people are in fundamental agreement. The
Parliaments of the 1620s did not urge subjects to take up arms against such
men as Laud or Maynwaring, though many members believed that both were
guilty of giving the king wicked advice. They did not advocate making war
on the king's evil advisers, for they hoped they could persuade the king by
other means. On the face of it, the impeachment of Maynwaring suggests that
many in Parliament found his ideas obnoxious; and the king's decision to
pardon him implies that Charles I was unconvinced of the error of Roger's
ways. But a recent revisionist account has suggested that Maynwaring's real
problem was less that he had unpopular ideas than that he chose his words
badly in expressing them. Rather like the careless and ham-fisted Cowell, it is
said, Maynwaring used vocabulary that people found inappropriate. It was his
insensitivity towards linguistic conventions which brought about his troubles.
The next section surveys the thesis that early-seventeenth-century politics was
structured around a series of linguistic conventions which served to maintain
consensus.

THE LANGUAGES OF POLITICS AND THE RULES STRUCTURING CONSENSUS

In the early days of revisionism, we were told that practically everyone in
England shared a single set of political and constitutional ideas. It was this
position that the first edition of *Politics and Ideology* set out to challenge. Some
revisionists still stick to their old guns. Conrad Russell, for example, takes the

110 Examples of illicit publications which permitted kings to be resisted or deposed in certain
circumstances include Paul Baynes, *The diocesans tryall* (Amsterdam 1621) 88–9, and John Ponet's
Short treatise of politike power (Paris 1639).
111 Burgess, *Politics of the ancient constitution*, 10–11. Arguably, Willet's position hardly deserves
to be called resistance theory at all: see n. 102 above.

line that the dominant ideology on the eve of the Civil War was one which stressed the rule of law but allowed monarchs to be resisted in self-defence.[112] His basic claim is that only very few people dissented from the prevailing theory, and that those few were mostly eccentric and ignored clerics. Russell's arguments have been discussed at length elsewhere in this chapter, and in the book itself. This section is about a second revisionist thesis, expressed most forcefully by Glenn Burgess.

Burgess accepts that there were several different political theories current in early modern England, but argues that their proponents lived together in harmony, since each of the theories (or 'languages', as Burgess often prefers to call them) served different but mutually compatible purposes. In particular, there was a 'theological language of politics' and a quite distinct 'language of common law'.[113] The theological language employed 'such terms as God, providence, grace and order', while 'the language of the law . . . talks about politics using such concepts as custom, precedent, rights and liberties, prerogatives and so on'.[114] In contrast to other revisionists, Burgess frankly admits that there was no 'uniformity of opinion (or even of theory)' in Jacobean times. His argument is that 'most players in the political game' recognised that 'there were a variety of languages of politics, each appropriate in some areas and for some audiences'.[115] Just which language was suitable in what circumstances was defined by 'the unspoken conventions structuring consensus'.[116] People lived in harmony with one another despite holding different political theories, for they all subscribed to certain unspoken rules telling them when it was permissible to express which ideas. Since the rules were unspoken, Burgess has had to reconstruct them from early-seventeenth-century practice. He argues that the 'dominant language' for the discussion of most domestic political issues was the common law. Theological language was used principally to 'make statements of *moral* duty', but 'in *political* matters' was 'vague and unspecific'.[117] Talk of the Divine Right of Kings included some high-sounding claims about the origin and nature of royal power, but these were left purposely vague and were intended only to inculcate a general respect for authority and to counter Catholic ideas on papal power, not to say anything concrete about the rights and duties of kings and subjects in England. While other revisionists argue that harmony reigned because everyone agreed, Burgess claims that consensus worked because people got along with each other despite disagreements.

It might be helpful to give a concrete example or two of the kind of thing that Burgess has in mind. He provides a detailed discussion of the cases of

112 Russell, *Causes of the English Civil War*, 131–3.
113 Burgess, *Politics of the ancient constitution*, 174, 119. A critique of currently fashionable talk about the 'languages' of politics is in Sommerville, 'The ancient constitution reassessed: the common law, the Court and the languages of politics in early modern England', esp. 43–5.
114 Burgess, *Politics of the ancient constitution*, 116.
115 Ibid., 145.
116 Ibid., 149.
117 Ibid., 119, 138.

Sibthorp and Maynwaring.[118] Both preached in favour of the Forced Loan of 1626–27, and their sermons were published with official approval. Sibthorp's work was licensed by the Bishop of London on Laud's instructions, while Maynwaring's book appeared by the king's own special command. This was in 1627, when there was no Parliament meeting and when Charles was employing coercion to get people to pay the Loan – a levy which many thought was illegal because it flouted the principle that taxation requires the consent of Parliament. People who refused to pay the Loan were imprisoned on royal orders but not charged, since the king did not want the legality of the Loan tested in court. In 1628, however, he decided to try to work with Parliament once more. The Parliament attacked the Loan, and in the Petition of Right they condemned it – and all extra-Parliamentary taxation – as contrary to the ancient law of the land. They also condemned the imprisonment of those who had refused to pay the Loan, and they investigated the sermons of Sibthorp and Maynwaring, though in the end only the latter was impeached. The House of Lords sentenced him to imprisonment during its pleasure, heavily fined him, and perpetually disabled him from holding any office in church or state. After Maynwaring had been impeached, and after Charles had approved the Petition of Right, Parliament finally voted the king taxes. Once he had been granted the cash, Charles pardoned and promoted Maynwaring. Later, he made him a bishop. When the Long Parliament met in 1640, it soon began inquiries into the writings of people like Maynwaring, who had argued strongly in favour of absolute royal power. Fearing that his manuscript work on the *Elements of Law* would be held against him, Thomas Hobbes took flight for France – the first of all that fled. As Hobbes told his friend John Aubrey, Maynwaring preached his own doctrine. If ideas like Maynwaring's were called in question, it seemed likely that Hobbes's would be too.[119]

When Parliaments were not in session, people like Hobbes and Maynwaring – and earlier Cowell – seem to have been perfectly safe. The absolutist ideas which they advocated were unpopular in Parliament, but far more acceptable to king and Court. At times when kings had to co-operate with Parliaments – usually because they needed money – outspoken absolutists could find themselves in danger – and this was a good reason for not being too outspoken. Maynwaring was especially trenchant in spelling out the practical implications of his views, and so he was punished. Others were more circumspect, but a number of people in Parliament believed that theories like his were alarmingly common, particularly amongst the clergy.[120] They punished him because they thought his views were widespread and influential, and not the ravings of a lone eccentric.

118 Ibid., 173–7. See also pp. 119–24 above.
119 John Aubrey, *'Brief lives', chiefly of contemporaries*, ed. Andrew Clark, 2 vols (Oxford 1898) I, 334. In 1641 Hobbes told Viscount Scudamore that he left England when he 'saw words that tended to aduance the prerogatiue of kings began to be examined in Parlament': *The correspondence of Thomas Hobbes*, ed. Noel Malcolm, 2 vols (Oxford 1994) I, 115.
120 See above, p. 111.

The general principles which underlay Maynwaring's arguments were, indeed, commonplace amongst highly-placed clerics, and shared by such writers as Filmer and Kynaston, both of whom had Court connections. Indeed, these last two made the practical consequences of their theory as evident as did Maynwaring himself. But it was the cleric who got into trouble. This was because his writings were published while theirs remained in manuscript until much later (Kynaston's work never has been printed), because his sermons were authorised by the king, and because he was associated with a hated royal policy – the Forced Loan. On the face of it, the reason why Maynwaring was attacked by members of Parliament seems clear: he was an absolutist who defended the Forced Loan, while they were anti-absolutists who said that it was illegal and unconstitutional. And it seems fairly manifest, too, that a leading reason why others did not spell out the implications of absolutist theory quite so publicly and in quite such detail as Maynwaring was that they wanted to avoid his fate. Maynwaring derived his central claims from the writings of other churchmen, including Saravia and Bishops Lancelot Andrewes and John Buckeridge. His general position was also close to that of such lay absolutists as Filmer and Kynaston. Not all that much later, Hobbes was to adopt a theory that he himself regarded as the same as Maynwaring's. Perhaps he had done so already. Certainly, he helped to collect the Forced Loan in Derbyshire.[121]

Let us turn now to Burgess's interpretation of the cases of Maynwaring and Sibthorp. He admits that their broad political theory was much the same as that of other clerics: 'In terms of basic theory there seems to be little to distinguish this pair from numerous other employers of the theological language of politics.' What separates them from the rest, says Burgess, is that they flouted the 'unspoken conventions structuring consensus' – just as Cowell had done earlier. In particular, they broke 'the convention requiring vagueness'.[122] According to Burgess

The Commons' Declaration against Manwaring also made it clear that the really obnoxious thing in his work was the destruction of the opinion that 'the free subjects of England do undoubtedly inherit this right and liberty, not to be compelled to contribute any tax, tallage, or aid, or to make any loans, not set or imposed by common consent.' The other things objected to in Manwaring's sermon were incidental to this central matter: he used the language of divine right not in its proper place but to undermine the role of the common law.[123]

One quite remarkable feature of this passage is that the words quoted from the Declaration say nothing whatever about the proper use of the language of divine right, but that Burgess nevertheless concludes that this was the 'central matter' at issue in the document. It is exceedingly hard to see how the

121 SP 16/79/67. I am grateful to Richard Cust for this reference.
122 Burgess, *Politics of the ancient constitution*, 174.
123 Ibid., 176.

Declaration supports the idea that what the Commons really disliked about Maynwaring was his linguistic insensitivity. In fact, they said nothing at all about it, either in the Declaration or anywhere else. They objected strongly to his views on royal power and especially to his claim that in emergencies the king could tax without consent. But they said not a word about his linguistic improprieties, and not a syllable to suggest that what they really found objectionable about him was his tactless and ham-fisted disregard for unspoken conventions regarding the use of language.

Of course, the English are well-known for social conventions which people from other countries sometimes find confusing and difficult to understand. If you pass the port the wrong way at dinner you run the risk of not being invited back. Such conventions are not wholly unspoken, but it can occasionally be hard to find out exactly what you have done wrong, and why the invitations stop arriving. Usually, though, a thorough search of books on etiquette will be enough to tell you where you have been going astray, and enable you to start filling your social calendar again. Burgess's account suggests that Maynwaring was taken to task for breaching unspoken conventions on the use of certain words and phrases. Oddly, however, no books of etiquette seem to have survived forbidding the use of theological language in political contexts, and neither the Commons nor Maynwaring appear to have suspected that he was impeached for using language badly. Nor did anyone else. Hobbes fled from England because he thought that his own views were close to Maynwaring's. But Hobbes used a secular and philosophical rather than a theological vocabulary. He was rightly fearful because he knew that what the Commons objected to was absolutist ideas, not inappropriate prose style.

Burgess argues that unspoken conventions on the use of language maintained political consensus under James I, but that in Charles's reign consensus decayed as the country slid into Civil War. If this is so, then clearly the unspoken conventions were extremely important in allowing the English to keep the peace despite their disagreements. And that raises the question of why the conventions remained unspoken, particularly when consensus began to break down and civil war loomed. Of course, we English are famous for our stiff upper lips, and our ability to endure hardship in silence. But surely someone would have tried to avert the catastrophe of war by reminding people of the unspoken conventions – if they had existed. Yet they remained unspoken until their recent discovery by Burgess.

Burgess informs us that one of the most important unspoken conventions demanded that theological talk about politics should be vague and should steer clear of sensitive practical questions about the rights and duties of kings and subjects in England. The mistake which such ham-fisted folk as Cowell, Maynwaring and Sibthorp made – he tells us – was to apply religious or scriptural conceptions to problems which people saw as essentially legal in nature, like royal rights of taxation.[124] If this were so, we would expect that

124 Ibid., 174.

members of Parliament who attacked Maynwaring and the rest would themselves have been careful to avoid theological language when they discussed English rights. And we might also expect that Parliament would have called in question any *anti*-absolutists who used theological terminology to talk about politics. In the 1630s writers such as Burton, Bastwick and Prynne employed religious language to launch scathing attacks on the king's evil advisers. Much of what they had to say was political in nature, yet they freely used theological language to say it. Burton, for instance, declared that the king 'hath entered into Solemne and sacred Covenant with all his people' to respect their just liberties, and 'according to the Patterne of God himselfe' 'to demaund of them no other obedience, but what the good lawes of the Kingdome prescribe, and require'.[125] In Burton's opinion, God Himself had established limited monarchy. His sermons *For God, and the King* were saturated in religious imagery, but nevertheless trenchantly attacked the king's regime, accusing it of acting illegally and unconstitutionally. Burton, Prynne and Bastwick seem to have been unaware of the convention requiring that people be vague if they applied religious ideas to politics. Failing to spot anything vague in their writings, Star Chamber sentenced them to savage punishment in 1637. Crowds lined the streets to cheer them as they were taken to gaol. When the Long Parliament met in 1640, the Commons freed them from prison, reversed the sentences against them, and treated them as heroes and martyrs. It did not hold their lack of vagueness against them, nor call them to account for ham-fistedly misusing religious language to talk about politics. The Commons disliked absolutist ideas and liked anti-absolutist ones. They seem to have been unconcerned with nuances of style or vocabulary.

In fact, early Stuart people often larded their language with religious phrases and scriptural citations, even when they discussed politics – and no one held it against them. Sometimes they used theological talk not just to enliven their speech, but to make a key argument on a precise legal or political point. In 1607, Nicholas Fuller drew on a number of biblical passages to show that the oath *ex officio* employed by High Commission was 'directly against the rule of the law of God', and ought therefore to be discontinued forthwith.[126] In the Commons that same year, a bill was discussed which would have given jurors the power to refuse to hear the testimony of witnesses they deemed unreliable. Sir Anthony Cope argued that they should be granted no such right, since the book of Deuteronomy showed that we must search before we can judge, and a jury can search only by hearing witnesses. Sir George More took the opposite view – but again used Scripture to make his case.[127] One of the hottest issues discussed by Parliament in 1628 was the Forced Loan and the

125 Henry Burton, *For God, and the king: the summe of two sermons preached on the fifth of November last in St. Matthewes Friday-Streete* (1636) 42.
126 Nicholas Fuller, *The argument of Master Nicholas Fuller, in the case of Thomas Lad, and Richard Maunsell, his clients* (1607) 11.
127 *The Parliamentary diary of Robert Bowyer 1606–1607*, ed. David Harris Willson (Minneapolis 1931) 359–60.

imprisonment without cause shown of people who refused it. To prove that such imprisonment had been wrong, Sir Edward Coke – that great champion of the common law – cited what he termed 'the chiefest authority', namely Scripture itself, and in particular the Book of Acts, where he found it written that it is unreasonable to imprison people and not to specify the crimes they are charged with (Acts 25:27).[128] In all these instances, and in many more, religious language was used quite uncontroversially not to be vague, nor to attack papists, but to hammer home concrete political points.

So it is not true that early Stuart people maintained consensus by adhering to the unspoken convention that theological talk should never be used in politics. Such talk was regularly so used, and mostly no trouble resulted. If people employed religious language to boost royal power too much then they could get in trouble with Parliament, as Maynwaring did. If they employed it to speak too unkindly of royal policy then the king and his supporters might call them to account (as they did Edmond Peacham in 1615, and the puritan triumvirate in 1637). No one was concerned with unspoken rules on the appropriate use of theological language – and that is why they were never mentioned.

It is true that divine right theorists usually avoided applying their ideas to concrete English circumstances in anything like as explicit a way as Cowell or Maynwaring. Burgess argues that this was because they wanted to maintain consensus, and deduces that people like Maynwaring were punished for infringing rules which most obeyed. But the cases of Cowell and Maynwaring themselves show that there were major disincentives to spelling out the practical implications of divine right thinking. There are other examples which confirm that point. In 1610, Richard Martin introduced a bill in the Commons calling for ferocious penalties against clerics who opposed the subject's liberties. He claimed that absolutist sermons were delivered daily, and he wanted the practice stamped out.[129] In 1627, the Bishop of London's chaplain was asked to license Sibthorp's notorious sermon in favour of the Forced Loan. He did so, but soon had second thoughts, and decided to consult the famous lawyer John Selden. Selden circumspectly refused to put his views in writing, but he told the chaplain that licensing the book had not been a good idea: 'If ever the Tide turn, and matters be called to a reckoning', he said, 'you will be hanged for publishing such a Book.' The chaplain took his advice, and scraped out his name from the licence.[130]

According to Burgess, the theories of people like Sibthorp were commonplace amongst clerics, but most wanted to maintain harmony and so refrained from spelling out the practical implications of their ideas; those who did spell them out risked severe punishment, for the authorities were also keen to safeguard consensus. On similar grounds, we can easily prove that harmony ruled in the Old Soviet Bloc, and, indeed, just about anywhere that people are

128 *PP 28*, ii, 102.
129 *PP 10*, ii, 328–9.
130 John Rushworth, ed., *Historical collections*, 7 vols (1659–1701) i, 444.

not actually fighting a civil war. True, there were dissidents in Russia and Eastern Europe. But most of them did not spell out the more extreme consequences of their thinking. This can be read as showing that they upheld unspoken conventions structuring consensus. Those who broke the conventions risked punishment, and a number were imprisoned or suffered worse fates. This can be used as evidence that society would not tolerate the extremist attacks on the consensual viewpoint of modern Maynwarings and Cowells, whose ham-fistedness marked them out for re-education. If this is consensus, it is difficult to see what counts as conflict. But revisionists insist that consensus *did* indeed prevail in England until quite shortly before the Civil War began. The conclusion to this Retrospect briefly surveys their views on the issue, and reflects in general on revisionism.

CONCLUSION: REVISIONISM, CONSENSUS, AND THE CAUSES
OF THE ENGLISH CIVIL WAR

Revisionists agree that consensus – not conflict – was the keynote of politics in England until shortly before the Civil War. But they do not agree on the nature of the consensus. According to J.P. Kenyon, early-seventeenth-century England was a place where everyone 'spoke the same language'[131] – by which he means not that they spoke English, but that they all endorsed the same political ideas and expressed them in the same vocabulary. On the other hand, Glenn Burgess specifically takes issue with Kenyon, rejecting the view that early Stuart England was 'some unlikely homogenised world in which everyone agreed and "spoke the same language"'.[132] According to Burgess, as we have seen, a number of different theories (or 'languages') were current, but their various proponents preserved harmony by silently endorsing unspoken rules structuring consensus – rules which eluded Kenyon and other revisionists, who do not mention them.

Although Burgess claims that a number of 'languages' were used in politics, he informs us that one of them was more important than the others. This was the language of the common law, which was (he asserts) not simply a language but a 'master-language'.[133] Englishmen in the early seventeenth century were, he tells us, 'typically, if to varying degrees, possessors of common-law minds'.[134] The 'common-law mind' was, indeed, 'a hegemonic *mentalité*', and the ancient constitutionalism with which it was linked was 'the shared language of an entire political nation'.[135] So although Kenyon was wrong to say that everyone 'spoke the same language', there was indeed a single shared language, and people typically possessed common-law minds, albeit to varying

131 Kenyon, ed., *Stuart constitution*, 9.
132 Glenn Burgess, review of Markku Peltonen, *Classical humanism and republicanism in English political thought, 1570–1640* (Cambridge 1995) paragraph 11, in Burgess's editorial in *Renaissance Forum* vol. 1, no. 1 (1996), at http://www.hull.ac.uk/renforum/v1no1/editoria.htm
133 Burgess, 'Common law and political theory', *Political Science* 40 (1988) 4–17, at 13.
134 Ibid., 4.
135 Burgess, *Politics of the ancient constitution* 231, 17.

degrees. There is a certain opacity or even confusion about some of this, and we might suspect that it was written in accordance with unspoken conventions requiring vagueness. For instance, it is not evident what is meant by the claim that the English all possessed common-law minds, though to varying degrees. On the face of it, this is about as helpful as saying that they all possessed wealth, though of different amounts – a perception which would be of limited use in the social and economic analysis of early modern England. The French almost all speak English to varying degrees, but despite the fears of the *Académie Française*, English does not yet seem to have become their hegemonic *mentalité*.

As we saw, Burgess took William Wilkes to be endorsing common law theory, since Wilkes quoted Fortescue. Of course, if we interpret any quotation from a common lawyer, however neutral or negative, to be evidence of approval, we can vastly swell the ranks of 'possessors of common-law minds'. Yet, despite using such generous criteria for what counts as one of these 'possessors' – criteria infinitely less strict than those he employs on candidate 'absolutists' – Burgess is able to produce remarkably few clear cases of common-law minds. He tells us, for instance, that a key thought which passed through such minds was that the Norman Conquest had no 'disruptive effects on legal continuity', but then presents evidence suggesting that few people took that line and that many argued the opposite. Perhaps the majority just possessed common-law minds in a very low degree.[136]

Burgess is also somewhat vague about *when* the 'common-law mind' became a 'hegemonic *mentalité*', and when it ceased to be one. He does tell us, though, that the 'classic age of common-law political thought, of ancient constitutionalism' was 'remarkably short. It took shape in the Elizabethan period, went through its "classic phase" in James's reign, and was gradually battered to death by his son.'[137] Perhaps it is no wonder that other historians have failed to spot the transient hegemony of the common-law mind. Conrad Russell, the *doyen* of revisionists, has written extensively on the Parliaments of the 1620s. In 1628 the Commons debated the subject's liberties at especially great length, and we might expect that then if ever they would have made plain the hegemony of ancient constitutionalism. Yet Russell concluded that Pym was 'one of the surprisingly few vocal adherents' of the 'doctrine of the ancient constitution' in that Parliament.[138] Sir Geoffrey Elton – the founding father of revisionism – held that the English possessed statute-law minds rather than common-law ones. In the 1530s, he argued, Thomas Cromwell had advocated the sovereignty of laws made by the monarch-in-Parliament, and this remained the agreed viewpoint long afterwards, though harmony was

136 J.P. Sommerville, 'The ancient constitution reassessed: the common law, the Court and languages of politics in early modern England', 52–4.
137 Burgess, *Politics of the ancient constitution*, 230.
138 Conrad Russell, 'The Parliamentary career of John Pym, 1621–9', in Peter Clark, Alan G.R. Smith and Nicholas Tyacke, eds, *The English commonwealth 1547–1660: essays in politics and society presented to Joel Hurstfield* (Leicester 1979) 147–65, at 161.

briefly and unaccountably disrupted in the 1640s, when the English started killing each other.

According to Elton, just about everyone agreed in rejecting the absolutist ideas of John Cowell. On the other hand, Kevin Sharpe suggests that Cowell's doctrine was in fact the standard position.[139] Like other revisionists, Sharpe stresses that consensus was the norm in early Stuart politics. Like the others, too, he has his own distinctive views on just what ideas it was that everyone endorsed. He does not always adhere to the (admittedly implausible) notion that consensus centred on theories of the sort that Cowell expressed – and that the Commons condemned. At one point, he affirms that the 'political theory of late sixteenth- and early seventeenth-century England was the theory of correspondency between the ordered macrocosm and the hierarchical microcosm of the state'.[140] But elsewhere he puts forward the rather different contention that the English did not really possess a political theory at all, since 'the unity of their realm was never fundamentally challenged' and therefore 'English writers needed never to argue a philosophy of state'. Instead, they busied themselves 'with policies and personalities rather than with powers or fundamental principles'.[141] It was only when civil war came, he assures us, that there 'arose the fundamental questions concerning why men should subject themselves to government, what rights they had and could or should surrender, what limits there were to authority'. As a result of the war, he proceeds, such a thinker as Hobbes was for the first time 'forced to answer questions that would have been, quite literally, unnatural to his predecessors', and it was after the war that Hobbes 'wrote the first work of political philosophy in England', namely *Leviathan.*[142]

On Sharpe's account, then, English consensus rested not on the common law theory of the ancient constitution, nor on a theory of Parliamentary sovereignty dating back to the age of Thomas Cromwell, nor even on unspoken conventions demanding vagueness, but on a wholly non-theoretical approach to politics, perhaps occasionally tinged with some notions about macrocosm and microcosm. Although Sharpe's position is very different from its revisionist rivals, it is perhaps no more convincing than the rest. At a general level, it is open to the objection that the England he describes resembles 'some unlikely homogenised world in which everyone agreed and "spoke the same language"' – to borrow Burgess's words. It seems implausible that the English wholly refrained from asking fundamental political questions, given that their educational system placed great weight on the writings of Aristotle, Plato and other political philosophers. We might expect that at least a few English thinkers would have been led to reflect a little upon royal rights and duties by such events as the papal deposition of Elizabeth I, or the Gunpowder

139 Sharpe, *Faction and Parliament*, 14–15. See above, p. 238.
140 Sharpe, *Faction and Parliament*, 28.
141 Sharpe, *Sir Robert Cotton, 1581–1631: history and politics in early modern England* (Oxford 1979) 223.
142 Sharpe, *Politics and ideas in early Stuart England: essays and studies*, 67–8.

Plot. The French religious wars generated a great deal of writing about fundamental questions of political theory, and this literature attracted much interest in England. Indeed, a good deal of it was translated into English.[143] This looks a little strange if the English were not interested in political theory. Turning from the general to the particular, Sharpe's thesis is also open to the simple but devastating objection that Hobbes wrote about fundamental issues of political theory well before the Civil War began, for he had completed the *Elements of Law* by May 1640, and *De Cive* before the end of 1641. Both of these volumes were works of political philosophy of the highest sophistication, and both put forward theories that were largely indistinguishable from the one he presented in *Leviathan*. Amongst the many other books of political philosophy produced in England long before 1642, we might mention Filmer's *Patriarcha*, Saravia's *De Imperandi Authoritate*, and Hooker's *Laws of Ecclesiastical Polity*. Manifestly, people in England were perfectly capable of asking and answering key questions of political theory decades before the Civil War. People after 1642 found it worthwhile to publish or re-publish many political writings that had been composed before that date – including works by Hooker, Parsons, Owen, Ponet, Buchanan, James I, Filmer and Hobbes.

To sum up, revisionist writers all assert that consensus reigned in early Stuart England, but all offer different and incompatible accounts of just what principles lay at the heart of English agreement. This is rather odd. If the evidence did indeed demonstrate – as revisionists say it does – that the English all agreed in endorsing one set of ideas, or perhaps a couple of sets with some unspoken conventions regulating relations between them, then we would surely expect that the same evidence would tell us what the ideas in question are. If explorers returning from some newly discovered tribe inform us that its members all speak the same language, we might have no reason to doubt them. But we are likely to grow suspicious if one of them goes on to say that the language is Greek, while another tells us it is Latin, and a third asserts that they actually speak both French and German but have rules dictating which they use when. Indeed, we might well conclude that the testimony of these explorers is not really a very good guide to the tribe's language – or languages. Scepticism on this score would grow if it turned out that the tribe had in fact been well known for centuries, and that it had been widely and uncontroversially acknowledged that it spoke Swedish, Finnish and Danish. Revisionists invite us to believe that able and assiduous historians have for centuries mis-described the early seventeenth century as an age of conflict, and that they themselves are the first scholars to have observed that it was actually a period of consensus, during which everyone spoke the same language (or perhaps two or three languages), though it is not clear what it (or they) were. There may be good reasons for arguing as the revisionists do. In the 1970s and

---

143 The influence of the French debates on English thought before the Civil War is discussed in two excellent books: J.H.M. Salmon, *The French religious wars in English political thought*, 15–79; and (for the late sixteenth century) Lisa Ferraro Parmelee, *Good newes from Fraunce: French anti-League propaganda in Late Elizabethan England* (Rochester, NY 1996).

1980s – when revisionism rose – Britain underwent economic decline that was clearly linked to social and ideological divisions. Public-spirited citizens, anxious to avert the decline, had a motive for arguing (and, in time, believing) that such divisions were not part of the fabric of British life, but aberrations that had no precedent even in early Stuart times – just before that greatest of aberrations, the Civil War. Perhaps there are more reasons why people have subscribed to revisionism. But conformity to the evidence is not one of them.

Suggestions for Further Reading

The notes and references above list many of the works in which particular points can be followed up, so a full-scale bibliography would be unnecessarily repetitive. More helpful, perhaps, might be a few words on where the major themes surveyed in this volume can be pursued. Anyone who wants more detailed bibliographical information should consult *The Royal Historical Society annual bibliography of British history*. This very useful work appears each year and lists a great many books and articles on British history. It is well indexed and conveniently arranged by period and topic. The paragraphs that follow inevitably omit many excellent and important writings, but they should at least enable the reader to get an idea of the contours of recent debate, as well as some guidance on older but still serviceable works.

Important original writings on political theory are printed – sometimes in full, sometimes in extracts – in David Wootton, ed., *Divine Right and democracy: an anthology of political writing in Stuart England* (Harmondsworth 1986). Wootton's introduction and editorial commentary are valuable. An excellent series of books has helped to enlarge the conventional canon of texts and so to transform the study of political thought in the past decade or so: the Cambridge Texts in the History of Political Thought (or Blue Books, as they are familiarly known). The Series Editors are Raymond Geuss and Quentin Skinner, and, formerly, Richard Tuck. Individual volumes normally contain accurate and reliable texts, informative introductions, and useful editorial material. Particularly important for students of early Stuart English thought are: Sir Robert Filmer, *Patriarcha and other writings*, ed. Johann P. Sommerville (Cambridge 1991); Sir John Fortescue, *On the laws and governance of England*, ed. Shelley Lockwood (Cambridge 1997); James Harrington, *The commonwealth of Oceana, and A system of politics*, ed. J.G.A. Pocock (Cambridge 1992); King James VI and I, *Political writings*, ed. Johann P. Sommerville (Cambridge 1994); and Thomas Hobbes, *Leviathan*, ed. Richard Tuck (Cambridge 1991; revised 1996) (in this book I have cited *Leviathan* in C.B. Macpherson's old Penguin edition because I imagine that it is the one to which most readers will have easiest access; Tuck's edition in any case contains a table converting page numbers from Macpherson's; two other excellent recent editions of *Leviathan* are those edited by Edwin Curley, and by Richard Flathman and David Johnston).

The vast bulk of early-seventeenth-century political literature is available only in the original editions, or in microfilms of them. Peter Milward's *Religious controversies of the Jacobean age* (1978) lists many important items, especially on church–state relations. Collections of statutes, legal decisions, and other constitutional documents include Sir G.W. Prothero, ed., *Select statutes and other constitutional documents illustrative of the reigns of Elizabeth and James I* (Oxford 1913); S.R. Gardiner, ed., *The constitutional documents of the puritan revolution 1625–1660* (Oxford 1906); and J.R. Tanner, ed., *Constitutional documents of the reign of James I* (Cambridge 1930). J.P. Kenyon, *The Stuart constitution: documents and commentary* (Cambridge 1966 and 1986) exists in two somewhat different editions, though there is a great deal of overlap between them.

Easily the best single-volume survey of early modern European political thinking is J.H. Burns and Mark Goldie, eds, *The Cambridge history of political thought 1450–1700* (Cambridge 1991). Quentin Skinner's *The foundations of modern political thought*, 2 vols (Cambridge 1978) is a fine study of Renaissance and Reformation thought. Richard Tuck's *Philosophy and government 1572–1651* (Cambridge 1993) is a highly original and imaginative – if not always convincing – account of its subject. The fullest general survey of political thinking in early Stuart England is Margaret Atwood Judson, *The crisis of the constitution: an essay in constitutional and political thought, 1603–1645* (New Brunswick, NJ 1949; reissued with a foreword by J.H. Hexter 1988). It is very rich in quotations from primary sources, but follows C.H. McIlwain too closely in seeing the Civil War as a great watershed which secularised English political thinking and led people to digest the concept of sovereignty. J.W. Allen's *English political thought, 1603–1660, vol. 1, 1603–1644* (1938) contains brief accounts of the ideas of a number of important writers, but the theorist-by-theorist approach has defects: it involves repetition and makes themes difficult to follow. W.H. Greenleaf, *Order, empiricism and politics* (Oxford 1964), R. Eccleshall, *Order and reason in politics: theories of absolute and limited monarchy in early modern England* (Oxford 1978), and Stephen L. Collins, *From divine cosmos to sovereign state: an intellectual history of consciousness and the idea of order in Renaissance England* (Oxford 1989) all make suggestive points but are much more difficult than Judson or Allen. Useful collections of essays on early modern British political thought include Nicholas Phillipson and Quentin Skinner, eds, *Political discourse in early modern Britain* (Cambridge 1993), and J.G.A. Pocock with the assistance of Gordon J. Schochet and Lois G. Schwoerer, eds, *The varieties of British political thought 1500–1800* (Cambridge 1993). On Scottish thought, fundamental works are Roger A. Mason, ed., *Scots and Britons: Scottish political thought and the Union of 1603* (Cambridge 1994); and J.H. Burns, *The true law of kingship: concepts of monarchy in early modern Scotland* (Oxford 1996). Two important collections of essays about Court life and culture also contain interesting work on political thought: Linda Levy Peck, ed., *The mental world of the Jacobean Court* (Cambridge 1991); and R. Malcolm Smuts, ed., *The Stuart Court and Europe: essays in politics and political culture* (Cambridge 1996).

The classic account of the Divine Right of Kings is J. Neville Figgis, *The Divine Right of Kings* (Cambridge 1914) – a fine introduction which deals with the whole of Europe but concentrates on France and England, as does Johann P. Sommerville, 'Absolutism and royalism', J.H. Burns and Mark Goldie, eds, *The Cambridge history of political thought 1450–1700*, 347–73. J.H. Salmon's very important *The French religious wars in English political thought* (Oxford 1959) is highly informative on the connections between French and English theories, both absolutist and anti-absolutist. Glenn Burgess, *Absolute monarchy and the Stuart constitution* (New Haven 1996) attempts to show that absolutism scarcely existed in early Stuart England. A more ambitious exercise, in a similar vein, is Nicholas Henshall, *The myth of absolutism: change and continuity in early modern European monarchy* (1992). It argues that there were virtually no absolutists anywhere. Both Henshall and Burgess achieve their goals largely by redefining absolutists in a way that ensures none can be found. Conrad Russell's 'Divine rights in the early seventeenth century', in John Morrill, Paul Slack and Daniel Woolf, eds, *Public duty and private conscience in seventeenth-century England: Essays presented to G.E. Aylmer* (Oxford 1993) 101–20, argues that practically everyone believed in the Divine Right of Kings in early Stuart times. A response to Russell and Burgess on Divine Right and absolutism is Johann P. Sommerville, 'English and European political ideas in the early seventeenth century: revisionism and the case of absolutism', *Journal of British Studies* 35 (1996) 168–94. Some of Russell's views are surveyed in John Sanderson, 'Conrad Russell's ideas', *History of Political Thought* 14 (1993) 85–102. A useful work on the theory and practice of the royal succession is Howard Nenner, *The right to be king: the succession to the crown of England, 1603–1714* (Chapel Hill 1995). Still very useful on James I is C.H. McIlwain's introduction to his edition of *The political works of James I* (Cambridge, Mass. 1918). McIlwain is especially strong on Jacobean controversies with Catholics. Hobbes is perhaps best approached through Tom Sorell, ed., *The Cambridge companion to Hobbes* (Cambridge 1996). His political theory is discussed in its historical context in Johann P. Sommerville, *Thomas Hobbes: political ideas in historical context* (1992).

Patriarchal social and political thinking has attracted quite a lot of attention lately, as has patriarchal practice. Some important works are Gordon J. Schochet, *Patriarchalism in political thought: the authoritarian family and political speculation and attitudes especially in seventeenth-century England* (Oxford 1975), reissued, with a new introduction, as *The authoritarian family and political attitudes in 17th century England: patriarchalism in political thought* (New Brunswick 1988); Susan D. Amussen, *An ordered society: gender and class in early modern England* (Oxford 1988); Amy Louise Erickson, *Women and property in early modern England* (1993); Anthony Fletcher, *Gender, sex, and subordination in England,*

1500–1800 (New Haven 1995); Mary Lyndon Shanley, 'Marriage contract and social contract in seventeenth century English political thought', *Western Political Quarterly* 32 (1979) 79–91; Constance Jordan, 'The household and the state: transformations in the representation of an analogy from Aristotle to James I', *Modern Language Quarterly* 54 (1993) 307–26; and Margaret R. Sommerville, *Sex and subjection: attitudes towards women in early-modern society* (1995). The most famous political theorist of patriarchalism was Sir Robert Filmer, who is the subject of James Daly, *Sir Robert Filmer and English political thought* (Toronto 1979) – a book which rather overplays Filmer's originality.

Catholic political thought is well served by Thomas Clancy's *Papist pamphleteers* (Chicago 1964) – though this concentrates on Elizabeth's reign – and his 'English Catholics and the papal deposing power, 1570–1640', *Recusant History* 6 (1961–62) 114–40, 205–27; 7 (1963–64) 7–10. A recent study of a very important Catholic is Michael L. Carrafiello, *Robert Parsons and English Catholicism, 1580–1610* (Selinsgrove, Pa., 1998). The use of natural law arguments against absolutism by non-Catholics has received less attention. Contrasting accounts of John Selden are in Richard Tuck, *Natural rights theories: their origins and development* (Cambridge 1979) 82–100; Johann P. Sommerville, 'John Selden, the law of nature, and the origins of government', *Historical Journal* 27 (1984) 437–47; Tuck, *Philosophy and government 1572–1651*, 205–21; and Paul Christianson, *Discourse on history, law, and governance in the public career of John Selden, 1610–1635* (Toronto 1996). On the Civil lawyers, there is a fine book by Brian P. Levack – *The Civil lawyers in England 1603–1641: a political study* (Oxford 1973). It includes a chapter on their political thought. Levack is also the author of 'Law and ideology: the Civil law and theories of absolutism in Elizabethan and Jacobean England', in Heather Dubrow and Richard Strier, eds, *The historical Renaissance: new essays on Tudor and Stuart literature and culture* (Chicago 1988) 220–41.

The links between puritanism and social and political thought are explored in two older but still stimulating works – Michael Walzer's *The revolution of the saints: a study of the origins of radical politics* (1966), and Christopher Hill's *Intellectual origins of the English revolution* (Oxford 1965) – and also in Margo Todd's *Christian humanism and the puritan social order* (Cambridge 1987), though this is largely on an earlier period. A very well-researched and subtly argued book is Peter Lake's *Anglicans and puritans? Presbyterianism and English Conformist thought from Whitgift to Hooker* (1988). Lake discusses the religious and political ideas of Presbyterians and their opponents in the late-Elizabethan period, but his book contains a great deal that illuminates Stuart debates. A good guide to historical thinking is Daniel R. Woolf, *The idea of history in early Stuart England: erudition, ideology, and 'the light of truth' from the accession of James I to the Civil War* (Toronto 1990). Woolf has much to say about political ideas as well as historical scholarship.

The standard survey of common lawyers' attitudes towards history and the constitution used to be J.G.A. Pocock, *The ancient constitution and the feudal law* (Cambridge 1957; reissued with a new retrospective essay 1987), but recently

Glenn Burgess has revised and refined a number of Pocock's positions in his *The politics of the ancient constitution: an introduction to English political thought, 1603–1642* (1992). Moreover, the views of both Pocock and Burgess have come under attack. Pocock's arguments on common law thinking are examined in Johann P. Sommerville, 'History and theory: the Norman Conquest in early Stuart political thought', *Political Studies* 34 (1986) 249–61. A discussion of the ideas of both Pocock and Burgess is in Johann P. Sommerville, 'The ancient constitution reassessed: the common law, the Court and the languages of politics in early modern England', in R. Malcolm Smuts, ed., *The Stuart Court and Europe: essays in politics and political culture* (Cambridge 1996) 39–64. A good brief introduction to common law political thinking is Corinne Comstock Weston, 'England: ancient constitution and common law', in J.H. Burns and Mark Goldie, eds, *The Cambridge history of political thought 1450–1700*, 374–411. Sir Edward Coke's thought is discussed in Burgess, *Absolute monarchy and the Stuart constitution*, chapter 6, and in James R. Stoner, Jr., *Common law and liberal theory: Coke, Hobbes, and the origins of American constitutionalism* (Lawrence, Kan. 1992), part 1. A useful discussion of Coke's political career in the 1620s is S.D. White, *Sir Edward Coke and 'the grievances of the commonwealth', 1621–1628* (Chapel Hill 1979). The role of lawyers in politics is surveyed in W.J. Jones's valuable *Politics and the Bench: the judges and the origins of the English Civil War* (1971), and there is some excellent material on the same subject in J.S. Cockburn, *A history of the English assizes, 1558–1714* (Cambridge 1972). Important books on particular themes in legal and constitutional history include Michael Mendle, *Dangerous positions: mixed government, the Estates of the Realm, and the Answer to the xix propositions* (University, Ala. 1985); Corinne Comstock Weston and Janelle Greenberg, *Subjects and sovereigns: the grand controversy over legal sovereignty in Stuart England* (Cambridge 1981); Clayton Roberts, *The growth of responsible government in Stuart England* (Cambridge 1966); Corinne Comstock Weston, *English constitutional theory and the House of Lords, 1556–1832* (1965); and J.W. Gough, *Fundamental Law in English Constitutional History* (1955). A collection of essays on various themes connected with Parliament and liberty is J.H. Hexter, ed., *Parliament and liberty from the reign of Elizabeth to the English Civil War* (Stanford 1992). The history of republicanism has recently been attracting a great deal of interest. J.G.A. Pocock's *The Machiavellian moment: Florentine political thought and the Atlantic republican tradition* (Princeton 1975) remains the most influential book on the subject. Two important recent works are Markku Peltonen, *Classical humanism and republicanism in English political thought 1570–1640* (Cambridge 1995), and Quentin Skinner, *Liberty before liberalism* (Cambridge 1998).

Good recent accounts of political history are: Mark Kishlansky, *A monarchy transformed: Britain 1603–1714* (1996), a very clear, readable narrative; Derek Hirst, *Authority and conflict* (1986), an excellent survey of English history 1603–58; and A.G.R. Smith, *The emergence of a national state* (second edition 1997), a good, up-to-date textbook, featuring short, straightforward chapters, and useful supplementary materials including maps and tables. The fullest narrative of

English politics is S.R. Gardiner's monumental *History of England from the accession of James I to the outbreak of the Civil War, 1603–1642*, 10 vols (1883–84). Its theme of mounting constitutional conflict is pursued in works on the four Parliaments of James's reign by W. Notestein, T.L. Moir, R. Zaller and R.E. Ruigh. But Gardiner's interpretation was attacked by G.R. Elton, 'A high road to civil war?' in C.H. Carter, ed., *From the Renaissance to the Counter-Reformation: essays in honor of Garrett Mattingly* (New York 1965) 325–47; reprinted in Elton's *Studies in Tudor and Stuart politics and government*, vol. 2 (Cambridge 1974) 164–82; and Conrad Russell, 'Parliamentary history in perspective, 1604–1629', *History* 61 (1976) 1–27. These two founding documents of the so-called 'revisionist' interpretation of the early seventeenth century were followed by a number of more detailed expositions of revisionism. Amongst the most important are other works by Russell: *Parliaments and English politics 1621–1629* (Oxford 1979); *The causes of the English Civil War* (Oxford 1990); *The fall of the British monarchies 1637–1642* (Oxford 1991); and *Unrevolutionary England* (1990). Paul Christianson takes a revisionist approach to political thinking in 'Royal and Parliamentary voices on the ancient constitution, c.1604–1621', in Linda Levy Peck, ed., *The mental world of the Jacobean Court* (Cambridge 1991) 71–95; and at greater length in *Discourse on history, law, and governance in the public career of John Selden, 1610–1635* (Toronto 1996). The longest of all revisionist writings is Kevin Sharpe's *The personal rule of Charles I* (1992), which runs to just under 1,000 pages. A monument of industry, it is also noteworthy as one of the most extreme of revisionist works. In *Politics and ideas in early Stuart England: essays and studies* Sharpe applies revisionist insights to the theory as well as practice of politics (1989). Two other revisionist heavyweights are Mark Kishlansky, who stresses consensus in the electoral politics of the period in *Parliamentary selection* (Cambridge 1986); and John Morrill, whose *The nature of the English revolution* (1993) is a convenient collection of his essays. Glenn Burgess combines Morrillian revisionism with a Pocockian stress on the importance of common law attitudes in his *Absolute monarchy and the Stuart constitution* and *The politics of the ancient constitution: an introduction to English political thought 1603–1642*.

Revisionists disagree with one another on many matters of detail, but they all argue that consensus rather than conflict was the keynote of the political and social history of early Stuart England, at least until quite soon before the Civil War began. This thesis has been questioned by a number of scholars who are sometimes collectively called post-revisionists. An important collection of post-revisionist essays is Richard Cust and Ann Hughes, eds, *Conflict in early Stuart England: studies in religion and politics 1603–1642* (1989). The two editors have each produced major studies which cast serious doubt on the revisionist thesis about social and political consensus. Richard Cust's *The Forced Loan and English politics 1626–1628* (Oxford 1987) is a lucid and superbly researched analysis of local and national politics at a critical period. Ann Hughes's *Politics, society and civil war in Warwickshire, 1620–1660* (Cambridge 1987) is an extremely fine study of an important county. Hughes is also the author of a very readable overview of *The causes of the English Civil War* (1991). Another highly important work, grounded in a mass of archival material, is Thomas Cogswell, *The Blessed Revolution: English politics and the coming of war, 1621–1624* (Cambridge 1989). Cogswell is also the author of another fundamental county study, on Leicestershire, to be published imminently; and of a very entertaining essay on 'Underground verse and the transformation of early Stuart political culture', in Susan Amussen and Mark Kishlansky, eds, *Political culture and cultural politics: essays presented to David Underdown* (Manchester 1995) 277–99. Underdown himself has repeatedly criticised revisionist ideas in beautifully written books which combine nuanced social analysis with engaging narrative history: *Revel, riot and rebellion: popular politics and culture in England 1603–1660* (Oxford 1985); *Fire from heaven: life in an English country town in the seventeenth century* (New Haven 1992); and *A freeborn people: politics and the nation in seventeenth-century England* (Oxford 1996). A lively, short book on Charles I is Michael B. Young, *Charles I* (New York 1997). In 'Revisionism revised: two perspectives on early Stuart Parliamentary history', *Past and Present* 92 (1981) 55–99, Theodore Rabb and Derek Hirst provide a fine statement of the points at issue in the debate between revisionists and their critics. A useful guide to earlier writings is Robert Zaller, 'The concept of opposition in early Stuart England', *Albion* 12 (1980) 211–34.

Early Stuart church history is perhaps best approached through Kenneth Fincham, ed., *The early Stuart church, 1603–1642* (1993), a collection which includes some outstanding essays. Patrick Collinson has written many important books and articles on the religious history of the sixteenth and seventeenth centuries, including *The religion of Protestants: the church in English society 1559–1625* (Oxford 1979). Outstanding works on religious thought include Peter Lake's *Anglicans and puritans? Presbyterianism and English Conformist thought from Whitgift to Hooker*, and Anthony Milton, *Catholic and Reformed: the Roman and Protestant churches in English Protestant thought, 1600–1640* (Cambridge 1995). A very important book is Nicholas Tyacke, *Anti-Calvinists: the rise of English Arminianism c.1590–1640* (Oxford 1987). Tyacke's views on the rise of Arminianism have been attacked in a number of works, including Peter White, *Predestination, policy and polemic: conflict and consensus in the English church from the Reformation to the Civil War* (Cambridge 1992), and Julian Davies, *The Caroline captivity of the church: Charles I and the remoulding of Anglicanism* (Oxford 1992). Tyacke has mounted a highly effective response in 'Anglican attitudes: some recent writings on English religious history, from the Restoration to the Civil War', *Journal of British Studies* 35 (1996) 139–67. In early modern times, debate about the church often concerned the clergy's claims to wealth and power. Modern ecclesiastical historians often ignore these issues, and concentrate on doctrinal questions, and the clergy's social functions. Many of the writings of Christopher Hill are outstanding exceptions to this rule, and his *The economic problems of the church* (Oxford 1956) is the classic study of the church as an economic institution.

Chronology

1525	Amicable Grant: Henry VIII's government tries to raise funds without Parliamentary consent, but cancels the levy in response to widespread opposition.
1558–1603	Reign of Elizabeth I.
1559	Act of Supremacy declares Elizabeth I Supreme Governor of the church, but leaves unresolved the question of whether the Supremacy is personal or Parliamentary.
1567–1625	Reign of James VI of Scotland.
1590	Publication of Hadrian Saravia's *De Diversis Ministrorum Evangelii Gradibus*, which defends divine right episcopacy, a theory which becomes increasingly fashionable.
1593	Publication by Elizabeth I's Printer of Hadrian Saravia's *De Imperandi Authoritate*, which defends absolute monarchy.
	Publication of first four books of Richard Hooker's *Laws of Ecclesiastical Polity*.
1598	Publication in Edinburgh of James VI's *The True Law of Free Monarchies*.
1599	Private printing of James VI's *Basilicon Doron*.
1603–25	Reign of James I of Great Britain.
1603	James I's *The True Law of Free Monarchies* and *Basilicon Doron* republished in London.
1604	Hampton Court Conference: James rejects puritan calls for reform of church.
	Church authorities introduce new ecclesiastical canons, and deprive clergy who refuse to accept them.
	Henry Jacob, William Bradshaw and others leave church and begin Independent/Congregationalist movement.
1604–10	James's first Parliament meets in several sessions.
1604	Goodwin v. Fortescue Case: House of Commons wins right to judge disputed elections after acrimonious dispute with James I.
	Form of Apology and Satisfaction drawn up by members of the House of Commons, asserting Parliamentary liberties.

1605 Publication of *Regales Disputationes*, defending absolute monarchy, by Alberico Gentili, Regius Professor of Civil Law at Oxford.
Discovery of the Gunpowder Plot, a Catholic conspiracy to blow up king and Parliament.

1606 Parliament passes new laws against Catholics, and introduces an Oath of Allegiance requiring them to renounce the pope's claims to power to depose heretical kings.
Pope condemns Oath of Allegiance.
The English clergy approve canons affirming the direct divine derivation of royal power.
Bate's Case vindicates the king's right to levy extra-Parliamentary duties on imports; Chief Baron Fleming's judgment suggests that the king has still wider powers.
Publication of an English translation of Jean Bodin's *Six Books of the Commonwealth*, the most famous work of French absolutist theory.

1606–7 Parliament rejects James's proposals for a full union between England and Scotland.

1607 Publication of *The Interpreter*, a law book by the Regius Professor of Civil Law at Cambridge, John Cowell; it argues that James I is an absolute monarch.

1608 James I publishes a defence of the Oath of Allegiance, beginning a long controversy with Catholics about church–state relations.
Lord Treasurer Salisbury levies extra-Parliamentary impositions on a wide range of exports as well as imports.

1610 Commons complain vigorously against Cowell, but James I intervenes before he suffers serious harm.
Commons condemn extra-Parliamentary impositions on trade in a bill and a petition.
Negotiations between king and Commons to arrange a lasting settlement of royal financial problems – the Great Contract – break down.
A bill introduced in the Commons for the severe punishment of absolutist clerics.

1611 George Abbot becomes Archbishop of Canterbury.
Cowell appointed to serve on the High Commission, the most powerful church court; also appointed are Sir Edward Coke and other common law judges, but they refuse, claiming that the court acts illegally.
Saravia's works reprinted by the Company of Stationers of London.

1614 Addled Parliament; Commons attack impositions; James I dissolves Parliament before it passes laws or votes taxes.

1616 James I dismisses Sir Edward Coke from his position as Chief Justice of the King's Bench, signalling to the judges that there are limits to their independence.

1617	James's favourite George Villiers becomes Earl of Buckingham.
1618	Publication of John Selden's *Historie of Tithes*, which casts doubt on the clergy's claims that they have a divine right to tithes; James I condemns the book and forbids Selden to respond to attacks on it.
	James I's *Declaration of Sports* encourages people to play sports on Sundays, annoying puritans.
	Bohemian Revolt against Austrian Hapsburgs.
1618–19	Synod of Dort: Arminian doctrines condemned, and Calvinist doctrines upheld, at an international conference which includes a delegation sent by James I.
1619	James I's son-in-law Elector Palatine Frederick V accepts the crown of Bohemia.
1620	Troops fighting on behalf of the Hapsburgs drive Frederick V from Bohemia.
1621	Parliament attacks monopolies, and impeaches Lord Chancellor Bacon and others.
	Without royal permission, the House of Commons discusses foreign policy and the projected marriage between Prince Charles and a Spanish Princess; after a bitter dispute the Commons pass a Protestation asserting their freedom of speech; James dissolves Parliament and tears the Protestation out of the Commons' Journal.
1623	Prince Charles and Buckingham go to Spain so that Charles can woo the Princess in person.
	Buckingham made a Duke.
	Frederick V expelled from the Palatinate by troops of the Hapsburgs and their allies.
	James I continues to negotiate for a Spanish marriage for Prince Charles, hoping that the Spanish Hapsburgs will help restore Frederick V to the Palatinate.
	Breakdown of Charles's negotiations in Spain; he and Buckingham return to England and soon call for war with Spain.
1624	Parliament, Charles and Buckingham agree on war with Spain.
	Publication of *A New Gagge for an Old Goose* by Richard Montagu; subsequent controversy centres on doctrinal disputes between Calvinists and Arminians; Montagu is attacked by Archbishop Abbot but defended by William Laud.
1625–49	Reign of Charles I.
1625	Charles I's first Parliament: the Commons break with tradition by voting the king customs duties (tonnage and poundage) for one year only and not for life; the Lords refuse to approve this, but the king collects the customs anyway – illegally; he also continues to collect impositions.
	Buckingham's naval expedition against Cadiz ends in fiasco.

1626	York House Conference on Arminianism fails to condemn it.
	Parliament attempts to impeach Buckingham; to protect his favourite the king dissolves Parliament before it votes money.
	Charles I introduces a Forced Loan to pay for continued English intervention in the Thirty Years War; he gaols refusers without bringing a charge against them.
	Dismissal of Sir Randal Crew from office of Chief Justice of King's Bench when he opposes Forced Loan.
1627	War with France; defeat of Buckingham while trying to aid French Protestants besieged in La Rochelle.
	Troops billeted on civilian homes; they are tried by martial law when they commit crimes against civilians, though the common law courts are open.
	Publication of sermons by Roger Maynwaring and Robert Sibthorp, defending the Forced Loan and absolute monarchy.
	George Abbot, Archbishop of Canterbury, suspended after refusing to license Sibthorp's sermon for publication; effective power over the church henceforth increasingly in the hands of William Laud and his supporters.
	Five Knights' Case: imprisoned refusers of the Forced Loan ask to be freed or charged, but the judges leave them in gaol.
1628	Parliament passes Petition of Right condemning the Forced Loan (and all extra-Parliamentary levies), and other recent royal policies; Charles I first refuses, then accepts the Petition.
	Parliament impeaches Maynwaring, then votes the king taxes; Charles takes the money and pardons Maynwaring.
	Charles I makes Montagu Bishop of Chichester.
	Assassination of Buckingham.
1629	The Commons attack Arminianism and the illegal collection of tonnage and poundage.
	2 March: the Speaker held in his chair while Sir John Eliot's three resolutions are read denouncing Arminianism and extra-Parliamentary levies of tonnage and poundage.
	Charles I dissolves Parliament and arrests Eliot, John Selden and others involved in the events of 2 March.
	Peace with France.
1629–40	Charles I rules without Parliament; this is the longest period without a Parliament since Parliaments began in the 1200s.
1630	Peace with Spain.
1632	Sir Robert Filmer completes a political treatise, probably *Patriarcha*.
1633	Abolition of Feoffees for Impropriations, a puritan financial organisation; their assets confiscated.
	Laud becomes Archbishop of Canterbury on the death of Abbot.
	Charles orders publication of *Book of Sports*, a reissue of his father's *Declaration of Sports*.

1634	Ship Money introduced in coastal counties.
1635	Ship Money introduced in inland counties; it becomes an annual levy.
1636	William Juxon, Bishop of London, made Lord Treasurer – the first time since the Reformation that a clergyman is Treasurer. Maynwaring made Bishop of St David's.
1637	The puritans John Bastwick, Henry Burton and William Prynne are branded and mutilated for publishing attacks on the Laudian regime. Charles I introduces a new Prayer Book in Scotland, arousing strong national and religious opposition.
1637–38	Hampden's Case: despite strong pressure from Charles I, the judges approve Ship Money by the narrow margin of only 7 to 5.
1638	Scottish National Covenant against Laudian policies; war between Charles I and Scots.
1639	Truce of Berwick between Charles I and Scots.
1640	April–May: Short Parliament, called to fund renewed war against Scots; it is so critical of Charles I's recent policies that he dissolves it before it votes taxes. May: Thomas Hobbes completes the trenchantly absolutist *Elements of Law*, dedicated to his patron the Earl of Newcastle, a leading courtier. The clergy adopt new canons, asserting the Divine Right of Kings and the duty of subjects to pay taxes. The Scots occupy Newcastle; Charles is forced to come to terms with them and to call a new Parliament. November: Long Parliament meets. Arrest of Laud and other leading royal advisers; flight of Hobbes and others. Root and Branch Petition in London calls for abolition of episcopacy.
1641	Charles concedes constitutional ground to his critics and wins increasing support. Triennial Act: future Parliaments are to meet at least once every three years. Execution of Thomas Wentworth, Earl of Strafford. Abolition of Star Chamber and High Commission. Abolition of Ship Money. Grand Remonstrance condemns many aspects of Charles I's past rule; the Commons approve it by the narrow margin of 159 votes to 148. Irish Revolt raises question of whether king or Parliament will control the army which will need to be raised to suppress the rebellion.

1642   Charles I leaves London.
Charles I and Parliament begin raising troops.
In his Answer to the Nineteen Propositions Charles I admits that he shares political power with Parliament, but rejects Parliament's demands.
Civil War begins.

Index

Cogswell, Thomas 225n4
coinage 97–8, 108
Coke, Sir Edward 45, 50, 79, 80, 122,
    128, 165, 166, 182, 204, 211, 212,
    219, 221, 227, 238, 260
  annual Parliaments, advocates 99–100
  artificial reason, concept of 84, 89,
    103
  attacked 112–13, 236
  career 82, 200–1
  common law and law of God 88
  common law and martial law 98
  common law and reason 87
  common law and statute 91–2, 93–4
  conquest, views on 65, 66n24, 67
  dispensing power, views on 169
  Fortescue and 83
  High Commission, views on 201–2
  history of the common law, views on
    85–6
  impositions, views on 141
  imprisonment without cause shown,
    views on 154–5, 156, 260
  influence of 78, 85–6, 103–4, 107
  insularity 78
  king bound by law 82, 96, 102, 162,
    163
  law of nature, views on 101, 102
  Littleton, views on 114
  maxims of the common law 90, 93–4
  monopolies 90, 144–5
  proclamations, views on 170
  sovereignty 159, 160n59
Coke, Sir John, Secretary 125, 129, 162
Collins, Samuel 36, 192, 193, 194
Collinson, Patrick 179n4, 180n7, 219n8
common law and lawyers 81–104, 158,
    169
  absolutism supported by 103, 151–3
  attacked 67–8, 81, 112–13, 114,
    236–7
  certainty of 143
  church and 199–205
  Coke on 82–3, 85–6, 87, 89, 90,
    91–2, 93–4, 96, 101–4
  custom and 84–7, 89, 90–1, 94, 101,
    113
  Davies on 41, 84–5, 88n16
  Hedley on 85, 86, 89, 91

  history and origins of 66–8, 85–7, 88,
    113
  individuals and 84, 100, 102, 144–5,
    150–1
  language of the 255, 261
  Norman Conquest and 66, 67, 86,
    87n12, 154
  sovereignty and 84–5, 92–3
common law mind, the 261–2
common law, the language of the 255,
    261
Common Prayer, Book of *see* Prayer
    Book
Commons, House of *see* House of
    Commons
communism 13, 135–6
Company of Stationers of London 12
compromise, attempts at 108, 123–33,
    165
Con, George 208
conciliarism 58, 178, 188, 189, 190
Congregationalism *see* Independency
conquest 28, 59, 65–8, 83
Conquest, the Norman 65–8, 83, 86,
    87n12, 113, 154, 262
  see also William I
consensus 2, 110, 127, 129, 168, 224–5,
    238
  linguistic conventions and 254–61
  origins of Civil War and 261–5
  see also unspoken conventions
    structuring consensus; unity
    between king and people
consent of individuals and origins of
    government 22, 23
Constitutions and canons ecclesiasticall
    (1640) *see* canons of 1640
contract, original 62–5, 102, 112, 122
  see also kings, origins of power of,
    from the people
conventions structuring consensus *see*
    unspoken conventions structuring
    consensus
Convocation 32, 167, 178, 196
Convocation Book (1606) *see* canons of
    1606
Cooke, James 192, 194
Cope, Sir Anthony 259
Cope, Esther 167n73, 235n37

Sacks, David Harris 245n80
Sackville, Edward, Earl of Dorset 157, 159
St Ambrose *see* Ambrose, Saint
St Bartholomew's Day massacres (24 August 1572) 58
St Edward *see* Edward the Confessor
St German, Christopher 88n15
St Gregory's, railing in of altar at 209
St John, Oliver, common lawyer 64, 74, 149, 167, 203n55
St John, Oliver, Wiltshire gentleman 138
St John's College, Cambridge 111
St Omer 56
St Paul's Cathedral 202
Salisbury 210
Salisbury, Earl of *see* Cecil, Sir Robert
Sallust 156n50
Salmon, J.H.M. 77, 78n52, 228, 264n143
salt 248
Saltern, George 86, 87n12, 88, 135
salus populi see public good; reason(s) of state
Samson 170
Sanderson, John 11n1
Sanderson, Robert, Bishop of Lincoln 37
Sandys, Sir Edwin 16, 59, 65, 79, 144, 145n24
Saravia, Hadrian 12, 51, 54n88, 249, 251, 264
  episcopacy by divine right 196
  king holds legislative power 40
  Maynwaring and 121, 257
  origins of government 12, 19, 22–3, 28
  Parliament 173, 174n86
  patriarchalism 34–5
  sovereignty, unlimited and indivisible 41, 42n68
  succession, king can alter 33n49, 34
Satan 183
Saul 45
Sawyer, E. 116n24, 117n24, 125n49, 185n15
Saxonhouse, Arlene 169n76
Saxons 86

Saye and Sele, Viscount *see* Fiennes, William
scandalous ministers, bill on 204–5
schism 131
Schochet, Gordon 17, 29n40
Sclater, William 20, 21n20, 25
Scot, Thomas (of Canterbury) 217–18
Scotland and the Scots 115, 141, 178, 188, 219
  resistance to royal policy, 1638–40 47, 49, 72–3, 80, 137, 220
  union with England, proposed 113
Scott, Thomas (pamphleteer) 49
Screech, M.A. 15n9
Scudamore, John, Viscount Scudamore 256n119
Sejanus 56
Selden, John 59, 60, 61–2, 78, 85, 168n74, 204, 211, 214, 216n2, 260
  act of Parliament may alter any part of Magna Carta 80
  against Coke on antiquity of English law 85, 86, 87
  bishops not really popish 181
  canon law 203
  clergy 204
  contractual nature of royal power 63, 101
  imprisonment, royal power of 155–6
  law of nature 21n20
  origins of government 19, 20–1, 61, 101
  prerogative, royal 96–7, 162
  proclamations 170
  property 135
  Sibthorp's *Apostolike Obedience* 260
  three estates 166
  tithes 204
self-defence 16–17, 250–2
  against kings, disagreement on 71, 73, 250–2, 255
  even slaves have right of 70
  Hobbes on 95, 252
  law of nature and 16–17
  papal deposing power and 184
  revisionists on 250–2
  see also resistance, theories of; self-preservation, property and

Strafford, Earl of *see* Wentworth, Sir
 Thomas
Strangeways, Sir John 149
Strier, Richard 51n82
Suarez, Francisco 76, 122, 177, 222
 extent of king's power depends on
  contract with people 62, 66
 king's power derived from people
  23–4, 58
 natural law permits monarchy,
  aristocracy and democracy 61
 papal deposing power, argues for
  184
 quoted in Parliament 1628 66,
  76–7
 taxation, views on 76–7, 122
subsidies 123, 144, 161
 decline in value of 221
 owed to king 68, 150–1
 redress of grievances and 171–2
succession 28, 32–3, 34
supply *see* subsidies; taxation and taxes
Supremacy, the Royal ecclesiastical 94,
  113, 114, 201
 episcopacy by divine right and 197–8,
  199
 Prynne on 205
 theory of 191–6
 see also Act of Supremacy (1559)
Sutcliffe, Matthew 11–12
Sutton, Thomas 200
Swales, R.J.W. 149n33
Swedish 264
Synod of Dort *see* Dort, Synod of
synods *see* councils, ecclesiastical

Tacitus, Publius Cornelius 15n9, 38n59,
  56, 57, 72
taxation and taxes 140–53
 subjects have duty to pay 68, 112,
  124, 150–1
 without consent 76–7, 124, 140–9,
  230, 237, 248, 252
 see also Forced Loan; impositions;
  Maynwaring; property; Ship
  Money; Sibthorp, Robert;
  subsidies; tonnage and poundage
Ten Commandments *see* Decalogue

Theodosius 194
theology and theological language 13,
  40, 112–13, 255, 258–60
 see also bible, political uses of the
Thirty Years War 77, 161, 207
Thomas, St *see* Aquinas
Thompson, Christopher 146n27
Thompson, Faith 119n34, 201n49
Thomson, Richard 186n17, 192, 199
Thornborough, John, Bishop of Bristol
  113
Thorne, S.E. 92
Tiberius 56
tithes 16, 179, 204, 210
Titley, Peter 120
Tolmie, Murray 199n43
tonnage and poundage 149, 212, 215,
  237, 244
 Charles I commands Commons to
  discuss 173
 Charles I's extra-Parliamentary
  collection of, attack of Commons
  on 1626–29 145–6
 in 1625 145
 recompense for king's protection of
  trade, seen as 141
Tooker, William 31, 51, 186n17
Tories 222
Tower of London 82
Trentman, John A. 16n9
Triennial Act (1641) 100, 250
Trinity Hall, Cambridge 113
triumvirate, puritan 260
 see also Bastwick, John; Burton,
  Henry; Prynne, William
'True presentation of forepast
  Parliaments' *see* Kynaston, Sir
  Francis
Tuck, Richard viii, 15n9, 21n20,
  21n23, 27n34, 29n39, 38n59,
  62n15
Tully, James 21n23
tunnage and poundage *see* tonnage and
  poundage
Turks 102
Tyacke, Nicholas 64n20, 143n19,
  180–1n7, 211n71, 212, 218n8,
  225n4, 262n138